CAPITALISM, TECHNOLOGY, LABOR

CAPITALISM, TECHNOLOGY, LABOR

A SOCIALIST REGISTER READER

EDITED BY
GREG ALBO, LEO PANITCH, AND ALAN ZUEGE

SOCIALIST REGISTER CLASSICS
VOLUME 2

Haymarket Books
Chicago, Illinois

Published in 2020 by
Haymarket Books
P.O. Box 180165
Chicago, IL 60618
773-583-7884
www.haymarketbooks.org
info@haymarketbooks.org

ISBN: 978-1-64259-134-7

Trade distribution:
In the US, Consortium Book Sales and Distribution, www.cbsd.com
In Canada, Publishers Group Canada, www.pgcbooks.ca
In the UK, Turnaround Publisher Services, www.turnaround-uk.com
All other countries, Ingram Publisher Services International,
ips_intlsales@ingramcontent.com

This book was published with the generous support of Lannan Foundation
and Wallace Action Fund.

Cover design by Eric Kerl.

Printed in Canada by union labor.

Library of Congress Cataloging-in-Publication data is available.

10 9 8 7 6 5 4 3 2 1

CONTENTS

CAPITALISM, TECHNOLOGY, LABOR: AN INTRODUCTION

Greg Albo

At seemingly every turn, the political economy of contemporary capitalism is being transformed by unprecedented scientific, industrial, and commercial innovations. This new technological infrastructure is most visible in the penetration of the information-communication sector, through the internet, social media, and digital surveillance, into every nook and crack of work and daily life. But the imprint of the new automation is registered, too, in each moment of the circulation of capital: in the electronic "bits and bytes" form in which credit money is now created, circulated, and regulated; in the robotics and telematics that set the pace of the labor process and direct the distributional logistics of commodity production; and in the algorithms which gather infinite blocks of "big data" made up of individualized preferences, "likes," "journeys," and above all track the consumer purchases that facilitate the realization of new production.

As this new phase of value production consolidates and gains pace, its social meaning—and implications for socialist strategy—warrant considered attention. Indeed, there already exists a small library of contending forecasts from governments, corporations, and unions on the ways workplaces are being refashioned; on the new economic sectors that are emerging, from the web-centered "sharing economy" to the "internet of things"; on the occupations and jobs at risk of disappearing; on the new STEM and coding competencies that will be necessary to find future employment at all; and on the policy mandates for the redesign of state apparatuses to aid social adjustments to "platform capitalism."

1

A very different remit, one that grounds the analysis of technological change in the capitalist dynamics of work and class, has always guided the *Socialist Register*. From its very first volumes, the *Register* warned against the "technological fetishism" that has accompanied each new cluster of product innovations and production techniques, and rejected the claims that these economic "advances" offered a technical fix for the class antagonisms and ecological dislocations of the outgoing, "archaic" era of capitalism. The essays in this collection, drawn from over five decades of the *Register*'s annual publication, locate the technological transformations of capitalism concretely and directly within the competitive imperatives for capitalists to accumulate without limit. But they also reveal the class and political barriers to this drive: all the new machines in the world cannot ensure the social and economic conditions for profitable accumulation, nor can they contain workers' struggles for improved wages and limits on the stresses of workplace intensification, or eradicate popular demands for cooperative production that extend to democratic control over technological change.

I.

The impact of new technologies on the working class and the labor movement has always been both controversial and central to the study of capitalism. The founding text of classical political economy, Adam Smith's *Wealth of Nations* (1776), opens with a detailed study of the division of labor in the "modern" pin factory, made possible by "the invention of a great number of machines which facilitate and abridge labor, and enable one man to do the work of many." And David Ricardo famously reworked the third edition of his *Principles of Political Economy and Taxation* (1821) to account for "the question of machinery" as the First Industrial Revolution gained steam and the displacement of labor became a source of political upheaval. But it was Karl Marx who insisted, in his critique of political economy in *Capital* (1867), that these developments first had to be located in capitalism as a historically specific mode of commodity production for the purposes of accumulating additional value in the form of profits. In Marx's analysis of capitalism's particular social relations of production and property, technological change occupies an especially prominent place.

Both the exploiting and producing classes, Marx argued, are subject to the imperatives of market competition for their self-reproduction.

For the working classes, skills and capacities to earn wages in the labor market become prerequisites for obtaining the means of subsistence. For the capitalist classes, market competition compels constant cost cutting to sustain competitive prices, particularly through continual innovation in new technologies in production, new products, and a constant reorganization of work. As early as *The Communist Manifesto* (1848), Marx and Friedrich Engels recognized in capitalism a "constant revolutionizing of production, uninterrupted disturbance of all social conditions, everlasting uncertainty and agitation. . . . The need of a constantly expanding market for its products chases the bourgeoisie over the whole surface of the globe. It must nestle everywhere, settle everywhere, establish connections everywhere." This vivid—even futuristic—phrasing still captures very well the general competitive imperatives that compel capitalism to endless accumulation, while inviting us to investigate anew the precise, concrete ways that the means of production are set in motion and a surplus extracted from workers, which vary greatly by firm, across time, and between places.

In the Marxist view of capitalist development, as recently laid out by David Harvey in his *Marx, Capital, and the Madness of Economic Reason* (2017), technological change is a systematic and cumulative process of revolutionizing the means of production while simultaneously extending private property controls over value chains that are steadily more interconnected and organizationally complex. Under the pressure of competition, capitalists search out new techniques, organizations, and markets that allow them to increase output and sell more cheaply, attaining extra profit and a larger market share from a competitive advantage in value extraction. Marx conceptualized this as a process of relative surplus value extraction (distinct from absolute surplus extraction, from working longer or more intensively) and identified this tendency as a distinguishing and necessary feature of the capitalist mode of production. Technological change thus raises the productivity of labor such that for a given unit of labor-time input of average quality, the volume of output increases, the total value produced remains constant, and individual commodity prices fall, but the share of value appropriated by capitalists increases (as the value of labor power declines with cheaper goods).

The "fetishism" that plagues conventional technology studies—not least in discussions of "full automation" today—is the tendency to explain these results as a consequence of the machines (or electronic devices) "in themselves"; and from there to posit technical fixes to socioeconomic problems, with heated warnings of the horrors that will unfold absent the necessary social adjustments to the new technological and market conditions. Far too often, social assessment and political calculations degenerate into forecasts either of apocalypse by machine, or of imagined technological utopias now enabled. In contrast, the essays in this volume advance a class analysis of technological change that mediates between the structural imperatives of accumulation, on one hand, and the active agency of workers struggling to shape their conditions of work, on the other, to draw out the specific ways that restructuring impacts on capital and labor.

It is one of the intrinsic features of capital accumulation that in pursuit of relative surplus value and competitive advantage through the adoption of new techniques, wage labor inputs into given labor processes tend to decline. The technical composition of the capital stock is thus typically characterized by a labor-saving/capital-using bias. In the process, wage labor and money capital are reallocated between old and new sectors of production; new producer services emerge to design, manage, and service the more complex capital stock; and more employment is allocated to distributional and commercial sectors as the mass of commodities in circulation expands with the increase in output levels. From another vantage, automation generates a reserve army of labor as employment levels in manufacturing decline and labor demand is redistributed between sectors, occupations, skills, and regions. Yet how this plays out between unemployment, allocations of work time, wages, and new employment is far from determined by technological blueprints set by engineering estimates of capital-labor ratios for specific jobs. These outcomes are always overdetermined by class struggle over the distribution and control of skills, jobs, and restructuring. What we are really dealing with, as Ursula Huws in one of her essays here insists, are new fields of accumulation and struggle.

A further competitive dynamic is unleashed by the dialectic between accumulation and struggle that investment in new techniques generates. Each individual capitalist pursues their own competitive advantage such that overaccumulated capital in some sectors may not be sustained (simply meaning the expected—or even any—rate of profit cannot be met). The various forms of credit capital advanced to firms for investments represents, moreover, not only claims on future profits but also the market validation of investments in particular technologies and organizational infrastructure in workplaces. If a crisis erupts from a decline in markets and profits, the bankruptcies of firms and deterioration of credit conditions create a spiral of idle capital and unemployed labor side by side, with the crisis spreading to other sectors in a common cyclical trajectory of "investment–accumulation–crisis–restructuring." Money values in all forms—speculative and loan capital, and productive and commodity capital alike—take a hit. Older vintages of technologies embodied in the capital stock can no longer be valorized, as ruthless competition between firms breaks out to preserve individual market shares. "The slaughter of capital values" was how Marx aptly described this. Crises thus always force the scrapping and redeployment of investments in productive capital (plant and equipment, infrastructure, logistics, and distribution networks) in an effort to restore profitability, to preserve the money capital necessary to invest in new techniques and capital stock, and to reestablish flows of credit money.

As firms scrap old technologies and adopt new ones in phases of crisis, the capitalist control of the production process, whether in producing services or material goods, raises another set of concerns. Capitalists are driven to redesign labor processes, to introduce new techniques in order to restore profitability, and to increase their control and flexibility in managing workers. Hence newer technologies tend to deepen the social and technical divisions of labor. As Harry Braverman forcefully demonstrated in his *Labor and Monopoly Capital* (1974), there is an incentive for capitalists to ensure that the fewest number of workers gain technological competencies while the largest number are flexibilized in their work deployment and their skills routinized and degraded. The host of technologically enabled developments that have so extended the world market and the international division of labor have taken a number of forms: the intensification of some labor processes into gigantic production sites, accompanied by the outsourcing and fragmentation of others; an increasing velocity in the turnover of fixed capital and the speed at which commodities and money circulate; the facilitation of further appropriations of the wealth of nature, and hunts for economic rents and transformations of labor reserves; as well as an infinite multiplication of new commodities. Technological change, in sum, is never innocent of a very powerful and deliberate class appropriation of the knowledge and self-governance capacities of workers, and at the same time it lays the material foundations for the ideological attribution of autonomous "production powers" to management and capitalist firms as such.

The confusion that accompanies every fetishization of technology arises from a fundamental misunderstanding of the new organizational forms that coincide with technological change: the continual evolution of "best means for given ends," as in the crude Weberian sense of instrumental rationality; or a consequence of the economic determinism of the forces of production, as with vulgar forms of Marxism. Rather, as the essays in this collection detail, organizational forms are not given by technologies with fixed technical coefficients of production and immutable social consequences. The introduction and application of new technologies on any substantial scale must always be located in relation to expanded capitalist reproduction, and to the purposes of the capitalist classes that control these technologies as their private property. It is capitalist social relations, as reflected in the class struggles embedded in the particularities of gender, race, and place, that structure the technical divisions of labor of modern firms, while the hierarchies and disciplines that govern labor power and workplace surveillance constitute the social architecture of technological change.

In *Capital*, Marx observes that "[t]echnology reveals the active relation of man to nature, the direct process of the production of his life, and thereby it also lays bare the process of production of the social relations of his life, and of the mental conceptions that flow from those relations." Marx traced these processes from the dispossessions of primitive accumulation all the way to the transition from the formal to the real subsumption of labor he observed in the techniques of the factory system of his time. But it can be seen today that the processes of dispossession and subsumption have no firm end point, as new technologies find ever more innovative ways to penetrate new spaces for accumulation and squeeze more labor out of labor time (such as the monitoring bracelets and computer logs that add an entirely new dimension of surveillance to the time and work-disciplines of capitalism). It is the error of technological fetishism to see science and technology per se as the solution to the social contradictions of laboring under capitalism, rather than as the evidence of capitalism's class divisions. The forces of production, it needs to be stressed, are always a result, and not a cause, of social relations. Primacy in social explanation must always be given to social forces and political struggles, not to engineers and scientists in isolated laboratories or, in the fashion of today, to the unique capacities of "creative" or "knowledge" workers.

II.

The *Socialist Register* emerged in 1964 as the postwar era hit full stride in one of the most sustained periods of accumulation in the history of capitalism. The war had delivered a massive and exhaustive restructuring of productive processes—ushering in the dedicated machinery, flow line assembly, skilled workers, and standardized products of the so-called Fordist labor process. This presented a host of new commodities and sectors in chemicals, autos, rubber, appliances, and electronics, to name but a few. With the new technologies having consolidated through the 1950s, the 1960s immersed all the core capitalist countries in a "great automation scare" of massive job losses as manufacturing employment fell relative to the volume of output and service sector employment grew. This was but one part, it was argued, of a wider "managerial revolution" that was compelling a general upgrading of skills, expansion of unique engineering and scientific qualifications, and ever more layers of "white-collar work" in administration, marketing, and finance. The traditional working class, it was argued, was in terminal decline amid the emerging "postindustrial society."

In its very origins, the New Left of the 1960s, and the *Socialist Register* in particular, took as one of their foremost tasks a dismantling of these narratives. In the *Register*'s first volume, Ernest Mandel offered a sharp rebuke to these theses in an essay titled "The Economics of Neo-Capitalism." Here Mandel argued that "technological innovation [in firms] . . . does not automatically flow from technological discovery," but that the postwar period had seen a "stepping up of the general rate of technological innovation . . . [due to] the logical link between technological innovation and the permanent arms race." This produced during the Cold War period a shrinking of the trade cycle and an accentuation of the "uneven development" between sectors and zones of the world. From this, Mandel offered a quite distinct Marxian explanation of the rise of managerialism in "technological innovation and the shortening of the life span of fixed capital . . . [requiring] more long term cost planning . . . made possible by the rapid progress of

computer techniques and their application to economic calculations."
The new productive capacity, in turn, mandated "development of the
techniques of marketing" and "planning techniques" introduced into
the state "to rationalize" capital investments.

With remarkable foresight to what would prove a central aspect of
the crisis of the 1970s, Mandel observed that the more technically sophisticated capital stock revealed "a growing contradiction between
the needs of neo-capitalist programming and trade union freedom of
bargaining for higher wages," which would in turn generate a further
"massive development of automation, the aim being the reconstitution of the reserve army of labor." It would be necessary in this context to push past "the essentially defensive strategy of the trade union
movement (against wage restraint, and for freedom of bargaining) . . .
without which the workers will be fighting a losing battle against the
technocrats and their employers." What this meant was that socialist
strategy could not, therefore, be for or against "technology," but rather
against the capitalist planning of firms, and should see that "workers'
control is a first and essential step toward . . . management of a socialized economy and toward industrial democracy."

Ralph Miliband's essay in the 1968 *Register*, "Professor Galbraith
and American Capitalism," offered a direct critique of the most force-
ful and encompassing formulation of the new industrial society thesis, J. K. Galbraith's *The New Industrial State* (1968), with its image of
vertically integrated corporations controlled by a "technostructure" of
white-collar specialists. Galbraith argued that there was no longer any
countervailing power outside the dominant capitalist corporations, and
that within the commanding heights of the economy, the new technostructure that emerged from the "logic of industrialization" had obscured the distinction between "employer and employee." Corporate
control came to be diffused and shared among a "very large" group
of people—ranging from technicians, scientists, market analysts, computer programmers, and industrial stylists, all the way to more routine
white- and blue-collar workers—"who bring specialized knowledge,
talent, or experience to decision making." Miliband observed that the
political remit of such an argument was of a piece with all those who
insisted, despite concern for the growing concentration of corporate
power under modern capitalism, that "the question of alternatives to
capitalism had been rendered obsolete by the internal developments of

the system itself." "[C]apitalism, the argument goes, has been so thoroughly transformed in the last few decades that the need to abolish it has conveniently disappeared." Miliband's devastating critique thus revealed the basic political contradiction underlying Galbraith's analysis:

> [T]he confusion and bafflement of the latter-day liberalism that Professor Galbraith represents, in regard to an "industrial system" that it approaches with a mixture of admiration and distaste, and whose basic irrationality, some aspects of which it perceives, it is either unable or unwilling to locate and transcend. . . . The tone is critical and so is the intent, but the result is all the same profoundly apologetic.

That Miliband's essay appeared in the midst of the radical political explosions of 1968 was more than coincidence. It captured, far more than did the Galbraithian fetishism of industrial technique, the increasingly diverse class contradictions of the contemporary capitalist system. More than a decade of industrial and public sector militancy had completely shattered the postwar political consensus, and it persisted right though the economic crisis of the 1970s until the profound defeats inflicted on trade unionism in the 1980s, amid the massive wave of industrial restructuring. Fordist labor processes were steadily replaced by the "new technologies" of microelectronics, which facilitated more flexible production techniques, "just in time" inventories and workers, the multitasking and multiskilling of core workers, and continual learning. The investments in these new flexible labor processes, moreover, encouraged a so-called hollowing out of old industrial centers, seen in a "vertical disintegration" of traditional corporate structures into de-unionized "greenfield" sites, and an internationalization of production chains into low-wage zones. In progressive circles, new theories began to circulate about the meaning of these technological developments and their consequences for the future of work and class formation. On the one side, André Gorz, Stanley Aronowitz, and Jeremy Rifkin, for a few prominent examples, began to bid "farewell to the working class" and foresee a "jobless future," and, thus, to overhaul completely the social agencies and imaginary of any potential noncapitalist alternative. On the other, Michael Piore and Charles Sabel, Robert Boyer, and Wolfgang Streeck trumped for revitalized production processes through more egalitarian, skill-intensive, and flexible labor regimes, variously tagged "flexible specialization," "post-Fordism," and "diversified quality production." The latter group, in particular, offered a renewal of social democracy and class compromise founded on the distributional logic of the new technologies.

This was, by now, familiar ground for the *Socialist Register* in rebuffing technology-centered contentions of a "disappearing proletariat," as Richard Hyman put it in the title of his 1983 essay. Hyman took as his target Gorz's claim, in his *Farewell to the Working Class: An Essay on Post-Industrial Socialism* (1982), that the "capitalist rationality" embedded in technical development of the forces of production foreclosed the agency of the "traditional" working class and, at the same time, created a "non-class of nonworkers," of "all those who have been expelled from production by the abolition of work." For Gorz, the "microprocessor revolution" accelerated the "process of marginalization, multiplying both unemployment and those employments designed simply to 'provide work,'" whose only exit was a societal realignment committed to the principles of "work less, consume better, live more." Hyman challenged Gorz's reliance on "assertion" more than on evidence of complex and uneven changes to working-class occupations and struggles for job controls in the labor process. And he argued that, as with other such futuristic postwork provocations, Gorz's contained more than a few confusions, not least in calling for the "abolition of work, before going on to insist that work *cannot* be abolished"; or in his bewildering claim that "the present forces of production are adapted specifically to capitalist priorities and hence inappropriate for socialism," while going on in subsequent discussion "to assume that current technology will be applied largely unaltered within the sphere of necessity in a socialist economy." Still, Hyman granted, Gorz's argument required socialists to adopt "a more detached and critical attitude to the state," very different from those that simplistically sought "to 'socialize' and manage more 'efficiently' the large-scale high-technology apparatus of contemporary capitalism."

In his 1985 essay "Marx, the Present Crisis, and the Future of Labor," Ernest Mandel showed that there was underway "a fundamental change of structure of the international capitalist economy, with a long-term fundamental shift in the weight, cohesion, and dynamic of wage labor, at the expense of that class." Building on his earlier piece in the 1964 *Register*, Mandel's monumental study *Late Capitalism* (1975) had periodized capitalism in terms of the intersections of cycles of class struggle, technological changes to the capital stock, and long waves of accumulation and profitability within a hierarchical world market. Now, in his *Register* essay a decade later, Mandel grasped the significance of developments of the 1980s in terms of a "growth of wage labor on a world scale" alongside a relative decrease of labor employed in the "largest capitalist factories." As a result, it was necessary "to take into consideration the precise effects of robotization on specific branches of industry that have played a key role in the organization and strength of the working class and the labor movement." And insofar as automated technology is always foremost deployed to increase the conditions of profitability and with the intent of "reducing labor's power of resistance at factory, industrial branch, or societal level," Mandel insisted that labor movement strategies that now embraced "national competitiveness" and "enterprise profitability" needed to be rejected in favor of a new focus on "a radical international reduction of the working week without a cut in weekly pay . . . [as an] absolute social priority."

If the essays by Hyman and Mandel reasserted the imperatives of class struggles over the remaking of labor regimes in the workplace, the point of Greg Albo's 1994 *Register* essay, "'Competitive Austerity' and the Impasse of Capitalist Employment Policy" was to challenge the viability of what Albo termed a new social democratic strategy of "progressive competitiveness." Conceived as a compromise at a national level with the consolidation of a neoliberal policy regime at a global level, this strategy was to be built on the rejection of a low-wage, low-skill, low-tax road to sustain corporate profitability, in favor of the adoption of new industrial policies encouraging the deployment of new technologies, high-skill workers, and new work organization in high value-added export sectors. But rather than offer a "high road" to better wages and job security, this path of binding workers into competitive partnerships with the companies, Albo showed, was likely to weaken the capacities of unions to resist concessions. The logic of competiveness was accepted as a parameter for collective action, such that "multiskilled core workers are pushed to work longer hours to recoup training investments, while peripheral workers and the unemployed scramble to get enough hours of paid work." In the face of stiffening competition and weak demand, amid a global neoliberal policy regime wherein states were continually cutting back social expenditures while increasing subsidies and corporate tax cuts to expand exports, "the progressive competitiveness strategy is forced to accept, as social democratic parties have been willing to do, the same 'competitive austerity' as neoliberalism." Breaking with this would require a more "inward-oriented" strategy that would build on "the principle of maximizing the capacity of different 'national collectivities' democratically to choose alternate development paths (socialist or capitalist), that do not impose externalities (such as environmental damage) on other countries, without suffering isolation and coercive sanction from the world economy."

By the turn of the millennium, it was increasingly evident that the various high-skill "progressive competitive" strategies had become little more than a tactical option for a few companies to pursue flexible production when precarity and outsourcing had reached their limits. The "connectivity" between locationally specific labor processes (even individual workspaces) and the circulation of money and commodities in the world market offered by the information and communication technologies (ICT) could already be seen pushing the boundaries of flexible accumulation even further. An evolving "platform capitalism" now placed the "professional middle class" and many skilled workers on perpetual work mode through the internet; contingent workers beginning from "zero-hour contracts" had to be available for work on a moment's notice; information was constantly "scraped" from all sources for possible conversion into a competitive advantage; and value chains, extended across the world market, traced through networks of logistics.

It was with these developing concerns in mind that the 2001 *Register*, titled *Working Classes, Global Realities*, focused its attention on the many misconceptions and realities of work in the "new economy." The essay here by Ursula Huws, "The Making of a Cybertariat? Virtual Work in a Real World," was pathbreaking. Arguing that the production of "material" commodities is only one source of value production in the "continuing seismic shifts in the social division of labor," Huws uncovered the ways "information workers" employed in "virtual production" were located in the capital relation, and became subjected to the same processes of automation as the manufacturing sector. For Huws, the distinctiveness of the modern "cybertariat," compared to traditional office workers, lies in the way that information technologies "blur the boundaries between work and consumption, constituting as they do a shifting interface between server and served" and, in home computer usage, become "an instrument both of production and of reproduction." In this respect, cyber-work repositions gender relations (without overturning patriarchal relations), dissolves old divisions between sectors, and tends to make tasks more standardized and routinized, rather than creative. Even if "a new cybertariat is in the making," Huws cautioned, "whether it will perceive itself as such is another matter."

In the same 2001 volume, Andrew Ross dismantled the most touted managerial ethos of the new economy: the "leveling of workplace hierarchies" through "flexible communal workspaces" with "dedicated computer workstations," and the like. The reality of the new "flexible style of corporate organization" embraced by the "software startup" culture, as Ross demonstrated in his essay "No-Collar Labor in America's 'New Economy,'" is long hours of work, falling pay, reliance on multiple job holdings, and lack of union protections. It is of no little irony that the new "knowledge factories" in New York's "Silicon Alley" "physically occupy spaces filled by manufacturing sweatshops a century ago." Showing how a new "automated Taylorism" that monitors webshop workers "through keyboard strokes, e-mail and voice-mail snooping, or surveillance cameras is now standard practice on the part of the majority of American employers," Ross posed one of the crucial challenges for both union and socialist organizing in the twenty-first century.

In the wake of the global financial crisis of 2008–2009, the restructuring of capital and work intensified the exploitative patterns identified by Huws and Ross. In her "A Tale of Two Crises: Labor, Capital, and Restructuring in the US Auto Industry" in the 2012 *Register*, Nicole Aschoff argued that "long-term trends of de-unionization, concessions, and isolation have paved the way for unprecedented concessions" for autoworkers with the bankruptcy and bailouts of GM and Chrysler. Aschoff revealed how the major auto multinationals are organizationally so very different than Galbraith's technostructure. Indeed, the internationalization of auto production, further enabled by the "rise of finance," also allowed a decentering of production zones and relations between parts companies and assemblers, in a "continual process of reorganization." Aschoff's conclusion is to the point: "[C]apital continually reinvents itself. . . . If auto unions are to recover from the crisis, they must also reinvent themselves."

In the wake of the crisis, such radical restructuring was hardly limited to manufacturing, as Huws explained in her important 2012 essay also included here, "Crisis as Capitalist Opportunity: The New Accumulation through Public Service Commodification." Privatization was in the process making "public services themselves . . . a site of accumulation that is crucial for the continuing expansion of international capital." The impact of "opening up of public services to the market" for work was creating a new "reserve army" of information workers "who, thanks to the standardization of white-collar work through the introduction of information and communications technologies, are increasingly able to carry out the tasks that had previously formed part of the job descriptions of civil servants or other public sector bureaucrats." With the public sector workforce becoming "subsumed into a larger mass of interchangeable labor," it is clear how much there is a need for new "forms of organization that recognize the common interests of a global proletariat."

The informational technologies analyzed by Huws are, of course, central to the dizzying speed at which commodities circulate through the massive distributional and retail networks of Amazon, Costco, and the like. These "new" forms of capital have their cognate in the "Walmart Working Class"—the title of Arun Gupta's 2014 essay in the fiftieth-anniversary volume, *Registering Class*. The Walmart proletariat forms in a matrix of distribution centers, each purposed to serve up to 150 retail stores and "to keep 'commodities in motion' as quickly as possible from manufacturer to stores." Adapting the industry term for its extreme "union avoidance" practices, Gupta argued that the "Walmart effect" is "shifting working-class employment from stable medium-wage jobs to a precarious low-wage service sector." Tracing new forms of union organizing in this "new economy," from OUR Walmart and the Warehouse Workers Organizing Committee to the Fight for $15, Gupta calls for "the rebirth of a strong left . . . with a vision that points the way beyond wages and consumption to economic democracy, to spur militant class consciousness and create the social space for it to spread."

All the essays brought together here reject the false notions that technologies either bring about postwork utopias or deprive workers of the capacity to struggle and transform their workplaces. And each essay, in its own way, points to the need for a constant renewal of class analysis based on a grounded understanding of the changes in work and labor processes within contemporary capitalism. The final two essays take this renewal of class analysis—a necessary precondition for the renewal of working-class politics—as their point of departure. Bryan Palmer's "Reconsiderations of Class: Precariousness as Proletarianization" argues that what has led many to see "precariousness as class formation" is a series of "working-class defeats [that] have, after decades of retrenchment, taken on a cumulative character, and the result is a class too often stripped of its seeming capacity to fight, its leadership increasingly characterized by caution and the sensibilities of an ossified officialdom." It is crucial in this context to understand precarity as a continual process of dispossession, Palmer insists, one which has always been integral to the insecurities of working-class life. Since precariousness "has always been the fundamental feature of class formation rather than the material basis of a new, contemporary class," then all proletarians suffer precarity and "have interests that coincide directly with this class of the dispossessed." In this way, Palmer concludes that "there are expanding possibilities for more effective politics based on class struggles in our times."

In "Class Theory and Class Politics Today," in the 2015 *Register, Transforming Classes*, Hugo Radice refutes the thesis of a new managerialism "heralding a 'postcapitalist' order based on technical rationality and economic efficiency," arguing that on the contrary, "the once-feted managerial revolution has very largely been reversed." Radice goes even further to declare that today "it would be hard to argue that there exists a [professional middle] class, in the Marxist relational sense, that is distinct from the working class and the capitalist class." While also taking stock of the "polarization and fragmentation" of working-class organization, politics, and ideology over recent decades, Radice insists that this signals the need for a "critique of the ways class has been understood" in the Marxist tradition. Insofar as the continuous technological change integral to capital accumulation "transforms the social division of labor both within society at large and within workplaces," a major challenge for class analysis is to develop "an alternative understanding of production and labor that can effectively integrate the sphere of reproduction." But, in opposition to the "realm of value and capital," also something more: "[t]o envision socialism as a realm of freedom, and develop social practices that can begin to realize it . . . [by starting] from use values, concrete labor, and social needs."

III.

The essays in this collection offer, then, a distinctive socialist contribution to the analysis of class and technology within capitalist relations of production. Across a five-decade span of publication of the *Socialist Register*, they advance a withering critique of the technological fetishism that has accompanied each new wave of innovation and each new crisis with its associated forced restructuring of capital, labor processes, and class relations. Such misconceptions arise, on the social democratic left as well as the political center and right, from the confusion that the increased concentration of technical and social control over massive fixed-capital complexes by corporations, and a "politics of production" of individual labor processes that is increasingly opaque and mediated by layers of management protocols, are technological inevitabilities. The essays assembled here point to what is missing in all variants of technological fetishism: both a theoretical understanding of the class dynamics that inevitably distort and circumscribe the process of technological change under capitalism, and the political imagination to see the enormous untapped potential that could be unleashed by enabling popular capacities for democratic planning around technological development and deployment in a different system of production.

As the essays here attest, "making the working class" today is far removed from a backward-looking quest to reassemble a "traditional" industrial working class, in the face of new technologies and sectors of accumulation, as more than a few lazy liberal critiques have charged. And it is even less an effort to discover an equivalent to the proletariat under the amorphous—indeed vacuous—conceptual label of the "multitude." It is, rather, to insist on a careful class mapping—what Marx called for at one time as a "class inquiry"—of the tendencies and forces that materialize from specific technological developments in new labor processes and occupational vectors. The digital platforms and distributional logistics of twenty-first-century capitalism offer a landscape of class formation and struggle quite distinct from the coal seams of the Industrial Revolution or the auto plants of the last century.

But if new, even better, class maps can help us clarify the political questions at hand, they do not settle them. New technologies have always provided capacities for individual capitalist groups to control ever-larger masses of capital, whether decentralized into individualized workstations or organized into intricate commodity chains linking nodes of massive fixed investments in industrial, commercial, and financial capital. Being only one part of a chain of value production can easily engender a sense of vulnerability and push workers into "productivity pacts" with employers that accept the disciplines and stratifications of market competition in return for job guarantees. It is simply not possible to offer a brace of policies—such as work sharing, skills adjustment, or basic income programs, in the common technocratic response to automation for a century now—to offset the impacts of technological change in the hope of a more "humane" capitalism. More ambitious reforms also need to take up work-time reduction, collective bargaining controls over work reorganization, upgrading of skills and standards to be cognizant of cyber-work, and prohibitions on work surveillance. Of course, such measures will be fiercely resisted by employers. Renewed technological change will always emerge to breach even limited constraints placed on capital, driven by the imperatives of competitive accumulation and the need to maintain capitalist control over productive assets and the deployment of labor power.

An interventionist socialist strategy to tackle these fundamental qualities of technological change cannot evade, therefore, the need for an explicit anti-capitalism. The dependence of production on labor processes that are increasingly "socialized" and interconnected (what Marx variously called the "collective worker" or the "general intellect") affords the working-class movement crucial production and distributional leverage points and, moreover, potentially opens the horizons of workers to the democratic control of capital and workplaces. In her famous pamphlet, *The Mass Strike, the Political Party and Trade Unions* (1906), Rosa Luxemburg argued that the economic struggle cannot be sealed off from the political struggle (or vice versa; "cause and effect here continually change places"). Liberal democratic institutions and parliamentary party practices, however, push toward their separation. But in certain conjunctures the two can fuse—for Luxemburg, this occurs when the mass strike emerging out of workplace struggles becomes the vehicle for common political action as "innumerable partial struggles [become] united in . . . common class action."

It is impossible to envision any transformative project intent on sub-ordinating technological developments to human needs—an essential feature of any viable socialism—without a struggle on the two fronts of the workplace and the state. The more capital accumulates, the more the capitalist state has to mobilize its administrative and fiscal capaci-ties, especially under neoliberalism, to support and instrumentalize the commodified production of knowledge and science. Conversely, as this volume maintains, it is only through the practices of decommodifica-tion and democratization of both work and state that the subordination of technology can be achieved, so that the socialist aspirations for social control of production and the development of free time apart from work might become practical realities.

In the long chapter on "Machinery and Large-Scale Industry" in *Capital*, Marx observed that in the wake of the Luddite movement in the first decades of the nineteenth century, "it took both time and ex-perience before the workers learnt to distinguish between machinery and its employment by capital, and therefore to transfer their attacks from the material instruments of production to the form of society which utilizes those instruments." Marx's political lesson, carried for-ward in the essays in this collection, remains just as relevant to the "digital capitalism" of today and the "future of work": the need to locate our political struggles not in the subjective social organization formed by the "device" (today's machinery), but "to transfer our at-tacks" to capitalism and its crippling modes of deploying technology in its never-ending quest for the accumulation of ever more capital.

THE ECONOMICS OF NEO-CAPITALISM

Ernest Mandel

The ten years up to 1964 will probably be regarded by historians as the heyday of neo-capitalism.* In Western Europe and in Japan, capitalism has enjoyed a rate of economic growth and of prosperity which was unknown even before World War I. In the United States, after the "lean years" of republican deflationary stagnation, the Kennedy administration seemed to have reversed the trend and to have pushed the economy back onto the road of growth. World trade has beaten all records (the volume of world exports of manufactured goods in 1961 was three times as large as in 1938 and more than twice as large as in 1950). Only the underdeveloped countries presented a black spot in this bright picture.

CAUSES OF GROWTH

One does not have to be an apologist for capitalism in order to recognize the facts of life, namely, that the system has witnessed in most of the industrialized countries (the United States and Britain being the two main exceptions) an exceptionally high rate of growth during the past decade. This growth, following in the wake of a large reconstruction of physical damage wrought by the Second World War, cannot be explained essentially by reconstruction activities, even though this was still continuing in some of the countries concerned (especially in

---

*   This essay was first published in *Socialist Register 1964* (London: Merlin Press, 1964).

German house building, an important support of the industrial boom in that country).

From the point of view of trade cycle history, we were obviously faced with a new "Kondratieff," or long-wave movement involving several normal cycles. The theory of the long-wave movements in the history of capitalism was first developed by the Russian economist N. D. Kondratieff,[1] and Joseph Schumpeter integrated it into his own explanation of the cyclical movement of capitalist production, set out in his magnum opus, *Business Cycles*. It has earned less interest in Marxist circles, though Trotsky used a similar idea in his famous report before the Third World Congress of the Communist International.[2]

Today, it appears that, contrary to what most economists—Marxists and non-Marxists alike—were thinking in the late thirties and the early forties, after a Kondratieff wave of long-term stagnation which started in 1913 and lasted till 1939, world capitalism entered in 1940 on a new long wave of accelerated growth, which will probably last till the second half of the sixties. All the main indicators point to that conclusion.

In Schumpeter's trade cycle theory, long-term waves of more rapid expansion are explained basically by a rapid succession of technological innovations, which tend to appear "in bunches." This same explanation seems sufficient to account for the long-term wave of accelerated growth which world capitalism witnessed since the beginning of World War II. We could even add that this movement of technological innovation—generally called the Third Industrial Revolution—has *a tendency to become permanent*, which is something quite new in the history of capitalism. There is an important economic reason for this, which we shall go into later in this study. But one peculiar origin of this *stepping up of the general rate of technological innovation* should be emphasized immediately: it is the logical link between technological innovation and the permanent arms race.

Traditionally, technological *innovation* happens to arrive in bunches because it does not automatically flow from technological *discovery*; many discoveries will be allowed to lie dormant as long as current technological processes (and the fixed capital investments which they imply) have not been thoroughly exploited. But what is common capitalist procedure in the field of industry would become pure suicide in the field of armaments. The basic conflict between the capitalist powers and the Soviet bloc being what it is, capitalist countries cannot indulge in the luxury of first thoroughly using up supersonic bombers before going into rocket production. On the contrary the logic of the arms race implies that each basic technological discovery must lead as quickly as possible to innovation (that is, to large-scale production) in order that the same, or more advanced technology, does not become the monopoly of a potential antagonist. It is this which condemned the "Blue Streak" [intermediate-range ballistic missile] project before it was completed. As a result of the arms race, therefore, the time lag between technological discovery and technological innovations tends to shrink or even disappear altogether. Although the big monopolies will resist the automatic transfer of these innovations from the armament sector to the civilian sector of production, the interpenetration of both these sectors,[3] as well as the threat that competitors will use these innovations in order to improve their individual position, results in the general rate of innovations being considerably accelerated.

From a Marxist point of view, the *shortening of the duration of the trade cycle* which coincides since 1940 with the new Kondratieff long wave of increased growth can be explained by this same factor of stepped-up technological innovation. For Marx, the length of the trade cycle depends essentially upon the period of renewal of fixed capital. This was traditionally an eight- to ten-year period. Quicker technological innovation means, of course, a quicker renewal of fixed capital, whose lifetime is considerably shortened as a result of "moral" obsolescence. We thereby get trade cycles of four to five years' duration instead of those lasting eight to ten years. If the rate of technological innovation were to slow down again (as a result of the beginning of partial disarmament, or of the main factors of the "Third Industrial Revolution" having spent themselves), the lifetime of fixed capital would again tend to grow, and the trade cycle would again become longer. There is some indication—as yet insufficiently confirmed—that this has already happened in the United States, since the 1960–61 recession.

THE ANATOMY OF NEO-CAPITALIST GROWTH

The history of capitalism has always been dominated by *uneven development*: between countries, between regions inside each country, between groups of industries, and between industry and agriculture. Germany, Italy, and Japan are the three major powers which in the past decade have shown a higher rate of industrial growth than all others, while the unevenness of regional growth, in these three economies as well as in Britain, France, Belgium, Holland, and the United States, is a phenomenon that has been much commented upon. It is therefore necessary to draw attention in the first place to the uneven growth of various branches of industry, which is one of the main keys for understanding the present capitalist world (and Mr. Khrushchev's speech to the Central Committee of the CPSU, in December 1963, shows that this is true not only of capitalist countries).

Between 1958 and 1962, overall industrial production rose by 34 percent in the six countries of the Common Market. During this same period, the output of cars rose by 70 percent, the output of machine tools for the metal industry by 100 percent, the output of plastics by 160 percent, and the output of synthetic fibers by 235 percent. Further: industrial equipment and vehicles, which in 1938 represented only 32.7 percent of Germany's exports, today represent 46.2 percent (1962); while in France, they represented 14.5 percent of total exports in 1938 but in 1962 this percentage was already 26.8 percent, and it reached 30.1 percent for Italy in the same year.

Even if we look at the United States, which from many points of view went through a phase of near stagnation during the same period, we discover that the chemical industry passed the 50 percent–increase mark over the 1958 level of output during the first half of 1963. As for electricity output, it is running at present at the monthly average of 90 billion kWh, against 66 billion kWh in 1959 and 60 billion kWh in 1958, again a 50 percent increase. The slower overall rate of growth of the American industry is a result of the *combination* of stagnation in the "older" industries (like steel, coal, and textiles) and fast growth in chemicals, electronics, and electricity.

It is demand generated by these quick-growing industries (to which the building industry must be added, at least in countries like Germany, Italy, and Japan) which explains the generally high level of expansion in most of the imperialist countries. In the same way, it is the key role played by the rapid growth of certain big imperialist powers (in the first place Germany and Japan) which explains largely the growth of all other imperialist powers, since these latter are their main trade partners.

This is especially true for Western and Central Europe. The economy of this part of the world has expanded, so to speak, as a *system of concentric circles*, with Western Germany's growth at the center. This growth has induced the growth of other countries whose economies are deeply integrated with that of Western Germany (Austria, Switzerland, Denmark), and it has further generated accelerated growth in all the Common Market countries. Even peripheral countries like Spain, Greece, and Ireland (and in the future possibly even Portugal and Turkey, if the expansion lasts long enough, which, however, is rather questionable) have been drawn into the same whirlpool of capitalist expansion.

Some proof of this "anatomy of growth" can be clearly given in an industry-by-industry breakdown of expansion figures, provided by Common Market statistics. For instance: between 1953 and 1960, Germany's imports of manufactured paper rose from 252,000 tons to nearly 1.2 million tons; total imports of the six Common Market countries rose from 628,000 tons to 2.4 million tons, of which only 35 percent came from Common Market partners, thus providing a huge supplementary market for countries like Austria, Sweden, and Finland. From 1954 to 1961, German output in the shoe industry rose from roughly 100 million to 150 million pairs of shoes a year; but during the same period, German *imports* of shoes rose by value from less than US$5 million to nearly $50 million. During the same period Italy's shoe *exports* rose from $20 million in 1956 to $125 million in 1961, of which $41 million worth went to Common Market countries. Another example is that of the wood and furniture industry. Western Germany's output doubled between 1953 and 1961, but its imports increased nearly fivefold between 1958 and 1962 (from $4 million to $20 million); and during the same period, Italian and Dutch exports both doubled, respectively, from $5 million to $10 million, and from $6 million to $12 million, of which in the case of Italy only 30 percent, but in the case of Holland more than 75 percent, were sold to Common Market countries.[4]

Why was economic growth so much quicker in Western Germany, Italy, and Japan than in the other capitalist countries, and why did these three countries play such a strategic role in the general economic growth of much of the Western world? Several important factors could be advanced in order to explain this phenomenon. The most important one, however, seems to have been the *exceptionally high rate of capital accumulation*, explained by a *very high rate of profit*, which in its turn depends upon a much lower level of wages compared with other capitalist countries; and the lower wage levels are to be explained by the *much larger reserve army of labor*.

Historical factors can easily explain these distortions between the wage rates in the early 1950s of the United States, Britain, Sweden, Belgium, and even France on the one hand, and Western Germany, Italy, and Japan on the other hand. The capitalist class in each of these three latter countries were provided with an exceptionally favorable combination of circumstances. In the first place, they each had an abundant manpower situation with large-scale unemployment, and therefore low wage-rates. In Italy it has been the underdevelopment of the Mezzogiorno that made Southern Italy into a vast reservoir of labor supply for the North; in Japan it was the combination of a "modern" and an "archaic" (traditional) sector of industry, with the latter providing large reserves of labor for the former; and in Western Germany there was the influx of more than ten million refugees. Secondly, there was an immense fund of technological knowledge and innovation developed during the previous decade in the Anglo-Saxon countries which offered many possibilities of very rapid increases in productivity. It was the existence of these two main factors which explained at one and the same time the extremely low initial levels of wages in these three countries at the beginning of their boom periods and the practicability of "buying social peace" in exchange for *regular annual wage increases of a rather broad scope* which did not cut into the high rate of profit. Given the extremely rapid rate of accumulation, the industrial structure of these three countries has been transformed within the last ten years.[5]

THE CONTRADICTIONS OF NEO-CAPITALISM

Neo-capitalism itself is the new modus operandi of the capitalist system, whose distinctive characteristics flow from the organic needs of capital itself, as well as from the system's attempt to answer the challenge of the worldwide progress of anti-capitalist forces (the Soviet bloc and the colonial revolutions). These characteristics can be summarized in the following way:

1. The stepped-up rate of technological innovation and the short-ening of the life span of fixed capital impose accurate calcu-lations of depreciation and obsolescence, and more and more precise *long-term cost planning* in general. These are made pos-sible by the rapid progress of computer techniques and their application to economic calculations.

2. Like the two previous ones, the Third Industrial Revolution implies again a tremendous increase in the volume of industrial production, and there is a new and sharpened contradiction between seemingly limitless productive capacities and the lim-its of effective demand of the "market." Increasing difficulties of realization of surplus value lead to a *constant increase of selling costs*, and to the development of techniques of marketing, mar-ket research, elasticity of demand calculations, together with the somewhat less sophisticated antics of publicity.

3. The necessity of avoiding at all costs a repetition of the 1929-type depression has become a life-and-death question for capitalism under the conditions of the Cold War and the rise of the anti-capitalist forces on a world scale. The techniques of anti-cyclical policies and the redistribution of purchasing power by each individual state are developed on an increas-ing scale. The state now guarantees, directly and indirectly, private profit in ways that range from concealed subsidies to the "nationalization of losses," and this aspect of contemporary capitalism now becomes one of its most notable features.

4. The combination of all these factors leads to a gradual intro-duction of "planning" techniques into the capitalist economy, which are fundamentally nothing else than integrated fore-casts of demand and output by employers' associations (based upon projection into the future of current trends, corrected by rough demand-elasticity calculations), and which serve to "rationalize" in a certain way capital investment.

Although most of these "plans" involve some large errors in fore-casting,[6] and have not been able at all to prevent the appearance of excess capacity on a wide scale, it would be wrong to deny their useful-ness from the point of view of the big monopolies. The French Com-missariat Général du Plan, the Dutch Planbureau, the Belgian Bureau de Programmation, and their Italian counterpart (recently imitated in Britain by the National Economic Development Council) certainly help the employers to make investment decisions on a more sophisticated basis than by the old rule-of-thumb methods. Usually, this help is appreciated, and when it is not, it is more for reasons of political bias and bigotry than from any fear that this form of programming will undermine free enterprise and capitalism in general.

But if neo-capitalism's successes certainly shine bright, in view of results obtained during the past ten years, its inner contradictions—which superimpose themselves, so to speak, on the general contradictions of the capitalist mode of production, which have not been eliminated in any way whatsoever—are also coming to the forefront.

In the first place, inasmuch as neo-capitalism generates a higher rate of growth, in order to make possible a quicker amortization of fixed capital, it also tends to depress the reserve army of labor, and even to lead to nearly full employment (what the employers, of course, will call overfull employment). It thereby destroys one of the basic mechanisms which make capitalism work. For once there is no large-scale unemployment; there is no institutional factor built into the economic system which can prevent trade unions from exploiting favorable market conditions for winning higher wage rates. And such continuously increasing wages rates enter, of course, into conflict with the need for a high rate of profit in order to finance the huge capital outlays which are at the very basis of neo-capitalism's growth policy.

There thus appears *a growing contradiction between the needs of neo-capitalist programming and trade union freedom of bargaining for higher wages*. The capitalists try to solve this contradiction in two ways: an economic way and a sociopolitical way (or a combination of both).

The *economic* solution is a change in the *nature* of investment, putting an end to "extensive" or horizontal investment (i.e., the creation of new plants and enterprises) and concentrating on "intensive" (or vertical) investment, i.e., on labor-saving devices. This explains the *massive development of automation*, the aim being the *reconstitution of the reserve army of labor* which will tend to come about when the annual growth in productivity outruns the annual growth in output. This is the economic force which helps to make technological innovation *permanent* in the present long-wave Kondratieff cycle.

In the United States, this solution has been successfully applied during the past ten years, with the result that there has been a steady growth in the volume of structural unemployment. Even during periods of rapid economic development, the large pool of unemployed remains. In 1962, for example, output grew by nearly 9 percent, but there were still throughout the period more than four million unemployed. It can be applied in an even more efficient way if it is combined with a growing export of capital toward economies with lower wage rates, the effect of which is to exert pressures on existing wage levels in the capital-sending country, or at least a pressure against any upward movement.

The success of this employers' policy in the United States can be measured by the slowing down in the increase of real wages during the last ten years compared with the rapid wage increases on the European continent and in Japan. It can be assessed, too, by the slow erosion of trade union strength, and the changed relationship of forces between employers and trade unions which has resulted from this new situation.

In Western Germany, as soon as the steady flow of refugees from the East started to dry up, and as the reservoir of manpower thus disappeared, money wage-rates started going up very quickly. As a result of this reversal of trends, West Germany's real wages rapidly became the highest of the big industrial powers in Western and Central Europe. And German capitalism immediately reacted in the same way as in the United States, as a result of which total industrial employment actually *went down* for the first time during the first half of 1963 (from 8,037,000 to 7,976,000), after having risen since 1960 by less than 4 percent, whereas industrial output, which had risen by more than 20 percent between 1960 and 1962, again rose in the first half of 1963, although only by 1.5 percent.[7]

The *sociopolitical* solution consists in bringing strong pressure to bear upon the trade unions, either to practice wage restraint in a voluntary manner, or to be restricted in their bargaining possibilities and in the legal right to strike (Taft–Hartley law in the US; French anti-strike laws; big financial penalties imposed upon "wildcat strikes" in many Western European countries; attempts to impose an "anti-strike law" in Belgium).

But these policies, however successful they may seem in the short run, are self-defeating in the long run in terms of the goals neo-capitalism has set itself. For a huge buildup of fixed equipment, financed by a large increase in the rate of profit, cannot but lead to a considerable growth in the productive capacity of society, including its ability to produce consumer goods. And this must conflict, sooner or later, with the decline in consumers' purchasing power which will result from the relative stagnation both of wage rates and employment.

In the same way, both the attempt to stimulate growth by mild inflation and to halt inflation by deflationary policies must in the long run become self-defeating. Creeping inflation is one of the basic contradictions of neo-capitalism and of welfare statism in general. It results both from organic developments of capital ("administered prices" under monopoly capitalism) and from the specific new characteristics of the epoch (huge increases in arms expenses and in unproductive outlays in general). Boom conditions normally generate price increases. In the long run, this creeping inflation erodes the purchasing power of the main currencies; disorganizes long-term investment operations; stimulates speculation of every kind, among which real estate speculation occupies a privileged position in most countries; and generally undermines the normal functioning of the system (and in the case of the United States, growing capital exports are, of course, one of the causes of the deficit in the balance of payments). Any attempts to come to grips with inflation through efficient deflationary measures only throttles economic growth as such, and leads to stagnation, as Tory Britain (and in a certain sense the US, under Eisenhower) have learned to their cost: the cure is deadlier than the illness.

These contradictions of neo-capitalism are not only of theoretical importance inasmuch as they prove that the system remains fundamentally what it has always been. They also lead to the conclusion that the present rate of growth cannot be kept up; that the Common Market countries will also witness recessions; and that the long wave of increased growth will probably come to an end sometime during the sixties. The fact that the economic growth of the underdeveloped countries has not kept pace at all with the growth of the industrialized countries; that trade between the industrialized countries has more and more been substituting itself for trade between the advanced and the underdeveloped world; and that therefore the underdeveloped countries can play less and less the role of a safety valve for the capitalist system as a whole reinforces these conclusions.

EXCESS CAPACITY:
THE "MEMENTO MORI" OF NEO-CAPITALISM

In my *Traité d'économie marxiste*, I already emphasized the trend toward increasing excess capacity in capitalist industry, as one essential by-product of the reduced recessions and the smoother operation
of the system during the present phase of accelerated growth. In the
boom year 1956, in the United States, the automobile industry worked
only at 72 percent of its capacity, and the radio and TV industry at 60
percent of its capacity. The previous year, these percentages were respectively 55 percent in vacuum-cleaner production, 46 percent in the
refrigerator industry, and 70 percent in the cotton industry.[8]

The same phenomenon has recently spread to Western Europe. In
the Common Market, excess capacity has appeared in several sectors:
e.g., refrigerators, sewing machines, synthetic fibers, shipbuilding. A
recent source indicates that in Western Germany, the overall rate of
utilization of productive capacity in industry has fallen from 93.8 percent in 1956 to 90.2 percent in 1960 and 84 percent in 1962.[9] But the
two most significant cases which merit more comment are those of the
European steel industry and the European automobile industry.

Excess capacity in the European steel industry has existed for several
years, and output has stagnated in the Common Market steel industry
since 1960. However, despite stagnation, investment has continued to
increase. A record investment of seven hundred seventy-five million
dollars in the steel industry of the Six [EU founders] in that year was
increased by no less than 45 percent in 1961; and the investment level
of 1962 was nearly double that of 1960.

The explanation of this investment boom in face of stagnating output is simple: a series of technological innovations (LD, rotor, and other
patents, all based on massive oxygen injection) are being applied on a
large scale, and these new methods will mean a substantial fall in costs.
The introduction of new methods is all the more necessary as stagnation in output and underutilization tend to raise costs and thereby
cut into the rate of profit, at the same time as increased international
competition sharply reduces export prices.

This is a good example of the limits of neo-capitalist programming;
and the attempt of each individual firm to arrive at maximum income
under the conditions of a relative stagnation of demand leads to a mad
scramble for cutting production costs. This results in a considerable

increase in total productive capacity in the industry, the outcome of which can only be redundancy in the future.

The facts are striking. While the global output of the steel industry of the Six has been stagnating for four consecutive years around 73 million tons a year, productive capacity for 1965 is expected to rise to around 95 million tons (some sources even quote 100 million tons). Similarly, the output of hot rolling mills for 1965 is expected to be in the neighborhood of 18 to 19 million tons, while productive capacity in that year would increase up to 35 million tons, if all current investment programs are fulfilled.[10]

The case of the Western European automobile industry is as significant as that of the steel industry. But whereas the steel industry illustrates the development of excess capacity under conditions of *relatively stagnating markets* (under the pressure of price reductions), the car industry illustrates the development of excess capacity under the pressure of *rapidly growing markets* (and the feverish attempts of each firm to conquer the biggest possible share of that "bonanza" market, which is rightly considered to be of relatively short duration).

Total annual output of private cars (i.e., excluding trucks) has risen from nearly 1 million in 1953 to 3.7 million in 1961 in the six Common Market countries. By adding British output, this makes a total output of 1.5 million cars in 1953 and 4.7 million cars in 1961 in Western Europe. The total number of all types of vehicles in the Common Market countries has risen during this same period from 5 to 15.7 million, in the Six plus Britain from 7.8 to 22 million cars.

Projecting current demand in the future and using certain coefficients in order to predict prices, income and demand elasticity on this basis, possible sales inside the Common Market of 3.5 million private cars in 1965 and of 6 million private cars in 1970 have been foretold. But current investment *leads to a productive capacity of 6.5 to 7 million private cars in 1965* in these six countries, and their projection toward 1970 even mentions the figure of 10 million. It is obvious that the excess capacity already existing today is going to be greatly increased during the next years, and that this in turn will encourage many firms to increase investment in order to cut costs.[11]

SOCIALISTS AND NEO-CAPITALISM

Socialists should view neo-capitalism as an essentially organic development of monopoly capitalism. This means that they can neither see
their task as the hastening of neo-capitalist reforms, nor in defending
more backward capitalists, who try to obstruct neo-capitalist reforms
because they cannot keep up with the pace of investment and competition. The approach must be the same as the one socialists took
traditionally toward capitalist concentration and monopolies, neither
"promoting" concentration in the name of efficiency, nor "defending"
technically backward firms in the name of economic freedom, but of
considering concentration as inevitable *within the framework of capitalism*,
while using the progress of concentration as a most powerful argument
in favor of introducing socialism.

Neo-capitalist "planning" is planning neither in favor of harmonious growth nor "in the interests of the nation," but planning in favor
of rationalizing the oligopolies' investments *in defense of private profit*.
Everything is geared, in the long run, toward this central goal: the protection, defense, and guarantee of private profit in the strategically central
areas of monopoly capital (and the sectional interests of other bourgeois
groups are likely to be quite ruthlessly sacrificed in the process).

Socialists should neither oppose to these planning techniques the re-
actionary ideal of laissez-faire nor support them as a "step forward," but
insist upon the reality of socialist planning which does not imply only
technical differences (such as a greatly increased volume of direct state
investment and an enlarged public sector which will make possible a
centrally planned direction of the economy) but which involves *social*
priorities quite different from those which obtain today. A series of
production priorities, established by democratic discussion, will begin
to make possible the creation of a genuine equality of opportunity for
all. These new economic and social objectives will not only provide
free medicine, free education, decent housing, and the possibilities of
creative leisure, but they will also permit the working class of the West
to make a necessary contribution toward the final emancipation of the
colonial peoples, not only from foreign oppression and exploitation,
but also from the consequences of underdevelopment.

Around these priorities, a series of production objectives will then
automatically organize themselves, and provide us with a pattern of

production for needs as opposed to the *production for profit* of today, which has aptly been described as involving

> the purposive creation of dissatisfaction: the stimulus to status-seeking through conspicuous consumption; the incitement to create social differences working on the knowledge which modern psychology has unearthed; the playing on the sense of insecurity to encourage the desire of people to identify themselves with groups, which are outwardly full of goodwill but fiercely competitive in reality; the use of human frailty for profit-making purposes when concentrated educational and psycho-therapeutical drives would be needed to mitigate them.[12]

Socialists should not accept the neo-capitalist myth about the welfare state and the mass consumer's society. They should oppose their own values of consumption to those of the system geared to the maximization of private profit for a few monopolies. They should challenge further the inability of neo-capitalism to change in any way the *autocratic structure of business*, which is the basis of the alienation of labor in contemporary industry.

For that reason, and also because it is the necessary answer to any campaign in favor of an "incomes policy" (everybody knows the wages bill, but since there are innumerable ways of hiding profits, in order to avoid tax payments, why should we believe any statement of profits from the employers?), the demand for *workers' control* is today the strategically central demand of socialists and of the labor movements in general.

Workers' control is a first and essential step toward socialist democratic planning—the only efficient answer to neo-capitalist-programming. It is the first step toward workers' management of a socialized economy and toward industrial democracy (and as long as the economy is capitalistic, workers should refuse all co-responsibility in management). The demand for it is the means of drawing the working class into the great debate around the aggregate volumes of wages and profits (surplus value) which the discussion around an "incomes policy" will inevitably lead to. And it will give the essentially defensive strategy of the trade union movement (against wage restraint, and for freedom of bargaining) the necessary militant and positive character, without which the workers will be fighting a losing battle against the technocrats and their employers.

PROFESSOR GALBRAITH AND AMERICAN CAPITALISM

Ralph Miliband

T HE intellectual defense of capitalism has long ceased to be confined to the simple celebration of its virtues; or even to the argument that, whatever might be said against it, it was still a much better system, on economic, social, and political grounds, than any conceivable alternative to it.* Such arguments are of course still extensively used. But they belong to an older school of apologetics; and for some considerable time now, many people, who see themselves as part of the "democratic left," as liberal and even radical critics of the existing social order, and as anything but its apologists, have argued that the question of alternatives to capitalism had been rendered obsolete by the internal developments of the system itself; capitalism, the argument goes, has been so thoroughly transformed in the last few decades that the need to abolish it has conveniently disappeared. The job, for all practical purposes, has been done by the "logic of indus- trialization," which is well on the way to erasing all meaningful differences between "industrial systems," whatever misleading labels they may choose to pin upon themselves. Dinosaur socialists will, no doubt, continue to peddle their unwanted ideological wares; for their part, serious men with a bent for reform will address themselves to the *real* problems of what Mr. Crosland long ago called "postcapitalist" societies.

The New Industrial State is a further version of this by now familiar thesis.[1] Professor Galbraith, however, does not conceal his belief that

---

★   This essay was first published in *Socialist Register 1968* (London: Merlin Press, 1968).

he is here unrolling a map of American capitalism (or of "what is commonly called capitalism") which is entirely new, and immeasurably more accurate than any previous one. The former claim is rather exaggerated, but it is perfectly true that there is much in his essay which is indeed new. The question, however, is whether what is new is also true, and whether the combination of old and new really does provide an accurate, reliable map of American economic life. The answer, as I propose to argue in this review, is that it does not; and that much more interesting than the revelation which it purports to bring about the true nature of American capitalism is what it reveals of the confusion and bafflement of the latter-day liberalism which Professor Galbraith represents, in regard to an "industrial system" which it approaches with a mixture of admiration and distaste, and whose basic irrationality, some aspects of which it perceives, it is either unable or unwilling to locate and transcend. It is not surprising that Professor Galbraith should sometimes be seen as a critic of the system and sometimes as its defender. For he is both, at one moment belaboring conservative economists, yet echoing, in more elegant language, their own vulgar apologetics, at another trembling on the brink of radical criticism, yet unable to jump. The famous style of exposition itself, the labored humor, the straining after ironic effect, the attempt at cool wit, all testify to the ideological tension. Professor Galbraith perceives that an advanced industrial system *requires* the transcendence of private appropriation, and much of his book is in fact a documented, though seemingly unconscious, comment on Marx's prediction that with the development of capitalism, "centralization of the means of production and socialization of labour at last reach a point where they become incompatible with their capitalist integument." But the central point of the book, which is also its central weakness, is that the "industrial system" has actually *solved* the problem, and that whatever adjustments it further requires can be achieved within its present framework, and without, perish the thought, the invocation of the old socialist gods. The tone is critical and so is the intent, but the result is all the same profoundly apologetic.

★ ★ ★

In *American Capitalism: The Concept of Countervailing Power*, first published in 1952, Professor Galbraith advanced the notion that while the growing concentration of economic enterprise might appear to entail a dangerous increase in the power of business, traditional liberal, not to speak of socialist, fears on this score were really misconceived: for the power of business was, he argued, effectively balanced and checked by a variety of forces and agencies, such as organized labor, other economic interests, the state, the consumer, and so forth. This notion of "countervailing power," coming as it did in the early days of an ideological, political, and military struggle which counterposed power-diffused democracy to monolithic communism was an exceptionally useful ideological weapon; and it served as one of the foundations of a theory of political pluralism which has since greatly prospered, to the point of becoming the dominant orthodoxy of Western political and social theories of power in capitalist societies: in these societies, a plurality of "interests" (classes being rather *vieux jeu*) compete under the watchful eye of a democratic state and achieve, as a result of that competition, a rough equilibrium in which everybody has some power and no one has, or can have, too much.

In *The New Industrial State,* Professor Galbraith has now come to discard the notion of "countervailing power." Unions, he now believes, are a declining force, consumers are the manipulated prisoners of induced demand, the state serves the goals of the "industrial system," and there is no "interest" remotely comparable in importance to the five or six hundred large corporations which are "the heartland of the modern economy."

Professor Galbraith writes:

> Nothing so characterizes the industrial system as the scale of the modern corporate enterprise. In 1962 the five largest industrial corporations in the United States, with combined assets in excess of $36 billion, possessed over 12 per cent of all assets used in manufacturing. The fifty largest corporations had over a third of all manufacturing assets. The 500 largest had well over two-thirds. Corporations with assets in excess of $10,000,000, some 2,000 in all, accounted for about 80 per cent of all the resources used in manufacturing in the United States. In the mid nineteen-fifties, 28 corporations provided approximately 10 per cent of all employment in manufacturing, mining and retail and wholesale trade. Twenty-three corporations provided 15 per cent of all employment in manufacturing. In the first half of the decade (June 1950 – June 1956) a hundred firms received two-thirds by value of all defense contracts; ten firms received one-third. In 1960 four corporations accounted for an estimated 22 per

cent of all industrial research and development expenditure. Three
hundred and eighty-four corporations employing 5,000 or more
workers accounted for 55 per cent of these expenditures; 260,000
firms employing fewer than 1,000 accounted for only 7 per cent.[2]

This is, indeed, impressive, and Professor Galbraith is certainly right
to place this formidable complex at the center of the picture, since
those who control it might also reasonably be thought to concentrate
in their hands a vast amount of power, not only economic but political
and cultural as well.

Not so at all, Professor Galbraith hastens to reassure us. For while *resources* are concentrated, *power* is not. Power, in the "industrial system"
is not in the hands of the old-style owner-capitalist, who has, he suggests, all but disappeared; nor of course is it held by essentially passive
shareholders; nor even by that managerial elite which had long been
claimed to have inherited the power of both. The people to whom
corporate power *has* passed, Professor Galbraith insists again and again,
is an entirely different element, so far overlooked by all other toilers
in this field, namely "the technostructure." On this, it is necessary to
quote Professor Galbraith at some length, firstly because much of his
thesis rests on this discovery, and secondly because it will be argued
here that the "technostructure" as the new repository of corporate
power is unmitigated nonsense.

The "technostructure" comprises a "very large" group of people
who "contribute information to group decisions" and who "extend
from the most senior officials of the corporation to where it meets, at
the outer perimeter, the white and blue collar workers whose function
is to conform more or less mechanically to instructions or routine. It
embraces all who bring specialized knowledge, talent or experience
to group decision-making." "It will be evident that nearly all powers
– initiative, character of development, rejection or acceptance – are exercised deep in the company. It is not the managers who decide. Effective power of decision is lodged deeply in the technical, planning and
other specialized staff."[3] Indeed, Professor Galbraith, later in the book,
goes even further. For, he tells us, "distinctions between those who
make decisions and those who carry them out, and between employer
and employee, are obscured[4] by the technicians, scientists, market analysts, computer programmers, industrial stylists and other specialists
who do, or are both. A continuum thus exists between the centre of

the technostructure and the more routine white-collar workers on the fringe."[5]

On this view, the demon Power has once again been exorcized, without the help of "countervailing power": for the "technostructure" is very large, and the power which accrues to it is therefore diffuse, shared—indeed, why not say it? Democratic.

★ ★ ★

In examining this remarkable argument, it may, to begin with, be noted that much of it rests on the by now well-entrenched notion of the separation of ownership from control, which Professor Galbraith pushes to its furthest limits: for him, those who control the corporations are now virtually ownerless, and ownership is in any event wholly irrelevant to corporate policy.

A considerable amount of evidence and argument, which Professor Galbraith does not discuss, has been produced over the years to rebut or at least to qualify this thesis; and some interesting further evidence against it has recently appeared in *Fortune* magazine.

In an article entitled "Proprietors in the World of Big Business," and concerned with ownership and control in the five hundred largest corporations in the United States, Mr. Robert Sheehan writes that "in approximately 150 companies on the current *Fortune* list (i.e. of the 500 largest industrial corporations) controlling ownership rests in the hands of an individual or of the members of a single family"; and, he adds, "the evidence that 30 percent of the 500 largest industrials are clearly controlled by identifiable individuals, or by family groups . . . suggests that the demise of the traditional American proprietor has been slightly exaggerated and that the much-advertised triumph of the organization is far from total."[6] Mr. Sheehan, it should be explained, also notes that he has used a very conservative criterion of control, i.e., that his list only includes companies in which the largest individual stockholder owns 10 percent or more of the voting stock or in which the largest block of shares—representing 10 percent or more of the total votes—is held by members of a single family. This, he points out, leaves out "coalitions" which may assure working control for small groups of associates in many companies; and also businessmen known to wield great influence with holdings of less than 10 percent. Even so, "at least 10 family-controlled companies rank among the top 100, and several of these are actively owner-managed"; and "approximately seventy family-named companies among the 500 are still controlled by the founding family."[7]

Even if these pretty severe qualifications to the thesis of the disappearance of the owner-controller are ignored (and Professor Galbraith was in no position to consider them, since they appeared after he had written his book), the question remains as to the managerial elite's relation to ownership. Professor Galbraith, as noted, wholeheartedly endorses the thesis of managerial ownerlessness. Thus: "stock holdings by management are small and often non-existent"; "even the small stock interest of the top officers is no longer the rule"; and so on.

This, too, however, is rather extreme. For, as one writer among many has noted, "the managerial class is the largest single group in the stockholding population, and a greater proportion of this class owns stock than any other."[8] Another writer notes that "a recent study by the National Industrial Conference Board shows that 73 percent of 215 top executives during the period 1950–1960 gained at least 50,000 dollars through the use of stock options, that 32 percent gained 250,000 dollars, and that 8 percent gained at least 1,000,000 dollars";[9] and by 1957, it may also be noted, option plans for the purchase of stock had been instituted by 77 percent of the manufacturing corporations listed in the New York or American Stock Exchange.[10] Managers, the evidence shows, are by no means as ownerless as Professor Galbraith, following many others, maintains.

On the other hand, how often ownership determines control is a rather more complex question. That it does not has, of course, been an article of faith with managerial revolutionists ever since Berle and Means claimed in 1932 that "ownership is so widely distributed that no individual or small group has even a minority interest large enough to dominate the affairs of the company."[11] This too has long been held to be far too categorical. There is dispersal of ownership (though even this should not be exaggerated), but, as Mr. Clive Beed of the University of Melbourne has recently argued, the method used by Berle and Means

> is unable to separate ownership from control because it does not establish empirically the proportion of votes needed for control in the real as distinct from the legal company situation . . . since ownership is very widely dispersed (among different names) in management controlled companies, either it could mean, with Berle and Means,

that no one individual or small group could gain sufficient votes for control, *or*, contradicting Berle and Means, that only a few percent of votes was required for control.[12]

Various such percentages have at one time or another been advanced. As Mr. Sheehan suggests, 10 percent is a very conservative estimate. Mr. Villarejo took 5 percent as the amount of stock required to control a corporation whose stock is widely dispersed, and found that in at least 76 of the 232 largest United States corporations, ownership on boards of directors was sufficient to ensure working control;[13] and Mr. Beed also notes that Professor Gordon's 1945 study, *Business Leadership in the Large Corporations*, on which Professor Galbraith greatly relies, held that 3 percent ultimate ownership might exercise control.[14] In fact, as Mr. Beed suggests, "the possibility of '*any percentage*' control does exist."[15] And where it does, that control-through-ownership is most likely to be in the hands of top managers. Moreover, one place where it is *not* likely to be lodged is in Professor Galbraith's "technostructure." For it is scarcely to be thought that "the technical, planning and other specialized staff" in which, according to him, "the effective power of decision is lodged" ("deeply") are to be counted among the "large owners" of corporate stock.

This, however, is by no means the main reason for thinking that the claim is invalid. For even if it is assumed—which is obviously often the case—that top managers do not exercise control through ownership, the notion that they do not exercise control *at all,* and that the men at the top of the corporate structure are, as Professor Galbraith claims, virtually powerless and ceremonial figures, whose function within the corporation is "to give the equivalent of the royal assent to agreements, contracts and indentures"[16]—this notion too must invite complete disbelief, the more so since Professor Galbraith provides no concrete evidence whatever to buttress his claim.

That claim, in fact, would appear to rest on an extreme "technocratic" view of the degree of influence which hierarchically subordinate technical experts of one sort or another (and the corporation is of course a highly hierarchical, and hierarchy-conscious organization) may wield with men upon whom the power of managerial decision rests. There may be "mature corporations" where the top men are *rois fainéants* or constitutional monarchs. But hard evidence to that effect is lacking. Professor Galbraith claims that the expert influence in the corporation is decisive. There is every reason to think that, here as in government, it is nothing of the kind. The expert does not decide policy: he works out how best to carry it out. In that role, he may well affect policy, but this is hardly synonymous with the dramatic reversal of roles—the experts on top, the managers on tap—which Professor Galbraith claims to be the present reality of the "industrial system."

★ ★ ★

Having lodged the "effective power of decision" in the "technostructure," Professor Galbraith proceeds to discuss the latter's "motivations." Since there is no good evidence to suggest that the "technostructure" does have such power, it might seem superfluous to follow him in this exercise. But since much that he has to say about the motivations of the "technostructure" also concerns wider issues of corporate policy, it is worthwhile persevering.

Theories of motivation have been closely linked with the thesis of ownerless management. That thesis was not, it may be surmised, so passionately embraced by so many writers because of its irresistible conceptual beauty. Ideology came into it as well. For from the view that the new class of managers neither owned the resources it controlled, nor was subject to the control of owners, it was but the shortest step, which was eagerly taken, to the claim that managers were, in their running of the corporation, moved by impulses altogether different from those of old-style capitalist owner-entrepreneurs, or from those of passive shareholders, and that these impulses were not only different, but *better,* less "selfish," more "socially responsible." It was this notion which Professor Carl Kaysen once epitomized in the phrase "the soulful corporation." "No longer the agent of proprietorship seeking to maximize return on investment," he claimed, "management sees itself as responsible to stockholders, employees, customers, the general public, and perhaps most important, the firm itself as an institution . . . there is no display of greed and graspingness;[17] there is no attempt to push off onto the workers or the community at large part of the social costs of the enterprise. The modern corporation is a soulful corporation."[18] This, incidentally, was also the view of Mr. C. A. R. Crosland, who wrote in *the Conservative Enemy* that "now perhaps most typical amongst very large firms, is the company which pursues rapid growth and high profits – but subject to its sense of social responsibility and its desire for good labour and public relations. . . . Its goals are a 'fair' rather than a maximum profit, reasonably rapid growth and the warm glow which comes from a sense of public duty."[19] Much the same view, it may be recalled, also found expression in a major Labour Party policy document, which proclaimed that "under increasingly professional management, large firms are as a whole serving the nation well."[20]

This notion of soulful managerialism has often been challenged on two different grounds. Firstly, on the ground that top managers do, as "large owners," often have a direct financial interest in "profit maximization." Thus, Mr. Sheehan, in the article quoted earlier, notes that "Chairman Frederic C. Donner, for example, owns only 0.017 percent of GM's outstanding stock, but it was worth about $3,917,000 recently. Chairman Lynn A. Townsend owns 0.117 percent of Chrysler, worth about $2,380,000. Their interest in the earnings of those investments is hardly an impersonal one."[21] And Professor Kolko also notes that "in early 1957, 25 General Motors officers owned an average of 11,500 shares each. Collectively their holdings would have been inconsequential if they had chosen to try and obtain control of GM through their stocks. Yet each of these men had a personal share of roughly half a million dollars in the company."[22] The largest part of managerial income may not be derived from ownership, or depend upon such ownership, but managers are hardly likely, all the same, to ignore their shareholdings in their view of what their firms ought to be about. As indeed why should they?

The second and more important reason why managers *are* concerned with "profit maximization" has been well put by Baran and Sweezy: "The primary objectives of corporate policy," they write,

> which are at the same time and inevitably the personal objectives of the corporate managers—are thus strength, rate of growth and size. There is no general formula for quantifying or combining these objectives—nor is there any need for one. For they are reducible to the single common denominator of profitability. Profits provide the internal funds for expansion. Profits are the sinews and muscle of strength, which in turn gives access to outside funds if and when they are needed. . . . Thus profits, even though not the ultimate goal, are the necessary means to all ultimate goals. As such, they become the immediate, unique, unifying, quantitative aim of corporate

policies, the touchstone of corporate rationality, the measure of corporate success.[23]

As it happens, the inventor of the "soulful corporation" himself concedes a good deal to this view. "It may be argued," Professor Kaysen writes, "that all this (i.e. the managers' multiple responsibilities) amounts to no more than long-run profit maximization, and thus that management in the modern corporation does no more than business management has always tried to do, allowing for changed circumstances"; furthermore "only the ability to continue to earn a substantial surplus over costs makes possible a variety of expenditures whose benefits are broad, uncertain and distant."[24] This is also Mr. Sheehan's conclusion: "Very few executives argue that the managers of a widely held company run their business any differently from the proprietors of a closely held company"; "it is unrealistic to assume that because a manager holds only a small fraction of his company's stock he lacks the incentive to drive up the profits."[25] Indeed, Professor James Earley has even gone further and suggested, very plausibly, that the modern manager may be better placed to pursue profit than the old-style entrepreneur, because with "the rapidly growing use of economists, market analysis, other types of specialists and management consultants by our larger businesses . . . profit-oriented rationality is likely to be more and more representative of business behaviour."[26]

For his part, Professor Galbraith will have none of this. Profit maximization, he holds, excludes other goals. But this can only be true if "profit maximization" is taken to mean, as Professor Galbraith appears to mean, a reckless and wholly irrational pursuit of immediately realizable profit, regardless of any longer-term consideration. And this is a purely arbitrary definition, which is applicable neither to corporate management, nor, for that matter, to owner-entrepreneurs.

In any case it is not the motivation of managers, but of the "technostructure" which, in Professor Galbraith's view, is what matters. The professional and salaried staff who mainly compose it are, he insists, even less concerned with "profit maximization" than top managers. This may well be the case, but would only be significant if one were to accept the view that the corporation "as an instrument of power" is used "to serve the deeper interests and goals of the technostructure." And there are no good grounds, as I have suggested, for accepting this view.

Even so, it may be worth examining what, according to Professor Galbraith, these "goals" of the "technostructure" are, since his discussion illustrates so well the extreme difficulty of finding a rationale for corporate enterprise clearly distinct from financial reward.

Despite solemn announcements of motivational revelations, the motives and goals which Professor Galbraith ascribes to the "technostructure" (purely on the basis of supposition and inference) turn out, upon examination, to be no different from the goals which have often been ascribed to top management—the survival of the firm, its growth, its independence from outside control. But these are precisely the kinds of issues which the technical and professional staffs within the corporation are least likely to be called upon to decide.

Nor is Professor Galbraith at all successful in locating the larger "social" goals which, he claims, move the "technostructure." "The individual," he tells us, "will identify himself with the goals of the corporation only if the corporation is identified with, *as the individual sees it,* some significant social goal." On the other hand, "the individual," he also tells us, "serves organization because of the possibility of accommodating its goals more closely to his own." But *then,* we also find that "he will normally think that the goals he seeks have social purpose," "for individuals have a well-marked capacity to attach high social purpose to whatever – more scientific research, better zoning laws, manufacture of the lethal weapons just mentioned – *serves their personal interest.*" Moreover, it does not appear to matter in the least *what* the corporation produces, whether "life-saving drugs" or "an exotic missile fuel, or a better trigger for a nuclear warhead."[27]

What this amounts to is that whatever "goals" members of the "technostructure" may have will be seen, *by them,* as having a "social purpose"; and whatever the corporation produces will be deemed, *by them,* to have an equally "social purpose." As Professor Galbraith puts it, "what counts here is what is believed."[28] But this surely renders the discussion of "goals" quite meaningless. For why should we accept the "goals" of the "technostructure" as having a "social purpose" simply because its members happen to *believe* this to be the case?

In any case, Professor Galbraith himself is compelled to attribute more importance to "pecuniary compensation" than many of his formulations would tend to suggest. For it appears that other "goals" only operate *after* a certain level of income has been achieved; it is only "above a certain level" that other motivations "may operate independently of income"; "the participants are well compensated" and "few regard their compensation with disinterest." On one page, "pecuniary compensation, as an explanation of effort, has now a much diminished role"; twenty pages later, "pecuniary compensation is an extremely important stimulus to individual members of the technostructure up to a point. If they are not paid this acceptable and expected salary, they will not work."[29] As a "general theory of motivation," these extraordinary contortions may be thought to leave something to be desired.

★ ★ ★

One of Professor Galbraith's most insistent themes is that modern economic life requires planning. But this requirement, it would appear, is already largely met in the American "industrial system": for the United States, *mirabile dictu,* is "a largely planned economy." This remarkable assertion rests on the notion that the "mature corporation" is able to plan because it is no longer subject to the vagaries of a market which it controls, or to the cold winds of competition; and its planning is the more secure in that the state controls aggregate demand: "[T]he firm is the basic planning unit in the western economies. In the Soviet system it is still the state."[30] This is surely pushing "convergence" beyond the bounds of sense. For whatever may be thought of Soviet planning, it is hardly to be assimilated to the "planning" of which Professor Galbraith speaks. Even if one leaves aside his dubious elimination of the market and of competition from the "industrial system," and his no less dubious assurance that the state has perfected its mechanism of control of aggregate demand (i.e., that depression is now not only unlikely but impossible), the planning in which individual corporations engage bears no relation to, and is in fact the opposite of, any meaningful concept of national planning. Professor Galbraith may *wish* to overcome the anarchy of production characteristic of his "industrial system"; but the wish ought not to be taken for a fact.

As for "state intervention," Professor Galbraith clearly sees that what he calls "the public sector," i.e., government expenditure, is the "fulcrum" for the regulation of demand. And he also notes that "plainly military expenditures are the pivot on which the fulcrum rests." This he finds regrettable. But all he has to offer, concretely, as an alternative to military expenditure is expenditure on space competition. "In relation to the needs of the industrial system, the space competition is nearly ideal." He is then moved to ask: "Are there not better uses for the resources so employed?" And he answers, in a remarkable and revealing phrase:

> There is no rational answer to these questions as there is none to a query as to why negotiated disarmament is inherently more danger-ous than a continuance of the weapons competition. *Truth in both instances is subordinate to need and the needed belief.* But this does not affect the value of the space competition in meeting the needs of the industrial system in a comparatively harmless instead of an extremely dangerous competition.[31]

This would do very well as a satire on the "industrial system," of the kind presented, deliberately or unwittingly, by *Report from Iron Moun-tain.* But Professor Galbraith is not here, to all appearances, in the least satirical. And his prescription therefore betokens, in the face of genuine human need, an illuminating willingness to sacrifice reason so as to meet the "need and the needed belief" of the "industrial system."

But what, in any case, if armaments expenditure is not simply pro-duced by a deluded view, as Professor Galbraith suggests, of the "Soviet threat"? What if it is the inevitable expression of the determination to maintain the largest-possible area of the globe open to the "indus-trial system," and to a consequent determination to counter by every means, including military means, all attempts to resist that penetra-tion? What, in other words, if military expenditure is the necessary concomitant of the expansionist needs of the "industrial system" itself? Professor Galbraith has not a word to say about *this* aspect of the "in-dustrial system," of its relation to the world, of its imperialist urges; and it is only by ignoring it, and by ignoring the supreme irrationality of his prescription, that he is able to urge "space competition" as an alternative to armaments.

In a sense, his default is all the greater in that he does see that the system "generally ignores or holds as unimportant those services of the state which are not closely related to the system's needs";[32] and that a state attuned to capitalist purposes therefore neglects those services.

Yet even here, there is a typical disregard of the *scale* of the human needs which are left unfulfilled. Professor Galbraith is of course con-cerned with poverty. But in *The New Industrial State* as in *The Afflu-ent Society,* he treats it as an all but marginal, "special" problem. The

latter book rendered an immense service to the "industrial system"
by helping to popularize the notion that capitalism had all but eliminated poverty, or that it had at least reduced it to marginal, "minority"
proportions. In *The Affluent Society,* he described poverty as mainly
confined to "special" sections of the population: either "some quality peculiar to the individual or family involved – mental deficiency,
bad health, inability to adapt to the discipline of modern economic
life, excessive procreation, alcohol, insufficient education, or perhaps a
combination of several of these handicaps – has kept these individuals
from participating in the *general* well-being"[33] (the notion that these
are qualities "peculiar to the individual" is distinctly odd, but let it
pass); or, alternatively poverty was an "insular" phenomenon, which
had "something to do with the desire of a comparatively large number
of people to spend their lives at or near the place of their birth."[34] In
either case, his readers, presumably mentally alert, healthy, disciplined,
sexually sophisticated, nonalcoholic, educated, and mobile, were given
to understand, for this was the theme of the whole book, that here *was*
a special problem, which might be thought to involve, since Professor
Galbraith did not venture figures, a quite easily manageable minority.
Poverty might be a "disgrace" to an "affluent society"; but the very
idea of the affluent society exiled the poor to its outer fringes and
greatly helped to obscure them from view.

It was not long after the publication of *The Affluent Society* that poverty was rediscovered in the United States (and in Britain), not as a
marginal and special phenomenon, on the way to eradication in "postcapitalist" societies, but as a literally massive phenomenon, of quite
gruesome proportions. Harry Magdoff has summarized thus, to take
but one example, the findings of an impeccably official Conference on
Economic Progress which reported in April 1962: "The simple summary of the Conference Report on the 1960 income situation in the
US is as follows: 34 million people in families and 4 million unattached
individuals (that is, unattached economically to a family unit) lived
in poverty; 37 million people in families and 2 million unattached
individuals lived in deprivation. The total of 77 million comprised
two-fifths of the US population in 1960."[35] This is not, as Professor
Galbraith had it, "private affluence and public squalor," but public
squalor *and* private poverty.

There is nothing in *The New Industrial State* to suggest that Professor Galbraith has taken note of such findings, nothing to qualify his view of poverty as a special, marginal, and easily soluble "problem." Certain "tasks"—"the care of the ill, aged and physically or mentally infirm, the provision of health services in general, the provision of parks and many other services"—"are badly performed to the general public's discomfort or worse. Were it recognized that they require planning, and in the context of a largely planned economy [*sic*] have been left unplanned, there would be no hesitation or apology in the use of all the necessary instruments for planning. Performance would be much better."[36] In fact, nothing is more certain than that it would require much more than "recognition" for performance to be much better. Here is not simply optimism but blindness to the reality which Professor Galbraith so insistently claims, throughout his book, to portray; and it is a blindness induced by the wish to see all "problems" of the "industrial system" as readily soluble within its framework, and without the need to look beyond it.

The final question raised by Professor Galbraith's modest discontents with the "industrial system" concerns the likely agencies of its reform. Not labor, certainly; for in that system, "everything is more benign. Compulsion will have receded. In consequence, there is little or no alienation; the way is open for the worker to accept the goals of the organization"; "interests that were once radically opposed are now much more nearly in harmony." Demand for change cannot, clearly, be expected from the happy industrial family which Professor Galbraith has conjured up; where, but fifteen short years ago, there were large reserves of countervailing power, there is now unalienated integration. But all hope is not lost, for there remains, in growing numbers and strength, the "educational and scientific estate." "It is possible," Professor Galbraith suggests, "that the educational and scientific estate requires only a strongly creative political hand to become a decisive instrument of political power."[37] "A decisive instrument of political power" is pitching it rather high, and the notion of people as "an instrument" of political power, decisive or otherwise, is ambiguous and unattractive. Still, there is everything to be said for the stress on the responsibility and possible power of intellectuals. But the question then arises—political power for what? Professor Galbraith has no serious answer to that question. In fact, his whole soothingly complacent view of the "industrial system" and of American society precludes him from providing such an answer. For all the verbal iconoclasm, and the seeming dismissal of "conventional wisdom" and orthodox economics, there is too much here of apologetics and obfuscation, too little genuine probing, too ready an acceptance of the "logic" of the system, too cramped a view of its contradictions, too much underlying intellectual and political timidity, notwithstanding the self-conscious *enfant terrible* posturings, for Professor Galbraith to speak seriously to the American condition, or to those who seriously seek to change it. For such people, *The New Industrial State* has little to offer, either by way of diagnosis, or of prescription. What it does offer is a further demonstration of the limitations, both in diagnosis and in prescription, of a type of liberalism which constitutes not an alternative but a variant of that conservatism which Professor Galbraith claims to condemn.

ANDRÉ GORZ AND HIS
DISAPPEARING PROLETARIAT

Richard Hyman

*F*arewell to the Working Class:[1] an apposite text to review in election week 1983?* The erosion of traditional Labour loyalties—first
through the relative or even absolute decline in the staple industries and
occupations in which Labourism was rooted, second through a switch
from political support and identity as an inbuilt reflex to more calcu-
lative and volatile electoral behavior—has been a topic of analysis and
debate for a quarter of a century. Three successive defeats for Labour in
the 1950s provoked influential assertions that the party's working-class
identification had become a fatal handicap,[2] as well as pleas for a dilution
of the state socialist objectives enshrined in the 1918 party constitution.[3]
Though apparent electoral recovery under Harold Wilson largely stilled
such controversies, mass unemployment and the rise of Thatcherism have
brought renewed attention to the political implications of the changing
composition and structure of the working class.[4]

In the agonizings which will inevitably follow Labour's new disaster, what can British socialists learn from experience and analysis
elsewhere? André Gorz is well known among the British left (and even
better in the United States) as a prolific essayist and polemicist. In his
early years profoundly influenced by Sartre, he has been a member of the
editorial committee of *Les Temps Modernes* since its formation in 1961;[5]
and has shown a distinctive capacity to apply a humanistic Marxism to

---

* This essay was first published in *Socialist Register 1983* (London: Merlin Press,
  1983).

the contemporary predicament and struggles of workers both nationally and internationally. His writings during these years have revealed
an uncanny aptitude to crystallize, and at times anticipate, innovatory
concerns among socialists: shop floor union rebellions, demands for
workers' control, the growth and seeming radicalization of technical
employment, the nature of capitalist control of the labor process, the
connections between work, consumption, and the environment.[6]

Farewell to the Working Class (first published in French in 1980) was
written after the defeat of the French left in 1978; and though no
overt reference is made to the immediate political context, the demoralization and recrimination of the period must have influenced the
writing of this book—accentuating its relevance for socialists today. It
is a work characteristic of Gorz's perceptive and rigorously (if often
selectively) critical intelligence; and characteristic also in its limited
overall integration. In its 152 pages the book provides a preface, an
introduction, nine main chapters, a postscript, and two appendices,
in the course of which a variety of themes emerge, combine, diverge,
disappear, and reappear. Rarely can so brief a work have been so dis-
cursively fashioned. Rather than attempting to impose my own structure, however, I propose to set out Gorz's arguments according to his
own format before offering a critical assessment of what I regard as the
central themes.

For the English reader, Gorz offers his own initial summary: "Nine
Theses for a Future Left." First, he defines his objectives as "the liberation of time and the abolition of work," insisting that within capitalism
work is always an externally imposed obligation rather than self-de-
termined activity. Second, he relates the contrast between work and
autonomous activity to that between exchange value and use value.
Thus the progressive abolition of waged work implies the reciprocal
liberation of productive activity from the domination of commodity
relations. Third, he argues that the abolition of work is already in process, as a result of mass unemployment. Current trends offer the alternatives of a society sharply divided between a mass of unemployed or
those in casual and marginalized work, and an advantaged minority
in relatively secure employment; or one in which socially necessary
labor is spread thinly among all who are available to work, freeing the
bulk of people's time for self-defined activities. Fourth, Gorz stresses
the inadequacy of the "right to work" as a political slogan. Full-time

employment for all is no longer possible, nor necessary or desirable. A guaranteed income for all, as commonly demanded by the left, would merely represent "a wage system without work": exploitation by capital would give way to dependence on the state, perpetuating the "impotence and subordination of individuals to centralised authority."[7] Instead, the aim should be "the right to autonomous production": access to means of production (in the form defined by Illich as "tools for conviviality")[8] so that individuals and grassroots communities can produce directly for their own use. One consequence would be to break down the division between social production and domestic labor.

Gorz turns to the question of agency. His fifth thesis is that the abolition of work is not a demand of immediate appeal to the minority of skilled workers still able to take pride in their occupation and exert some control over the labor process; their response to changing technology is typically negative and defensive. But the abolition of work could win the support of routine employees in boring jobs, whom he describes as "a non-class of nonworkers." Restoring skill and creativity to the bulk of work, he insists as his sixth thesis, is not an option. While some aspects of capitalist work organization and its application of high technology may be rejected, the rapid production of use values which is the precondition of a major reduction in working time requires "a standardisation and formalisation of tools, procedures, tasks and knowledge. . . . The socialisation of production inevitably implies that microprocessors or ball-bearings, sheet metals or fuels are interchangeable wherever they are produced, so that both the work and the machinery involved have the same interchangeable characteristic everywhere." Seventh, the socialization of production also limits the scope for self-management. Autonomous collective decisions within productive units can do no more than adjust the details of each unit's integration within the overall social division of labor. Such forms of decentralized democracy "may eliminate the degrading character of work, but they cannot endow it with the characteristics of personal creativity." In his eighth thesis Gorz distinguishes his view of the "non-class of nonworkers" from the classic Marxist conception of the working class as historical actor. They are a "non-class" because they share "no transcendent unity or mission, and hence no overall conception of history and society." Their concerns are parochial and individualistic; but because of their tendency to reject "law and order, power and authority" they are the potential vehicles of a libertarian social movement. The final thesis is that such a movement is "fragmented and composite . . . by nature refractory towards organisation," and suspicious of large-scale political projects. A possible consequence is that "spaces of autonomy from the existing social order will be marginalised, subordinated or ghettoised."[9] What is required is a synthesis of autonomous movement and political struggle, of a form which Gorz does not attempt to predict or prescribe.

The main text of *Farewell to the Working Class* begins with a critique of Marx, challenging two fundamental principles: that the development of productive forces within capitalism creates the material basis for a socialist society; and that the working class engendered by capital is the inevitable agent of its overthrow. On the contrary, insists Gorz: the productive forces functional to the capitalist mode of production are antagonistic to an alternative socialist rationality; while "capitalism has called into being a working class (or, more loosely, a mass of wage earners) whose interests, capacities and skills are functional to the existing productive forces and not directly consonant with a socialist project."[10] Marx's theory of the proletariat was essentially metaphysical: the working class as historical subject transcended the concrete reality of empirical workers, its revolutionary essence deduced from a critical engagement with Hegelian philosophy. "It is not a question of what this or that proletarian, or even the whole proletariat, at the moment *regards* as its aim. It is a question of *what the proletariat is,* and what, in accordance with this *being,* it will historically be compelled to do": in this famous passage from *The Holy Family,*[11] argues Gorz, are the roots of Marxist substitutionism. The philosophers of revolution best understand the proletariat's essential nature; this revolutionary essence cannot be contradicted by historical experience, which at most is evidence of temporary deviation from the inevitable path; the question how workers *might become* revolutionary does not require serious attention.

Gorz adds that a mystical vision of the proletariat does not merely pervade the writings of the 1840s, but frames the analysis of *Capital* itself. The possibility of communist revolution is located in the destruction of the artisan character of work, in the transformation of concrete into general abstract labor, in the submersion of workers' limited particularistic interests within an overarching class identity. Reduced by capital itself to interchangeable components of labor in general, workers have no possibility of redemption short of appropriation of "the totality of productive forces." But does this mean that they *can* and *will* embrace such a mission? This was unproblematic for Marx, says Gorz, because he already *knew* that the proletariat was revolutionary.

Yet the account of factory labor presented at length in the first volume of *Capital* is a catalog of degradation: the destruction of creative ability, the suppression of intelligence, the habituation to servility. Was this the agent of revolution? Gorz argues that from the *Grundrisse* onward, Marx envisaged the reemergence of the confident and assertive artisan within capitalist industry itself:

> He anticipated a process in which the development of the productive forces would result in the replacement of the army of unskilled workers and labourers – and the conditions of military discipline in which they worked – by a class of polytechnic, manually and intellectually skilled workers who would have a comprehensive understanding of the entire work process, control complex technical systems and move with ease from one type of work to another. . . . He was convinced that the figure of the polytechnic worker embodied the reconciliation of the individual proletarian with the proletariat, a flesh-and-blood incarnation of the historical subject.[12]

But modern capitalism has followed the opposite path: not only manual workers, but also technicians and supervisors, have increasingly lost control over the production process; expansion of the power of the collective worker has been associated with the destruction of the power of individuals and work groups.

Only when viewed *from above,* Gorz continues, does the working class possess an organic unity. Hence the collective appropriation of the productive forces cannot reflect workers' own initiative: it can only be undertaken from above in their name. A system in which a "workers' state" sustains and amplifies the productive forces developed by capitalism cannot avoid "a quasi-military hierarchical set of relationships and a substantial body of staff officers and quartermasters," workers' continued subordination being underpinned by a set of principles "akin to the ideology of the bee-hive."[13]

If one aspect of proletarianization is the destruction of creativity and autonomy within work, another is the worker's definitive status as wage laborer:

> As long as workers own a set of tools enabling them to produce for
> their own needs, or a plot of land to grow some vegetables, and
> keep a few chickens, the fact of proletarianisation will be felt to be
> accidental and reversible. For ordinary experience will continue to
> suggest the possibility of independence: workers will continue to
> dream of setting themselves up on their own, of buying an old farm
> with their savings or of making things for their own needs after they
> retire. In short, "real life" lies outside your life as a worker, and be-
> ing a proletarian is but a temporary misfortune to be endured until
> something better turns up.[14]

Perceptive bourgeois rulers may indeed seek to preserve such fragments of autonomy for workers, precisely because they inhibit identification with a general class of dispossessed proletarians. For the same
reason, the labor movement has traditionally proved hostile to workers'
attempts to preserve or construct areas of individual autonomy, seeing
these as detrimental to the broader class struggle. But in fact, says Gorz,
the alienation of the "pure" wage slave is not expressed in a generalized
challenge to capitalist relations of production; at most, conflict with
capital is normally manifest in routinism, passive sabotage, impotent
resentment; and in a politics which focuses on the state as provider of
satisfactions and resources for workers' passive acceptance. The culture
of proletarianization generates no vision of the collective negation of
workers' subordination to capital.

Gorz directs this argument specifically at strategies based on the
demand for workers' control. "The factories to the workers" was a slogan which could appeal to an artisan elite, to whom capitalist managers represented arrogant usurpers of workers' legitimate autonomy and
culture. No such response is to be anticipated from a more fully proletarianized labor force. Moreover: traditional notions of workers' control
(and associated movements to form revolutionary workers' councils)
flourished when capitalist industry was relatively decentralized, when
"the site of production was also the site of power." But economic concentration and technological interdependence entail that today, workers' control at factory level can involve at best a limited power of veto,
not directive control. Similarly, such bodies as factory councils may
succeed in modifying aspects of management policy and practice, but
cannot impose a major shift in priorities and strategies; hence their
real function is to provide a representative mechanism accommodating

workers to the dictates of capitalist production. Indeed, the same type of limitation applies at higher levels of aggregation:

> The obstacle standing in the way of workers' control, power and autonomy is not merely legal or institutional. It is also a material obstacle, which derives from the design, size and functioning of factories. It ultimately derives from the "collective capitalist" responsible for the management of all factories. For the great secret of large-scale industry, as of any vast bureaucratic or military machine, is that *nobody holds power*. Power in such organisms does not have a subject; it is not the property of individuals freely defining the rules and goals of their collective actions. Instead, all that can be found – from the bottom right up to the top of an industrial or administrative hierarchy – are agents obeying the categorical imperatives and inertias of the material system they serve. The personal power of capitalists, directors and managers of every kind is an optical illusion. It is a power that exists only in the eyes of those lower down the hierarchy who receive orders from "those above" and are personally at their mercy.[15]

To "capture" the productive system without transforming its structural dynamics would permit no alteration of substance.

Gorz reiterates this contention in a chapter which contrasts "personal" and "functional" power. The former is associated with superior skill, aptitude, training; those who deploy such power must be ready to demonstrate these qualities in order to establish the legitimacy of their position. Anarcho-syndicalist challenges to management prerogatives were typically associated with craftsmen who denied the superior competence of their appointed supervisors. But power today is characteristically bureaucratic: authority is legitimated by the position occupied rather than the personal qualities of the occupant. When power is personal, a change of personnel may permit far-reaching practical consequences; when it is functional, little can be expected from a change of officeholders. As a result,

> the concept of seizure of power needs to be fundamentally revised. Power can only be seized by an already *existing* dominant class. Taking power implies taking it away from its holders, not by occupying their posts but by making it permanently impossible for them to keep their machinery of domination running. Revolution is first and foremost the irreversible destruction of this machinery. It implies a form of collective practice capable of bypassing and superseding it through the development of an alternative network of relations.

Such an institutional transformation can in turn transform the nature of functional power; but it cannot abolish such power altogether, for a new institutional order will necessarily contain positions of authority. Gorz's prescription is thus to impose strict bounds upon functional power, and "to dissociate power from domination."[16]

From the elusiveness of the ruling class, Gorz returns to the ambiguities of the working class. In complete proletarianization, the reduction of all specialized competencies to the level of generalized, homogeneous abstract labor, Marx premised the growth of working-class unity. Yet the aspiration to displace capitalist management of production requires workers committed to their own productive identity and confident of their ability to take control: a commitment and confidence destroyed by proletarianization:

> Loss of the ability to identify with one's work is tantamount to the disappearance of any sense of belonging to a class. Just as work remains external to the individual, so too does class being. Just as work has become a nondescript task carried out without any personal involvement, which one may quit for another, equally contingent job, so too has class membership come to be lived as a contingent and meaningless fact.
>
> For workers, it is no longer a question of freeing themselves *within* work, putting themselves in control of work, or seizing power within the framework of their work. The point now is to free oneself *from* work by rejecting its nature, content, necessity and modalities. But to reject work is also to reject the traditional strategy and organisational forms of the working-class movement. It is no longer a question of winning power as a worker, but of winning the power no longer to function as a worker. The power at issue is not at all the same as before. The class itself has entered into crisis.

Just as the rise of capitalist production created the working class, so its crisis and decay are creating the "non-class of nonworkers," encompassing "all those who have been expelled from production by the abolition of work. . . . It includes all the supernumeraries of present-day social production, who are potentially or actually unemployed, whether permanently or temporarily, partially or completely."[17]

Transient, marginal, insecure, "they do not feel that they belong to the working class, *or to any other class.*" For the postindustrial proletariat, work is simply "the contingent form of social oppression in general."[18]

The microprocessor revolution will accelerate this process of margin-alization, multiplying both unemployment and those employments de-signed simply to "provide work."

What Marx referred to as production for production's sake, accu-mulation for accumulation's sake, Gorz defines as "productivism." The advance of capitalist technology has largely eliminated the *need* to work, but within capitalism it results in an ever more desperate drive to produce more, and more destructively. "The forward march of pro-ductivism now brings the advance of barbarism and oppression." "The threshold of liberation," Gorz continues, "can only be crossed at the price of a radical break, in which productivism is replaced by a different rationality. This rupture can only come from individuals themselves."[19]

More specifically, the break can only come from those who are driven to reject the work ethic. Gorz regards the social aspirations of his "non-class" as essentially negative: "to regain power over their own lives by disengaging from the market rationality of productivism."[20] They hold no common or coherent vision of the type of society in which this aim might be realized; their aspirations are essentially in-dividualist, closer to traditional bourgeois thought than to orthodox socialism. The socialist ideal, as articulated by Marx, assumed that individual fulfillment could be unproblematically achieved within collectivized production; and conversely, that the free association of producers would be the sufficient foundation of a socialized economy. Gorz denies this. Small-scale communities may be able to function on the basis of spontaneous collaboration, but grassroots collaboration alone will not sustain a complex large-scale economy with an elaborate social and geographical division of labor.

Under socialism, he insists, economic planning directed toward the attainment of collectively defined goals cannot be the unmediated ex-pression of aggregated individual preferences:

> However open and sincerely democratic the process of consultation, the plan schedule and objectives will never be the expression of a common civic will or of grass-roots preferences. The mediations which made it possible to coordinate broad social options with grass-roots preferences will be so complex and so numerous that the local community will be unable to recognise itself in the final result. This result – the plan – will inevitably be the work of a state technocracy obliged to make use of mathematical models and statistical materials

which in itself can only imperfectly control because of the very large number of inputs, variables and unforeseeable elements. Thus the plan will never be a "photograph" of everyone's preferences, but will have to adjust each sub-set of preferences in the light of all the other sub-sets and of the technico-economic constraints upon their coherence. In the last analysis, "democratic elaboration" of the plan does not allow each and all to become the subject of that voluntary social cooperation through which "the associated producers" are supposed to impose their common will upon the society they seek to create. Instead, the plan remains an "autonomised result," intended by no one and experienced by all as a set of external constraints.

If a socialist economy required workers' unconditional commitment to the plan *because* it embodied their collective interests and wishes, the experience would indeed be even more oppressive than under capitalist market relations. This is the crucial weakness of contemporary socialist ideology: bourgeois apologists have learned to appeal successfully, through their emphasis on the need for individual choice, "to the lived experience and aspirations of the post-industrial proletariat, as well as the major part of the traditional working class." Most reject the authoritarian connotations of socialism in favor of "a private niche protecting one's personal life against all pressures and external social obligations."[21] Rejecting the work ethic, seeking satisfaction in a realm of (at least apparent) autonomy from the world of work, the "post-industrial neo-proletariat" is repelled by conventional models of socialism and does not fully recognize that its demands are incompatible with capitalism.

What alternative social order might capture their imagination? Marx himself at times bespoke the diminution of work as the externally directed component of social production, and the enlargement of creative activity outside the domain of economic rationality. Ending the equation of work with full-time wage labor would enlarge the scope for all to engage in "raising children, looking after and decorating a house, repairing or making things, cooking good meals, entertaining guests, listening to or performing music";[22] not least among the consequences would be a possible abolition of the traditional sexual division of labor.

In elaborating this vision, Gorz draws explicitly on both Illich and Bahro.

The priority task of a post-industrial left must therefore be to extend self-motivated, self-rewarding activity within, and above all, outside the family, and to limit as much as possible all waged or market-based activity carried out on behalf of third parties (even the state). A reduction in work time is a necessary but not a sufficient condition. For it will not help to enlarge the sphere of individual autonomy if the resulting free time remains empty "leisure time," filled for better or worse by the programmed distractions of the mass media and the oblivion merchants, and if everyone is thereby driven back into the solitude of their private sphere.

More than upon free time, the expansion of the sphere of autonomy depends upon a freely available supply of convivial tools that allow individuals to do or make anything whose aesthetic or use-value is enhanced by doing it oneself. Repair and do-it-yourself workshops in blocks of flats, neighbourhood centres or rural communities should enable everyone to make or invent things as they wish. Similarly, libraries, places to make music or movies, "free" radio and television stations, open spaces for communication, circulation and exchange, and so on need to be accessible to everyone.

The interrelationship of work and autonomous activity is crystallized in the concept of a "dual society," premised in turn on the insistence that "contrary to what Marx thought, it is impossible that individuals should coincide with their social being, or that social being should encompass all the dimensions of individual existence."[23] Emotional, affective, and aesthetic experiences are essentially subjective; their subordination to impersonal social norms spells oppression. In this realm of individual choice, Gorz adds, is the only terrain for morality.

The obverse of this argument Gorz has already presented: individual autonomy is impossible within the area of social production governed by scarcity and necessity. The much-quoted passage from the third volume of *Capital*,[24] he suggests, is often misunderstood:

The actual wealth of society, and the possibility of constantly expanding its reproduction process . . . do not depend upon the duration of surplus-labour, but upon its productivity and the more or less copious conditions of production under which it is performed. In fact, the realm of freedom actually begins only where labour which is determined by necessity and mundane considerations ceases; thus in the very nature of things it lies beyond the sphere of actual material production. Just as the savage must wrestle with Nature to satisfy his wants, to maintain and reproduce life, so must civilised man, and he must do so in all social formations and under all possible modes of production. With his development this realm of physical necessity expands as a result of his wants; but, at the same time, the forces of production which satisfy these wants also increase. Freedom in this field can only consist in socialised man, the associated producers, rationally regulating their interchange with Nature, bringing it under their common control, instead of being ruled by it as by the blind forces of Nature; and achieving this with the least expenditure of energy and under conditions most favourable to, and worthy of, their human nature. But it nonetheless still remains a realm of necessity. Beyond it begins that development of human energy which is an end in itself, the true realm of freedom, which, however, can blossom forth only with this realm of necessity as its basis. The shortening of the working-day is its basic prerequisite.

Within the "realm of necessity," freedom can be only partial and restricted, even given the most democratic social and economic arrangements; real freedom is possible only in the context of activities not directed to sheer subsistence. Gorz links Marx's distinction to that made by Illich between manipulative institutions and conviviality. Unless socialism is conceived in terms of self-sufficient small-scale communities with preindustrial technology (a recipe for back-breaking toil, restricted culture, and suffocating interpersonal relationships) much social production (telephones, bicycles, computers) will remain standardized, depersonalized, and intrinsically unsatisfying. Such other-directed work cannot be eliminated; but ideally its extent can be minimized; it can be distributed equitably; and it can be utilized to produce goods and services which genuinely enhance the quality of life.

The final chapter in the main body of the book takes issue with another established doctrine of the left: the withering away of the state. In bourgeois society, the expansion of state functions is in part a necessary socialization of costs evaded by individual capitals, in part a repressive guarantee of social order. But as with other-directed work, argues Gorz, the functions of the state cannot be abolished under socialism, even though they can and must be reduced. If it *were* possible to do away with the state, then the conflation of state and civil society would paradoxically diminish individual autonomy; for social order could be maintained only through an inflexible adherence to standardized norms and obligations.[25] Echoing his earlier discussion of "functional power," Gorz defines the socialist objective as "the abolition not of the state but of domination." The role of the state can diminish only as *other* sources of social and economic dominance are neutralized. This depends in turn on the mobilization of struggle from below:

> The state can only cease to be an apparatus of domination over society and become an instrument enabling society to exercise power over itself with a view to its own restructuring, if society is already permeated by social struggles that open up areas of autonomy keeping both the dominant class and the power of the state apparatus in check. The establishment of new types of social relations, new ways of producing, associating, working and consuming is the fundamental precondition of any political transformation. The dynamic of social struggles is the lever by which society can act upon itself and establish a range of freedoms, a new state and a new system of law.[26]

Such struggles constitute the domain of politics: an essential mediation between the spheres of autonomy and necessity—before, during, and also after a transition to socialism.

In a postscript and appendices, Gorz explores further the connections between work, politics, technology, and ecology. In capitalism, consumption is subordinated to the dictates of profitable production; and waste, destruction, and triviality are built into both. Were the principle of accumulation to be replaced by that of sufficiency, existing technical resources would permit the satisfaction of needs though a small expenditure of labor, opening a substantial space for autonomous creativity. The application of microelectronics could in principle greatly accelerate the opportunity to "work less, live more."[27] (In a concluding "utopia," Gorz specifies three pivotal principles: work less, consume better, and reintegrate culture with everyday life.) Enhanced choice by individuals of their expenditure of social labor (and corresponding income), and its phasing over the week, year, and even lifetime, is immediately feasible and increasingly reflects workers' own express wishes. A "politics of time" could thus represent the key to a realistic socialist program with genuine popular appeal.

Farewell to the Working Class is provocative in both senses of the word: it stimulates fresh perspectives on a range of vital issues for socialist theory and practice; but is often overanxious to stress the novelty of the positions adopted in opposition to "orthodox Marxism." Its structural looseness is allied with a journalistic breathlessness of style, often at the

expense of precision and analytical acuity. Thus it is perplexing that
Gorz defines his objective as the abolition of work, before going on
to insist that work *cannot* be abolished; the revised (and less dramatic)
goal must be to overcome the dominance of other-directed labor in
social existence. It is equally bewildering that, having argued at the
outset that the present forces of production are adapted specifically to
capitalist priorities and hence inappropriate for socialism, he appears
in all subsequent discussion to assume that current technology will be
applied largely unaltered within the sphere of necessity in a socialist
economy. Likewise it is frustrating, given the emphasis on the need to
differentiate power from domination, that the criteria for this distinction are nowhere defined.

Gorz as *prestidigitateur:* seemingly striving to make his thesis *appear*
more daring than is actually the case. The illusion is helped along by a
tendency to straw mannerism in the presentation of "orthodoxy" as a
foil to his own analysis. The treatment of "Saint Marx," as Gorz terms
him in the opening chapter,[28] arguably trivializes the evolution of his
arguments over the four decades of his writing, suppresses many of the
nuances of his theories, and neglects the extent to which he can be associated with contradictory positions on many key issues. I shall pursue
these questions while focusing on what I see as the four main themes of
the book: the critique of Marx's theory of the proletariat; Gorz's own
conception of the "neo-proletariat"; the case against "oversocialized"
conceptions of socialism; and the alternative model based on a "dual
organization of social space."

Gorz reiterates a now-familiar argument in insisting on the idealism
of Marx's vision of the revolutionary proletariat.[29] Bahro has recently
offered a cautious statement of the case: in the writings and actions
of Marx and Engels "it seems to me that their entire concept of the
proletariat was never completely free from the Hegelian antithesis between (rational, essential) reality and (merely empirical, accidental) existence."[30] Gorz is more forthright: "Marx's theory of the proletariat is
not based upon either empirical observation of class conflict or practical involvement in proletarian struggle."[31] This is, to say the least, an
undialectical interpretation: Marx and Engels were surely profoundly
influenced by their involvement with the empirical working class, but
their vision of the proletariat was refracted by their philosophical po-
lemic with the young Hegelians. Marx philosophically discovers the

proletariat as agent of world revolution (in the *Introduction to the Critique of Hegel's Philosophy of Right*) only *after* moving to Paris in the autumn of 1843 and experiencing a working class which "pulsed with all the political and social movements from liberal reform to revolutionary communism."[32] Engels, in England from the end of 1842, was caught up in the ferment of militant Chartism.

Thus it is incorrect to regard Marx's theory as without empirical foundation. What *can* plausibly be argued is that the time and place in which Marx and Engels encountered the working class were exceptional; and that they were encouraged to treat the militant socialist worker as prototypical because the stereotype meshed so neatly with their unfolding world-historical analysis. The extrapolation of the struggles of the 1840s into proletarian revolution was an act of faith, the predicted transition from "class in itself" to "class for itself" resting on no more than a loose analogy with the rise of the bourgeoisie. Certainly it is not unreasonable to maintain that faith became increasingly blind when, despite the collapse of the upsurge of 1848, the grave-digging inevitability of victory was so confidently reiterated.[33] Like Bahro, Gorz quite rightly argues that this conviction has involved a mythologized proletarian ideal; and that the failure of the empirical working class to conform to the prescribed model has encouraged all manner of substitutionist tendencies and projects.

Yet Marxism also contains a divergent conception, in which workers' common class identity and political insurgency are not a mechanical outcome of material necessity. The long *practical* involvement of Marx and Engels in the international working-class movement reflected a *contingent* theory of revolution: a task to be actively accomplished, not passively awaited. Marx does not "guarantee the success of the revolution in advance or take it for granted. He only indicates its possibilities historically."[34] Significantly Lukács, after starting with the "essentialist" position of Marx in *The Holy Family*, concludes that "the objective theory of class consciousness is the theory of its objective possibility"; and that the scientific analysis of the conditions for the development of this potential is thus a priority for Marxists.[35]

It is important to disentangle several distinct sources of Marx's identification of the working class as agent of revolution. First was the search for a "universal class" to set in place of Hegel's state bureaucracy; and the discovery of the proletariat as a class whose "radical chains" entailed that its particular emancipation could be achieved only through *general* social emancipation. Second was the anthropological conception of purposeful social labor as the defining characteristic of humanity, its "species being"; the proletariat's function was the embodiment of this human creativity. Third was the connection with the "philosophy of practice": if consciousness and action combined dialectically with material reality to transform social existence, the labor process could be viewed as the elemental form of human praxis and proletarian revolution its crowning manifestation. The fourth reflected the labor theory of value: if labor was the foundation of social productivity, it seemed to follow that the working class was pivotal for social transformation. The final proposition was that of (relative) immiseration: as the principal victims of capitalist "progress" and capitalist crisis, workers would surely be driven to revolt, and would continue to revolt until they had eliminated the underlying causes of their misery.

These arguments are evidently varied and differ in the degree to which they are "philosophically" and "empirically" derived. In sum they cannot be dismissed as cavalierly as Gorz imagines. Yet it is true that Marx's analysis contains an apparent contradiction which he seems nowhere to have appreciated. If capitalist production progressively degrades and disables the proletariat, reducing the worker to a "crippled monstrosity," how can the worker then take the stage of history as a "newfangled man" who overturns capitalist relations of production and domination and ushers in a new social order?

Gorz's answer, as has been seen, is that Marx envisaged the reappearance of the artisan in the guise of the polytechnic worker in high-technology industry. This is surely a perverse reading of Marx. Perhaps a couple of *aperçus* within the rich and visionary complexity of the *Grundrisse* are open to this interpretation;[36] but throughout the whole body of Marx's writings is a consistent and altogether-contrary thesis, and one to which Gorz himself alludes. Though the development of capitalist science and technology provides the material prerequisites for the emancipation of labor, by reducing necessary labor time and immensely increasing productivity, the actual consequences are not liberating but enslaving. The individual worker is no longer identifiably productive; established skills are eroded and displaced; the worker is subordinated to the machine; wages are depressed as women and children are employed in place of adult men; both the intensity and the length of the working day are increased. To quote from *Capital:*

> Factory work exhausts the nervous system to the uttermost; at the same time, it does away with the many-sided play of the muscles, and confiscates every atom of freedom, both in bodily and in intellectual activity. Even the lightening of the labour becomes an instrument of torture, since the machine does not free the worker from the work, but rather deprives the work itself of all content. Every kind of capitalist production, in so far as it is not only a labour process but also capital's process of valorization, has this in common, but it is not the worker who employs the conditions of his work, but rather the reverse, the conditions of work employ the worker. However, it is only with the coming of machinery that this inversion first acquires a technical and palpable reality. Owing to its conversion into an automaton, the instrument of labour confronts the worker during the labour process in the shape of capital, dead labour, which dominates and soaks up living labour-power. The separation of the intellectual faculties of the production process from manual labour, and the transformation of those faculties into powers exercised by capital over labour, is, as we have already shown, finally completed by large-scale industry erected on the foundation of machinery. The special skill of each individual machine-operator, who has now been deprived of all significance, vanishes as an infinitesimal quantity in the face of the science, the gigantic natural forces, and the mass of social labour embodied in the system of machinery, which, together with those three forces, constitutes the power of the "master."[37]

Marx assumed that workers were *bound* to rise up against such denial of their humanity. One might suspect that his image of the revolutionary proletarian was colored by the qualities of those activists with whom he collaborated: Parisian communists, survivors of Chartism, delegates to the First International, German social democrats. Did he regard these "organic intellectuals"—no doubt disproportionately drawn from an artisan stratum—as typical, or at least prototypical, of the proletariat in general? This may in part explain his view of the working class. But probably more important was the fundamental principle of Marx's epistemology: the educative power of experience and action. *Struggle* was the yeast in the development of consciousness; revolutionary confidence and commitment would be fostered by a perhaps-lengthy learning process based on collective action. And here, indeed, is one possible line of explanation of the failure of revolutionary expectations: that workers learned the *wrong* lessons! Gains *could* be made piecemeal, positions defended, areas of relative autonomy secured; many workers, and particularly those with enduring records of collective struggle, did have more than their chains to lose. In other words: against Gorz's thesis that full proletarianization made revolutionary consciousness impossible, it could be argued that it was the partial and uneven character of proletarianization which had this effect. In was Marx's prognosis of complete homogenization of labor which proved inaccurate; and thus his prediction of the revolutionary outcome of such homogenization was never put to the test.

Why does Gorz invent this allegedly Marxist concept of the neo-artisan? The cynic might reply: as a foil for his own notion of the neo-proletarian. The thesis that advanced capitalism gave birth to a new category of polytechnic workers was not Marx's, but rather the enthusiasm of a number of left-wing French sociologists in the 1960s.[38] Gorz himself was clearly influenced by this tendency, though more skeptical than some of his contemporaries.[39] But his treatment of the "non-class of nonworkers" is no more satisfactory than the account of the "new working class" presented by Mallet and others two decades ago. Indeed, Gorz replicates many of the weaknesses which he claims to have discovered in Marx's theory of the traditional proletariat.

The Gorzian analysis is unconvincing at a number of different levels. First, contemporary workers are contrasted with the stereotype of a traditional skilled craftsman: the bearer of class consciousness, anti-capitalist assertiveness, and aspirations for workers' control. This model clearly owes a great deal to the specifically French context, in which many features of artisan production were an enduring element in capitalist development and made their mark on the character of the labor movement. Nevertheless, Gorz's socialist (or anarcho-syndicalist) craftsman is a highly romanticized stereotype, while his account of the transition from occupationally conscious artisan to alienated mass worker is absurdly simplistic. The dynamics of capitalist production relations, with their complex patterns of division of labor and hierarchies of control, have always involved elaborate trajectories of skill, deskilling, and at times re-skilling. Ever since the early nineteenth century, socialists and capitalists alike have repeatedly discerned the final abolition of skill and associated job controls. From Marx's notion of "real subsumption" within the "modern industry" of the mid-nineteenth century, to Braverman's account of the "degradation of work" in the twentieth,[40] to Gorz's present work, the story is remarkably the same. Yet the question seems unavoidable: How is it that any skills or worker autonomy are left to be degraded?

The answer is of course that trends within the capitalist labor process are always contradictory and uneven, and mediated by class struggle. Transformation is rarely as abrupt and decisive as the most highly dramatized accounts suppose. To establish his argument that a new epoch has arisen, Gorz should pay far more heed to the criticisms he himself directs against Marx. What is needed, in short, is less *a priori* assertion and far more detailed evidence.

Even were Gorz's general diagnosis of the trends within the labor force accepted, there is a second problem: the very notion of a "non-class of nonworkers." In employing this term, he neatly contradicts his own prior arguments: for if work is *defined* as heteronomous and alienated labor, then those in the "secondary labor market" performing the most degrading tasks in the most uncongenial conditions are surely *quintessential* workers, it would appear that Gorz is here entangled in his own rhetorical devices: not the best posture for analytical illumination.

More substantively, the whole treatment of the "neo-proletariat" follows French sociological tradition in fusing actuality with aspiration. Who *are* the "marginalized majority"? What do the situations of the jobless school-leaver, the underemployed graduate, the deskilled professional, the unemployed industrial worker, or the redundant executive have in common? And what do their *perceptions* of these situations, and their responses to them, have in common either? What evidence is there that, as Gorz insists, such groups typically reject work, and with it authority in general? Like so many French theorists of "postindustrialism," the grandiose vision overwhelms critical perception. Indeed Gorz blithely contradicts his own thesis with the argument that unskilled and alienated workers, far from rejecting work and management control, commonly embrace passivity, eschew initiative, and seek to extend commodity relations.[41] Nor is it evident that the unemployed customarily turn against work. "Gis a job" is not the cry of those who have abandoned the work ethic; there is by now extensive evidence that many unemployed experience guilt and psychic deprivation; that possession of even an oppressive and damaging job is an essential part of their social identity and self-esteem.

There is little evidence, either, that hierarchy and authority have lost their legitimacy in the eyes of the "neo-proletariat." Would that it were so! Today in Britain, the notion of "de-subordination" seems a little less convincing than a decade ago. Unemployment, economic crisis, and insecurity have evoked an authoritarian rather than a libertarian response. Thatcher's appeal to the Victorian virtues of hard work and law and order has clearly won substantial backing within the working class—as, of course, did the imperialist pomp and bloodletting in the South Atlantic. Nor did the ranks of the un- and under-employed strike an obviously discordant posture on either occasion. In short, the anarchic neo-proletariat seems a rather less plausible construct than Marx's original notion of the revolutionary working class.

I have devoted some space to Gorz's treatment of the working class in Marx and in contemporary society, since his title indicates this as his central concern. But I suspect that many readers might consider more important the issues indicated in his subtitle: *An Essay on Post-Industrial Socialism.*

The dominant conceptions of socialism for the past century have defined a pivotal function for the state, as owner/controller of the means of production and as provider of collective services. The reform/revolution debate has centered primarily on whether the state's strategic functions should be enhanced by constitutional gradualism, by a radical seizure of its apparatus, or by its destruction and replacement by a new workers' state. For Fabians and social democrats, the consolidation of the state as general social representative may be the ultimate goal; for Marxists, merely a transitional stage to the suppression of class antagonisms which permits its own "withering away." Uniting these diverse conceptions is an acceptance—whether enthusiastic or apologetic—of a bureaucratic model of socialism.

Implicit in these traditions is an "objectivist" view of the state: a set of institutions, positions, and officials with prescribed functions, their powers underwritten by "special bodies of armed men, etc." This is a perspective increasingly under question, as the traditional equation of socialism with state control is itself challenged. Both doubts were well articulated in a study published after Thatcher's first electoral victory:

> For as long as we can remember, the question of the transition to
> socialism has been polarized between two positions: on the one hand
> gradualism, on the other "the seizure of state power." But recently
> there seems to have been an increasing recognition that this debate
> is sterile. The obvious lack of possibilities for reform, coupled with
> our eye-opening experiences of "participation," have disabused us
> of hopes in gradualism. There is no way that society can be trans-
> formed through institutions that have been developed precisely to
> take away our power.
>
>   On the other hand, a politics which pins everything on "the sei-
> zure of state power" leaves many socialists feeling uncomfortable.
> They are skeptical about the possibility of overnight change, know-
> ing it will be difficult to generate popular support for socialism when
> the question of just what it is we are fighting for is left so unreal.
> Neither capital nor the state can be seized, because they are not *things*.
> They are *relations* which cannot be grasped and held down, they have
> to be unmade. In a strange way our critique of the "seizure of state
> power" line shares much with our doubts about gradualism: "captur-
> ing power" by either means is not the same thing as taking control.[42]

It is today a familiar argument that within capitalism, the state form
replicates the pattern of social relations of production; while under
"actually existing socialism," the similarities are more notable than the
differences. Whether this is explained in terms of the dictates of accumulation, the pervasive influence of commodity relations, or the
distinctive interests and perspectives and relative autonomy of the state
bureaucracy, it is evident that socialist strategy requires a more detached and critical attitude to the state.

The problem of the state is directly reflected in the constituency to
which socialism should appeal. For British socialists and labor movement activists, "public enterprise" and the "welfare state" are typically
regarded with pride and without question as signals of socialist advance.
Arguments to the contrary have normally been associated with attacks
by right-wing social democrats on the nationalization commitment in
the Labour Party constitution. The whole tenor of the debate indicates,
however, that the mainstream of labor movement thought it out of
touch with popular opinion. Almost certainly, for most members of the
working class the welfare state is not *their* welfare state. The services
provided are typically inadequate, hemmed in by bureaucratic regulation, subject to inexplicable delay. The manner of delivery is often

grudging, patronizing, humiliating. Nationalization is rarely seen as advantageous either to employees or to consumers. State officialdom is widely regarded as arrogant, incompetent, unaccountable. The whole apparatus of state activity is generally perceived as an ever-increasing burden on the incomes of ordinary workers.

Of course some of these arguments and attitudes represent popular mythology, fanned by political misinformation and media hostility. But the stereotypes have proved so powerful because they resonate with people's real experiences. There can be no prospect of mobilizing popular support for an extension of state activity, or even to defend what already exists, if the state is popularly viewed as impoverishing and oppressive rather than liberating and enriching. This point, too, has been well made before:

> Our daily contact with the state is a crucial arena of class struggle. In the past, however, if as socialists we have concerned ourselves with struggles with the welfare state at all, we have tended to concentrate on questions of resource provision: more and better housing, more hospitals, better teacher–pupil ratios and higher pensions. Increasingly, however, we are coming to realise that it is not enough to fight to keep hospitals open if we do not also challenge the oppressive social relations they embody, that it is insufficient to press for better student–teacher ratios in schools if we do not also challenge what is taught or how it is taught. Socialists involved in struggles over resources are realising that many people choose precisely *not* to give their support to "fighting the cuts," defending or extending the state apparatus, because they quite reasonably have mixed feelings about the social relations which state institutions embody.[43]

The question of quantity, one might say, is subsidiary to that of the quality of state activity.

Hence it is not surprising that Labour manifestos and "alternative economic strategies" based essentially on a policy of more—more nationalization, more state services, more controls over private economic activity—have failed to win enthusiastic backing. On the contrary: Tory deployment of the rhetoric of individual choice and personal freedom suggests a far more sensitive understanding of working-class aspirations.

Against this background, Gorz's discussion of the interrelationship between state, socialism, and individualism is of urgent import. Some of his arguments on the themes of self-determination in personal life and in grassroots collective relations have become familiar through the women's movement and libertarian socialist currents. His distinctive contribution is to link these concerns to a more abstract analysis of the spheres of individual autonomy and collective control, and to a critical assessment of the nature and limits of state activity under socialism.

The propositions which Gorz develops stand or fall independently of his prior analysis of the "neo-proletariat." In my view, his emphasis on the inevitable space between individual and social being is wholly persuasive. The necessity of macro-social determination of many aspects of collective life does not entail that individuals will experience true freedom in submission to such control. Nor should socialism imply the socialization of all aspects of everyday life: diversity and creativity require the preservation of private social space. Also persuasive is Gorz's insistence that state power *is* necessary within any form of socialism, but that equally essential are autonomous collectivities to sustain the maximum possible self-determination and also to curb any tendencies to state aggrandizement.

Gorz's argument on this score is clear and convincing, and particularly relevant in Britain today. The traditional program of state socialism repels more than it attracts, and for reasons which socialists should consider legitimate. The model of "actually existing socialism" is rejected by most workers themselves as drab, monolithic, and oppressive. It is not enough to insist that socialism here would be different; it is a question of demonstrating how and why this should be so. To do this, we on the left must agree ourselves where we are going; must redefine for our own day a social vision which recaptures from the right the appeal to individual freedom while sustaining the traditional principles of conscious collective determination of social existence.

Marxists, as Bahro has commented, "have a defensive attitude towards utopias. It was so laborious to escape from them in the past. But today utopian thought has a new necessity."[44] How many of us have found it easy to dismiss those questions which occur to anyone but passionate believers in socialism as an abstract ideal: How would the major practical problems of social and economic organization be resolved under socialism?

Of course we can't offer detailed blueprints; of course it is absurd to speak of releasing collective creativity and then lay down the lines which must be followed. But is it unreasonable to expect some sort of answer to such questions as: What will happen to the motor industry? Will the private car survive? What about motorways? How will a national road network be determined, and who will build it? With this, as with myriad other areas of possible inquiry, the ritual response that the workers will decide for themselves when the time comes sounds suspiciously like a lack of vision or of honesty. The case for socialism carries little conviction unless at least some plausible *options* can be spelled out.

Bahro, it will be recalled, outlined what he termed "the economics of the cultural revolution" according to five central principles: "the goal of production as rich individuality"; "a new determination of the need for material goods and the availability of living labour from the standpoint of the optimization of conditions of development for fully socialized individuals"; "a more harmonious form of reproduction"; "accounting for a new economy of time"; and "individual initiative and genuine communality."[45] Gorz develops his utopia along parallel lines, popularizing many of the themes from Bahro's weightier tome, and adding a distinctively "green" complexion to the argument: a reflection of his previous insistence that "the ecological movement is . . . a stage in the larger struggle."[46]

As has been seen, Gorz seeks to eschew *both* those forms of economic strategy which merely aim to "socialize" (and manage more "efficiently") the large-scale high-technology apparatus of contemporary capitalism; *and* the diametrically opposed conception of a return to "primitive communism," with material life restricted to production with rudimentary equipment in small communities. His notion of a "dual society" is more than a simple compromise; it is an imaginative synthesis which demands close critical consideration by socialists.

There are four problems in his analysis which I would wish to emphasize. The first is a highly diffuse perspective of the obstacles and enemies confronting a struggle for the type of society proposed. "In modern societies, power does not have a subject": Gorz's thesis is scarcely novel.[47] But does this mean that socialists have merely to dismantle an impersonal "system"? And in the short term, does it make *no* difference who occupies positions of "functional power"? Capitalism indeed sets oppressive limits to the options available within its framework; but precisely because its operation is internally contradictory, those who exert political and economic management and direction can and must choose among alternatives. And if the discretion of *individual* rulers is limited (though given the supermarketed ersatz charisma of contemporary political leaders, and the extensive patronage at their disposal, surely far from insignificant), the power of the *ruling class* may be far more momentous.[48] Gorz's abstract and elusive references to "domination" hint at this, but he nowhere confronts the problems inherent in a socialist challenge to the mechanisms and vested interests of class rule.

This issue connects with a second: Gorz oscillates between a highly determinist model of the "juggernaut of capital," and (no doubt reflecting his existentialist background) a tendency to voluntarism and idealism. The sway of capital is at times attributed, not to material relations but to the "rationality of productivism"; its abolition thus demands a transformation in social philosophies, "the rejection of the accumulation ethic." Correspondingly, freedom is to be achieved "by a constitutive act which, aware of its free subjectivity, asserts itself as an absolute end in itself within each individual."[49] This is sheer mysticism. It is right to insist that the abolition of capitalism must be a cultural as much as a material revolution; but Gorz here seemingly proposes that socialism will be established through spiritual conversion alone.

The third problem is also related: like Bahro, Gorz is very imprecise in locating the *agency* of socialist advance. Given his stress on the individualism, the nonclass identity of the "neo-proletariat," what is it that can give their gratuitous subjective acts a common direction and purpose? He speaks of "the movement formed by all those who refuse to be nothing but workers," and insists portentously that "only the movement itself, through its own practice, can create and extend the sphere of autonomy";[50] but this is the sum total of Gorz's guide to strategy. Implicit in such remarks is an assumption of spontaneous collectivism, akin to that which Gorz derides in Marx's treatment of the working class, but far less grounded in evidence and analysis. A century of debate on socialist political strategy—the party, parliamentarism, reform/revolution—is not engaged or contested; it is simply ignored.

The fourth problem is of a different order. In discussing the integration of different systems of production, and the relationship between state and civil society, Gorz appears to assume a specifically national context. Despite the attention in many of his previous writings to issues of internationalism, this dimension is absent here. How would the movement toward socialist production relations and a "dual society" confront the problems of the world market, the sway of multinational capital, the policies of domination of the superpowers? Is *world* revolution a necessary condition of transformation in individual societies—and if so, does this not multiply the problems of strategy and organization among socialists? And on a global scale, is the conquest of the sphere of necessity as close to our grasp as Gorz's discussion assumes?

On issues such as these, *Farewell to the Working Class* provokes far more questions than it resolves. In what is not designed as a fully fashioned manifesto, this is not necessarily a weakness. "There is no wealth but life": Ruskin's maxim, the inspiration of so many early British socialists, was expunged from the consciousness of later generations of bureaucratic and technocratic social democrats. Even radical currents within the labor movement are typically marked by the philistine priorities of capitalist production. Campaigns for the right to work, demands for workers' control, implicitly accept the segmentation of life into a (dominant) sphere of full-time wage labor and a (subordinate, devalued) sphere of activity outside the bounds of commodity production.

There have of course been challenges to this dominant "workerism," not least under the impact of feminism. On the left, declining faith in Leninist orthodoxies has been associated with renewed discussion of strategies for humanistic/libertarian socialism; but attention has been mainly concentrated in narrow intellectual coteries; in particular it is hard to detect more than a token influence within the organized labor movement.[51] Symptomatic is the fate of *A Life to Live,* written by Clemitson and Rodgers in response to mass unemployment and the 1979 election defeat, an eloquent plea for a right to a fuller life as an alternative to both unemployment *and* employment.[52] Specifically addressed to the unions and the Labour Party, their case for a worthier demand than the "right to work" has seemingly passed unnoticed.

Institutionalized within the sclerotic structures of the labor movement, British socialism has become modest and banal in its long-term vision, even when superficially radical in its short-term program. Utopian imagination—the tradition of William Morris—is more often an embarrassment than an inspiration. As 1983 has brutally demonstrated, official socialism, with its "combination of narrow trade unionism and failed state intervention,"[53] no longer has a popular constituency. No more do the industrial and political organizations of labor possess a language with which to relate to those they supposedly represent. Will the current crisis stimulate an effort to rediscover the essence of socialism, in a form appropriate to the closing years of the twentieth century, and in terms which can inspire more than a dedicated minority? Gorz's utopia provides a valuable contribution to such a quest.

MARX, THE PRESENT CRISIS, AND THE FUTURE OF LABOR

Ernest Mandel

I.

For several years, the *political* thesis that human emancipation can no longer rely on the "proletariat," the class of wage labor, has been increasingly buttressed by economic arguments.* Some posit that wage labor is receding rapidly from its position as the main sector of the active population, as the result of automation, robotization, mass unemployment, growth of small independent business firms, et cetera (Gorz, Dahrendorf, Daniel Bell, Hobsbawm).[1] Others state that there is no future for humankind (and therefore for human emancipation) as long as "classical" industrial technology and thence "classical" wage labor are maintained at their present level because such a situation would lead to a complete destruction of the ecological balance (Illich, Bahro, Gorz).[2] The present crisis is therefore seen not as a typical crisis of overproduction and overaccumulation. It is seen as a fundamental change of structure of the international capitalist economy, with a long-term fundamental shift in the weight, cohesion, and dynamic of wage labor, at the expense of that class, as a "crisis of the industrial system."

Can this hypothesis be verified empirically? If not, what is the meaning and what are the long-term potential consequences of growing structural unemployment, which, in and by itself, is an undeniable

---

* This paper was initially delivered to a colloquium "The Future of Human Labour" organized by the Institute for Marxist Studies at the Vrise University, Brussels, February 14–16, 1985; it was first published in *Socialist Register 1985/86* (London: Merlin Press, 1986).

phenomenon? If yes, what is the explanation of the phenomenon of the supposed "decline of the working class" as an objective phenomenon? What are its potential economic consequences?

II.

Empirically, the *basic* trend which is statistically verifiable is that of the growth of wage labor on a world scale, and on all continents, and not that of its absolute or relative decline. If one looks at the International Labour Organization statistics, one can see this at first glance. When I say basic trend, I mean of course not three-month or six-month variations, but five- or ten-year averages. Even since the beginning of the present long economic depression, for example since 1968 or since 1973, this remains the predominant tendency.

The verification of this tendency implies a series of conceptual precisions:

(a) that one does not reduce "wage labor" to "manual labor in large-scale industry" (Marx's definition of the "total worker," *der Gesamtarbeiter,* in *Capital, Volume 1,* and in the unpublished section 6);

(b) that one defines "wage laborers" (proletarians) in the classical way as *all those who are under economic compulsion to sell their labor power* (excluding thereby only those managers and high functionaries who have high incomes which allow them to accumulate sufficient capital to be able to survive on the interest of that capital);

(c) that one does not reduce the proletariat to productive workers but includes in it all unproductive wage earners who fall under condition b, as well as all unemployed who do not become self-employed (see Marx's *Capital,* Rosa Luxemburg's *Einführung in die Nationalökonomie,* and the general concept of the "reserve army of labor"); and

(d) that one gives an objective and not a subjective definition of the class of wage labor (class in itself); i.e., that one does not make its existence dependent on levels of consciousness.

This implies, among other things, that wage labor in agriculture (e.g., India) and in the so-called service industries is wage labor to the same extent as wage labor in mining and in manufacturing industry. With that criterion the statistical evidence that we are still witnessing a growth and not a decline of the "world proletariat" is undeniable. The total number of nonagricultural wage earners in the world today is somewhere between seven and eight hundred million, a figure never attained in the past. Together with agricultural wage earners, it reaches one billion. This is confirmed by the following data even concerning the imperialist countries:

Table 1. Changes in Annual Civilian Employment of Wage Earners (Annual Average, 1973–1980)

Norway	+2.5%
Portugal	+2.5%
United States	+2.2%
Australia	+1.1%
Italy	+ 1.1%
Denmark	+0.8%
Japan	+0.8%
Austria	+0.3%
France	+0.2%
Belgium	0.0
United Kingdom	−0.1%
West Germany	−0.2%

Source: ILO, World Labour Report (Geneva: ILO, 1984)

There remains the problem of the relative decrease of wage labor employed in the largest capitalist factories, i.e., of a relative deconcentration of labor accompanying a further concentration and centralization of capital. This has been the tendency since the beginning of the present slump in the imperialist countries, not in the semi-industrialized ones and not on a global scale, where concentration of labor continues to advance. Whether in the metropolis this is only a conjunctural phenomenon like the relative decline of the "old" industrial branches before large-scale plants appear in "new" branches, or whether it has become a long-term trend, remains to be seen. We will have to wait at least till the 1990s before we are able to draw definite conclusions in that respect.

III.

The short- and medium-term impact of full-scale automation or robotization on total employment (the number of wage laborers employed) has been practically nil till the beginning of the seventies
(taking into account shifts of employment between branches, which
are of course very real), and remains modest today and for the foreseeable future. Recent OECD studies predict that between now and the
nineties, robotization will cut somewhere between 4 and 8 percent of
all existing jobs *in the West* (and between 2 and 5 percent of all existing
wage jobs on a world scale).[3] It does not add how many new jobs will
be created in the industrial branches producing robots and automatic
machines. Predictions vary wildly between the "optimists" and "pes-
simists" in that regard. But even if we follow the most pessimistic predictions, according to which the number of new jobs created in these
new industries will be negligible, the total number of wage earners
employed will still constitute the overwhelming majority of the active
population till the end of the century (between 80 and 90 percent of
the population in the West, Eastern Europe, and the USSR).

So there is no objective ground for speaking of a "decline of the
proletariat" in an objective sense of the word.[4] This does not mean that
one should underestimate the dangerous potential of long-term mass
unemployment. This has basically two causes in the capitalist countries:

(a) the decline of rates of growth during the long depressive wave,
rates of growth which fall below the average rate of growth of productivity of labor (third technological revolution); and

(b) the impossibility of the economic system absorbing population
growth into employment under these same circumstances, all other
things remaining equal.

In addition, we have to take into consideration the precise effects
of robotization on specific branches of industry which have played a
key role in the organization and strength of the working class and the
labor movement, e.g., the automobile industry in the United States and
Western Europe.[5] Here, the prospects are threatening and should be
understood before it is too late (as has been unfortunately the case in
the steel and shipbuilding industries).

The consequences of growing long-term structural unemployment
(in the West: from ten million around 1970 to thirty-five million today
and forty million in the mid-eighties) are a growing fragmentation of

the working class and the danger of demoralization, already visible in certain sectors of the proletarian youth (e.g., Black youth and Spanish-speaking youth in the United States and in certain regions of Great Britain),[6] who have *never* worked since they left school and are in danger of not finding jobs for many years to come.

Japanese socialists[7] have tried to study the effects of new technologies, especially on the automobile industry. Also stressing qualitative aspects of the changes (loss of skills, increase in accidents, emergence of new layers of workers and of skills, et cetera), the authors find a reduction of shop floor workers of around 10 percent at the most highly "robotized" automobile plant in Japan, Nissan's Murayama Plant, between September 1974 and January 1982, accompanied, however, by small increases in white-collar personnel. Even the Japanese "company unions" seem worried by these developments, "life-long employment" still the rule in Japan notwithstanding.[8]

IV.

The only serious answer to the growth of massive structural long-term unemployment during the present long depression is a radical international reduction of the working week without a cut in weekly pay: the immediate introduction of the *thirty-five-hour week*. This means the spread of the existing workload among the whole proletariat without loss of income (12 percent of unemployment can be suppressed by every worker working 12 percent weekly hours less), and with obligatory additional hiring and the reunification of the working classes torn apart by unemployment and fear of unemployment. This should be the central strategic short-term goal of the whole international labor movement, in order to prevent the relationship of forces between capital and labor from being changed in a serious way at the expense of labor. The longer-term perspective is the thirty-hour week.

All considerations about "national competitiveness" and "enterprise profitability" should be abandoned in favor of that absolute social priority. One could easily prove that from a global and international—not single-firm—point of view, that this is also the most economically rational solution. But of course capitalist "rationality" *is* single-firm based "rationality," i.e., *partial* rationality, which leads more and more to *overall* irrationality. The disastrous political risks of massive unemployment, both nationally and internationally, do not need to be stressed.

Marx was unequivocally clear on both issues: the beneficial effects of a radical reduction of the working week without reduction in pay, and the need for international solidarity of labor to substitute itself for "national" (or regional, or local, or sectoral, or even one-corporation) solidarity between workers and capitalists.

It is sufficient to quote Marx's "Inaugural *Address of the International Workingmen's Association*" (First International): "Past experience has shown to what extent the neglect of the fraternal links which should tie and inspire the workers of different countries to firmly stand together in all their struggles for emancipation, is always punished by the common failure of their unconnected attempts." And in his quarterly report on the activity of the General Council of the WMIA, Marx wrote: "And even its national organization easily leads to failure as a result of the lack of organization beyond national boundaries, as all countries compete on the world market and mutually influence each other. Only an international union of the working class can assure its final victory." In an even more categorical way, Marx stated in his instructions to the First International's General Council delegates to the 1867 Geneva Congress of that organization: "We declare the limitation of the working day to be a precondition, without which all other endeavors for amelioration and emancipation must fail."[9]

V.

The struggle between the forces which push in the direction of long-term massive structural unemployment on the one hand, and of a new radical reduction of the working week on the other, are intimately related to the two basic motive forces of bourgeois society: capital's drive to increase the production of relative surplus value, i.e., the development of the "objective" (objectivized, materialized) productive forces, machinery, machine systems, semi-automized systems, full-scale automization, robots on the one hand; the counterpressure of the class struggle between capital and wage labor on the other. One of the main analytical achievements of Marx consisted precisely in indicating the *dialectical* (not mechanical, of the Malthus-Ricardo-Lassalle type) *interrelation between the two.*

The increase in mechanization has a *contradictory* effect on labor. It reduces skills, suppresses employment, bears down on wages through the rise of the industrial reserve army of labor, effects which can be partially offset through the increase in the accumulation of capital ("economic growth"), international migration of labor, et cetera. But likewise, the increase in the mechanization of production tends *to increase the intensity of the work effort* (physical and/or nervous), and therefore exercises objective pressure in the direction of a reduction of the working week. This second effect has often been overlooked by working-class militants, including socialists and Marxists. It is strongly emphasized by Marx.[10]

But capital will not grant this physically and economically indispensable reduction of the working week out of the kindness of its heart. It will only do so after a fierce struggle between capital and labor.

Workers' rebellion—as Marx called it—can, however, only be (temporarily) successful under relatively favorable relationships of forces. *These are created by the effects of employment and organization of labor of the phase prior* to the long-term depression and surge of unemployment. And precisely in the late 1970s and '80s, the international (especially the Western European) proletariat entered the growing confrontation with capital around the issue "austerity versus shortening of the working week without a reduction in take-home pay or social security allowances," with a much-increased numerical, organizational, and militant strength accumulated during the 1950s, '60s, and early '70s, i.e., during the period of the long-term postwar "boom." *It is for that reason that resistance of the working class against the austerity offensive will increase, will spread, will become periodically explosive, and will tend to be generalized* nationally and internationally. It is for the same reason that the capitalist class will not find it easy to implement its own historical "solution" to the present depression.

Precisely because the *organic strength* of the working class (wage labor) is so large at the outset and in the first phase of this depression, the outcome of this intensified class offensive of capital against labor is far from certain. The likelihood that the proletariat will suffer a crushing defeat as in Germany in 1933, Spain in 1939, or France in 1940 in any of the larger capitalist key countries in the foreseeable future is limited.

This does not imply that a proletarian-socialist solution of the crisis is certain or already visible on the horizon. The main obstacle for such a crisis is *subjective* and not objective: the level of consciousness of wage labor and the capacity of its leadership are still absolutely inadequate. But this means that at least the *objective possibility* of a socialist working-class solution of the crisis of humankind remains with us. The rest depends on the socialists themselves: their awareness of the gravity and the risks implied in the crisis (the very physical survival of humankind is now at stake); the impossibility of solving it within the framework of generalized market economy, i.e., "exchange value production," i.e., capitalism; the necessity to develop an anti-capitalist program of action starting from the real, existing concerns and needs of the real, existing wage laborers, in all their varieties; the necessity to unite this mighty force into a battering ram to shake the fortresses of capital; the necessity to organize for the overthrow of capitalism.

VI.

Let us now make the hypothesis that all this will be disproved by experience during the coming decades; that both for economic reasons (robotization) and political ones which we allegedly "underestimate," wage labor will decrease considerably between now and the end of the twentieth century; that therefore the proletariat has already started to decline objectively (both in numbers and inner cohesion) and that for the same reason its *objective capacity* to transform society in a socialist sense will also decline more or less steadily. In that case, one should not only say "goodbye" to the proletariat. One would also have to say:

    —"goodbye" to socialism and any realistic (materialistically based) project of human emancipation; and

    —"goodbye" to the market economy and capitalism itself.

One of the basic theses of Marx, to which no evidence can be opposed on the basis of the last one hundred years of experience, is that only the class of wage labor acquires through its place in capitalist production and bourgeois society those "positive qualities," i.e., the capacity for massive (self-)organization, solidarity and cooperation, which are the *preconditions* for a socialist solution of the crisis of humankind. These qualities do not *automatically* create the emancipatory revolutionary role of the proletariat; they only lead to a *social potential* of that nature. But no other social class or layer has a similar potential, neither Third World peasants, nor revolutionary intellectuals, and certainly not technocrats and functionaries. Other social classes and layers have a huge revolutionary anti-capitalist (anti-imperialist) "negative" potential, e.g., the peasantry in underdeveloped countries. But history has proved again and again that they don't have the "positive" potential for conscious socialist organization.

On the other hand, if a massive substitution of "living" by "dead" labor (robots) leads to a massive absolute decline of wage labor, it is not only the future of the proletariat and of socialism which is threatened. It is the very survival of the capitalist market economy which becomes more and more impossible. This is expressed in a graphic, somewhat simplified way, by the already-classical dialogue between the factory manager and the trade union militant:

> —"What will become of your trade union strength when all the workers will be replaced by robots?"

> —"What will become of your profits in that case? Your profits are realized through the sale of your goods; robots unfortunately don't buy goods."

Marx foresaw that development more than 125 years ago, in his *Grundrisse* (which, incidentally, confirms the point which I have made many times that, far from being an "economist of the nineteenth century," he was a visionary who detected trends which would only come into their own in the late twentieth century). He wrote there:

> But to the degree that large industry develops, the creation of real wealth comes to depend less on labour time and on the amount of labour employed than on the power of the agencies set in motion during labour time, whose "powerful effectiveness" is itself in turn out of all proportion to the direct labour time spent on their production, but depends rather on the general state of science and on the progress of technology, or the application of this science to production. . . . Labour no longer appears so much to be included within the production process; rather, the human being comes to relate more as watchman and regulator to the production process itself.[11]

And again:

> *The theft of alien labour-time, on which the present wealth is based*, appears a miserable foundation in face of this new one, created by large-scale industry itself. As soon as labour in the direct form has ceased to be the great well-spring of wealth, labour time ceases and must cease to be its measure, and hence exchange-value [must cease to be the measure] of use value. *The surplus-labour of the mass* has ceased to be the condition for the development of general wealth, just as the *non-labour*

of the few, for the development of the general powers of the human head. With that, production based on exchange value breaks down.[12]

Obviously, this development cannot fully unfold under capitalism, because precisely under capitalism, economic growth, investment, the development of machinery (including robots), remain subordinated to the accumulation of capital, i.e., to the production and realization of surplus value, i.e., to profits for individual firms, both expected profits and realized profits. As I already indicated in *Late Capitalism* more than ten years ago,[13] under capitalism full automation, the development of robotism on a wide scale, is impossible because it would imply the disappearance of commodity production, of market economy, of money, of capital and of profits. (Under a socialized economy, robotism would be a wonderful instrument of human emancipation. It would make possible the reduction of the working week to a minimum of ten hours.[14] It would grant men and women all the necessary leisure for self-management of the economy and society, the development of a rich social individuality for all, the disappearance of the social division of labor between the administrators and the administered, the withering away of the state and of the coercion between human beings.)

So what is the most likely variant under capitalism is precisely the long duration of the present depression, with only the development of partial automation and marginal robotization;[15] both accompanied by large-scale overcapacity (and overproduction of commodities), by large-scale unemployment, and large-scale pressure to extract more and more surplus value from a number of *productive* workdays and workers tending to stagnate and decline slowly, i.e., growing pressure to overexploitation of the working class (lowering of real wages and social security payments), to weaken or destroy the free organized labor movement and to undermine democratic freedoms and human rights.

VII.

In his *Grundrisse,* Marx not only foresaw the basic trend of capitalist technology toward the progressive expulsion of human labor from the process of production. He also foresaw the basic contradictions this trend would lead to under *capitalism:*

—Huge overproduction, or, what amounts to the same, under-capacity.
During the last recession (1980–1982), over 35 percent of the capacity of output of US industry remained unused. If one also deducts
arms production—useless from a reproduction point of view—one
arrives at the staggering amount of nearly 50 percent of America's
productive capacity not being used for productive purposes.[16]

—High unemployment. Marx opposes the emancipatory *potential* of automation and robotism—its capacity to increase greatly the amount
of human leisure time, time for full development of the all-round
personality—to its oppressive tendency under *capitalism.* He synthe-
sizes this opposition precisely as being that between a class society
and a classless society.

In a class society, appropriation of the social surplus by a minority means *capacity of extending leisure time for only a minority,* and therefore reproduction on a larger and larger scale of the division of society
between those who administer and accumulate knowledge, and those
who produce without or with only very limited knowledge.[17] In a classless society, appropriation and control of the social surplus product by
all (by the associated producers) would mean a radical reduction of labor
time (of necessary labor) *for all,* a radical extension of leisure *for all,* and
thereby the disappearance of the division of society between administrators and producers, between those who have access to all knowledge
and those who are cut off from most knowledge. In a striking passage of
the *Grundrisse,* linked to the above-quoted passage, Marx writes:

> *The creation of a large quantity of disposable time* apart from necessary
> labour time for society generally and each of its members (i.e. room
> for the development of the individuals' full productive forces, hence
> those of society also), this creation of not-labour-time, appears in
> the stage of capital, as all earlier ones, as not-labour-time, free time,
> for a few. . . . But its tendency always, on the one side, *to create dis-
> posable time, on the other, to convert it into surplus labour.* If it succeeds
> too well at the first, then it suffers from surplus production, and then
> necessary labour is interrupted, because *no surplus labour can be realised
> by capital.* The more this contradiction develops, the more does it
> become evident that the growth of the forces of production can no
> longer be bound up with the appropriation of alien labour, but that
> the mass of workers must themselves appropriate their own surplus
> labour. Once they have done so – and *disposable time* thereby ceases
> to have an *antithetical* existence – then, on one side, necessary labour

time will be measured by the needs of the social individual, and, on
the other, the development of the power of social production will
grow so rapidly that, even though production is now calculated for
the wealth of all, *disposable time* will grow for all. For real wealth is
the developed productive power of all individuals.[18]

And Marx indicates how, *under capitalism*, science, the results of
general social labor, i.e., general social knowledge, gets systematically
divorced from labor, how—a striking anticipation of capitalist "robotism"—science under capitalism becomes *opposed* to labor.[19]

VIII.

How does capitalism try to overcome this growing new contradiction,
resulting from the reduction of the absolute amount of human labor
necessary to produce even a growing mass of commodities saleable
under the present (i.e., bourgeois) conditions of production and distribution? Its solution is that of the *dual society,* which divides the present
proletariat into two antagonistic groups:

—those who continue to be included (or are newly incorporated,
especially in the so-called Third World countries) into the process of
production of surplus value, i.e., into the *capitalist process of production*
(be it for tendentially declining wages); and

—those who are expelled from that process and survive by all kinds
of means other than the sale of their labor power to the capitalists (or
the bourgeois state): welfare; increase of "independent" activities;
becoming small-scale peasants and handicraftsmen; returning to domestic labor (women); "ludic" communities, et cetera.

A transitional form of "dropping out" of the "normal" capitalist production process is "Black" labor, "precarious" labor, "part-time jobs," et
cetera, hitting especially women, youth, immigrant workers, et cetera.

Table 2. Part-Time Employment in 1979

	Percent of Total Employment	Percent Female Labor
West Germany	11.4%	91.5%
Belgium	6.0 %	89.3%
Denmark	22.7%	86.9%

	Percent of Total Employment	Percent Female Labor
US	17.8%	66.0%
France	8.2%	82.0%
Italy	5.3%	61.4%
Holland	11.2%	82.5%
UK	16.4%	92.8%

Source: ILO, World Labour Report (Geneva: ILO, 1984)

. What is the *capitalist rationale* of that dual society? It is a gigantic historical turning of the clock backward on one key issue: *indirect (socialized) wages.*

Through a long historical struggle, the working class of Western Europe, Australia, and Canada (to a lesser degree that of the United States and Japan) had conquered from capital that *basic cement of class solidarity* that wages should not only cover the reproduction costs of *actually employed* living labor, but the reproduction costs of the proletariat *in its totality,* at least on a national scale: i.e., also the reproduction costs of the unemployed, sick, old, invalid male and female workers and their offspring. That is the historical meaning of social security, which is part and parcel of the wage bill (its socialized part, or at least that part of wages which "transits" through the hands of social security institutions).

Through pressure in favor of a *dual society,* part-time labor, casual labor, "dropping out of the rat race," et cetera, capital now wants to reduce its wage bill to directly paid-out wages only, which will then inevitably tend to decline as a result of a hugely inflated industrial reserve army of labor. It already succeeds with that goal with the mass of the "casual" and "precarious" laborers, who generally do not enjoy social security benefits. It wants to realize the same gains with regard to the unemployed as such.

In other words: the "dual society" *under capitalism* is nothing but one of the key mechanisms to increase the rate of surplus value, the rate of exploitation of the working class, and the mass and the rate of profit. Any excuse of a "sophisticated" nature for supporting *this goal of capital* (be it "Third World–ism," ecologism, "the immediate realization of communism," the desire to "break up the consumption norm," et cetera) is in the best of cases a mystified capitulation before bourgeois ideology and capital's economic purposes, in the worst of cases a direct help to the capitalist anti-working-class offensive.

To advocate that unpaid labor should spread, even for "socially useful purposes," when there is a huge number of unemployed, is not to build "cells of communism" inside capitalism; it is to help the capitalists divide the working class through a new rise in unemployment, to help them increase profits.

But it is more than that. It puts new and formidable stumbling blocks on the *really emancipatory potential* of new technologies and "robotism," inasmuch as it tends to perpetuate, in an elitist way, the subdivision of society between those who receive the necessary leisure and potential to appropriate all the fruits of science and civilization—which can only occur on the basis of the satisfaction of elementary fundamental material needs—and those who are condemned (including those who condemn themselves through self-chosen asceticism) to spend more and more of their time as "beasts of burden," to quote again Marx's eloquent formula.

The real dilemma, which is the basic historical choice with which humankind is faced today, is the following one: *either a radical reduction of work time for all*—to begin with the half-day of labor, or the half-week of labor—or the perpetuation of the division of society between those who produce and those who administer: the radical reduction of the work time *for all*—which was Marx's grandiose emancipatory vision—is indispensable both for the appropriation of knowledge and science by all, and for self-management by all (i.e., a regime of associated producers). Without such a reduction, both are utopias. You cannot acquire scientific knowledge nor manage your own factory, neighborhood, or "state" (collectivity) if you have to work at drudging mechanized labor in a factory or an office eight hours a day, five or six days a week. To say otherwise is to lie to yourself or to lie to others.

The emancipatory potential of robotism is that it makes socialism, communism, much easier, by making a twenty-hour, fifteen-hour, or ten-hour working week possible *for all*. But any step in the direction of the *dual society,* even with the best of intentions, goes in the diametrically opposed direction.

We leave aside the question whether "labor" reduced to twenty or fifteen hours a week is still "labor" in the classical sense of the word.[20]

We also leave aside how far the development of the individual, to quote Marx again, is a development in which "productive" activities remain separated from cultural, creative, scientific, artistic, sportive, purely recreative ones, in which, in other words, Lafargue's famous *droit à la paresse* becomes realized. Human happiness certainly does not depend on strenuous permanent activity, although a certain minimum amount of physical and mental activity and mobility seems to be an absolute precondition for a healthy growth, including the growth of the mind.

But independently of any consideration of that nature—the future of labor in the secular sense of the word—one conclusion seems inescapable: What will happen to human labor and to humanity is not predetermined mechanically by technology or science, their present trends and the obvious dangers which they encompass. It is determined, in the last analysis, by the social framework in which they develop. And here the difference between a development in the framework of capitalism, competition, market economy on the one hand, and socialism, i.e., collective property and collective solidarity through the rule of the associated producers, through the mastery of all the producers over all their conditions of labor as a result of a radical reduction of the (productive) work time, is absolutely basic.

The employers (and the bourgeois state) can likewise be helped in their strategic goal of introducing the *dual society* by the workers' obviously ambiguous attitude toward wage labor, toward work under capitalism, and work in the modern factory in general.

It is true that workers are forced, *under capitalism*, to be attached to full employment in order to receive a full (direct and indirect) wage. The alternative, again *under capitalism,* is a sharp decline in their standard of living, i.e., material and moral impoverishment and degradation.

But likewise, the workers are clearly aware of the increasingly degrading character of capitalist labor organization and capitalist productive effort, especially under the conditions of extreme parcellization of labor (Taylorism). Precisely when their standard of living is going up, as it did in the period 1950–1970, the needs of "work satisfaction" and of increased leisure (increased health, increased culture, increased self-activity) take on a new dimension. This became strikingly evident through and after the May 1968 explosion.[21] This awareness still exists—and employers as well as the bourgeois state consciously try to capitalize upon it in order to make the appeal for the *dual society* appear as something else from what it really is: an attempt to have the working class itself pay the burden of unemployment, and thereby sharply increase the mass and rate of profit.

In the same way as the demagogic outcry that the workers (why not the capitalists?) should share their income with the unemployed, and as the myth that "excessive wages and social security payments" are really responsible for the crisis, all the talk about "meaningless labor which you had better do away with" is therefore today nothing less than an ideological weapon of the capitalists in their class struggle against wage labor for lowering the worker's shares in the national income.

IX.

We have likewise to stress that any idea that present-day "dirty," nature-destroying, or directly life-threatening technology is an "inevitable" outcome of the inner logic of natural science, has to be rejected as obscurantist, ahistorical, and, in the last analysis, an apologia for capitalism.

Under capitalism, technology develops in the framework of money-costs accounting and money-profit projection for the individual firm. Hence general social costs, human costs, ecological costs, are "discounted," not only because they are "externalized" (i.e., individual firms do not pay for them), but also because they appear often much later than the profits which the new technology permits on a short- or medium-term basis.

Examples of such technological choices which were profitable from the individual firm's point of view but irresponsible socially, as a whole, in the long run are the internal combustion engine for vehicles and the detergent (versus soap) washing agents. In each of these cases choices were involved.

These were by no means the only technologies existing at these points of time.[22] On the contrary: many alternatives were present. The choices were not made for reasons of "purely" scientific or "technical" preferences. They were made for reasons of profit preferences by *specific* branches of industries, or better still, leading firms in these branches, i.e., power relations inside the capitalist class. No "technological determinism" was or is deciding humanity's fate. What is at stake is a socio-economic determinism, in which material interests of social classes or fractions of classes assert themselves, as long as these classes or fractions of classes have the actual power to impose their will (guided by these interests) upon the whole of society.

There is nothing new in understanding that technology developing under capitalism is not the only possible technology, but *specific* technology introduced for specific reasons closely linked to the specific nature of the capitalist economy and bourgeois society. Karl Marx was perfectly aware of this. He wrote in *Capital,* Volume 1:

> In modern agriculture, as in urban industry, the increase in the productivity and the mobility of labour is purchased at the cost of laying waste and debilitating labour-power itself. Moreover, all progress in capitalism is a progress in the art, not only of robbing the worker, but of robbing the soil; all progress in increasing the fertility of the soil for a given time is a progress towards ruining the more long-lasting sources of that fertility. The more a country proceeds from large-scale industry as the background of its development, as in the case of the United States, the more rapid is this process of destruction. Capitalist production, therefore, only develops the techniques and the degree of combination of the social process of production by simultaneously undermining the original sources of all wealth – the soil and the worker.[23]

Marx also stressed that this tendency of applying specifically capitalistic technologies—i.e., only technologies which lead to an increase in the production of surplus value—implied that new techniques had to be not only means for reducing the value of labor power, for cheapening consumer goods, and for economizing constant capital (cheaper machinery, raw materials, and energy). They could also be means for breaking or reducing labor's power of resistance at factory, industrial branch, or society's level:

> But machinery does not just act as a superior competitor to the worker, always on the point of making him superfluous. It is a power inimical to him, and capital proclaims this fact loudly and deliberately, as well as making use of it. It is the most powerful weapon for suppressing strikes, those periodic revolts of the working class against the autocracy of capital. . . . It would be possible to write a whole history of the inventions made since 1830 for the sole purpose of providing capital with weapons against working-class revolt.[24]

The history of the introduction of numerically controlled machine tools after the big 1946 strike wave in the United States is a striking confirmation of this rule.[25] Actually, when the balance sheet is made "after the facts," today less than 1 percent of the machine tools used in US industry are numerically controlled ones. But the scare created by their initial introduction was sufficient to break union power at the machine tools–producing plants.

A similar function is being played at present by the scare created in the trade union movement and the working class by the "suppression of labor through robots." Reality is still far removed from anything of the kind, as is indicated by the following table:

Table 3. Robots per 10,000 Wage Earners in Manufacturing Industry, 1981

	1978	1980	1981
Sweden	13.2	18.7	29.9
Japan	4.2	8.3	13.0
W. Germany	0.9	2.3	4.6
United States	2.1	3.1	4.0
France	0.2	1.1	1.9
Britain	0.2	0.6	1.2

Source: L'Observateur de l'OECD 123 (July 1983)

And to quote *Electronics Week,* "Even if the use of robots increases as predicted . . . by 1990, this would still affect only a few tenths of 1% of all employees in the industrialised countries, industry sources estimate."[26]

It is necessary to answer this scare *by familiarizing workers with computers,* by demanding that working-class children's schools should put computers at their disposal without any costs. This year up to five million "personal" home computers are supposed to be sold in the United States. Competition is ferocious. Prices will fall accordingly. Trade unions and other working-class organizations should see to it that workers and employees learn to master these mechanical slaves, whether or not endowed with "artificial intelligence." Then the scare will recede, and the working class will view new machines as it came to view old ones: as *instruments of labor* which can be transformed from instruments of despotism into instruments of emancipation, as soon as the workers become their collective masters.

Postcapitalist societies like that of the USSR generally borrow capitalist technology and suffer in addition from the consequences of bureaucratic management and bureaucratic power monopoly, i.e., the absence of free critical public opinion. But in a regime of associated self-managing producers under a socialist democracy with a plurality of political parties, no such constraints would operate. There is no reason to assume that such producers would be foolish enough to poison themselves and their environment, as soon as they knew the risks (when the risks are unknown, this is not due to too much but to too little scientific knowledge!). There is no reason to assume that they could not use machinery, including robots, as tools for the reduction or suppression of all mechanical, uncreative, burdensome, tedious, i.e., wasted, human labor, as instruments for making possible the reunification of production, administration, knowledge, creative activity, and full enjoyment of life, after having transformed them for that precise purpose.

X.

There remains one unanswered question, a question which Marxists have not taken up till now because it was not posed before humanity. But after dwelling for decades in the realm of science fiction and futurology, this question has now been brought to the threshold of the materially conceivable, as a result of the huge leaps forward of applied science and technology in the last decade: could human labor construct machines which could escape the control of humanity, become completely autonomous of men and women, i.e., intelligent machines, and machines with a potential to rebel against their original creator? After a certain point, would robots start to build robots without human instructions (without programming), even robots inconceivable to humanity and largely superior to them from the point of view of intelligence?

In the abstract, such a possibility certainly is conceivable. But one should circumscribe more precisely the present and reasonably foreseeable material framework of the problem, before getting hysterical or feeling doomed concerning human mastery over machines.

To build a "perfect" chess-playing machine, which has an answer to *all* possible combinations (10120), you would need *a number of combinations which far exceeds the number of atoms in the universe.* To have an existing computer calculate all numbers with 39,751 digits in order to discover a possible prime number among them, *it would take more time than the age of the universe up till now.* But with the help of the same existing computers, *human intelligence,* in the month of September 1983, actually discovered such a prime number with 39,751 digits (which, if fully printed, would extend for sixty meters) at Chippewa Falls, Wisconsin.[27]

Furthermore, there are fifteen billion nerve cells and fifteen trillion synapses in the human brain—in *one* human brain—a figure today's computers cannot compete with in any foreseeable future.

So the days in which we could become controlled, overwhelmed, mastered, by our chippy friends and slaves, are still far, far off. They are all the more so as humanity, i.e., human labor, commands their production and determines their calculating power. If necessary, humanity can decide to limit or stop the development of that power, or even to stop the production of robotized computers and computerized robots altogether. They are human tools, subordinated to specific human purposes. Humanity can avoid begetting sorcerers' apprentices, if it gains full control over its own tools and products.

But there we are at the heart of the matter: the structure and the laws of motion of *human society and economy.* That is what the problem is really all about, and not the undefined potential of mechanical calculating tools.

If humanity becomes master of its society, of the social organization of labor, of the goals and purposes of labor, i.e., master of its own fate, then there is no danger of it becoming enslaved by thinking computers. But that presupposes abolition of private property, market economy, competition, and "sacred egoism" as the main incentive for social labor. That presupposes a labor organization based upon cooperation and solidarity for the common good, i.e., self-managing socialism. If we don't achieve that mastery, then the threats are innumerable: nuclear annihilation; suffocating in our own excrements, i.e., ecological destruction; massive poverty and decline of liberty; universal famine. Possible enslavement by machines would be only one of the threats, and probably not the worst.

What is therefore the rational kernel of that irrational scare is the fact that the changes in human consciousness necessary to bring about a socialist world might be rendered more difficult by the *short-term effects of new communication techniques on human thinking and sensibility,* inasmuch as these techniques are subordinated to particular goals of privileged social groups (ruling classes and *strata*). Substitution of videocassettes for the written book; extreme narrowing of choices between conflicting sets of ideas; decline of critical thought and of research free from the tyranny of short-term "profits"; decline of the theoretical, synthetical, imaginative thinking in favor of narrow pragmatism and shortsighted utilitarianism (generally combined with a generous zest of mysticism and irrationalism regarding "broader" issues): there is the real danger that the robot and computer reshape our way of thinking,[28] but not through the fault of these poor mechanical slaves themselves but through the fault of those social forces who have an immediate social interest in achieving these disastrous effects.

Likewise, *human brains helped by computers* can more easily oppress, repress, exploit, enslave other human beings—the oppressed and exploited social classes in the first place!—than could human brains without computers. And this is so not because of the "wickedness" of the computer or of applied science, but because of the wickedness of a given type of society, which creates the temptation and the incentives for such types of behavior and endeavor.[29]

Against these dangers we must mobilize, not under the slogan of "Down with science and its dangerous potential," or "Destroy the computer," but under the slogan "Let humanity become master of its social and technical fate, master of its economy and of all the products of its manual and intellectual labor." That is still possible today. That is more necessary today than it ever was before.

•

"COMPETITIVE AUSTERITY" AND THE IMPASSE OF CAPITALIST EMPLOYMENT POLICY

Greg Albo

I. THE IMPASSE OF CAPITALIST EMPLOYMENT POLICY

Keynes closed his *General Theory* with the warning that "it is certain that the world will not much longer tolerate the unemployment which, apart from brief intervals of excitement, is associated – and, in my opinion, inevitably associated – with present-day capitalistic individualism."* Despite Keynes's conviction that "a right analysis of the problem [would] cure the disease," present-day capitalism is again associated with mass unemployment.[1] This represents a remarkable reversal of the postwar "golden age" of high growth and low unemployment. In the period from 1966 to 1973, a state of virtual full employment was reached, with unemployment falling below 3 percent in many states, with Germany and Japan even suffering serious labor shortages. From the oil shock of 1973 to the 1981–82 Volcker recession, mass unemployment spread across the OECD area, accompanied by accelerating inflation, giving rise to the awkward, if descriptive, term "stagflation." Despite the recovery of the mid-eighties and the squashing of inflation, the majority of the advanced capitalist bloc continues to be characterized by low productivity increases, "jobless growth," and steadily mounting unemployment. Even in the case of what often has been misleadingly referred to as the "great

★   This essay was first published in *Socialist Register 1994* (London: Merlin Press, 1994).

North American jobs machine," unemployment has failed to drop back to precrisis levels.

The stagnation of industrial production since the recession of 1991–92 has added further to employment problems. The subsequent "sick recovery" has shown scarce job prospects (with rates of new job creation in North America running at about one-quarter of previous recoveries). Stagflation has fallen into "disinflation" but still without growth. Across the OECD zone unemployment rates are now typically double, and often three and four times, what they were during the "golden age of capitalism." The proportion of the population actually engaging in paid work contributing to the total social product has, for the most part, been declining.[2] Fewer people are working at full-time jobs—and often at longer hours—while more people are not getting enough—or any—hours of work. The proportion of the population dependent on income transfers has, consequently, been secularly increasing.

The shift in the principal doctrines of employment policy since the onset of the crisis has been, perhaps, even more remarkable than the rise in unemployment. The postwar period was dominated by a form of Keynesianism commonly referred to as the "neoclassical synthesis," or, less favorably, by Joan Robinson as "bastard Keynesianism."[3] This Keynesian view held that the unemployed were involuntarily out of work and represented unutilized resources that could be mobilized to increase output. Capitalist economies, Keynesians argued, can get stuck at high levels of unemployment: nominal wages tend to be "sticky" downwards so that real wages might not fall to clear the market; similarly, declines in interest rates might not cause capitalists to invest and thereby to take up more workers. In either case, there is a lack of *effective demand* due to the collapse of the marginal efficiency of capital (expected profits). Full employment can be restored only by raising effective demand by increasing private or public consumption, bolstering investment levels, or by finding new foreign markets. The point was well summed by Keynes in *The General Theory*.

> The celebrated optimism of traditional economic theory—which has led to economists being looked upon as Candides who, having left this world for the cultivation of their gardens, teach that all is for the best in the best of all possible worlds provided we will let well alone—is also to be traced, I think, to their having neglected to take account of the drag on prosperity which can be exercised by

an insufficiency of effective demand. For there would obviously be a natural tendency toward the optimum employment of resources in a society which was functioning after the manner of the classical postulates. It may well be that the classical theory represents the way in which we should like our economy to behave. But to assume that it actually does so is to assume our difficulties away.[4]

Following the stagflation experience, there are few adherents to the Keynesian view today that increasing aggregate demand, in either the form of consumption or public investment, will have much effect in stimulating economic growth or lowering unemployment. Even when there exists real effective demand shortfalls at the national level, due to slower investment or to the pursuit of restrictive budgetary policies to control domestic costs for international competitiveness, particularly by the G7 group at the core of the world economy, it is doubtful that a stimulative package would call forth private sector investment at levels high and enduring enough to recreate an economic boom. It is even more unlikely that demand stimulation at the national level—or even the supranational level such as Europe—can solve the long-period unemployment problem now exists. (Nor can the international mechanisms and institutions that might supply stable, long-term, balanced aggregate world demand be identified or foreseen.)

The general crisis of unemployment since 1974 has shattered postwar capitalist employment policy centered on Keynesianism. All sides of the political spectrum have seemed to come to agreement on two fundamental points as necessary to soak up the massive global labor surpluses: the need to provide a supply-side stimulative package to spur renewed accumulation; and maintenance, if not strengthening, of a liberal regional and global trading regime, through the economic integration proposed by the European Economic Community and the North American Free Trade Agreement, or via the multilateral General Agreement on Tariffs and Trade.

The right's supply-side strategy has focused on breaking the institutional rigidities built into the Fordist postwar system that limited market discipline, protected workers' bargaining power, and, through productivity sharing, maintained aggregate demand. Improved market flexibility would, it is contended, increase the returns to capital and, in turn, the rate of capital accumulation. The social democratic left's supply-side strategy has also attempted to increase flexibility and competitiveness, but in this case by stimulating the introduction of flexible automation through the systematic introduction of new technologies by industrial policies and tax incentives and by developing highly skilled workers through modernized training regimes. In either the neoliberal or "progressive competitiveness" strategies, the employment policy conclusions run parallel: rapid economic growth, export-oriented industrial policies, and freer trade are the only hope to bring unemployment back down to the "full employment" levels of the postwar "golden age of capitalism." There is no alternative to supply-side strategies of "liberal productivism" for each firm, region, or country to win a place in the competitive battle for world market shares and to solve the unemployment crisis.

The neoliberal view, in its original monetarist or more recent variants, contends that unemployment is a *specific, individual, voluntary* problem of the labor market.[5] Individual firms and workers voluntarily make, accept, or refuse wage offers. Unemployment is essentially a result of real wages asked being too high and profits too low, consequently leading to fewer job offers, a lower rate of investment, and the use of labor-saving techniques. Attempting to lower real wages through inflation, as Keynesian stimulus does, soon leads to workers' wage expectations adapting, leaving the aggregate labor supply unchanged. Unemployment remains at its natural, or voluntary, rate of unemployment (which is redefined more precisely as the non–accelerating inflation rate of unemployment). Demand stimulus, therefore, does not affect real output and thus levels of employment in the long term.

In this view, lowering the natural rate of unemployment depends upon lowering inflation, so that capitalists can have more certainty about their investments, and deregulating nonmarket barriers which prevent real wages from falling in the labor market and thus preventing new hires and higher levels of productivity and investment. The measures to improve labor market flexibility are primarily "defensive" in nature; that is, they involve rolling back institutional securities for workers built into the postwar labor market and welfare state. This defensive flexibility includes: reducing trade union power; minimizing the welfare disincentives to work; improving information flows and labor mobility; leaving investment in training to individual decisions on their "human capital" needs; and eliminating market restraints, such as minimum wages and unemployment insurance, which limit downward wage flexibility. By moving to an unregulated free market, economic adjustment would instantaneously produce market-clearing wage levels (with the principle of substitutability of labor and capital making any bias to capital-using technological change unimportant except for determining the rate of growth). In effect, Say's Law is restored, and all unemployment is a voluntary, individual choice given existing competitive conditions in the market.

In one form or another, the neoliberal approach has dominated the agenda of employment policy since the late 1970s. It has not stood up very well against actual economic experience. At the most basic level, the neoliberal position has never provided a satisfactory explanation as to why the natural rate of unemployment should vary so much over time, between countries, or for any number of institutional reasons. Rather than exhibiting any tendency "toward an optimum employment of resources," more than anything else, as Keynes warned, the natural rate seems to track the historical rate of unemployment. Bringing down the rate of inflation and increasing wage flexibility through the 1980s has not meant a reduction in unemployment. On the contrary, fiscal and monetary restraint have contributed to the deflationary tendency of the crisis by squeezing down social and wage costs, thereby taking demand out of the system (in the process seriously damaging the neoclassical notion of a vertical Phillips curve at a natural rate of unemployment).

Indeed, the spread across the capitalist bloc of neoliberal policies of keeping wage increases below productivity growth and pushing down domestic costs has led to an unstable vicious circle of *"competitive austerity"*: each country reduces domestic demand and adopts an export-oriented strategy of dumping its surplus production, for which there are fewer consumers in its national economy given the decrease in workers' living standards and productivity gains all going to the capitalists, in the world market. This has created a global demand crisis and the growth of surplus capacity across the business cycle. The structural asymmetries in the payments position of the major countries, notably the deficit of the United States which has played the role of absorbing other countries' export surpluses since the postwar period, have thus proven intractable. As a result, unemployment is spiraling upward even in the center economies of Japan and Germany, which are running payments surpluses. So long as all countries continue to pursue export-led strategies, which is the conventional wisdom demanded by IMF, OECD, and G7 policies and the logic of neoliberal trade policies, there seems little reason not to conclude that "competitive austerity" will continue to ratchet down the living standards of workers in *both* the North and the South. Only the most dogmatic of market economists, of which there are all too many today, can still hold that neoliberal policies offer a route out of the jobs crisis. (Or they must at least concede that these policies can only be sustained by further "Brazilianization" of having the working classes of the North and the South bear the burden of adjustment imposed by the contradiction between the international payments constraint and export-oriented policies.)

II. COMPETITIVENESS AND THE PRODUCTION OF SKILLS

The social democratic supply-side perspective also stresses the need for labor market flexibility "to compete in the new global economy" to maintain domestic employment. In this case the focus is less on increasing wage and market flexibility, which, it is argued, has caused the income and work polarization of the 1980s. Rather, the notion is of an offensive flexibility whereby the training of highly skilled workers contributes, or indeed causes, the successful integration of new technologies and flexible workplace adaptation to shifting market demand for products. The lack of an appropriate skill profile of the labor force and a dynamic training regime, this view contends, causes a mismatch between workers' skills and the demand for labor as a result of technological change. The mismatch is registered in slow industrial adjustment to market changes and thus higher rates of unemployment. By retraining and adjusting workers' skills, the dislocations from technological change will eventually work themselves out as firms adapt to the new competitive conditions at higher levels of output. In its essence, this position was elaborated best by Joseph Schumpeter:

> Economists have a habit of distinguishing between, and contrasting, cyclical and technological unemployment. But it follows from our model that, basically, cyclical unemployment is technological unemployment. . . . We have seen, in fact, in our historical survey, that periods of prolonged supernormal unemployment, coincide with the periods in which the results of inventions are spreading over the system.[6]

The high unemployment levels confronting the advanced capitalist countries today, then, are caused by a shift to a new technological
paradigm: the end of the mass production processes of Fordism and
the transition to the new flexible work processes and automated factories brought about by the microelectronics revolution. The period of
economic transition across this "industrial divide" can be shortened,
however, by retooling of factories and rapid adjustment of work skills
to meet the new competitive conditions. This position suggests that
supply, in this case the supply of skilled labor, will create its own demand, and that the processes of national adjustment, and existing demand conditions, provide no significant long-term barrier to lowering
unemployment. Successful microeconomic adjustments on the supply
side will lead to desired macroeconomic results on the employment
side. This view can be termed the *"progressive competitiveness"* model—
adapted by social democratic parties across the OECD and by the
Democratic Clinton regime in the United States—of creating globally competitive, high value-added firms using highly skilled workers.
Training policy is, in this model, the cornerstone to job creation and
an alternate response to the "competitive austerity" resulting from neoliberal labor market strategies.

But how should we think of training policy within capitalist societies, and can we infer the employment conclusions drawn by the
"progressive competitiveness" strategy? Since the publication of Harry
Braverman's remarkable book *Labor and Monopoly Capital,*[7] there has
been a veritable explosion of studies of the capitalist labor process.
Braverman's own view that the structural tendency of modern capitalism is to uniformly extend Taylorism, and thus deskill workers,
is limited. Not only does he fail to fully account for a differentiation
of skills across occupations; his thesis also appears historically bound
to the deep separation of conception from execution characteristic of
Fordism. Yet, even more insensitive to skill differentiation has been
the view, associated with Michael Piore and Charles Sabel's *The Second
Industrial Divide,*[8] that microelectronics leads to a uniform process of
skill enrichment. This latter sentiment has characterized most recent
writings on the skills impact of the new production concepts and is
central to the progressive competitiveness model.

The real lesson of the many studies of the labor process, however,
is that a *social choice* is involved in the organization of the workplace,

albeit a choice severely constrained by the relations of production particular to capitalism.[9] This dynamic relationship between technological changes, work organization, and skills has been neglected until
recently.[10] Depending on whether one was reading the economics or
sociology literature, technology or organizations caused a certain type
of labor process and hence a specific national growth model. But as
Michael Storper notes: "In reality, both 'firms' and 'industries' are being redefined, such that the notion of returns as strictly internal loses
its meaning in any dynamic, historical sense. In sum, in functioning
industrial systems, both the division of labour and technological innovations tend to be endogenously and dynamically reproduced and are,
in turn, mutually reinforcing."[11]

An important factor affecting this social choice—little considered
because of the assumption of either progressive or regressive advance of
worker skills through the growth of the market—is the "technical capacities" of the national labor force and the role of the training process
in determining what goes into the labor process. With the old technological paradigm of Fordism in decline, the development of "technical capacities" also raises fundamental political questions. If the labor
movement should support the end of Taylorism—one of its historical
demands for the reuniting of head and hand—on what basis should it
commit itself to upgrading the skills of workers so as to expand the capacities for self-management? How should the productivity gains from
more flexible work processes be shared out so as to increase employment and equalize income?

The failure to take up these questions, at least within North America, is witnessed most clearly in the "human capital school," the position which has dominated the analysis and policies of training since the
1960s, and is most associated with neoliberal employment policies.[12]
The conceptual core of human capital theory is the view that individuals invest in themselves (in job search, information sources, qualifications, migration) for the sake of future monetary returns—a return
on investment in skills (nonpecuniary returns from education being
ignored or reduced to a monetary value). As one of the founders of the
school, T. W. Schultz, put it:

> Laborers have become capitalists not from a diffusion of the own-
> ership of corporation stocks, as folklore would have it, but from the
> acquisition of knowledge and skill that have economic value. This

knowledge and skill are in great part the product of investment and, combined with other human investment, predominantly account for the productive superiority of the technically advanced countries.[13]

At the level of the firm, individual enterprises respond to relative costs of factor inputs, including varied types of skilled labor, and then set the demand for labor. Even with nonhomogeneous units of labor, production functions substitute units of labor and capital at the margin with no substantive, or at least dynamic, variation in technique. At the level of the individual, price signals are sufficient to yield the required investment in skills and thus supply of skilled workers. For firms or individuals training occurs by comparing the cost of investing in skills with the additional revenues earned. In short, human capital theory suggests that the labor market yields *private* market signals to individuals which are not at variance with the *social* signals for the economy and society as a whole.

But the treatment of skills as acquired individual attributes tradable in the market, and thus a claim for a high wage based on a high marginal productivity, is seriously flawed. One of the tenets of dual labor market theory which still merits attention is that the labor market is something less than homogeneous in its treatment of individual workers and in its structure. The earnings of workers are significantly influenced by factors such as gender, age, race, and social origin, so they cannot be reduced simply to a return on investment in human capital. As well, systematic barriers to occupational mobility and employment instability for one group of workers can be contrasted with the stable employment advance through internal labor markets of firms for other workers.[14] Regardless of whether such a strong dualism should be attributed to technology and market structures, specific skills learned through on-the-job training tend to be limited to core workers in technically advanced firms. The market alone does not provide either adequate skills or stable employment. Thus, the dualists pointed out, if investment in skills is important, it is unlikely to be adequately provided in terms of volume or of equal access for all workers by the market. Public programs for training and employment are essential.[15]

Apart from the lack of training due to differences of industry structure, there are additional reasons to suggest that the problems of market failure extend to individual firms and eventually across the economy.[16] Firm investment in training resides with the individual worker and not in physical assets; the "human capital" attached to the trainee is thereby mobile. This is especially the case for what Gary Becker calls "transferable skills and competencies."[17] These general skills will increase individual productivity equivalently for any enterprise, and contrast to the specific training that increases individual productivity primarily in the firm providing the training (although little training is completely specific to a single firm). Skills provided by general training are, consequently, in danger of being "poached": individual firms may forego the costs of training, finding it instead to their advantage to bid trained workers away from the training firm by providing a higher wage. If this occurs on a wide-enough scale, training firms would cease to train, for they would lose their investments. In other words, markets with "poachers" and "trainers" are unstable; market failures in this type of "employer-centered" system will lead to skill shortages. So governments, again, have a role to play in the provision of training either by a grant-levy scheme to equalize private training or through institutional public training programs providing a collective good.

The expansion of state training programs in the 1960s and '70s to cope with the problem of poaching sparked a further response, particularly in Britain, Canada, and the United States, from human capital theorists to reestablish the primacy of a private market in training—a response now embedded in the neoliberal labor market policies of the Anglo-American countries.[18] The human capital theorists contended that, at least theoretically, the market would provide specific skills. Yet they also agreed that firms would be unwilling to finance *general* training that involved costs that could not be recouped because of poaching. The problem, however, was not market-based training, but trainee wages that were too high relative to their marginal product. If these wages were brought in line, either by wage subsidies or lowering trainee allowances and minimum wages, poaching would be pointless as all firms would undertake training. The market would again supply price signals appropriate to socially efficient training levels.

This neoliberal strategy of privatizing training had disastrous consequences for workers and skills training throughout the 1980s as firms failed to provide adequate levels of trained workers, and workers dropped out of training programs because of a lack of decent living allowances. Unskilled workers on training programs, moreover, often became little more than subsidized waged labor, especially in the

British and Canadian training programs, on the basis that any paid work provided basic training for further employment. The return to market-driven training, therefore, represented the market failures of insufficient volumes of training and a social polarization among the recipients of training.

The "progressive competitiveness" advocates of training policies for more flexible workplaces, moreover, began to point to more fundamental limits of market-driven training which were blocking skills adjustment (and thus allowing unemployment unnecessarily to climb). The problem of training market failure, for example, meant that a labor market intelligence network was still required, but the rush to privatization had seriously compromised the capacities of the labor exchanges (a key project of social democratic reformers since the turn of the century). For instance, formal training for higher education or technical training tends to leave the costs (foregone income and direct outlays) with the individuals. As predicted by human capital theory, "workers pay for their own schooling." But imperfections in the capital market, especially equal access to loans for trainees of different social origins, will remain. Substantial financial programs and trainee allowances—which also involve occupational-selection decisions by the state on what to provide funding for—will be required. There is, furthermore, unlikely to be perfect information about occupational choices, for youth and older workers in particular, so skill "investments" will not necessarily be efficient. The typical activities of labor market boards—counseling, job banks, placement, mobility—remain imperative if the market is not to undersupply skills. Limiting skilling to calculations of returns on investment will, in fact, yield fewer returns in terms of skilled workers than if training and education are viewed as social rights to be guaranteed by the state.

A period of transition between techno-social paradigms will compound all these problems into serious obstacles to adjustment and high unemployment. The problem of poaching, for example, will tend to intensify in market-driven training systems in a transitional period. Few skills are exclusively firm specific, and bidding wars will ensue for workers with the new skills in demand. So unless rigid internal labor markets are in place, or the firm is in a monopsony position, capitalists will, in general, underinvest in training. Firms in a competitive cost crunch, moreover, are likely to cut training costs as a first step to cutting labor costs (as has happened as a result of more open economies and import pressures during the 1980s). As a result of these two pressures, skill shortages will appear in recoveries from recessions which, in turn, will spur poaching from weaker firms (many of which will be startup new-technology companies). In a period of a technological paradigm shift, training failures will inevitably lengthen the period of adjustment and provide the basis for wrenching levels of unemployment for countries pushed down the neoliberal path as weak firms lose their skilled workers and competitive edge.

Finally, the neoliberal defense of market-based training, critics pointed out, depends upon static parameters in the demand and supply of labor in the short period (and pure flexibility of skills and wages in the long period). This assumes that individual capitalists know *ex ante* the appropriate skills to even new techniques and that *ex post* these skills will be supplied to meet the aggregate needs of all capitalists. But this is not likely, given the fallacy of composition problems underpinning the logic, to be the case. An *oversupply* of high-level general skills in the labor market will in fact make for an easier transition to more advanced production techniques and a more flexible workforce to meet changing market demands. This is the foremost principle drawn by the "progressive competitiveness" strategy from the training policy debate: product strategies are linked to available skills and technological advance places a premium on highly skilled workers.

The systemic failure of the market to provide comprehensive training suggests that skills may be seen best as a "public or collective good." In a powerful series of essays, Wolfgang Streeck has argued precisely this point:

> [T]he fundamental uncertainty for employers recovering their training expenses in an open labour market . . . turns skills, from the viewpoint of the individual employer, into a collective good. If an employer provides training, he is no more than adding to a common pool of skilled labour which is in principle accessible to all other employers in the industry or locally, many of which are his competitors. . . . As a result, there will be a chronic undersupply of skilled labour. . . . In this sense, I regard skills as an example of what I described as collective, social production factors which capitalist firms, acting according to the rational utilitarian model, cannot adequately generate or preserve.[19]

This is an important conclusion, and one that can be widely endorsed: if left to the market, training will occur, and powerful corporations like IBM may even provide high-quality training and develop strong internal labor markets, but these will be isolated "islands of excellence." Nonmarket training institutions are essential to the adequate provision of skills (particularly to the access to skills by individual workers in marginalized social groups). A neo-corporatist training regime, as argued by Streeck and endorsed by the "progressive competitiveness" strategy, would be a preferred option to the market.[20] In this view, firms, regulated by corporatist structures like the German works councils, are the ideal places for training. State training programs, like markets, may equally fail to provide the needed "collective skills good." Schools are not the ideal places to create work skills, even if the skills needed are general and polyvalent. This does not mean that formal classroom training is absent—even the famous German apprenticeship system includes this component; but it does mean that on-the-job training is suited best for producing the dynamic training regime and skills attributes, including the "socialization in work-related values," demanded by "the new competitive conditions in world markets."[21]

The obstacles to a successful corporatist strategy along German lines are enormous in the Anglo-American countries, where the experience of on-the-job training is mixed and the political conditions to produce works councils are decidedly remote. Even when the state has extensively regulated on-the-job training, it often has meant little more than firms providing brief, firm-specific training for semiskilled workers. In introducing the Japanese flexible work processes, firms have used training as much for the inculcation of "corporate culture" as for actual skills training. On-the-job training for peripheral workers, moreover, has often simply meant brief periods of employment without the skills upgrading necessary to improve labor market chances in the long term (and certainly not the development of the skills requisite for more active citizenship in the broader community). Publicly provided programs, and institutional training centers supplying formal qualifications, have been essential to providing skills and broadening access to training. A strong public core to training is often seen, therefore, as necessary in North America to facilitate adjustment to the new work processes and to have productivity gains spread across the national economy.

These three principal means of regulating the training of workers—the market, corporatist institutions, or the state—are rooted in
different societies in quite distinct ways. In Japan, a highly segmented,
formal schooling is followed by extensive training at the firm level,
with the firm's investment maintained by extremely rigid internal labor
markets. Germany appears as the example par excellence of corporatist
regulation of training. An extensive adult and secondary vocational education structure is added to a highly developed apprenticeship system,
jointly regulated by unions and management through works councils.
Sweden, in contrast, has a strong public component to training, particularly for the unemployed and to encourage worker mobility, su-
pervised by the National Labour Market Board. The North American
"market model" of training has been more varied and institutionally
unstable: Canada and the United States have alternatively relied upon
"poaching" skilled workers from other nations through immigration,
public training programs targeted at the disadvantaged or the highly
qualified, and firm-specific market-supplied skills.

These different national forms of producing skills have become important, according to the progressive competitiveness model, to current industrial restructuring. The production of skills and the type of
national training regime are important not just for flexibility in general
but for the *kind* of flexibility firms will adopt. The old mass production
processes of Fordism tended to rely on a sharp separation of conception
and execution. The rigid differentiation of tasks produced a skill polarization: conception concentrated in specialist technical skills in design
offices; skilled manufacturing and trades jobs filled by apprenticeship
or specialist training; and a mass of unskilled assembly jobs with limited specific training tied to a minute division of labor. In contrast,
flexible automation tends to use reprogrammable technologies to reintegrate production and design.

Work organization can consequently be more flexible, in responding to differentiated product demand. Flexible automation, moreover,
requires workers that are more flexible, emphasizing multitasking and
multiskilling, general skills rather than specific ones, and analytic and
problem-solving abilities rather than mere procedural capacities. Thus
skills are likely to be decisive to a reorganized labor process—both to
exploit the potential productivity of new technologies and to involve

workers directly in improving productivity—for firms attempting to export high value-added products.[22]

Yet just as Fordism differed between nations, the "progressive competitiveness" strategy contends there is unlikely to be a uniform adaptation of a new form of work organization under a regime of flexible automation. As Arndt Sorge and Malcolm Warner have emphasized, training and qualification structures appear linked to technological adaptation but are embedded in national traditions.[23] The availability of highly skilled workers in countries with strong training institutions permits quick redeployment of labor to new technologies and products, which, in turn, helps preserve the skills base and competitiveness. In contrast, in countries with weak skilling structures and old products, a low skills equilibrium seems to develop which forces downward economic adjustments to compete on the basis of costs. In other words, there appear to be national forms of flexibility, dependent upon the training regime, in responding to market uncertainty and new product demands. The task of employment policy is, then, to upgrade the national training regime. Within social democratic thinking, this conclusion has been most forcefully stated by Canada's United Steelworkers:

> What has become known as the high-skill business strategy refers to a cluster of business strategies that are compatible with secure jobs providing fair wages. . . . The high-skill option requires businesses to pursue strategies of increasing value-added rather than strategies to reduce labour's share in existing value-added. . . . We need enlightened management who recognize the importance of competing in higher value-added markets on a high-skill basis. . . . Once there is a commitment to truly developing worker skills and their roles in a workplace, workers will be partners in building toward sustainable prosperity in their workplaces and communities.[24]

If a country, or region for that matter, is to keep its export share, or increase it to boost employment levels, employment policy must have as its central concern the production of skills. Training leads to jobs, and highly skilled training is the basis for the good jobs in high value-added, globally competitive firms that will put an end to "competitive austerity."

The training policy regime advocated by the progressive competitiveness strategy is superior to the neoliberal model in terms of both the analysis of market failure in the provision of skills and the positive role that training can play in adjustment. The insight that training structures can act as a leverage to improve firm-level adjustment to the demand and quality of products, for instance, is important. Similarly, the conclusion that highly skilled, involved workers can begin to reverse the deskilling of work under Taylorism, and add to labor productivity, is a result with important implications for the labor movement as a whole. To the extent that worker involvement and training policy are collectively negotiated with organized workers at the plant level, and through elected works councils at the sectoral level, there is the *potential* capacity to make material advances to worker self-management that has been limited by the management-rights clauses that were part of the Fordist productivity-sharing bargain.

But it is not possible to generalize, as is done by the progressive competitiveness strategy, that upgrading skills in line with the new technologies will resolve the problem of unemployment. This position must assume that levels of unemployment have not been secularly increasing for some time (a questionable proposition for the OECD zone). It must further assume that the volume and distribution of hours of work is, more or less, already adequate. Present unemployment can then be posed as essentially an adjustment problem caused by lags in skill development in response to new technologies and competitive conditions. These assumptions are problematic: numerous studies have shown that the level of unemployment has been increasing for some time for any degree of capital utilization, suggesting a growing surplus labor force; as well, the level of unused capacity has been increasing, indicating growing demand problems. In these conditions, training will raise the average level of skills, but it will not mean more jobs will be available.

The progressive competitiveness strategy hinges, then, on sustained high rates of growth in world (not necessarily national) markets to lower unemployment. This depends upon a number of equally strong and dubious assumptions. It depends, for example, on higher value-added production spreading across the national economy so as to replace lower value-added standardized production being lost to low-wage producers and regions. This entails the very large risk that the deindustrializing sectors will decline at a faster rate, and with greater employment losses, than the rate of expansion of sectors of high technology. The high-technology sectors being boosted must also see no cost advantage to moving to low-wage production sites (although there is ample evidence that they do and that developing countries are able to supply skilled workers). Export growth in high-technology sectors, moreover, must be more rapid than previous levels of export growth if unemployment is not to grow because of higher capital–labor ratios in these sectors relative to the declining low-wage sectors.

It is an extremely suspect proposition that rapid-enough accumulation can be achieved in world markets to accommodate all the countries and regions engaged in this high-growth, high-productivity, high-tech export-oriented strategy. That would take a near miracle in itself. Yet more basically the extension of the export-oriented strategy beyond a single country ignores the simple problem of who is going to bear the payments deficits as all companies and countries squeeze costs to pursue the high value-added, export-oriented industrialization strategies that is to solve the national unemployment crisis. Will it be the deficit-plagued United States and Canada? Will it be the export-oriented Japanese and German economies engaged in their own fiscal crises and trying to maintain payments surpluses to expand their spheres of influence? Can the Asian "miracle economies" suddenly reverse their industrial structures and become launched on an import binge? Or, perhaps, the devastated economies and workers of Africa and South America could do the world economy a good turn?

The asymmetry of all countries pursuing export markets can only add to the competitive pressures to bargain down national wage and social standards. As low-wage zones increasingly adopt leading-edge technologies—as mobile productive capital from the North establishes new plants in these zones because of their own high-technology strategies—the downward wage pressure will accelerate (as it must with global labor surpluses). But, as has become all too evident, the bargaining-down process takes demand out of the system, with no clear compensating source, precisely when more output is being put on the world market. The cumulative effect is to add to the realization problems of growing surplus capacity and a further spiral of unemployment. The distribution of hours of work also polarizes to meet the new competition: multiskilled core workers are pushed to work longer hours to recoup training investments, while peripheral workers and the unemployed scramble to get enough hours of paid work. The progressive competitiveness strategy is forced to accept, as social democratic parties have been willing to do, the same "competitive austerity" as neoliberalism, and further "Brazilianization of the West," as a cold necessity of present economic conditions.

III. BEYOND "COMPETITIVE AUSTERITY"?

The relationship of training regimes to overall employment policy retains a central importance. New qualifications and skills may affect the speed of adjustment for individual firms, or even countries if a strong training regime has been institutionalized. But there is no reason that this should increase the general volume of employment particularly as other firms and regions adopt (as they appear to be doing) the same progressive competitiveness strategy. Under these conditions national (or regional) employment is increased only to the extent somebody else (or some other region) is bested and put out of work. The distribution of work, but not its aggregate volume, is altered: the result is better-skilled workers but unemployed in the same number (or higher if all countries pursue cost cutting to improve export competitiveness and take demand out of the system). Indeed, the rationalization of production from the new work processes has not meant higher world growth rates, so that productivity gains have largely been at the expense of employment, causing the "jobless growth" phenomenon. The productivity growth from new technologies has consequently been profoundly inegalitarian: the permanently displaced workers and unemployed suffer declining living standards; the retrained multiskilled worker often gains in greater job security and lower consumer costs; and the owners of capital, and their managers, take all the increases in productivity and output.

The danger in the present situation—and it is already a feature of current international conditions—is to push every country, and even the most dynamic firms embracing the new work processes, toward competitive austerity. Robert Boyer has captured well this dilemma:

> On the one hand, there is the opportunity to mitigate some of the worst features of fordism: less need for a hierarchy exercising authoritarian control, the possibility of doing away with tedious, dangerous, or purely repetitive jobs, opportunities of raising qualifications through general and adequate technical training. . . . But on the other hand not all companies or sectors are in a position to adopt this strategy: falling back on cheap, unskilled labour is a great temptation – and a very real danger, particularly as minimum wage levels

are lowered. . . . Equally, it is not certain that computerization will undermine the historical division between manual labour and intellectual work. If some repetitive tasks can be abolished and others made potentially more varied and interesting, the rationalization and taylorization of intellectual work itself may occur.[25]

If the "worst features of Fordism" are to be avoided, then the question of unemployment must be directly confronted.

There have been few credible explanations of the postcrisis divergence in unemployment rates to be found in any of the explanations from either the demand or supply side. Numerous cross-national correlational studies seem to have conclusively demonstrated that there is no simple, uniform relationship between economic variables and the level of unemployment.[26] In general these studies have found various political variables, such as the extent of corporatism, the composition of the governing block, to be more telling. The conclusion drawn from the "politics matter" studies is bold, and strikingly at odds with mainstream economic thinking: "mass unemployment is unnecessary; full employment is a matter of (social democratic) political will." This conclusion can be sustained, however, only at the most general level, in that some states have done better in *containing* the growth of mass unemployment, even while all states have been doing worse in employing their labor forces. It does point, however, in the direction of studying the particular history and economic institutions of national employment policies.

As Göran Therborn's book *Why Some Peoples Are More Unemployed Than Others* argues, the postwar national routes to employment success and unemployment disaster have been diverse. Some states, such as Sweden and Japan, have managed to perform relatively better in terms of unemployment, while other states, such as Britain, Canada, and the Netherlands, have become high-unemployment disasters. The allocation of unemployment within national labor forces, moreover, is distributed in strikingly different ways. Unemployment in Italy, for example, has tended to fall disproportionately on the young and women, whereas in Britain it has fallen more on males. Germans have withdrawn from the labor market with sharp declines in labor force participation (especially for older workers). The Swedes, in contrast, have expanded public employment and massively increased part-time work. North Americans have allowed the part-time, peripheral workforce to grow; at the same time average hours of work among core workers has increased. Although labor reserves appear as a fundamental feature of capitalist production within all these countries, and have grown in importance since the crisis, capitalist societies exhibit an extraordinary range of possibilities for the distribution of paid work and social arrangements for containing unemployment.

Even in the narrow Keynesianism of the neoclassical synthesis, there was an important rejection of some of the defenses of pure market economies. Keynesian reasoning laid to rest the doctrine of Say's Law—a mainstay of neoclassical economics since the nineteenth century—that supply creates its own demand by generating the income to purchase the output produced, making slumps, and labor surpluses, impossible. The Keynesian revolution suggested that capitalist economies, and especially labor markets, are not self-adjusting to fluctuations in supply and demand: as a result of expectations about the future, market adjustments can move as easily away from "full employment equilibrium" as toward it. This conclusion contained a broader implication, one little noted except within the Marxian tradition: economic adjustment takes place in real *historical time* and under the constraint of existing *economic institutions*.

Michal Kalecki pointed out that there are essentially three ways to bolster effective demand for employment: deficit spending through higher public investment or subsidies to private consumption; stimulating private investment by lowering interest rates or tax concessions; and, finally, redistribution of income (and work) from higher- to lower-income classes. The policy path pursued over the postwar period has had important implications for the postcrisis capacity of national states to contain unemployment.

Keynesian policies relied extensively on fiscal policy (and partly monetary policy) attempting to stimulate private investment, and much less on deficit spending, increasing consumption, or redistribution. This budgetary approach entailed keeping private sector growth rates as high as possible through ever-greater cuts in corporate taxes, subsidies, and tax incentives to keep investment levels increasing, and to offset the capital-using bias of technological change (given relatively constant hours of work and distributional shares). The economies of North America were the examples par excellence of this method of keeping employment high. As traded goods began to occupy an increased share of domestic production, the national economies which had adopted this strategy have had to engage in ever-increasing levels of competitive bargaining to attract or keep capital. The weak labor market and training structures developed over the postwar period added to the North American employment problem: skilled workers had either been "poached" from Europe or left to the random individual decisions of the private sector; the rapid labor supply growth which had fed postwar "extensive accumulation" now translated into the massive growth of low-waged job sectors; and workers with "good jobs" in unionized firms were forced into concessions bargaining to keep capitalists in their communities and to hold off the swelling rolls of unemployed and low-paid workers queuing up for the good jobs promised by the "American way of life."

Although deficit spending was never extensively engaged in for macroeconomic stabilization, European states, more than North American ones, stimulated public investment and expanded the size of their public sectors, using the investment as a platform for continual modernization of infrastructure and industry. But the end of the "golden age" and the competitive pressures of more open economies also showed the limits of this strategy. To the extent the European statist strategy disengaged a larger proportion of annual output from the market economy, and to the extent it contributed to the maintenance of a labor-process model using the most advanced techniques and work processes effectively involving workers, this method helped to stabilize employment fluctuations and to keep employment high.

But the "Eurosclerosis" disease of institutional rigidities in the labor market that served as the basis for containing unemployment became an obstacle with increased capital mobility: European capitalists took their investments to where wages and work standards were lower or where the rate of return was higher (as in the United States), effectively shutting down domestic accumulation. To try to keep investment at home and to hold market shares, European states also have been forced to hold back the public sector, to allow increased industrial rationalization and shedding of workers, and to raise interest rates. France's socialist reflation of the early 1980s, for example, had more successes than often given credit for, in terms of avoiding the extensive downturn of the rest of the OECD area, and in rationalizing industry from nationalizations. But the Keynesian reflation could not be sustained on its own against a world economy marching to the tune of restraint and capital mobility. The jobless rates in France, therefore, did not stay down once the reflation ended. The French socialists subsequently moved toward the neoliberal approach of stimulating private investment, following the route adopted elsewhere, but had even less success in containing the drift toward persistent double-digit unemployment. As a result of these forces, mass unemployment has spread across the European states as well, notably in Germany, France, and Italy, which had adopted the public sector route to maintaining high employment. Along with North America, they too have pursued neoliberal adjustment policies and export-oriented development at the end of the 1980s, allowing unemployment to rise (although still distributing it differently).

Kalecki's first two ways to full employment, deficit spending and stimulating private investment, appear to have reached their limits as a means to avoid competitive austerity. This leaves the third option to full employment of redistributing income, and, more particularly today, of redistributing work. Kalecki's third option of redistributing income was barely evident at all (and of work even less so) over the postwar period. The maintenance of private ownership of the means of production limited the possibilities for redistribution of income, for it also would have sacrificed Keynes's famous "animal spirits" inducement to invest. This was, as Leo Panitch has argued, one of the main failures of the income policies to constrain wage pressures that were a part of full-employment economies: they attempted to freeze the distributional shares of income between the social classes and fell apart on the basis of that contradiction.[27]

Redistribution of income was limited, therefore, to countries that could build up solidaristic institutions within the labor market to redistribute wages to the lower-paid, and that had the political capacity to drive up tax rates to provide a pool of funds to be redistributed through the welfare state. This situation was limited, for the most part, to Sweden. But even in this case, with the foremost political conditions for maintaining employment, the economic strategy still entailed the postwar Fordist fixation of keeping growth rates as high as possible, to avoid disturbing the unequal class structure by promising workers a share of growing output, and rationalizing the industrial structure to maintain export markets. As the golden age growth slowed, the Swedish model, too, confronted difficulties in containing unemployment: the solidarity-wages policy and tax loads both reached an impasse vis-à-vis workers initially, and subsequently capitalists. Sweden, therefore, had to engage in a continual series of competitive devaluations to export its unemployment elsewhere, and to maintain the competitiveness of its export-driven economy. Sweden's active labor market policies also had to change emphasis by the end of the boom in the 1970s from aiding adjustment to directly supporting employment.

As the golden age was ending, therefore, the Swedish model was under strain. The Meidner Plan to socialize capital in the late 1970s attempted to confront these difficulties directly by radically extending social ownership. But the labor movement was only able to advance the plan in a most limited, and essentially irrelevant, way. The defeat of the Meidner effort to bring capital more firmly under democratic control prepared the basis for the reversals of the 1980s. Swedish capital began to break openly with the postwar compromise, attacking the welfare state, opposing further tax burdens (despite the enormous concentration of wealth), and actively internationalizing financial and productive capital. The increased capital mobility, at the same time the social democratic government sought to improve profits to maintain its export-oriented strategy, eventually raised a new limit on Swedish employment policy: it blocked Sweden's ability to use competitive devaluations to export its unemployment.

The maintenance of low unemployment through the 1980s consequently depended less on Sweden's progressive competitiveness strategy, as social democrats continue to try to argue, and more on *"shared austerity"* among the Swedish working class through the "spreading of employment." These policies have included the holding back on the rationalization of plants, the extension of public sector employment, and reductions in the average hours worked per worker. Yet even *"shared austerity"* had reached its limits in the early 1990s. It could only be sustained as long as the labor market institutions built up over the postwar period had the ideological support for solidaristic wage and work policies among workers, *and* Swedish capital was willing to allow a *national* bargain to share productivity gains. With the fall 1991 election of a bourgeois government, neither condition still held. As a result, Swedish unemployment rapidly shot up, more than doubling in a year, in the process destroying the illusions which have captivated social democrats around the world of an export-led progressive strategy for competitiveness.

The Swedish experience of "shared austerity" contains two important lessons for socialist economic strategies. The first is that the employment impact of slower economic growth can be distributed in different ways, although they largely entail spreading employment across the working class. With limited or declining employment growth in the manufacturing sector, the spread of well-paid work depends upon workers as a whole paying more taxes, taking home less pay, and working less. This has the positive benefits of increased leisure and better public services and environment, but less private consumption.

The second lesson is that it is difficult politically to sustain employment-spreading as long as it is limited to "socialism in one class" or if capital is freed from having to make a national bargain. The social democratic left's response to the economic crisis throughout the 1980s has been that capital could not be attacked. Above all else, profits had to be improved for international competitiveness and thus to sustain employment and the welfare state. With the end of the Swedish experiment in "shared austerity," this is no longer a plausible line of argument. This strategy has allowed capital to free itself from national controls and the traded sector to dominate domestic production needs. Not even Swedish social democracy has been able to withstand the vicious circle of competitive austerity. The global Keynesianism or supranational regulation that might manage the world market has proven a deceptive political project and an elusive means of economic management. There is no intellectually honest response from the left to the economic crisis, particularly with respect to unemployment, that does not involve political restraint on the power of capital and a substantial redistribution of work and resources.

The impasse of capitalist employment policy is linked, based on the preceding analysis, to two broad factors: the crisis of Fordism and the end of Keynesian employment policies on a national basis; and the growing contradiction between the openness of national economies in terms of trade and capital mobility and the lack of regulation, and the seeming impossibility of doing so under the present international regime, of the world market. The left's economic alternative must address both sides of the crisis. Two general principles seem central. First, the view, now accepted among social democrats, that the growth of unemployment is inevitable must be rejected: unemployment is the basis for the splitting of society into those who have paid work in core jobs and those excluded from either work or stable employment. The left's economic alternative must advance the principle that democratic citizenship proceeds from the right to work and the right to a decent income. Second, the political compromises at the international level necessary for long-term stability must be built around the principle of maximizing the capacity of different "national collectivities" democratically to choose alternate development paths (socialist or capitalist) that do not impose externalities (such as environmental damage) on other countries, without suffering isolation and coercive sanction from the world economy.[28]

The implications of these principles is consistent with the analysis of employment policy that redistribution is central to addressing unemployment. An alternative model will have to entail a radical redistributional shift in terms of resources and new institutional structures: from the traded-goods sector to the local and national economies; from the highest paid to the lowest paid; from those with too many hours of work to those with too few; from management-dominated labor processes to worker-controlled; and from private-consumption-led production to ecologically sustainable economies. A redistributional employment policy would contain some of the following components.

INWARD INDUSTRIALIZATION

It is difficult to envision either stable macroeconomic conditions or alternate development paths with continued internationalization of production. The export-oriented strategies which have spurred competitive austerity will have to be replaced, therefore, by a process of inward industrialization. The inward-oriented strategy does not imply closing the economy from trade, but rather a planned expansion of domestic services and production to expand employment and increased control over the international economy to reinforce stable and divergent national macroeconomic conditions.

International trade will obviously remain important to reach certain economies of scale and to transfer new products and processes. But international trade and financial rules need to be restructured so as to allow for diversity of economic models rather than the homogeneity of "competitive austerity" now demanded by IMF adjustment procedures. Inevitably this points to managed trade between national economies and reforming international institutions to impose symmetrical adjustment on deficit and surplus countries. Confronting present imbalances, for example, will require debt relief for the countries of the South and Eastern Europe so they can shift to meeting domestic consumption needs and expand trade within their zones.

Protectionism will also have to be allowed. It has proven impossible for surplus countries to inflate enough, or deficit countries to deflate enough, to restore balance (without further devastating job losses). Social tariffs are important to allow countries to adopt advanced environmental and work standards without loss of jobs and international sanction from "worst-practice" production methods.

The corollary to diversity of development paths is the reintegration of national economies. The expansion of employment will depend, most notably, upon the redevelopment of urban economies and the fostering of a self-managed sector for community welfare and collective leisure.[29] Similarly, the limitations of market instability on employment will require the extension of national and sectoral planning structures to encourage future core industries, control the open sector, and establish sustainable production. Inward industrialization will mean, therefore, production and services more *centered* on local and national needs where the most legitimate democratic collectivities reside.

DEMOCRATIC WORKPLACES

A part of the economic crisis lies on the supply side in the impasse of the Fordist labor process and the transition to flexible automation. Under the pressures of competitive austerity it is the "worst features of Fordism"—speedup, continued fragmentation of work, increased supervision of workers—which are going ahead. Even if there are productivity gains to be had by increased worker input into production, the political risk this entails for capital in terms of worker self-management has meant opposition. Capital will prefer to continue with Taylorism or negotiate involvement with the fewest workers possible. As the basis for the wage bargain, such a labor process will contribute to the polarization of the labor market. An alternative model will, therefore, have to transform work relations. The left's project here has been long-standing: the collective negotiation over the terms of involvement in the labor process and an end of Taylorism. This will, of course, imply negotiation over training and skills, but also move to incorporate product design and quality, and even sectoral planning over what to produce.

REDISTRIBUTION OF WORK

The crisis of Fordism has not only lowered the rate of productivity increases, it has also concentrated these gains in the hands of capital. It is fundamental to an alternative economic model to redistribute existing output more justly and to share out further productivity gains equally. There are two important parameters to this principle to be accounted for. A just distribution of output requires that the unemployed be incorporated into the waged economy. As well, if sustainable production is a constraint, then increased production through working just as many hours is not a priority. Instead, existing work and future productivity gains would have to be shared so as to employ the jobless at decent incomes and increase free time as a central social objective. The employment crisis can only be resolved by directly confronting the redistribution of work hours and income.[30] The social democratic embrace of Keynesianism, and now progressive competitiveness, always sought solutions to unemployment and class divisions through faster growth and more output. This must now be firmly rejected as both unviable and undesirable.

As an economic system, capitalism rationalizes social life for economic ends. This includes, as a fundamental element, the extension of work time to lower costs. But the drive to continual technological change from competition also reduces the number of hours of work required to produce a given level of output. Thus, as an economic system, capitalism tends to produce long hours of work for some and a lack of hours, or unemployment, for others. The labor movement has consistently had to apply its alternate logic on this system to free time for leisure and ensure that work is solidaristically shared. Some of the dimensions of redistributing work are, although politically difficult, straightforward: overtime limits, restrictions on "double-dipping" by professionals, extension of vacations, flexible work-scheduling, increased possibilities for unpaid leave, yearly education and training days, and collective negotiation by worksite of job sharing to spread existing work. The major dimension for dealing with unemployment is, however, a reduction of standard work time that is sharp and general.

To be at all effective in dealing with current unemployment levels, it must be faced that the hours reduction will have to be accompanied by a decline in real wages (partially offset by productivity gains and a decline in unemployment claims) so as to redistribute both work and income. It is precisely because wages will have to shift in the short run that work-time reduction must be solidaristic: apply equally to the public and private sectors and squeeze wage differentials so as to preserve the purchasing power of the lowest-paid. As unemployment declines, productivity gains can then be shared out in both increased purchasing power and declines in work time. The struggle over the re-distribution of work and income must become central to employment policy if the unemployment crisis is to be addressed.

EMPLOYMENT PLANNING

The components of an alternate employment policy have in common the need for economic planning to constrain the market. Capitalist employment policies have typically left employment planning to the aggregate assessment of labor market trends and the targeting of train-ing. The local component of employment planning has been labor exchanges, which served as labor market intelligence networks and a location for job listings and counseling. Even the Swedish labor market boards never developed a local planning capacity or direct democratic accountability to the communities they served. Indeed, they have never been able to fully move beyond their adjustment role for com-petitiveness allocated to them under the Swedish model. An alternative employment policy will have to develop local democratic administra-tive capacities for both the technical and political basis to address the redistribution of work.

Democratic employment planning has a number of dimensions. The "golden age" simply ignored environmental issues, but it seems clear that an alternate model must have this as a binding constraint on production. This will have to be encompassed within employment planning for sustainable production and will entail "dirty" industries of declining jobs, the distributional consequences of slower growth, and the planning for new employment in non-resource-intensive ser-vices. With the dramatic lowering of the amount of labor employed in the manufacturing sector, employment planning will have a large component directed at the service sector. This should radically center our attention on the type of service sector that should be supported in terms of jobs and organizational structure. In particular, employment should be developed in the so-called third sector, that is, the self-managed community services (either newly formed or partly devolved from traditional state administration) such as cultural production, environmental cleanup, education, and leisure. In order to absorb the unemployed, these activities will have to be planned. Locally elected labor market boards—which would govern over all work-related issues—should have as part of their mandate the determination of socially useful activities and the planning for local employment.

The present political situation of competitive austerity does not lend itself to an alternate economic policy. It cannot proceed simply on the basis of economic necessity. The basis for an alternate social project must be found on the political grounds of social justice and the extension of democracy, as a substantial redistribution of resources and power lies at the heart of any real solution to the contemporary unemployment crisis.

IV. MASS UNEMPLOYMENT AND NATIONAL ECONOMIC POLICY

It would be rash to be optimistic on the future of the labor market and unemployment in the advanced capitalist zone. The constraints of the international order on national employment policy are severe. The pressures produced by open economies, with extensive capital mobility and global labor surpluses, have gutted the capacity of national governments to regulate employment levels through the type of aggregate measures that were part of postwar Keynesianism.

Many Keynesians concede that the increased openness of economies and the internationalization of production has shifted the economic terrain. "Keynesianism in one country" is no longer seen as viable as demand stimulation on a national basis is simply dissipated through either imports or capital outflows. Reflation will, therefore, have to take place on a supranational basis. This view has been argued by many advocates of economic integration associated with international economic institutes, and by a significant section of the social democratic movement. They seek to either coordinate a worldwide reflation or to re-create a viable economic space so that stimulation is not lost through leakages.[31] Yet even if the two premises of this view are granted—the combination of unused capacity and economic openness—its viability is deeply suspect. There are no substantive mechanisms for coordination or instruments for reflation at the international level; nor is the political means by which they could be implemented apparent, given the competition which still exists between capitalist nations and the spatial specificity of production structures. It is quite unclear, therefore, what it means to reduce unused capacity (and unemployment) at the international level, as this includes the vastly different national production structures and unemployment experiences of, for example, Japan, Canada, and Britain. Does global stimulation increase the exports of— and consequently reduce the unemployment of—the industrial belts of Japan or the Atlantic provinces of Canada? In any respect, this solution returns to the myopic social democracy of the postwar period of attempting to resolve the capitalist unemployment problem through higher growth, with the distribution and production questions being ignored and the environmental one ultimately being damned.

Much of the social democratic movement has consequently drifted to subnational levels of government, or specific industrial sectors, where some level of industrial capacity exists, and developed the "progressive competitiveness model" as an alternative to neoliberalism and Keynesian reflation. Training policy has become the centerpiece of this strategy: employment will result from highly skilled workers improving the competitiveness of high value-added firms selling on the world market. But this export-oriented strategy, too, has become incorporated in the pressures producing competitive austerity throughout the world economy and converged with neoliberalism. Its advocates must confront the harsh fact that it is not the Anglo-American countries who are converting to the Swedish or German models, but Germany and Sweden who are integrating the "Anglo-American model" of income and work polarization. Toyota is laying off and breaking lifetime employment guarantees, the Volvo plant in Kalmar is closing and the post-Fordist future of full employment in high value-added export-oriented firms now looks like one of the most potholed detours taken by the left in the 1980s.

As the golden age of capitalism was at its end in the 1970s, Joan Robinson, the foremost analyst of postwar employment policy, made the following bitter observation on the Keynesian experience: "Growth of wealth has not after all removed poverty at home, and 'aid' has not reduced it abroad. Now unemployment exacerbates social problems and embitters politics. In this situation, the cry is to get growth started again."[32] Two decades later, with a persistent lengthening of the unemployment queues, the supply-side "cry to get growth started again" is even more pitched. But now there is clearly even less reason to believe, and ecological and redistributive reasons actively to oppose, the supply-sider's proposition that better microeconomic performance leading to faster economic growth is capable of resolving the capitalist unemployment problem. Upon surveying the wreckage produced by these views, there is, indeed, good reason to adopt Robinson's dismay.

Yet there is as well, on this point, a lesson still to be absorbed from Keynes on national economic policy:

> If nations can learn to provide themselves with full employment by their domestic policy (and, we must add, if they can also attain equilibrium in the trend of their population), there need be no important economic forces calculated to set the interest of one country against that of its neighbours. There would still be room for the international division of labour and for international lending in appropriate conditions. But there would no longer be a pressing motive why one country need force its wares on another or repulse the offerings of its neighbours, not because this was necessary to enable it to pay for what it wished to purchase, but with the express object of upsetting the equilibrium of payments so as to develop a balance of trade in its own favour. International trade would cease to be what it is, namely, a desperate expedient to maintain employment at home by forcing sales on foreign markets and restricting purchases, which, if successful, will merely shift the problem of unemployment to the neighbour which is worsted in the struggle, but a willing and unimpeded exchange of goods and services in conditions of mutual advantage.[33]

Keynes's position still seems to be essentially correct. It strikes at the core of the present impasse of capitalist employment policy, where the demands for rationalization of all aspects of economic and social life for international competitiveness, so as to dump unemployment on other regions and countries, have become incessant. But for an employment policy to move beyond competitive austerity today, however, will require a much bolder political, economic, and ecological project than Keynes himself was ever capable of envisioning.

THE MAKING OF A CYBERTARIAT?
VIRTUAL WORK IN A REAL WORLD

Ursula Huws

I t is possible to argue that in the aftermath of 1989 a single global economy is in formation.* As the World Trade Organization dismantles any
remaining checks on the free movement of capital, goods, services, and intellectual property between countries, transnational corporations have an
open field. With the terms of employment of a growing proportion of the
world's population determined either directly or indirectly by these same
corporations, the conditions would seem, at last, to have arrived to render
possible the fulfillment of Marx's injunction at the end of the *Communist
Manifesto*: "Workers of the world unite." But are there in fact any signs that
a global proletariat with a common consciousness is emerging?

This essay takes as its starting point a conception of capitalism as a
dynamic force whose engine proceeds by the interrelated processes of
commodification and accumulation. On the one hand it seeks insatia-
bly for new commodities from the production of which surplus value
can be extracted, and on the other for new markets to fuel its voracious
expansion. New commodities arise either from the drawing into the
cash economy of activities which were previously carried out by unpaid
labor, for gift or exchange, or by the elaboration of existing commodities. Human activities and needs thus stand at either end of the process:
production and consumption. The inevitable impetus is toward a complete industrialization of the globe, with the entire population involved

---

*   This essay was first published in *Socialist Register 2001* (London: Merlin Press,
      2001).

on the one hand in contributing toward the production or circulation of commodities and the capital accumulation process in some capacity, and on the other in an ever-greater dependence on the purchase of these commodities for their survival.

The commodification process entails continuing seismic shifts in the social division of labor. This is not the place to describe in detail how, for instance, subsistence agriculture gives way to forms of farming locked into the market by the need to acquire such things as seeds, tools, and fertilizer, as well as to sell its produce, or how in the process new social categories are created, such as the landless rural wage laborer or the plantation manager. Or how the resulting changes in a rural economy force peasants to send their children to the city as factory workers. Or how the automation of factories leads to a growing complexity in the division of labor which generates new groups standing between the paradigmatic proletariat and bourgeoisie: the foreman, for example, or the skilled draftsman, or the purchasing manager. Or how these groups in turn are threatened or reconstituted at the next twist of technological development. Here it is enough simply to point out that their rise or demise affects not only the composition of the labor force—the organization of production—but also the structure of the market—the organization of consumption—since each of these groups buys commodities as well as sells its labor.

This point becomes particularly relevant when we come to discuss the current wave of technological change—the widespread use of information and communication technologies (ICTs)—because these, unusually in the history of automation, are technologies of both production and consumption. The possession or lack of these technologies is therefore likely to create a major new fault line running through entire populations. The "digital divide" is the currently fashionable term for this fault line.

But before examining these new demographics in detail, it is necessary to take a step back and define what work it is we are talking about, by no means an easy task.

I.

While thinking about this essay, I wrote in a newsletter:

> Recent work has raised in a very acute form the problem of how to
> name the kinds of work which involve telematics. Even the tradi-
> tional terms are unsatisfactory. "White collar" implies a particular
> kind of male office worker who probably ceased being typical (if he
> ever was) sometime in the 1950s. "Non-manual" denies the physical
> reality of pounding a keyboard all day. "Office work" links it to a
> particular kind of location when the whole point of recent devel-
> opments is that they mean such work can be done anywhere. And
> most of the newer terms are even worse. "Telecommuter" applies
> only to those people who have substituted one kind of location (the
> home) for another (the city centre office). "Teleworker" again tends
> to be restricted in practice to those workers who have relocated and
> cannot be applied to that whole class of workers whose work is *po-
> tentially* delocalizable. Some commentators have come up with cate-
> gories like "digital analyst" or "knowledge worker" but – apart from
> sounding rather pretentious – these tend to suggest a sub-category
> of work towards the top end of the skill scale. On the other hand
> "information processor" falls into the opposite trap of suggesting
> that it applies only to the more routine work, like data entry. I no-
> tice that the European Commission's "New Ways to Work" unit
> has lately taken to talking about "e-work" and "e-workers." This is
> certainly in tune with the current fashion in New Labour Britain,
> where recent government statements on the "Information Age" pol-
> icy include reference to the appointment of an "e-minister" to be in
> charge of "e-business" and an "e-envoy" to ensure that the policies
> are directed towards "e-inclusion." Perhaps "e-work" is indeed the
> least bad option.[1]

I was interested to receive the following reply from Alice de Wolff, a
researcher based in Toronto:

> I was amused by your discussion about what to call "it." We have
> had constant, very similar discussions about "the" term. . . . Our
> experience is that there are two issues – one, to find an adequate
> description, and two, to find one that the workers involved relate to.
> We haven't managed to bring them together in any satisfactory way.
> When we use language other than "office workers," or "administra-
> tive professionals" (not my favourite), or "administrative assistants,"
> the people who do the work don't think it's about them. I am most

comfortable with "information workers," because I actually think it describes much of the work very well, and suggests a central location in the "information economy." I use it, and "front line information workers" when I'm speaking with groups of office workers, and think it works well when used in context. But if we try to use it as a title of a document, event, etc., very few people relate.[2]

This encapsulates very well the tension which underlies any discussion of class: between class as an analytical term (objective class position) and class as an aspect of personal identity (subjective class position). This in turn reflects the broader tension between structure and agency as conceptual frameworks for understanding the dynamics of social and economic change. I would not wish to minimize the difficulties of resolving these tensions in relation to other class categories, such as the "working class" or the "peasantry." Nevertheless, the fact that such difficulties should arise so acutely in this context (which, for lack of a better term, I will call "office work" for the moment) is indicative of a particular lacuna in the history of socialist thought.

With a few notable exceptions, the literature on office work leaves a distinct impression that on the whole socialists would rather not think about the subject at all and, when they have reluctantly had to do so, have been at a loss as to how to categorize office workers and whether to place them, with Crompton and Gallie, respectively, in a "white-collar proletariat"[3] or "new working class";[4] to follow Lenin or Poulantzas[5] in locating them as part of a petty bourgeoisie whose interests lie with small employers and are opposed to those of manual workers; or to hedge their bets along with Wright, and regard them as occupying "contradictory locations within class relations."[6] Marx supplies a modicum of support for each of these positions. In his account, the inevitable proletarianization of the petty bourgeoisie (craft and own-account workers and small employers) sits side by side with an equally inevitable expansion in the numbers of employed clerical workers (whom he terms "commercial wage workers"). However, he refuses the status of proletarian to the latter, stating that "the commercial worker produces no surplus value directly" because "the increase of this labour is always a result, never a cause of more surplus value." Furthermore, he is of the opinion that "the office is always infinitesimally small compared to the industrial workshop."[7]

This is not the place for a detailed overview of debates about class. It is worth noting, however, that some degree of muddle about where to locate office workers seems to persist whether class is defined in relation to occupation (which corresponds, as Marshall et al. have pointed out, with categories defined by the technical relations of production);[8] to the social relations of production (the ownership or non-ownership of the means of production); to the social division of labor; to comparative income, to caste-based or other culturally constructed hierarchies (Weber's "status groups"); or to some empirically constructed stratification lacking any coherent conceptual underpinning, as in most official statistical categorizations.

II.

During the nineteenth century there were reasonable empirical grounds for regarding "clerks" as male. In the British Census of 1851, over 99 percent of people listed in this category were men. Despite an accelerating entry of women into the clerical workforce from the 1870s onward, until the 1960s most theorizing about the class position of office workers continued to be rooted in the assumption that they were masculine. The two classic studies of office workers in the postwar period, Wright Mills's *White Collar*[9] and Lockwood's *The Blackcoated Worker*[10] reveal this assumption only too clearly in their titles, which also, in their different ways, represent a sort of verbal throwing up of the hands in defeat at the problem of how to construct a conceptually coherent definition of office work. If there is no other feature which uniquely delineates office workers from the rest of the workforce, we can feel these authors thinking, then at least they have their clothing in common.

Although one can sympathize with the label problem, such blindness is staggering. While these books were being written, women (clad, no doubt, in brightly colored New Look shirt waisters or pastel twin sets) were entering office work in unprecedented numbers, so that by the time of the 1961 census they represented about two-thirds of all clerical workers, in both Britain and the United States[11]—a proportion which had risen to three-quarters by the 1971 census. Wright Mills does in fact devote six pages of his 378-page opus to a discussion of the "white-collar girl" but characterizes her mainly in terms of her love life. A discussion of gender plays no part in the formation of his bleak conclusion (essentially derived from Lenin) that white-collar workers will never develop distinctive forms of political agency and that even if they did, "their advance to increased stature in American society could not result in increased freedom and rationality. For white-collar people carry less rationality than illusion and less desire for freedom than the misery of modern anxieties."[12] There is a blurred recognition in these authors' work that office workers cannot be regarded as a single homogenous entity. But this is combined with a strange reluctance to anatomize the differences within the broader category, which can seem on occasion like a willful refusal to see the obvious. This obliviousness offers a clue to the more general neglect of office work in socioeconomic analysis, and, more specifically, in socialist discourse. It confronts the analyst in a particularly acute form with the unresolved "woman question" which has been flapping about the attic of Marxist theory since its inception.

Most theories of class, at least until the 1960s, assigned women unproblematically to the class position of their fathers or husbands. If they were not economically dependent on these men and played an independent role in the economy (something with which some theorists were already uncomfortable), then this did not pose major problems because they would normally occupy positions in the same class as these fathers or husbands: the wives and daughters of factory workers would also work in factories; the wives and daughters of rentiers would also be rentiers, and so on. (Marx's argument that domestic servants did not form part of the proletariat caused a few hiccups here, but not major ones, since servants were regarded as part of an obsolescent class and anyway merged into the reserve army of the lumpenproletariat from which there could be movement in and out of the proletariat without upsetting any important theoretical applecarts.) In other words arguments could be developed on the assumption that peoples' class positions *as citizens* (in which the basic unit is the household) were the same as their class positions *as workers* (in which the basic unit is the individual); and, indeed, that the former derived from the latter. While women are regarded simply as members of households, no tension between these different identities need arise and movements between classes (for instance by "marrying up" or "marrying down") can be dealt with under the heading "social mobility."

The minute female office workers are treated *as workers*, however, this simple mode of analysis breaks down. One is forced to confront the awkward fact that office workers may occupy a different class position from their husbands or fathers. The most thorough empirical study of class position in the UK of which I am aware concluded that "fully half of the conjugal units in our sample are cross-class families, using the three-category version of Goldthorpe's class schema."[13] Similar disparities arise using other classification methods, such as the Registrar General's categories used in UK official statistics, or Wright's neo-Marxist scheme.

This has implications not only for an analysis of the workforce but also for more general social analysis: if it is taken seriously, the household can no longer be perceived as a coherent political unit but must be recognized as fissured and complex; the atom must be split.

For the new generation of political analysts who came to adulthood in the 1960s and '70s, a serious examination of office work *as work* posed enormous theoretical challenges, and this may be the most charitable explanation of why it was, comparatively speaking, so neglected as a subject among those who were attempting to retheorize class politics at the time. There is perhaps another more personal reason, rooted in the class origins of this new generation of left intellectuals. In the UK, at least, the postwar welfare state opened up new forms of upward mobility for men and women of working-class origin. Selection at the age of eleven filtered a high-achieving minority into grammar schools from which they could enter the expanding university system. The novels and plays of the period are full of the class guilt which ensued. The act of leaving one's father's class was experienced acutely as an act of betrayal, but this was intertwined with an intoxication at the intellectual freedom of the new life of mental work. An oedipal delight at escaping from the authority of this father was combined with a romantic sense of loss and exile from the warmth and solidarity of a working-class community which was simultaneously both safe and claustrophobic, both politically revolutionary and morally oppressive. These were the upwardly mobile sons of the blue-collar heroes of Sennett and Cobb's *Hidden Injuries of Class*,[14] the "brainy" (and by implication effete) students who sat indoors revising for their university entrance examinations while their sneering mates who had left school at fifteen flaunted their new leather jackets and motorbikes and spent their weekly wages

on taking bouffant-haired girlfriends down to the Palais to rock and
roll on a Friday night. They felt both superior to and excluded from
this new consumerist working-class culture and this, perhaps, inspired
in them a permanent desire to earn the respect of these by now ideal-
ized working-class men. If they thought about women office workers
at all, it was most usually as class accessories of the bourgeoisie. One
archetype of the period is the secretary who acts as a gatekeeper for her
boss. With her crisply accented "I'm sorry but he's in a meeting right
now" and her unattainable sexual attractiveness, she can humiliate the
working-class shop steward who is trying to gain access quite as effectively as the snootiest of head waiters. If any independent political
agency is attributed to her at all it is (perhaps with some unconscious
projection) as a traitor to the working class.

Only some explanation like this, it seems to me, can make sense of
the subsequent political development of this generation of male left
intellectuals: the romanticization and stereotyping of specific forms of
working-class life long after many of their features had already passed
into history; the almost fetishistic preoccupation with certain types of
male manual work (coal miners, auto workers, truck drivers, dockers);
the anxious and competitive display of their own working-class ante-
cedents; the insistence that feminism was middle class and alienating to
"real" working-class men.

In most cases it was not until the dawning of the 1980s that in their
political imaginations these analysts were able to accept that proletarian
men were as likely to be picking up the kids from school while waiting for their wives to get home from the office as to be coming home
grimy from the pit or factory expecting to find a meal on the table.

III.

Perhaps because he had enough direct experience of manual work to
have no need to prove his political virility in this respect, it was Harry
Braverman who constituted the honorable exception to this pattern
and undertook, in his monumental *Labor and Monopoly Capital*,[15] the
first serious theoretical engagement with white-collar work which recognized the office as a differentiated locus of struggle between capital
and labor. Braverman also demonstrated a link between technological change and change in the division of office labor. His (essentially
Marxist) "degradation" thesis was later challenged from a Weberian

perspective by Goldthorpe, who argued that the empirical evidence (derived from a study of census data) did not support the proletarianization hypothesis but that on the contrary what was taking place was the development of a new "service class."[16] Perhaps more importantly than whether Braverman was "right" in the particulars of his analysis, this debate, coinciding as it did with a tremendous flowering of thoughtful feminist speculation about the relationship between class and gender, between paid and unpaid work, the nature of "skill," and the explanation for gender segregation in the labor market,[17] opened up an immense and fertile field of inquiry.

The resulting literature covered an enormous range: agitprop handbooks designed to rouse office workers to action, like those by Tepperman and Gregory in the United States or Craig in Britain; serious academic studies, like those by Crompton and Jones in Britain or Game and Pringle in Australia; and more journalistic overviews giving anecdotal support to the proletarianization thesis, like those by Howe, Howard, or Siegel and Markoff in the United States or Menzies in Canada.[18]

As well as raising a range of interesting questions, this added immeasurably to the store of empirical knowledge of the working conditions of office workers and the ways in which these were being transformed under the combined impact of the restructuring of markets, the ideological triumph of neoliberalism, and the impact of technological change. Most of these studies, however, reflect the fact that they took place within specific geographical locales. The labor markets they analyze are generally national or regional ones, and the workers' positions are mapped against those of their compatriots in other industries or occupations within these national labor markets. Although there have been a number of studies of globalization of blue-collar work, little account is taken of the implications of the relocation of nonmanual work across national boundaries. A partial exception is a series of small-scale empirical studies of data entry workers in developing countries,[19] which implicitly follow Braverman's degradation thesis by drawing direct comparisons with the conditions of women workers in production work. What is missing is an analysis which examines the position of these office workers both in their own local labor markets and in relation to their comparators in other countries.[20] This is an enormous task which I do not dare to attempt here. Instead, what I will try to do in the next section of this essay is to clear away some of the underbrush which is currently impeding clarity of thought in order to specify the sorts of questions which researchers will need to address to produce the evidence which might render such an analysis possible in the future.

IV.

Let us begin by outlining some of the dimensions of the problem. Office workers (to stick, for the time being, with this unsatisfactory term) can be defined in at least six different ways: in terms of the *functional relationship of their work to capital*; their *occupations* (their place in the technical division of labor); their *social relation to production* (the ownership or non-ownership of the means of production); their place in the *social division of labor* (including the gender division of labor in the household); their *comparative income* (and hence their market position as consumers); and their social "*status*." Definitions constructed in these different ways are not necessarily coterminous and produce shifting and overlapping groups, riven with internal contradictions. And, of course, the structural categories thus created may not be recognized as relevant by the office workers themselves, who, in their upward or downward or horizontal trajectories across the boundaries between them, may prefer to differentiate themselves by quite other criteria—their educational qualifications, for instance, or their consumption habits, or where they live, or, like Wright Mills and Lockwood, the clothes they wear to work.

Any analysis is further complicated by the fact that the empirical data, in the form of official statistics, are constructed using classification systems which do not map neatly onto any of these analytical categories. Nevertheless, let us recapitulate the evidence, such as it is, in relation to each of these approaches.

First, in terms of its *relation to capital*, office work can be regarded as covering the following functional categories: (a) design or elaboration of the content of products and services—including such things as software development, copy editing, the design of websites, product design, et cetera; (b) purchase of inputs to these products or services and their sale—the army of clerks whose numbers, according to Braverman, multiply exponentially as the number of transactions increases, because of the need for the value of each transaction to be recorded by a "mirror" in a system which "assumes the possible dishonesty, disloyalty or laxity of every human agency which it employs";[21] (c) management

of the production and distribution processes and of the workers themselves—descended from the eighteenth-century "timekeeper," this
class now includes a range of human resources management and supervisory functions as well as logistical tasks; (d) circulation—much
of the banking and financial services sector falls into this category,
as do some accounting and retail functions; (e) reproduction of the
workforce—activities associated with teaching, childcare, healthcare,
social work, et cetera; (f) local, national, or international government
functions connected with the provision of infrastructure, market management, and policing the population.

Of these categories, only (c) and (d) correspond to Marx's "commercial workers" of whom he maintained that "the commercial worker
produces no surplus value directly . . . the increase of this labor is
always a result, never a cause of more surplus value."[22] Category (a)
makes an input to the product in the form of knowledge in much the
same way that a craft worker contributed skill in the past. Its existence
as a separate nonmanual task is thus merely a reflection of an increase
in the division of labor. Workers in this category, it can be argued, contribute directly to the creation of surplus value in so far as the product
of their labor is appropriated from them by the employer.

Such a typology could have been sketched out at any time in the last
two hundred years. However, applying it in any specific case has been
rendered immeasurably more complicated as the years have gone by
and the division of labor has grown more complex.

Perhaps the most important change which has taken place is the increasing commodification of "service" activities. In the comparatively
simple markets which Marx and Engels observed, it was feasible to
regard the archetypal capitalist commodity as a physical object made in
a factory, designed either to be sold to another capitalist as a means to
produce other physical objects (for instance a loom, a vat, or a printing
press) or to be sold to a wholesaler or retailer for final consumption by
the consumer (for instance a shirt, a bar of soap, or a newspaper). Since
then, enormous elaborations have taken place. Each of the types of activity outlined above has itself become the basis of a host of new commodities, ranging from software packages to mind-controlling drugs,
from electronic surveillance systems to credit cards, from educational
CD-ROMs to baby alarms. Although the principles of economic analysis remain essentially the same,[23] breaking their production down into

their component parts and plotting their interactions with each other
and with the fulfillment of the primary functions outlined above is an
intricate and time-consuming business. Indeed, in some cases the process can appear like zooming in on fractals, a descent into ever-smaller
wheels within wheels, as with the seemingly inexhaustible inven-
tiveness of capital each area of human activity becomes the basis for
profitable new commodities.[24] Within the production process of each
commodity, even if it is carried out within a parent organization as a
sort of sub-loop in the production process of another, the whole range
of activities (design, management, execution, delivery to the customer)
is reproduced in miniature. And the task of assigning workers according to their functional relation to capital is rendered even more difficult
by the increasingly complex division of labor within functions.

Analysis is complicated still further by changes which have taken
place in the ownership structure of corporations. The combined effects of privatization, the disaggregation of large organizations into
their component parts, convergence between sectors, cross-ownership,
and "vertical integration" have made a nonsense of the tidy traditional
divisions between "primary," "secondary," and "tertiary" sectors, and
between the "public" and "private" sectors of the economy as well
as between the sub-sectoral categories within these devised by government statisticians. The new "multimedia" sector, for instance,
brings together organizations traditionally classified in many different
places, including the public sector (state broadcasting corporations);
metal-based manufacturing (computer companies, via their software
divisions, and electronics manufacturers); printing and paper manufacturers (publishers); record and tape manufacturers; toy manufacturers
(the ancestors of some computer game companies); business and financial services (independent software companies which are not branches
of computer manufacturers); film distributors; and telecommunications
companies. Convergence is taking place in many other areas of the
economy too, for instance between banking and retailing, and (thanks
to biotechnology) between pharmaceuticals and agriculture.

Not only are the old sectors dissolving and new ones forming;
there are also complex interrelationships between the corporate actors involved. Some have entered into shifting alliances to carve up
particular markets or to collaborate in the development of new products;[25] others have bought stakes in each other (i.e., in firms which

the public imagine to be their competitors), and mergers, de-mergers and takeovers are announced continuously. To make matters even more complicated, in addition to these external realignments, most companies are also involved in a continuous process of internal reorganization, whereby individual functions are transformed into separate cost or profit centers, or floated off as separate companies. Add to this the impact of outsourcing to external companies and we arrive at a situation where corporations can no longer be regarded as stable and homogenous. Rather they must be seen as mutually interpenetrating entities in constant flux, held together by an elaborate web of contracts which are in a continuous process of renegotiation. The sectoral classification of the "employer" to which any given worker is assigned is an almost-accidental by-product of all these shenanigans, and this makes it impossible to use official statistics, at least in their present form, as a basis for serious analysis.

A second method of defining office workers is in relation to their *occupations*—the tasks that they carry out—or their labor process. Where workers have been able to organize effectively in the past and set up professional associations or trade unions, and especially where negotiation has succeeded in making recognized qualifications a basis for limiting entry to particular trades or professions, these occupations can be said to be largely socially defined, their boundaries made explicit in these negotiations and their practices defined by custom and by the vigilance of the actors who stand to gain from the continuation of these forms of closure (to use Parkin's Weberian term).[26] In most cases, however, the tasks carried out by any given group of workers are determined in large part by the technical division of labor and their labor processes are thus shaped by the design of the prevailing technology (which, it must be added, is itself shaped by the assumptions of those who commission it, and in which the existing social relations of production are therefore already embedded).

Even in the occupational groups which have defended their inherited working practices most strongly against the assaults of the last quarter century, it has been impossible to resist entirely the impact of information and communications technologies. Even doctors and lawyers, these days, not to mention telephone engineers, generally check their own e-mail from time to time, and the expectation of a personal secretary has all but disappeared among executives under the age of about forty-five, except for those who are very senior indeed. Meanwhile, across the rest of the workforce, an extraordinary and unprecedented convergence has been taking place. From tele-sales staff to typesetters, from indexers to insurance underwriters, from librarians to ledger clerks, from planning inspectors to pattern cutters, a large and increasing proportion of daily work time is spent identically: sitting with one hand poised over a keyboard and the other dancing back and forth from keys to mouse. Facing these workers on the screen, framed in pseudo bas-relief, are ugly grey squares labeled, in whatever the local language, "File," "Edit," "View," "Tools," "Format," "Window" or "Help," the ghastly spoor of some aesthetically challenged Microsoft employee of the late 1980s. Gone are the Linotype machine, the Rolodex, the card index, the sheaves of squared paper, the mimeograph, the drawing board, the cutting table, the telex machine, and all the other myriad tools of the mid-twentieth century, the mastery of which entitled one to a specific designation—the proud ownership of a unique skill. Gone too is the shared identity with other holders of that same skill. It must be remembered, of course, that the security bestowed by possessing these skills was often the security of the straitjacket. Limited transferability meant increasing vulnerability with each wave of technological innovation, but specialist skill ownership did offer a basis for organizing and playing some part in negotiating the terms on which the newer technology would be introduced.

The skills required to operate a computer and its various communications accessories should not, of course, be mistaken for the totality of the requirements of any given job. They are often ancillary to other "core" skills—the skills required to do "the job itself." However, these too may be undergoing a process of modification (which could take the form of routinization, or full commodification) which is changing their nature. Social workers, for instance, may find themselves filling out standard forms on screen instead of writing, or delivering in person, more nuanced and qualitative professional reports on their clients; teachers may find themselves administering standard tests; insurance loss adjusters may have lost the discretion to decide what compensation a claimant should receive; internet journalists may be required to write to tightly defined standard formats; while architects may be reduced to recombining standard components instead of designing freely "from scratch." Often these transformations are disguised by a change in the division of labor. The job description of a professional may be stripped down to its core and the numbers of such staff reduced, while the former components of the job which are capable of routinization are transferred to lower-skilled workers. Thus, for instance, routine inquiries to a computer help desk may be dealt with by the use of automated e-mail responses or by more junior staff, with only the really difficult problems routed through to the more highly paid "expert." Or sick people may be encouraged to call a call center staffed by nurses before making an appointment to see a doctor, as in the UK's NHS Direct.

In general, it can be asserted that the number of tasks involving standard generic computer-related skills is growing rapidly, whether this is measured in terms of the numbers of people whose jobs involve these skills exclusively or in terms of the proportion of the time spent on these tasks by workers whose jobs also require other skills (or, indeed, both). This has curious and contradictory consequences. The fact that the skills are now generic has made it easier to skip laterally from job to job, company to company, and industry to industry. But by the same token each worker has also become more easily dispensable, more easily replaceable; the new opportunities thus also constitute new threats. The combination of this new occupational mobility with the huge expansion of the potential labor pool has also made it much more difficult to build stable group identities based on shared skills. Attempts to construct barriers around skill groups are thwarted by the speed of change. Any investment of time and effort in learning a new software package may be wiped out in a matter of months by the launch of a replacement. Existing hierarchies are challenged at precisely the moment that new fault lines are created. At the head office, e-mail brings senior and junior members of staff into direct communication with each other, cutting out middle layers of management, and a strange new camaraderie develops between colleagues of different grades as one shows the other how to eliminate a virus or unzip an obstinate attachment. But simultaneously an unbridgeable gulf may have opened up between these same head office staff and their fellow employees at a remote call center or data-processing site.

When the only thing which can be predicted with certainty is that there will be more change, it is difficult to generalize broadly about occupational trends: while some processes are Taylorized and deskilled, others become more complex and multiskilled; while some groups are excluded, others find new opportunities opening up. An interesting empirical study recently completed in Canada by Lavoie and Therrien explored the relationship between computerization and employment structure. Following Wolff and Baumol[27] these researchers divided occupations into five categories: "knowledge workers," "management workers," "data workers," "service workers" and "goods workers," and concluded that the category in which there was the greatest growth associated with computerization was not, as popular mythology would have it, the "knowledge workers" but the "data workers"—those who "manipulate and use the information developed by the knowledge workers."[28] This provides some support for the argument that the trend toward routinization outweighs, in numerical terms, the tendency for work to become more creative, tacit, and multiskilled.

The official statistics contain no categories labeled "website designer" or "call center operator" or any of the other new occupational categories which are emerging, although these figure in job advertisements and are clearly operational in the labor market. The question is, how permanent are they likely to be? And will they form the basis of new collective identities? Or will workers choose to group themselves in relation to some other variable, such as the employer they work for, or the site where they are based? The answer to this question will be a crucial determinant of the extent to which new class identities will develop independently of geography, and of the potential for organizing at a transnational level.

A third approach to characterizing office workers involves analyzing their *relationship to the means of production*. Put crudely, in the classic Marxist formulation, if workers own the means of production, they are part of the bourgeoisie; if they are waged workers working for an employer who owns the means of production (and thereby produce surplus value), then they can be assigned to the proletariat. Self-employed workers and proprietors of small firms, in this model, belong to a petty bourgeoisie which will in due course be steadily squeezed out in the primary struggle between capital and labor, its members pauperized or proletarianized, except for a lucky few who become capitalists.

But this model too is becoming increasingly difficult to apply to office workers. First, the tendency of self-employment to die out has obstinately refused to take place. Although it has not expanded at the rate hoped for it by neoliberals during the 1980s, self-employment remains fairly constant, at least in most developed countries. Across the European Union, for instance, the self-employed constituted a hardly varying 15 percent of the workforce over the two decades from 1975 to 1996.[29] This catchall statistical category of course includes a range of different class positions. At one extreme are the self-employed with a few employees, who can perhaps be regarded as petty bourgeois in the classic sense; then there are genuine freelances, who work for a range of different employers; and at the other extreme are casual workers whose self-employed status is a reflection of labor market weakness—people who lack the negotiating muscle to insist on a proper employment contract even though they are effectively working for a single employer. Despite the lack of change in their overall numbers, the evidence from the UK suggests that the composition of this group is changing, in the direction of the casual end of the spectrum. A study by Campbell and Daley found that the proportion of self-employed people with employees fell from 39 percent to 31 percent between 1981 and 1991,[30] while Meager and Moralee found that new entrants to self-employment were more likely than their earlier counterparts to be young, female, and entering relatively low value–added service activities. After analyzing data from the British Household Panel Survey, they concluded that the chances of a self-employed person being in the lowest earning category (the lowest 10 percent) were three times those of an employee. Even when an allowance was made for the underreporting of income by the self-employed, the chances were still twice as high.[31]

Self-employment is not necessarily a permanent state, however. Another study by Meager and Moralee, based on a longitudinal analysis of European Labor Force Survey data, uncovered high rates of inflow and outflow.[32] This makes it difficult to regard self-employment as a stable marker of class identity; for some it might merely be a staging post between different jobs.

Another factor which makes it difficult to regard the self-employed as a separate category is the increasing tendency to manage employees "as if" they are self-employed or, to use Rajan's phrase, to insist on "mindset flexibility."[33] Practices such as management by results, performance-related pay, and contracts in which working hours are not specified combine with intensified pressures of work and fear of redundancy to produce a situation in which the coercive power of the manager is internalized. The pace of work is therefore driven by a self-generated compulsive drive rather than the explicit external authority of the boss. Closer to the piece rates of the putting-out systems than the time-based pay (albeit with machine-paced work) of the factory, this method of management muddles the relationship between worker and employer, a muddle which is intensified when there is also a physical separation between them. One worker in seventeen in the British workforce, and a slightly higher proportion in North America, Scandinavia, and the Netherlands (though less in the rest of Europe) now works from home at least one day a week, using a computer with a telecommunications link to deliver work.[34] Of these, nearly half are formally self-employed. Since most of these workers own their own computers, it might be tempting to regard them as twenty-first-century equivalent of home-based handloom weavers, but can standalone personal computers really be regarded as the means of production? A loom can be used to produce cloth quite independently of any other loom, whereas in most cases the value of the computer to the employer rests on its being linked to others, in a system which is not owned by the worker.

This is a moot point, which there is no space to investigate further here. It relates interestingly, however, to another question which has some pertinence. At least in a highly commodified economy, it is arguable that in order to make sense of the individuals' general relation to capital (and hence their class position), it is necessary to consider not only their relation to the means of production but also to the "means of consumption" or "means of reproduction."[35]

The inexorable process of commodification has resulted in the decline of consumer service industries and their replacement by capital goods. In order to service themselves and their families, get themselves to work, and otherwise function, it is increasingly necessary for workers to invest in such capital goods, from cars to washing machines. In addition, the only way to achieve a decent standard of housing is to purchase their own homes. The need to pay for all these goods locks workers ever more tightly into the market. As Andrew Carnegie was shrewd enough to notice over a century ago, a working class which owns its own housing is the best-possible protection against strikes and uprisings.[36] It is then at least arguable that the degree to which they have succeeded in purchasing these things might affect workers' subjective view of their own class position. Whether it could be said to constitute an objective difference is a matter for investigation. There may be an analogy between workers' relationship to the "means of reproduction" and their relationship with the "means of production" according to which the homeowner occupies a position analogous to that of the independent craft worker, or the proprietor of a one-man business. This analogy can be taken further: the division of labor in "reproduction work" does not necessarily just involve householders themselves. Some workers may also employ cleaners, childcare workers, or other servants, thus occupying a place in the division of labor in reproduction work which is the equivalent of that of a small employer in production. This issue is especially important in considering the class position of the "new" information workers in developing or newly developed countries, where the employment of servants, including live-in servants, is more common. In Hong Kong, for instance, Greenfield reports that it is usual for skilled manual workers, such as engineers, and lower-paid office workers, such as call center workers, direct sales persons, or mobile and paging company workers, living in low-rent accommodation, to employ a live-in domestic "helper."

> Working families whose incomes simply cannot accommodate a domestic helper still hire them, then exert extreme pressure on their helpers to minimize costs so that they can "get their money's worth." There is even a growing tendency to hire "cheaper" Indonesian domestic helpers than Filipinas who number 350,000. It is interesting to note that in the aftermath of the Asian financial crisis the Hong Kong government intervened to alleviate the hardship of the average Hong Kong family by freezing the wages of domestic helpers![37]

The use of nonoccupational variables to assign workers to a class position is, to the best of my knowledge, untested and requires further analysis. It is particularly interesting in the context of the growth in homeworking, however, since the homeworker pays for many of the things more usually provided by the employer: the work space, storage space, heating, lighting, insurance, setting-up and putting-away time, management and monitoring (in the form of self-management, filling in reports and timesheets, et cetera), as well as incurring various risks to health and security. The home computer plays an interesting and ambiguous role in this, since it is an instrument both of production and of reproduction, as likely to be used for ordering the groceries or doing the kids' homework as for the work itself.

Information and communications technologies play a pivotal role in blurring the boundaries between work and consumption, constituting as they do a shifting interface between server and served. An order for an airline ticket, for instance, may be transmitted over the telephone and keyed in by a call center worker or entered directly onto the airline's website by the customer; the labor of data entry may be either paid or unpaid. It is therefore difficult to separate a discussion of the division of labor in paid "production" work from a more general discussion of the division of labor in unpaid, "consumption" work, which, highly gendered as it is, brings one to the more general discussion of the *social division of labor*, the fourth category in our list, but one which is beyond the scope of this essay to address in detail.

Our fifth category is the simple empirical one of *relative income*. For those wishing to model society as a tidy hierarchical pyramid this has posed problems for over a century. The poor but genteel clerk who earns less than the vulgar navvy features in many nineteenth-century novels, from Dickens to Gissing, and survives well into the twentieth century, for instance in Forster's *Howards End*, Grossmith's *Diary of a Nobody*, and some of Orwell's gloomier grubby-net-curtained novels. This clerk is presented as having traded money for a foothold (albeit precarious) in the middle classes and forms a male counterpart to the impoverished but well-educated governess hovering uneasily in an ambiguous social space between the servants' quarters and the drawing room (although his origins are likely to be humbler than hers, and his accent more suburban, his gender depriving him of the ever-latent potential for class elevation or downfall which constitutes the inherent inner drama of the feminine state).

The separation of status from income underlies most systems of class ranking, even the most empiricist and least theoretically grounded. It is explicit, for instance in the rationale for the Registrar General's categories which are used for class analysis in the British official statistics. A paper written in 1928 by a senior official at the General Register Office argued against classification by income, asserting that "any scheme of social classification should take account of culture . . . [which] the occupational basis of grading has a wholesome tendency to emphasize." In his opinion the criterion should be "the general standing within the community of the occupations concerned."[38]

Crompton and Jones note that there was parity between the earnings of male clerks and skilled manual workers from 1918 to 1936. For the next four decades, clerical workers' earnings declined in relative terms so that by 1978 they earned less than the average for all manual workers, with even the average wage for semiskilled male manual workers exceeding that for male clerical workers. The earnings of female clerical workers were even lower, of course: rising from 42 percent of men's in 1913 to 57 percent in the mid-fifties and 74 percent by the end of the seventies.[39] By the end of the 1990s, the hourly earnings of women clerical workers had reached 80 percent of men's across the European Union.[40] Clerical workers clearly fall below most manual workers in terms of their purchasing power.

Now that much information-processing work can be moved from region to region and country to country using electronic links, it becomes necessary to compare earnings between countries as well as within them. Such comparisons are difficult to make with precision because of variations in the structure of taxation and benefit systems, but in the form of "total labor costs" they figure prominently in the calculations made by employers when deciding what functions to locate where. And there are of course major differences. According to figures from the UN Conference on Trade and Development, in 1994 the average annual salary of a software programmer in India was US$3,975, compared with $14,000 in Malaysia, $34,615 in Hong Kong, $31,247 in the UK, $45,552 in France, $46,600 in the United States, and $54,075 in Germany.[41] It is important, however, to be aware that such differences may be transient. The very success of the software industry in Bangalore, for instance, has resulted in a rapid inflation of local salaries which are now considerably higher than in other parts of India, such as Calcutta, where the supply of such skills still greatly exceeds demand, and in other parts of the world, for instance Russia, where routine programming activities, such as coding, are now subcontracted from India. Khilnani describes the impact on the local labor of the large-scale influx of foreign multinationals into Bangalore: "These companies have transformed the wage structure of the Indian professional world. They are able to offer Indians in their late twenties salaries not even reached at the retirement points of Indian public enterprise salary scales."[42]

It is possible that such developments may signal the beginning of a global convergence in wages for workers with such specific and definable IT skills in activities which are capable of being carried out independently of location. Such a convergence, if it were taking place (and so far too little empirical research has been carried out to substantiate this), would imply a substantial gain for workers in developing countries combined with a reining in of real wage increases (if not an actual decline) in developed countries. That such increases would trickle down into the rest of the local economy in the developing countries cannot, however, be taken for granted. New forms of polarization might well develop between the holders of delocalizable jobs and workers whose jobs are geographically fixed. The extent to which the delocalizable jobs will take root in any given geographical spot is also dependent on a number of variables. If they take the form of labor-only subcontracting, then their anchoredness is highly contingent. There is always a choice open to the ultimate employer whether to send the jobs to the people or bring the people to the jobs, in the process which is known in the software industry as "body shopping." For at least two decades it has been a common practice for planeloads of software engineers to be flown on demand from India to London, Frankfurt, Los Angeles, or other sites where their skills are needed. Typically, in the 1980s and early 1990s, they were employed by subcontractors. In 1992, liberalization of trade made it possible for the first time for software to be exported from sites in India, and a large-scale software export industry grew up based in Bangalore, and later in other centers such as Hyderabad, Poona, and Chennai. However, employers still retain a choice, and both the United States and most European countries have recently loosened their immigration procedures to make it easy to get green cards for software engineers with scarce skills. Where there is a global market for skills, the employer's choice whether or not to relocate is therefore mirrored by the worker's decision whether to migrate or stay put.

Not all the new delocalized work involves technical software skills. In many developing countries there has also been a major growth in lower-skilled clerical work, such as data entry and typing, and in call center work. Here the earnings may well compare unfavorably with those of well-organized production workers. Gothoskhar describes how "in the Indian context, the pay-levels of the younger call-center workers may be much lower than those of middle-aged blue-collar workers." However, she goes on to point out that a comparison based only on income may be misleading in terms of defining their class position: "[T]he very criteria of recruitment of these workers as of today are such that they are from two-income families, mostly from 'white-collar' parents, people with an education in English and so on. This today at least excludes people from lower castes, people from the rural areas, and people whose parents are from what may be called the 'traditional working-class' families."[43]

This brings us to the sixth category, a class definition based on a notion of *status*. This term, in its Weberian sense, can be extended to cover a range of different variables including ethnicity, language group, religion, skin color, caste, or even the condition of slavery. The structure of most labor markets (and the history of most labor movements) bears powerful testimony to the force of such differences in creating patterns of inclusion and exclusion, privilege and deprivation. Labor markets are segmented along racial lines in North America, Europe, Australia, and Japan quite as much as (if sometimes more covertly than) they are in many developing countries. However, the fault lines may fall somewhat differently. One important factor is language. Entry to the new world of information work is crucially dependent on the ability to understand, speak, and write English, or, in some parts of the world, French, Spanish, German, Japanese, or Arabic. In countries where this is not the native language, this is likely to be the prerogative of the highly educated. Immediately, the threshold is raised above that required in the imperial parent economy. Relative wage levels and differences in the supply of and demand for labor also play their part, of course. It is therefore not unusual to find the sorts of work which are carried out by school-leavers, or graduates from junior college, in the United States being carried out by graduates or postgraduates in a developing country. Sinclair Jones studied a medical transcription center in Bangalore carrying out work for doctors in the United States. She reports that in the US the work was done by homeworkers, paid a piece rate for the number of lines typed, who would normally be educated only to community college level, but that applicants in India generally arrive with a master's degree. Nevertheless, "[e]ven though there is a rather paradoxical disparity between the qualifications base of the US and Indian workers there are still huge cost advantages to undertaking this work in India. For graduates in India with, for example, a Master of Arts, there are limited options for employment. As an English teacher in Bangalore they might earn around Rupees 3,000 per month (approx. US$75)." However, in the transcription center, "a good transcriptionist with two years' experience earns between 7,500 and 9,500 rupees per month (US$190–$240), while some are earning over 12,000 rupees (US$300) per month. This compares with workers in the US who earn between $1,800 and $2,400 a month. The experienced Indian medical transcriptionist is then about eight times cheaper than a US counterpart."[44] Her social status in the local economy will nevertheless be quite different.

This has implications for how office workers identify their own interests and their potential for making common cause with other workers doing identical work in other countries. This question is complicated by another issue. Where workers are employed by foreign companies, the exploitation of labor by capital may not be regarded as such but rather as an imperial exploitation of natives by colonialists.[45] Instead of perceiving their interests as being aligned with those of other workers employed by the same multinational companies, they may see their interests as national ones, best served by aligning themselves with local capitalists against the imperializing outsiders. Such attitudes are likely to be reinforced by encounters with racist attitudes among the workers of the developed world.

We must conclude that although there is considerable potential for the emergence of a common class consciousness among information-processing workers, based in a common labor process, common employers, and a common relation to capital, powerful counterforces are present which seem likely to inhibit this development, the greatest of which, perhaps, is racism.

There is considerable evidence of successful organizing by the new "e-workers" within countries, as indicated by the 1999 strike by call center workers at British Telecom in the UK and unionization among data entry workers in the Caribbean[46] and in Brazil.[47] There is also some evidence that when selecting locations, employers consciously avoid areas where workers are likely to organize. In her study of the medical transcription center in Bangalore, Sinclair Jones reports that

> the informant did comment that in the early stages they had considered establishment in Kerala on the basis that it has extremely high literacy levels. However, Kerala also has high levels of industrial organization

and the company decided not to take the risk. This kind of service provision is extremely vulnerable to stoppages given the commitment to rapid turnaround and the company management actively seeks to avoid becoming exposed to attempts at organizing labour.[48]

However, examples of such organization across national boundaries are few and far between. One notable exception is the agreement covering call center workers jointly signed with Air Canada by the Canadian Auto Workers and their sister unions in the UK and the United States. In general, though, the evidence of resistance by these workers comes in more sporadic and anarchic forms, such as the writing of viruses or other forms of sabotage.

One factor which will undoubtedly influence the propensity of workers to organize and take militant action will be the extent to which this is likely to be in their own economic best interests. If low-level office work is perceived as the bottom rung of a ladder which can be scaled successfully by keeping on the right side of the boss, then hard work, keeping one's nose clean, and sycophancy will offer the best route to advancement. If on the other hand no promotion prospects seem likely, for instance because the higher levels are located on another site halfway across the globe, or because only men, or only white people, or only people of a certain nationality or caste ever get promoted, then the best way to better one's income may well seem to lie in making common cause with one's fellow workers. Once again, we find that gender and race play a crucial role in determining class identity.

It is apparent that a new cybertariat is in the making. Whether it will perceive itself as such is another matter.

NO-COLLAR LABOR
IN AMERICA'S "NEW ECONOMY"

Andrew Ross

A dvance waves of the new no-collar work first swept across Wall
Street when office managers, conceding a barely begun struggle,
declared "casual Fridays" as the order of the day.* Dress codes and other
protocols of workplace formality were to be relaxed on the least industrious day of the work week. While starchy diehards growled about the
abatement of the American work ethic, evangelists of "reengineering"
welcomed the custom as a bold innovation; workers would feel their
personality was being acknowledged, and that their workplace was less
alienating on the day it was most perceived to be so. Introduced by the
employer, this new custom ironically evokes memories of Saint Mon-
day, the pre-Taylorist working-class tradition of mass absenteeism at the
close of the weekend. After all, casual Friday was intended to energize
white-collar workers by making them feel at home, rather than at work;
all the more present for feeling like an absentee.

Far from spontaneous, casual Friday is part and parcel of the new-
wave managerial ethos that preaches the leveling of workplace hierarchies. Employees are to feel empowered and individualized, workplaces
are to feel fluid and recreational, and work is to be liberated from rigid,
bureaucratic constraints. After several decades in which Americans
were encouraged to find the true meaning of themselves in leisure time
and consumption, work, according to this ideal, is once again the place

---

* This essay was first published in *Socialist Register 2001* (London: Merlin Press, 2001).

where our identity is to be most deeply felt and shaped. Perhaps this is just as well. The United States boasts an economy where the amount of leisure time available to workers has been in steady decline since the early 1970s, and where chronic overwork, and not unemployment, is the primary feature of the labor landscape. Since there is no easy return to the days when a clear demarcation between work and leisure existed, the efforts of the new managerialism are aimed at dissolving the boundaries as much as possible.

For the most advanced and entrenched examples of this ethos, you would have to pay a visit to New York's "Silicon Alley," where the webshops of the "new economy" have been at this game since the mid-1990s, when startup companies first began to colonize Manhattan's downtown manufacturing loft spaces. In those fledgling days, the physical culture of the new media workplace was more or less an extension of the grungy artist's loft. When dot-com mania broke out, and the Alley was flooded with venture capital, ritzy designers were hired to create set piece interiors. Trophy environments at companies like Screaming Media, DoubleClick and Oxygen Media featured flexible, communal spaces, where cubicles were banished and walls were rendered translucent. The office was reimagined as a giant, multi-purpose playroom for an ever-shifting team of workers. Cool, buzzworthy graphics are flung across the walls and ceilings. Pool tables in game rooms, basketball courts, and wellness relaxation spaces are a relief and counterpoint to the omnipresent but deftly decentered computer workstations. Who would ever want to go home? Silicon Valley had pioneered an earlier version of the informal workplace, where whiz kids didn't have to grow up and leave the never-never land of adolescence where the thrill of exploration and invention was unsullied by the external, social world. Silicon Alley, the "capital of content," upgraded the informality by adding all the hip features of an urban artist lifestyle.

THE RISE OF FREE AGENTS

For the new economy's boosters, these environments are much more than real estate icons, they are the ultimate physical embodiment of all the "flexibility" talk that has dominated corporate culture for the last twenty years. Indeed, they house internet industries that sprang directly from the head of the restructured economy of flexible accumulation and which at the turn of the new century were pumping fresh, hot air into the wobbly, digital stock bubble. As numerous commentators have described, this economic restructuring, begun in the mid to late 1970s, eliminated an enormous number of stable, high-wage union jobs and resulted in the normalizing of low-wage temp work for a large segment of the labor force. The two decades between 1973 and 1993 showed a steady decline in full-time jobs, and a rise in part-time employment, from 16.6 percent to 18.8 percent of the general workforce, almost all of the increase resulting from *involuntary* contingent work, and most of it in temporary-help employment.[1] In the technically skilled echelons of the new information industries, a deluxe form of temping emerged as the model pattern of employment, much hyped, and much over-rated. Well-paid technicians, engineers, and designers became inde-pendent contractors, eschewing benefits, pension packages, and other forms of job security for the freedoms offered by contingent work. "Employees without jobs," they moved from company to company, "pollinating" the seeds of innovation, according to the new flexible style of corporate organization.[2]

Over the course of the 1990s, this model was much emulated. "Consultant" became the fastest-growing job description, if not the fastest-growing job category, and segued into the phenomenon of the "free agent"—in new economy parlance, a skilled but flexible worker with no enduring company loyalties beyond the terms of the contract. The corporate crusade to downsize and shed its permanent workforce seemed to have met its perfect love match; workers who do not want a regular paycheck or any form of benefits from the companies for which they occasionally work. For the most fortunate, the freelance lifestyle is a heady potion, and their fantasies of autonomy (while still being paid by the Man) are seized on and glorified as a way to sell the profile of flexible labor in general. As a result, projected tallies for these "free agents" are inflated, as many as thirty-three million according to some internet industry boosters.[3] But who are these autonomous agents, and how voluntary is their employment condition?

According to the latest US Bureau of Labor Statistics (BLS), for 1997, there were 5.6 million workers with contingent jobs (employ-ment not expected to last for more than one additional year), most of whom are young and female, predominantly concentrated in low-wage temping, and 53 percent of whom would have preferred a job that was permanent. "Workers with alternative arrangements" (numbers that

overlap with those of contingent workers) include independent contractors, on-call workers, day laborers, temporary help agency workers,
and workers provided by contract firms. The independent contractors (8.2 million, and 6.3 percent of the workforce) are concentrated
in managerial, professional, sales occupations, and in the construction
and services industries, and are more likely to prefer their employment
arrangements than workers in other categories like on-call (2 million)
and temps (1.1 million). Among these 8.2 million are the much-her-
alded knowledge workers, labeled as free agents. Yet, between 1995
and 1997, when the knowledge industries were booming, there was
a decline in the number of independent contractors, while all other
categories, including those for contingent work, were little changed in
those same two years.[4]

In March 2000 *New York Times Magazine* devoted an issue to the
"new American worker." The issue focused on the concept of the free
agent as a symptom of the shift away from the "organization man"
of postwar corporate culture, where company loyalty was regarded as
a long-term two-way contract between employers and white-collar
employees. With the replacement of conformity by innovation, and
a large permanent workforce by temporary employee pools, a contract labor market is coming into its own, whereby free agents bid for
jobs offered by employers on auction websites like Bid4Geeks.com and
Monster.com. In the most breathless of these articles, Michael Lewis
lumps together all of the categories of "workers with alternative arrangements" to estimate the number of free agents at 12 million (out of
a national workforce of 131 million), and avers that their typical mode
of self-presentation usually includes

> piercing some highly unlikely body part and cultivating an air of total
> independence. Actually, what these people all were, or appeared to
> be, were artists. They kept artists' hours. They wore artists' clothes.
> They had persevered [in] the sort of odd habits that membership
> in any group—other than the group "artists"—tends to drum out
> of people. Maybe the most interesting thing about them was their
> lack of obvious corporate attachments. Corporations usually paid for
> their existence, but otherwise seemed to have no effect on their lives.
> If forced to discuss the companies that paid the bills, these people
> tended to be dismissive, or at the very least, ironic.[5]

In another article, which debunks the romance of the free agent nation, Nina Munk cites a new media marketing consultant who, with her laptop and cell phone, is using an offbeat Greenwich Village cafe, Les Deux Gamins, as her portable office—"It makes me feel like I'm in Paris," she says, "like Hemingway at Les Deux Magots." Munk points out that more than 60 percent of these workers earn much less than full-timers in comparable jobs, and that the lure of liberation from routine work seems to result in people putting in more hours than they would at a regular, comparable job.[6]

THE LEGACY OF THE STARVING ARTIST

The references by Lewis and Munk to artists and writers are crucial. A large part of the attraction of the free agent profile draws on the appeal to bohemian glamor. What are the consequences of this desire to assume the trappings of the artist? First of all, let us be clear that it is an invitation to underpayment. Artists' traditions of sacrificial labor are governed by the principle of the cultural discount, by which artists and other arts' workers accept nonmonetary rewards—the gratification of producing art—as compensation for their work, thereby discounting the cash price of their labor. Indeed, it must be acknowledged that the largest subsidy to the arts has always come from workers themselves. The mythology of the "starving artist" is rooted in the political economy of the creative professions, and the historical legacy of their emergence from the mold of aristocratic patronage.[7]

Just as important, however, is the serviceability of the artist's flexible labor. Since flexible specialization was introduced as a leading industrial principle, the number of artists employed in the general labor force (defined in decennial census data and annual BLS reports as eleven occupations: artists who work with their hands, authors, actors and directors, designers, dancers, architects, photographers, arts teachers, musicians/composers, et cetera) has swelled from year to year. According to the National Endowment for the Arts's annual summaries of BLS tabulations, this number more than doubled from 1970 to 1990, showing an 81 percent increase in the course of the 1970s (while artists' real earnings declined by 37 percent), a 54 percent increase in the 1980s, a slight decline in the depression of the early 1990s, and a renewal of growth ever since, reaching a peak of two million in 1998. In 1997, artists were enjoying a growth rate in employment (at 2.7 percent) that

far outstrips the general workforce (1.3 percent) and even that of other
professional specialists (2.4 percent).[8] These are impressive numbers,
but they do not tell a simple story. To figure in the BLS survey, "one
must be working during the survey week and have described that job/
work as one of eleven artist occupations." Respondents are asked to
describe the job at which "they worked the most number of hours in
the survey week." Artists working more hours in other jobs outside
the arts are classified as employed in those other occupations. By 1998,
these amounted to an additional 330,000, for a total of 2,280,000 artists employed in the workforce.[9] Randy Martin points out that these
requirements gloss over the verifiable existence of full-time jobs within
that occupational sector: "One works in an occupation, a sector, but
has the flexibility to remain unattached. The artist can secure an identity for a day's wage, but the rest of the week remains unsecuritized."[10]
Because of the high degree of self-employment, and because they are
most likely to have other jobs to support a creative trade that habitu-
ally employs them for only a portion of a workweek, employment and
earnings data on cultural workers have always been unreliable. Even in
the most highly unionized entertainment guilds, where the majority
of members cannot find work on any given day, the dominant employment model is casual employment on a project-by-project basis. Loyalty is to the guild or craft or union, rather than to a single employer.[11]

There may be more going on here than the sleight-of-hand interpretation of statistics to paint a rosy picture of job creation in the arts.
Whether or not we can verify a proliferation of new jobs, it is clear that
the "mentality" of artists' work is more and more in demand. In respect both to their function and the use of this work mentality, it looks
as if artists are steadily being relocated from their traditional position
at the social margins of the productive economy and recruited into
roles closer to the economic centers of production. Indeed, the traditional profile of the artist as unattached and adaptable to circumstance
is surely now coming into its own as the ideal definition of the postindustrial knowledge worker: comfortable in an ever-changing environment that demands creative shifts in communication with different
kinds of employers, clients, and partners; attitudinally geared toward
work that requires long, and often unsocial, hours; and accustomed, in
the sundry exercise of their mental labor, to a contingent, rather than

a fixed routine of self-application. A close fit, in other words, with the profile of the free agent.

NET SLAVES

In light of this artist profile, let us take a closer look at employment patterns in the new media industries of New York City. The backbone of the Silicon Alley workforce in the pioneer phase of this new urban industry was staffed by employees—"creative content-providers," or digital manipulators in website and software development—who had been trained primarily as artists. Deeply caffeinated eighty-five-hour workweeks without overtime pay are a way of life for webshop workers on flexible contracts, who invest a massive share of sweat equity in the mostly futile hope that their stock options will pay off. Even the lowliest employee feels like an entrepreneurial investor as a result. In most cases, the stock options turn into pink slips when the company goes belly-up, or, in some cases, employees are fired before their stock options are due to mature. Exploitative manipulation of this mode of employee recruitment and retention has resulted in several major lawsuits that have rocked the industry. Yet the lure of stock options remains very strong, largely as a result of the publicity showered on the small number of employees who have struck gold in a high-profile "IPO" (initial public offering) among the maze of new ones on the stock market.

Only 2.7 percent of workers in computer and electronics belong to unions (as compared to 56.2 percent in steel) and webshop workplaces are entirely nonunionized.[12] For several fledgling years, about half of the jobs were filled by contract employees or perma-temps, with no employer-supported healthcare. With the explosive growth of the last two years, the number of full-time workers has increased noticeably (by 57 percent annually). Yet in the most recent industry survey, the expected rate of growth for part-time (30 percent) and freelance employment (33 percent) still competes with that for full-time job creation (38 percent). Evolving patterns of subcontracting in Silicon Alley are not so far removed from those that created offshore back offices for data processing in the Caribbean, Ireland, and Bangalore, or semiconductor factories in countries that also host the worst sweatshops in the global garment industry.[13] Most revealing, perhaps, is that in 1997 the average full-time salary (at $37,000) was well below the equivalent in old media industries, like advertising (at $71,000) and television broad-casting (at $86,000).[14]

As noted earlier, the webshops physically occupy spaces filled by manufacturing sweatshops a century ago. Artists who took over these manufacturing lofts from the 1950s onward enjoyed wide-open floors where work space doubled as living space. This live/work ethos was embraced, to some degree, by the upscale cultural elites who later consolidated "loft living" as a real estate attraction, and it has been extended now into the funky milieu of the webshops, where work looks more and more like play. In the most primitive startups, the old sweatshop practice of housing workers in the workplace has also been revived. Bill Lessard and Steve Baldwin, authors of *Net Slaves*, an exposé of industry working conditions, report on this phenomenon: "We were up in Seattle on the book tour, and we visited a friend who's working for a startup that has installed beds in cubicles and is providing three meals a day. As if they were in a U-boat fighting a war! There are companies bragging about this kind of mistreatment!" Lessard and Baldwin sketch a portrait of an industry that benefits from the hag-iographical "myth of the 22-year-old code-boy genius subsisting on pizza and soda and going 36 hours at a clip." Employees' quality of life approaches zero as a result, in "the complete absence of a social life, a lousy diet, lack of exercise, chain smoking, repetitive stress disorders, and, last but not least, haemorrhoids. . . . There's going to be a lot of sick people out there in a few years, and worse, they won't even have any health benefits."[15]

All in all, the new media workplace is a prescient indicator of the near future of no-collar labor, which combines mental skills with new technologies in nontraditional environments. Customized work-places where the lines between labor and leisure have dissolved: hori-zontal networking among heroic teams of self-directed workers; the proto-hipster appeal of bohemian dress codes, personal growth, and nonhierarchical surroundings; the vague promise of bounteous re-wards from stock options; and employees so complicit with the culture of overwork and burnout that they have developed their own insider brand of sick humor about being "net slaves," i.e., it's actually cool to be exploited so badly. Industrial capitalists used to dream about such a workforce, but their managerial techniques were too rigid to foster it. These days, the new-wave management wing of the new economy worships exactly this kind of decentralized environment, which "liberates" workers by banishing constraints on their creativity, and delivers meaningful and non-alienated work for a grateful and independently minded workforce.

At a time when this managerial revolution is "liberating" employees, the workplace on the other side of the professional divide is more and more subject to automated forms of Taylorism. Worker monitoring, whether through keyboard strokes, e-mail and voicemail snooping, or surveillance cameras, is now standard practice on the part of the majority of American employers. Among service workers, human relations software is widely used for tracking, job timing, and to introduce speedup, yet the practice is also moving into white-collar professions. The most infamous example is the regulation of physicians' schedules by health-management organizations under the rubric of managed care. Alpha professionals, like doctors, are increasingly experiencing a loss of autonomy in the workplace, and are turning to union organizing as a result.

A VOLUNTEER LOW-WAGE ARMY

Labor history is full of vicious little time warps, where archaic or long-foresworn practices and conceptions of work are reinvented in a fresh context to suit some new economic arrangement. The "sweating" system of farming out work to competing contractors in the nineteenth-century garment industry was once considered an outdated exception to the rule of the integrated factory system. Disdained as a preindustrial relic by the apostles of scientific management, this form of subcontracting is now a basic principle of almost every sector of the postindustrial economy and has emerged as the number one weapon in capital's arsenal of labor cost-cutting and union busting. Where once the runaway shops were in New Jersey, now they are in Haiti, China, and Vietnam. So, too, the ethos of the autonomous artist, once so fiercely removed from industry's dark satanic mills and from the soiled hand of commerce, has been recouped and revamped as a convenient, even alluring, esprit de corps for contingent work in today's decentralized knowledge factories. Indeed, the "voluntary poverty" of the déclassé Bohemian artist—an ex-bourgeois descendant, more often than not, of the self-exiled romantic poet—may turn out to be an inadvertent forerunner of the discounted labor of the new industrial landscape.

In the academic sector in the United States we find a similar story about sacrificial labor. Indeed, the rapidity with which the low-wage revolution has swept through higher education in the last fifteen years was clearly hastened along by conditions amenable to discounting mental labor. For one thing, the "willingness" of scholars to accept a discounted wage out of "love for their subject" has helped not only to sustain the cheap labor supply but also to magnify its strength and volume.

The most obvious index of the changes in the academic labor force can be found in the rise of part-time employment, for that is how the payroll has been trimmed most dramatically. In 1970, the proportion of part-time faculty stood at 22 percent. By 1987, part-timers held 38 percent of faculty appointments, and ten years later, the proportion had risen to 42.5 percent. In addition, by 1988, the proportion of full-time faculty not on a tenure track had risen to 20 percent.[16] Even among full-time faculty, the rate of compensation is depressed. Salary levels remain below those of 1971, and the gap between faculty salaries and those of other highly educated professionals has widened considerably. Faculty earned 13.8 percent less than professionals with a similar education in 1985, a gap that almost doubled by 1997, with faculty earning 24 percent less.[17] Employers have long relied on maintaining a reserve army of unemployed to keep wages down in any labor market. Higher education is now in this business with a vengeance. In addition—and this is the significant element—its managers increasingly draw on a volunteer low-wage army. By this I do not mean to suggest that adjunct and part-timer educators eagerly invite their underpayment and lack of benefits or job security. Nor are they inactive in protesting and organizing for their interests. Rather, I choose the term to describe the natural outcome of a training in the habit of embracing nonmonetary rewards—mental or creative gratification—as compensation for work. As a result, low compensation for a high workload becomes a rationalized feature of the job, and, in the most perverse extension, is regarded as proof of the worth of the academic vocation—underpayment is the ultimate measure of the selfless and disinterested pursuit of knowledge.

In some respects, the peripatetic regimen of the freeway flyer is germane to the eccentric work schedule of the traditional academic, who commonly observes no clear boundaries between being on and off the job, and for whom there is often little distinction between paid work and free labor. For the professionally active full-timer, this habitual schedule is bad enough. For the part-timer, desperate to retain the prestige of being a college teacher, the identity of being a switched-on, round-the-clock thinker, eager to impart knowledge, and in a position to freely extend her or his mental labor feeds into the psychology of casualized work and underpayment. The industrial worker, by comparison, is not beset by such occupational hazards.

Again, what we see is the fabrication of a model "flexible employee" out of the cloth of a customary training in the amateur ideals and irregular routines of mental labor which can be roundly exploited by cost-cutting managers in search of contingent labor. Because of the elective component of this situation, capital, it might be said, as part of its ceaseless search for ways to induct workers in their own exploitation, may have found the makings of a *self-justifying* low-wage workforce, at the very heart of the knowledge industries so crucial to its growth and development.

THE MENTAL PRICE SYSTEM

My conclusion leaves us with some difficult questions. Are we contributing involuntarily to the problem when we urge youth, in pursuing their career goals, to place principles of public interest or collective political agency or creative expression above the pursuit of material security? In a labor environment heavily under the sway of neoliberal business models, is it fair to say that this service ideal invites, if it does not vindicate, the manipulation of inexpensive labor?

Fifteen years ago, this suggestion would have seemed ludicrous. Labor freely offered in the service of some common benefit or mental ideal has always been the informal economic backbone that supports political, cultural, and educational activities in the nonprofit or public interest sectors. Selfless labor of this sort is also a source of great pleasure. The world that we value most—the world that is not in thrall to market dictates—would not exist without this kind of volunteer discounted labor. But what happens when some version of this disinterested labor moves, as I have suggested here, from the social margins to core sectors of capital accumulation? When the opportunity to pursue mentally gratifying work becomes a rationale for discounted labor at heart of the key knowledge industries, is it not time to rethink some of our bedrock pedagogical values? Does the new landscape of mental labor demand more than the usual call for modernizing the politics of labor in the age of dot-com and dot-edu (the age of the Yale

Corporation, the Microserf, and the consolidated push of Time Warner-Bertelsmann-Disney-CNN-Hachette-Paramount-News Corp)?

On the one hand, there are sound reasons for retaining such ideals and traditions. Unpopular forms of intellectual, artistic, and political expression cannot and will not thrive unless they are independent of commercial or bureaucratic dictates. But these conditions of independence can no longer be "defended" stubbornly and solely as a matter of humanistic principle, or as the freestanding right of a civilized society. When capital-intensive industry is concentrated around vast culture trading sectors, when media Goliaths feed off their control of intellectual property, and when the new vested interests routinely barter discount wages for creative satisfaction on the job, the expressive traditions of mental labor are no longer ours simply to claim, not when informal versions of them are daily being bought off and refined into high-octane fuel for the next generation of knowledge factories.

Insofar as we participate in this economy as scholars, activists, or artists, there is a responsibility to recognize the cost of our cherished beliefs in political and educational ideals. These ideals come at a price, and managers of the new economy are taking full advantage of the opportunities that exist for capitalizing on our neglect of that price. Our first challenge, then, could be to assess the special conditions for pricing wages for thought, under which "free time" is systematically converted into un- or under-compensated labor (just as the hidden costs of the unwaged domestic labor of women have had to be acknowledged). Do such special conditions exist, or is pricing subject only to what the market will bear? As socialists, we know that the market does not function as an objective gauge of supply and demand—no more for sweatshop workers in an offshore free-trade zone than for CEOs in a tax-free zone of the Fortune 500. Ideas about the value of work and the worth of those who do certain kinds of work play a critical role in the price system, to use Veblen's pet phrase, and they must enter into our economic reckoning. Accordingly, we must remember that knowledge and rules of thumb passed on in a traditional craft are intellectual assets that will be stripped by managers looking for a comparative advantage. It was so in the steel mills where Frederick Taylor worked up his theories of scientific management, and it is little different in the knowledge factories of today.

Some part of the challenge also lies in organizing the unorganized, in this case those whose professional identity has been based on a sharp indifference to being organized. The sectors I have been describing here draw on an intimate and shared experience of the traditions of sacrificial labor. Yet they are divided by singular craft-like cultures, and by a tangle of class distinctions. Those most in denial (the most secure) will swear off any and every affinity. It will take more than a leap of faith to establish solidarity among mental labor fractions divided by the legacy of (under-the-table or above-the-salt) privileges passed down over centuries. Nevertheless, while the chief blight of these centuries had been chattel slavery, serfdom, and indentured labor (and we are not done with these), we must now respond to that moment in the soulful lullaby of "Redemption Song," where Bob Marley soberly advises us: "Emancipate yourself from mental slavery."

A TALE OF TWO CRISES: LABOR, CAPITAL, AND RESTRUCTURING IN THE US AUTO INDUSTRY

Nicole Aschoff

Much of the global auto industry went into a well-documented free fall following the 2007 financial meltdown.* The US market was hit particularly hard. The collapse in credit for dealers and consumers combined with skyrocketing fuel prices and wary consumers led to an evaporation of demand. US assemblers saw sales drop 50 percent and foreign assemblers 40 percent in 2009 to settle at an almost thirty-year low of 10.4 million vehicles in the United States.[1] Chrysler and General Motors's bankruptcy filing that year seemed to signal the long-prophesied downfall of Detroit. Citing the negative economic repercussions of the industry's collapse, the US state threw the assemblers a lifeline, trading financial assistance for reorganization. GM and Chrysler emerged from bankruptcy with fewer plants, dealerships, and brands; a new ownership structure; and a mandate to produce smaller, "greener" vehicles. In the process unionized autoworkers became partial "owners" of the "new" automakers and agreed to sweeping concessions in wages and benefits that put them on par with nonunion assembly workers in the US.

While the financial crisis and ensuing auto crisis did force significant change upon the industry, these changes do not represent a fundamental break from the past. Instead, the primary consequence of the crisis has

★   This essay was first published in *Socialist Register 2012* (London: Merlin Press, 2012). I would like to thank Sam Gindin and Pankaj Mehta for commenting on an early draft of this paper.

been to accelerate and reinforce ongoing processes of capitalist restructuring, largely at the expense of autoworkers. In fact, GM, Chrysler, and Ford have benefited from the recent crisis. It allowed the Detroit Three to rapidly regroup after their competitive strategy of the last two decades failed. This pattern of crisis followed by restructuring is endemic to the auto industry, particularly in big, competitive markets like the US. Assemblers have enacted multiple waves of restructuring in the US since the 1980s that, combined with increasing foreign investment, have resulted in a constantly evolving industry. The recent crisis represents a continuation of these dynamics. Thus, from the perspective of capital, the present crisis can be largely situated within the ongoing process of restructuring occurring in the industry.

The same cannot be said for unionized autoworkers in the US. The Detroit Three in partnership with the US government exploited the doomsday atmosphere surrounding the crisis to push through concessions that fundamentally undermine the power of the United Auto Workers (UAW) to protect and improve the working lives of its members. While US autoworkers' fortunes have oscillated in synch with the booms and busts of the industry, their overall trajectory during the past three decades has been one of decline and disorientation. Long-term trends of de-unionization, concessions, and isolation have paved the way for unprecedented concessions. The recent crisis has essentially erased the postwar gains of unionized autoworkers in the industry.

Hence, the crisis has had divergent consequences for capital and labor. For capital it has triggered a rapid restructuring and the restoration of profits, while for workers it has compounded the precarious position of unionized autoworkers by reversing decades of hard-won gains. To better understand the crisis and its differing consequences for capital and labor, it is necessary to situate it within a historical context. Doing so allows us to gain a clearer perspective on the nature of the crisis and, importantly, explore possible avenues for workers to regroup and fight back.

CRISIS FOR CAPITAL

In the fall of 2008, the US auto industry looked like it was headed for disaster. Chrysler and GM reported losses for the year totaling eight billion and thirty-one billion dollars, respectively. The turmoil in financial markets beginning a year earlier caused the market for asset-backed securities to dry up. Almost overnight, consumers found it difficult to finance vehicle purchases, and dealers were unable to get credit to purchase inventory from assemblers. Detroit was affected more severely than foreign assemblers because of its overreliance on both the SUV (sport utility vehicle) segment (which had contracted because of skyrocketing fuel prices) and, in the case of GM and Ford, their finance subsidiaries. But the crisis was not confined to US assemblers. The industry is tightly interlinked with complex, overlapping supply chains. For this reason, the collapse in credit markets rapidly generated a chain reaction that threatened the survival of assemblers, suppliers, dealers, workers, and the communities who depend on them, particularly in states like Michigan, Kentucky, Ohio, Indiana, Alabama, and Tennessee.[2]

GM and Chrysler announced in late 2008 that they would not have enough cash to continue running operations by 2009 unless they received financial support from the US government. Despite widespread public opposition, in December 2008 the Treasury Department established the Automotive Industry Financing Program (AIFP) under the Troubled Asset Relief Program (TARP). Through the AIFP, the Treasury extended loans of $4 billion and $13.4 billion respectively to Chrysler and GM. The loans were conditional and required the assemblers to submit viability plans to cut costs and streamline operations in line with their declining market share. The assemblers submitted these plans in February 2009 and requested additional financial support because they continued to burn through cash. In March of that year the Obama administration rejected their proposals as "not sufficient to achieve long-term viability" and demanded the assemblers "take more aggressive action as a condition of receiving additional federal assistance." GM and Chrysler were given sixty and thirty days to achieve Obama's restructuring goals or else declare bankruptcy and be forcibly restructured by the US state. Both firms failed to meet their deadlines and declared bankruptcy.[3] Ford had sufficient cash reserves and negotiated a $9 billion emergency credit line, and so managed to avoid bankruptcy.

The bankruptcy process for both firms was classified as a "court-supervised asset sale." GM and Chrysler both sold their "good" assets— the parts of their companies that they wanted to keep—to the "new" GM and Chrysler. Undesirable assets and debt remained at the "old" companies and were liquidated through a longer bankruptcy process. The goal of the court-supervised asset sale was to get the companies out of bankruptcy quickly, thus accelerating their turnaround.[4]

Chrysler, already majority-owned by Cerberus Capital Management (CCM), was divided between Fiat, the UAW Voluntary Employees' Beneficiary Association (VEBA) fund, and the US and Canadian governments, who would be minority stakeholders.[5] Eight assembler and supply plants were slated to close. To create the "new" GM, fourteen assembly and parts plants and three warehouses were slated to close; the Hummer, Pontiac, Saab, and Saturn divisions were sold or discontinued; and GM was divided between the US government, the UAW and Canadian Auto Workers, the Canadian government, the provincial government of Ontario, and unsecured GM bondholders. Although Ford didn't declare bankruptcy, it also restructured. It sold its Jaguar and Rover divisions to Tata in 2008, reduced its share in Mazda to just 3 percent, and in 2010, discontinued its Mercury brand and sold Volvo to Geely.[6]

The automotive crisis and forced bankruptcy restructuring of GM and Chrysler were significant events for both the industry and the individual firms. The state's intervention and financial assistance allowed the assemblers to rapidly streamline operations and decrease capacity, allowing them to focus on profitable divisions. But the crisis was not the culmination of an overall pattern of decline, nor was it a game-changing event that forced abrupt change on the industry. Instead, the restructuring that occurred was part of an *ongoing* reorganization of the global automobile industry, especially in "replacement" markets like the US. For years global assemblers have been overhauling operations and designing new strategies to cope with increased competitive pressures. In this section we will situate this restructuring within a broader historical context to shed light on the significance of the crisis for capital.

US assemblers have been reorganizing their operations almost continually in the US market since the 1980s, in an attempt to maintain market share in the face of growing competition from foreign assemblers located in the US and abroad. With the emergence of Japanese and European competitors in the 1960s, US assemblers gradually lost their monopoly over the global auto industry, especially as imports began to encroach on their home market in the 1970s. To cope they first began to move production of parts and some assembly to the US South and Mexico as a way to cut costs. However, as imports continued to increase, US assemblers pressured the Reagan administration for import restrictions on foreign cars. The resulting "voluntary" export restrictions catalyzed a wave of investment by Japanese assemblers and suppliers into the US during the 1980s.

Foreign firms first moved into the Midwest to take advantage of existing supply networks. However, beginning in the late 1980s foreign supplier investment in the US increased significantly, allowing foreign assemblers to migrate investment southward to take advantage of lower-cost labor.

In response to growing competition on their home soil, US assemblers spent billions restructuring operations during the 1980s. They closed coastal assembly plants and reopened plants in the country's interior to be close to the country's transportation nerve center, while simultaneously moving more low value-added production to low-wage sites in Mexico.[7] US firms also moved away from producing smaller cars, ceding these segments to Japanese and European manufacturers and focusing on large cars and light trucks.[8] During the late 1980s US assemblers expanded into other brands and segments to improve profitability. For example, GM spent billions acquiring the niche brands Lotus and Saab, Ross Perot's computer company EDS, and Hughes Electronics, as well as other ventures in financial services and defense contracting.[9]

The geographical dynamism of the 1980s continued in the 1990s and 2000s. As Figures 1 and 2 show, investment during the last two decades was spatially dynamic, with growth and decline in investment occurring simultaneously, especially in the Midwest.

Figure 1: Reported Assembler Investment, 1988–2006

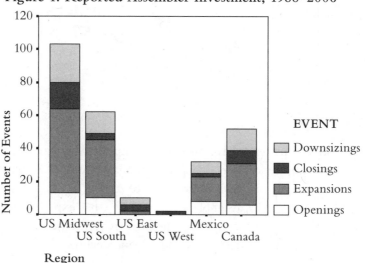

Source: Data is from the Automotive Investment Patterns (AIP) database constructed by the author.[10]

Japanese assemblers expanded production in the US and were joined by European assemblers and global suppliers, mainly from Europe and East Asia. This influx of production was coupled with strategies undertaken by US assemblers and some parts suppliers to lower costs by moving to Mexico and retool existing production in the Midwest. Rather than a unidirectional movement of production from traditional manufacturing regions to low-wage sites in the US South and Mexico, the investment pattern in the North American auto industry during the past three decades has been characterized by a reorganization of production, resulting in an "auto alley" stretching from the Great Lakes to the Gulf of Mexico.[11]

Figure 2: Reported Supplier Investment, 1988–2006

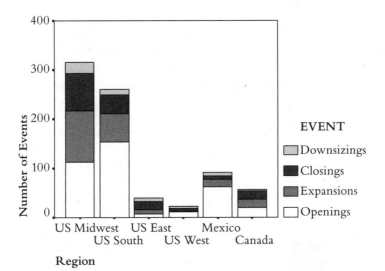

Source: AIP database.

Investment patterns have also been temporally dynamic, with no overwhelming trend of decline during the last two decades but rather a cyclical pattern of growth and decline. As Figure 3 illustrates, reported investment by assemblers and suppliers has experienced peaks and troughs over time in line with broader trends in the economy, but has consistently showed a mix of growth and decline.

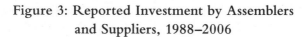

Figure 3: Reported Investment by Assemblers
and Suppliers, 1988–2006

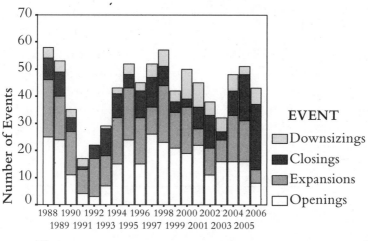

Source: AIP database.

Much assembler investment during the past two decades is characterized by retooling existing plants or opening new plants to produce
trucks (light trucks, SUVs, and minivans). While the US market is
generally considered a stagnant "replacement" market because market
saturation is high, its market for trucks has exhibited high growth rates,
especially in the 1990s. Light trucks accounted for more than half the
total value of all US auto sales by the late 1990s.[12] The widespread
popularity of trucks combined with their only marginally higher input demands made them a very profitable offering for assemblers. As
shown in Table 1, both US and foreign assemblers shifted their product
mix definitively toward trucks between 1995 and 2005. US assemblers
decreased cars and increased trucks, while foreign assemblers increased
both kinds of investment.

Table 1: Automobile Production in North America by Region (1995, 2005)

1995	US Midwest	US South	US East	US West	Mexico	Canada	Total
US Cars	2,812,610	1,335,068			339,798	679,057	5,166,533
US Trucks	3,362,022	1,111,537	436,725		61,716	961,350	6,033,350
JV Cars	367,093			229,393		116,610	713, 096
JV Trucks				123,257		59,258	182,515
Asian Cars	1,233,261	333,236			54,700	196,269	1,817,466
Asian Trucks	99,514	132,554					232,068
Euro Cars		11,876			156,422	7,588	175,886
Euro Trucks							0
Total	7,874,500	2,924,271	436,725	352,650	712,636	2,020,132	14,320,914
2005							**Total**
US Cars	1,709,434	354,493			408,805	982,403	3,455,135
US Trucks	3,794,246	1,699,974	14,489		483,395	759,159	6,751,263
JV Cars	272,632			248,471			521,103
JV Trucks				158,927		189,997	348,924
Asian Cars	1,236,663	383,252			343,684	424,560	2,388,159
Asian Trucks	481,130	745,448			66,111	266,952	1,559,641
Euro Cars		124,846			300,386		425,232
Euro Trucks		95,558			1,009		96,567
Total	7,494,105	3,403,571	14,489	407,398	1,603,390	2,623,071	15,556,024

Note: Vehicles are noncommercial. "Trucks" includes light trucks, SUVs, and minivans. Chrysler is considered a US firm in 1995. J.V. refers to East Asian / US joint-venture assembly plants. Source: Production data compiled by author from Automotive News Market Data Book (Detroit: Crain Communications, 1996 and 2006).

In addition to retooling for increased truck production, during the 1990s and early 2000s GM and Ford tried to improve market share and profitability through internal restructuring. Ford bought Volvo, Rover, Aston Martin, and Jaguar, and increased its control over Mazda; GM bought Hummer, Daewoo, and a controlling share of Isuzu. US firms also reshuffled their existing structures during the 1990s: GM sold Lotus, EDS, and Delphi, while Ford spun off Visteon.[13] As GM and Ford "de-verticalized" their supply operations, independent suppliers found the need to expand, and former in-house suppliers developed new partnerships with foreign assemblers, pushing them to open new plants.[14] As illustrated in Figure 2, many suppliers, both foreign and of North American origin, were pressured to follow assembly plants in order to retain or get contracts. Tier-one suppliers also evolved to take on more responsibility for manufacturing and design.[15] For example, in the late 1990s Delphi was asked to coordinate Mercedes's entire supply chain, stretching fifteen hundred miles from Juarez, Mexico, to Tuscaloosa, Alabama.

Restructuring in North America during the 1990s was part of a global process of restructuring. Whereas new assembly capacity in the 1980s was mostly of Japanese origin, in the 1990s American, European, and Korean firms began rapidly increasing investment in emerging markets. Global assemblers looked to corner new growing markets in countries like Vietnam, China, India, Pakistan, and the Philippines where market saturation rates were very low. Trade barriers were also relaxed in many countries during the 1990s, and with Triad (North America, Western Europe, and Japan) market competition increasing rapidly, global assemblers hoped to develop new avenues of future growth. However, the potential of these markets seemed uncertain after the Asian economic crisis. By the end of the nineties, many analysts suggested that firms had overestimated demand in emerging markets, and global assemblers and suppliers continued to rely on profits from Triad markets, particularly the US market.[16]

At the same time Ford and GM evolved to rely more heavily on their finance divisions (Ford Credit and GMAC) as a source of revenue and to compensate for their difficulty generating profits outside of truck production. The cost of credit was relatively low during the late nineties, allowing Ford and GM to gain huge profits from finance. In a highly competitive and cyclical industry like auto, revenue from credit activities is attractive because it represents a more steady income stream than profits from productive activities. Profits from their finance subsidiaries enabled GM and Ford to prop up unprofitable segments (like existing car models) worldwide while simultaneously acquiring new firms and expanding into developing markets. It is estimated that finance contributed 54 percent of Ford's net income in 1996,[17] and in the 1989–2006 period 93 percent of GM's consolidated net income was produced by GMAC.[18] While these statistics tend to overstate the role of finance because the finance subsidiaries were subsidized by the automakers through purchase incentives, GMAC and Ford Credit were nonetheless an important source of profit. For example, between 2001 and 2006 GM received over eight billion dollars in cash dividends from GMAC.[19]

The rise of finance also supported the industry as a whole during this period. As Krippner argues, free-flowing credit—a result of US state policies in the 1980s and '90s—"fueled asset price bubbles in financial markets and real estate markets."[20] These bubbles, particularly the housing bubble, created a consumption boom as homeowners took advantage of declining interest rates to refinance their homes, often borrowing additional funds to spend on home improvement, debt, and, luckily for the auto industry, new vehicles.[21] Ford and GM were able to use easy credit conditions to offer substantial incentives to new customers, maintaining sales for US assemblers in the face of growing competition. The housing boom also provided an additional revenue stream for GM and Ford because GMAC and Ford Credit were heavily entrenched in mortgage markets. By 2006 GMAC's ResCap operation was servicing $412 billion of mortgages and owned $69 billion in mortgage loans, totaling almost 40 percent of GMAC's receivables.[22]

GM and Ford's strategy of relying on trucks and finance to support their global operations was successful during the nineties. They regained the market share they had lost during the 1980s because SUVs delivered excellent margins and credit was cheap. But, because US firms used earnings from trucks and finance to prop up unprofitable segments rather than develop new offerings in other segments, they were left vulnerable to decreasing market share. Asian (and European) manufacturers took advantage of the product gap and at the same time started offering more vehicles in the segments where US assemblers were popular. As the market slowed down after 2000, US firms' market share continued to slide and factories were kept running by huge rebates and fleet sales. The subprime mortgage crisis put an end to this dead-end strategy. Ford Credit's and especially GMAC's (majority-owned by CCM after 2006) exposure to the imploding housing market, in combination with the industry slowdown and Detroit's sliding market share, created a perfect storm for the subsidiaries and all but locked them out of the credit markets when the financial crisis hit.[23]

Broadly speaking, the crisis showed the limits of growth in replacement markets like the US, Europe, and Japan. The ten-year production and sales boom in the US from 1995 to 2005 simply heightened competition in a market already characterized by overcapacity. With demand stalled in the US and Europe, and future sales uncertain, US firms began to ramp up efforts to expand faster into developing markets, especially those that were relatively unscathed by the downturn, like China and India. In 2009 total new car sales in BRIC nations (Brazil, Russia, India, and China) amounted to twenty million units, roughly one-third of the global total, and it is estimated that by 2050 half of all cars worldwide will be sold outside the Triad region. China overtook the US in 2009 as the largest domestic market for automobiles in the world, and is currently GM's largest market. Toyota, Ford, and Honda are all increasing productive capacity in China, scrambling to catch up with Volkswagen, GM, and Hyundai, who invested early and have a firm grasp on the market. VW alone controls nearly 20 percent of the Chinese market. Smaller assemblers are also keen to expand in China because of its large appetite for luxury vehicles. China is now BMW's second-largest market and the third-largest market for Jaguar Land Rover.

India has also seen extremely rapid growth—in 2009 its domestic market for passenger cars grew by over 25 percent. In the past two years Ford, Nissan, GM, Toyota, Honda, and Volkswagen have all expanded their productive base in India, building new assembly plants and expanding their supplier networks. Ford has recently announced that India will be its new small-car hub and has begun exporting Ford Figos from India to South Africa. Recent investments, combined with the massive presence of Subaru in India, have pushed India ahead of Japan as the largest global producer of "basic" low-cost cars. Thailand and Indonesia have also seen a surge in new investment. Ford has designated Thailand as its export hub to the ASEAN (Association of Southeast Asian Nations) region and is in the process of constructing a new assembly plant there, and Volkswagen is constructing its first assembly plant in Jakarta.

However, while new growth is likely to be concentrated in countries like China, India, and Brazil, most experts agree that the lion's share of automotive production and sales will take place in North America, Western Europe, and Japan for the near future. The clustering of skilled labor, sunk capital, and well-established supply bases in combination with political pressure push assemblers and suppliers to continue investing in or near traditional manufacturing regions. Indeed, after a brief hiatus following the automotive crisis, new productive investment has resumed in the US. Kia opened a plant in West Point, Georgia, in 2009 to produce Sorento crossovers and is currently expanding the plant to build sedans. After decades of producing exclusively in

Mexico, Volkswagen is opening an assembly plant and supplier park in the US. VW's complex in Chattanooga, Tennessee, will start producing midsize sedans in 2011. And Toyota has restarted production of Corollas at its new plant in Tupelo, Mississippi.

The Detroit Three are also building new capacity. GM is investing $336 million to retool its Detroit-Hamtramck plant to produce the Volt as part of its new "green" strategy.[24] Chrysler is investing $600 million to retool its Belvidere, Illinois, plant, replacing the Dodge Caliber with a new small car. Detroit assemblers also remain heavily invested in SUVs. With demand spiking for these vehicles once again, particularly for smaller crossovers, assemblers are restarting production at shuttered plants. GM is currently developing the next-generation Cadillac Escalade and Chevy Suburban, because it argues there are still few major players in this segment of the auto industry. In December 2010, Ford announced it was investing $600 million in its Louisville, Kentucky, plant to build small SUVs.

In addition to new investment, US assemblers have been raking in profits since the crisis. Ford actually gained market share in 2009 and 2010, posting its highest profit in a decade to become the world's most profitable auto company. GM's November 2010 IPO illustrates perhaps best of all the upswing of the industry. It pulled in over twenty billion dollars in the offering, signaling a growing investor confidence in the future of the company, and the US auto industry. GM is also developing a new finance subsidiary called GM Financial to offer leases and subprime loans in an effort to sell more vehicles and compete with its former subsidiary GMAC (now called Ally).[25]

So then, what has been the impact of the automotive crisis for the Detroit Three? The crisis forced the industry to regroup after the boom of the 1990s fizzled and easy credit conditions disappeared. US firms in particular have had to readjust after their trucks and finance strategy proved unable in the long run to prop up the rest of their operations. But this evolution has not been earth-shattering—the "new" US auto manufacturers are essentially slimmer versions of the old ones. Using the financial assistance and authority of the US state, they've simply eliminated some unprofitable lines and cut their costs faster than they would have otherwise, allowing a rapid turnaround to profitability. Although credit is less available, US firms will continue to rely on finance as a source of profit and cushion against the cyclicality of the industry.

They are also moving slowly into the (notoriously unprofitable) small car market and will continue to focus on SUVs, with a slight shift toward smaller SUVs.

Recasting the recent crisis in a historical context shows that it is part of a continual process of "creative destruction" in the auto industry over the past three decades, with firms opening plants, closings plants, buying companies and then spinning them off later. Rather than an overall pattern of decline, or an abrupt shift after the crisis, the dynamics of the industry are better understood as a continual process of reorganization. The inherent cyclicality of the industry combined with rising competition both in the US and globally suggests this kind of restructuring will be a permanent feature of the industry.

CRISIS FOR LABOR

When Chrysler and GM asked the US government for financial assistance in late 2008 the public response was unenthusiastic to say the least. A wide spectrum of voices blamed the industry crisis on high-cost labor, with the general sentiment: "US taxpayers should not bail out the UAW."[26] This perspective was echoed by the US government. When it did finally agree to extend Treasury money to GM and Chrysler, one of its main conditions was that the assemblers restructure their labor agreements to match those at nonunion assemblers in the US. This is ultimately what has occurred. By the spring of 2009 the UAW had agreed to implement a tiered wage system for all new hires in which wages were cut in half to around $14.50 an hour, a six-year wage freeze on all new GM and Chrysler hires, a strike ban until 2015 for Chrysler and GM workers, the elimination of the Jobs Bank, and a host of other concessions.[27]

This victory of capital over the UAW was a long time coming. While the industry has been cyclical with its upswings and downswings in sales and production, and constant restructuring, the situation for autoworkers since at least the 1980s has been a steady downward trend in terms of unionization rates, bargaining power, and workplace rights. Just as the recent financial crisis allowed US assemblers to quickly restructure their productive operations, it also gave them an opportunity to speed up the dismantling of their labor agreements. They used the shock of the financial crisis and swift downturn in the auto industry to extend concessions originally applied only to certain groups of the

UAW to the whole membership. In this section we will embed the recent crisis and its impact in the broader narrative of decline and disorientation experienced by US autoworkers over the past three decades. A crucial factor in the weakening position of US autoworkers has been the restructuring of the industry described above. The influx of new, nonunion investment, coupled with significant movement of production to low-wage sites in the US South and Mexico, has put a great deal of pressure on unionized workers. The influx of nonunion, foreign suppliers has been particularly damaging. By the 1990s, US assemblers could for the first time legitimately threaten to outsource components, modules, and even whole systems away from their in-house parts suppliers and workers to new companies, often located only a short distance away. In the 1970s and increasingly in the 1980s, the Detroit Three began sourcing many low value-added products, like wiring harnesses and spark plugs, from low-wage plants in the US South or Mexico, but remained dependent on in-house parts manufacturers for more complex and higher value-added components. The influx of tier-one suppliers like Bosch and Denso in the 1990s and 2000s, and rising competition among supplier firms, allowed US firms to shift the power dynamic and demand major concessions from workers (and suppliers) at the local level in exchange for the "right" to continue making a product.[28]

De-verticalization has been compounded by the inability of the UAW to organize new investment by assemblers and suppliers. While the total number of jobs in the US auto industry stayed relatively constant from 1950 to 2005, dropping in the years since, the number of unionized workers has declined sharply over the past three decades. This is partly a result of dramatic productivity gains at the Detroit Three—they simply need fewer workers to produce the same number of cars—and partly a result of outsourcing and Detroit's decreased market share. Although estimates vary, the US auto industry today is between 30 and 50 percent unionized, compared with 90 percent in the early 1980s. UAW membership dropped from 1.5 million in 1979 to just 557,099 at the beginning of 2006. Today it is less than 350,000, with about two-thirds of membership actually employed in the auto sector. New investment simply hasn't been unionized. Suppliers created two hundred thousand jobs between 1990 and 2000 alone, but the number of these jobs that are union is negligible. Fewer than 30 percent of suppliers are unionized despite the fact that over 70 percent of production workers in the industry are employed by suppliers.[29]

Rising numbers of nonunion jobs combined with decreasing numbers of union members has isolated unionized auto workers, making them more vulnerable to concessions, particularly at the local level. UAW attempts to stem trends of outsourcing and attrition through the development of cooperative relationships with the Detroit Three have proven ineffective. This has pushed local unions to negotiate directly with assemblers to save jobs. Throughout the 1990s unionized locals agreed to reorganizing production, implementing work teams and flexible "production cells" in exchange for promises of investment in plants and new products. But these moves have rarely prevented outsourcing and have ultimately undercut the union's power in a classic divide-and-conquer scenario.

The dismantling of worker gains at Delphi is an important example of the weakening of the UAW because it served as a template for concessionary bargaining prior to and during the recent auto crisis for the workers at the Detroit Three.[30] Delphi is the former in-house parts manufacturer for GM. It was consolidated during the 1990s and spun off as an independent entity in 1999, making it for a time the largest supplier in the world. Delphi workers were members of the UAW and at the time of the spin-off were covered under the same contract as GM.

With Delphi's primary customer GM's market share sliding and the UAW national contract up for renegotiation in the fall, in early 2003 Delphi began publicly complaining about its labor costs, citing high wages and legacy costs as major impediments to future growth. The company had readily matched the GM contract in the 1999 negotiations and had even given hourly workers a raise, but by 2003 it was calling for a new order. It argued that if it could cut its workforce by five thousand and implement a tiered wage structure, it would be competitive with nonunion suppliers in the US like Johnson Controls and Lear.[31] The UAW agreed. Using an undemocratic "supplemental agreement" to the national contract, Delphi and the UAW executive board negotiated the tiered structure in 2004, in which new workers would be paid half the wage of existing workers. In return for its cooperation Delphi promised to keep open three "threatened" plants in Michigan, Alabama, and Kansas.[32]

A year later, after Delphi was charged with fraud by the Securities and Exchange Commission for systematically "overstating its assets and understating its liabilities," the company again demanded concessions.[33] It brought in Steve Miller—the CEO known for taking Bethlehem Steel into bankruptcy, dumping its pensions onto the Pension Benefit Guaranty Corporation, and cutting off health insurance for retirees—to pressure workers to reopen their contract. Miller argued that if Delphi couldn't reach agreements with GM and the UAW to cut its labor costs substantially, it would not last until the 2003 UAW contract expired.[34] It proposed cutting wages to ten dollars an hour, eliminating cost-of-living allowances (COLA) and the Jobs Bank, and reducing benefits, vacations, and holidays.[35] The company also wanted greater leeway to hire temporary workers. Miller famously quipped: "Globalization has taken away the ability to have someone who mows the lawn or sweeps the floor get $65 an hour."[36]

When Delphi declared bankruptcy in the fall of 2005, the message to workers was the more cuts the union provided, the more factories Delphi would keep open and vice versa. The Delphi bankruptcy was the biggest bankruptcy to date in the auto industry and workers (and the UAW) were under enormous pressure to make concessions. As the editor of *Automotive News* presciently opined:

> Whether the unions willingly negotiate or the bankruptcy court voids Delphi's labor agreements . . . wages and benefits will be cut, plants will close and workers will lose their jobs. It is inevitable. . . . [T]here is no way to stop what is part of the natural order because protectionism cannot work. . . . Once the new competitive equilibrium is set during the Delphi reorganization, it will become the standard for other suppliers and the bogey for the Big 3 when they head into bargaining in 2007.[37]

The UAW yielded to the pressure, negotiating a "special attrition program" in which twenty-four thousand jobs were cut, and all new hires were temporary or second-tier workers. After the agreement the company went on a hiring spree of temporary workers in places like Milwaukee and Alabama. Delphi went further with its demands, filing a request with the bankruptcy judge to cancel its labor agreements with the remaining workers unless they agreed to additional concessions. The UAW ultimately approved the elimination of COLA, the Jobs

Bank, and defined pensions, and agreed to the sale or closure of twenty-four plants in the US.

Although various industry and bankruptcy experts challenged the validity of the filing and the financial crisis at Delphi, the company's actions elicited little opposition from the UAW leadership.[38] In fact, the UAW didn't even show up to court on the day of the filing. The union accepted that previous gains were no longer sustainable. Speaking to rank and filers in 2006, UAW President Ron Gettelfinger argued: "This isn't a cyclical downturn. The challenges we face aren't the kind that can be ridden out. They're structural changes, and they require new and farsighted solutions."[39]

These "farsighted solutions" have since become apparent. The UAW's failure to resist Delphi's concessionary demands laid the groundwork for an almost-identical scenario at the Detroit Three. As predicted, during the 2007 contract negotiations Detroit made a push to extend the Delphi concessions to unionized assembly workers across the industry. Again the UAW went along, agreeing to tiered wages and a separate health and pension plan for new "noncore" workers such as materials movers, general stores managers, and finished vehicle drivers. Wages for noncore work were modeled after the second-tier wages negotiated at Delphi. The UAW also agreed to take on healthcare responsibility for workers and retirees through its VEBA, removing the costs from Detroit's books.[40] Despite these concessions, when GM and Chrysler asked the US government for financial assistance in late 2008, the UAW was publicly excoriated. According to the White House press secretary, Detroit had "unworkable labor contracts" and was operating under an "obsolete business model." Politicians argued that unionized labor "had brought the industry to its knees," its "affluent wages and benefits prevent[ing] the Detroit automakers from successfully competing."[41]

A key condition for receiving financial assistance from the US state was that GM and Chrysler "make every effort to achieve labor cost parity with the [nonunion] transplants."[42] In particular it demanded that GM and Chrysler "(1) achieve total compensation packages (wages and benefits) competitive with transplants, (2) apply work rules that are competitive with transplants, and (3) eliminate any compensation or benefits, other than customary severance pay, to employees that have been fired, laid off, furloughed or idled."[43] These demands by the state put the UAW in a very tough position. By saying that worker concessions were the only way GM and Chrysler would survive, the US state made it nearly impossible to construct an alternative that wouldn't isolate the UAW further.

The UAW ultimately agreed to concessions in May 2009 that expanded the 2007 givebacks.[44] The new concessions extended second-tier (half-pay) wages to all new hires, loosened restrictions on the use of temporary workers, cut supplemental unemployment benefits (SUB pay), eliminated COLA, froze wages for new workers at GM and Chrysler for six years, and barred GM and Chrysler workers from striking until 2015. Despite these concessions the Treasury determined that the companies had still not implemented satisfactory viability plans and required them to declare bankruptcy. The bankruptcy restructuring compounded the concessions by closing plants and forcing workers to compete for the remaining jobs. The bankruptcy restructuring also deepened autoworkers' dependence on Detroit's profitability because it transformed the UAW and the VEBA into a partial "owner" of GM and Chrysler.

While the industry has rebounded in the two years since the crisis, the situation for autoworkers has only worsened. The experience of workers at GM's Lake Orion, Michigan, plant is telling. As part of its post-bankruptcy agenda to develop profitable small cars, GM decided to retool the idled plant to build the subcompact Aveo and compact Verano. However, GM and the UAW Executive negotiated a secret agreement in which only 60 percent of laid-off employees would be brought back at tier-one wages. The rest of the workforce would be forced to come back at a second-tier wage of $14.50 an hour, stay on layoff, or transfer two hundred fifty miles to GM's Lordstown plant. This came as a shock to workers who voted in 2009 to extend second-tier wages only to new hires. The justification for this new arrangement was that in order to produce a profitable small car, the UAW and GM had agreed to "work together . . . to arrive at innovative ways to staff these operations" in the 2009 contract.[45] Apparently "innovative" staffing is code for low-cost labor.

These trends are likely to continue. GM and Ford recently announced that they will hire at least thirty-six thousand new workers over the next few years, all at a second-tier wage. With demand having rebounded, factories are running all out with workers clocking maximum overtime. Under the current national contract Detroit can hire up to 25 percent of their total workforce at second-tier wages.[46] In addition, Detroit is implementing strategies targeted at individual plants to lower labor costs and expand its second-tier workforce. For example, at a parts plant in Saginaw, GM workers voted to "buy down" their wages. Workers would receive a forty-thousand-dollar payout if they agreed to decrease their wages from $18.50 to $12 an hour.

And with many workers making half what they used to, GM has announced that it will invest more in labor-intensive production because its costs are more manageable now that the UAW allows a range of employment options including tier-one and tier-two workers, flex workers who work two to three days a week, temporaries and workers on "temporary assignment."[47] GM has also opened a nonunion plant in Brownstone, Michigan, near Detroit, to produce lithium-ion batteries. It is GM's first nonunion plant in over three decades. Of the thousands of laid-off workers in the area, none were called in to the plant. This is significant because GM claims to be channeling its resources toward this kind of technology in the future. Is nonunion production its future too?

One thing is certain. The recent crisis has meant something very different for workers and capital. After years of complaining about the drag of labor costs, US assemblers have finally managed to downgrade their working conditions to match nonunion plants. After the concessionary model proved easy to implement at Delphi—not a single workday was lost in opposition—it was only a matter of time before it was extended to workers at the Detroit Three. When the industry hit the skids in 2008, Detroit and the US government seized the opportunity, reversing nearly every gain unionized autoworkers made in the post–World War II period.

Thus, instead of conditions at nonunion foreign assemblers improving over the years to match those of US assemblers, US assemblers in partnership with the US state have simply pushed down working conditions to match those of nonunion firms. GM now pays only $2 more per hour in labor costs than Toyota, compared with industry estimates of over $30 an hour in recent years.[48] And new assemblers feel little pressure to offer wage parity. Wages at the Hyundai plant in Alabama and the Kia plant in Georgia start at about $15 and max out at $21 an hour. Volkswagen's Chattanooga workers will start at $14.50 and top out at $19.50, with workers in the supplier park making about $10 an hour. But nonunion autoworkers aren't complaining. West Point,

Georgia—the site of Kia's new assembly plant—was once a textile town, until textile firms abandoned the town in favor of low-wage sites outside the US. Kia jobs are a godsend compared with available service jobs. The plant received forty-three thousand applications for the original twelve hundred assembly jobs.

While Detroit has been working toward this outcome for years, it's worth emphasizing that the US government played a direct role in the restructuring and forced concessions. Its demand for work rules and wages to match nonunion firms effectively negates the right of workers to collectively bargain to better their wages and working conditions. Work in the auto industry is dangerous, grueling, and alienating. The gains that autoworkers achieved over the years mitigated the difficulties of the job to a small degree and allowed workers to support a family and send their kids to college. On second-tier wages UAW families are eligible for food stamps. The dismantling of autoworker gains in recent years has also opened the door to similar moves by other manufacturers. Harley Davidson, Mercury Marine, and Kohler have all erected two-tier systems.[49]

BEYOND THE CRISIS

Needless to say the atmosphere at unionized assemblers and suppliers is tense, especially with contract negotiations between the UAW and Detroit coming up in September 2011. Despite the renewed profitability of Detroit, reversing the tiered wage system is not on the agenda for the UAW. The union believes lower wages are essential to Detroit's survival. According to UAW President Bob King, "We know it's pretty hard to support a family and everything on a $15 an hour wage, but we also know that we have to keep General Motors and Ford and Chrysler competitive."[50]

With tiered wages off the table, the UAW is planning a push to organize nonunion plants in the US instead. But it won't try to organize from the ground up as in past failed attempts to organize nonunion assemblers. This time the union will borrow a tactic from the Service Employees International Union (SEIU) and try to convince nonunion assemblers like Nissan and Toyota to voluntarily sign a "non-disparagement agreement," in which each side agrees not to censure the other during the campaign, thus promoting a fear-free election environment. The UAW believes that workers are afraid to join the union because the company will move to a low-wage, nonunion site if they do. By establishing neutrality and emphasizing the UAW's mission to "add value" and promote the employer's success, the union believes both auto manufacturers and workers will see the benefit of the union. If auto manufacturers do not agree to neutrality agreements, the UAW plans to pressure them through a political smear campaign highlighting assembler abuses in the US and abroad.[51]

The deep-seated anti-union attitude of foreign assemblers in the US makes the viability of this plan doubtful. Foreign assemblers like Nissan and Honda have taken great pains to avoid unions. It seems highly unlikely that now, when their market share is strong, their brands are popular, and the UAW is the weakest it has been in decades, that they will voluntarily invite the union in. But, whether the plan is practical or not, the nature of the strategy indicates a deeper problem within the UAW. The underlying premise is that workers are too afraid of capital flight to organize, so instead, the union will bypass the rank and file and go directly to management to ask its permission to unionize the plant. This not only destroys the potential of empowering rank-and-file workers, but also justifies management's use of capital flight and plant closure to repress workers.

While the threat of plant closure is real—workers do lose jobs to capital mobility and imports—it is necessary to put globalization and capital mobility in perspective. As we showed in the first part of this essay, the restructuring of the auto industry over the past three decades is not a simple globalization story of investment leaving for low-wage sites. Instead, it has been a story of constant restructuring with growth and decline occurring simultaneously in time and space. By not challenging popular accounts of globalization and capital mobility in the US auto industry, the UAW gives support to management threats to move if workers unionize or try to protect their rights from concessions. And as the recent crisis highlighted, concessionary bargaining has no end. The more the union gives, the more it is asked to give, dividing workers, undermining solidarity, and destroying the viability of the UAW. The message to both union and nonunion autoworkers should be that the auto industry is here to stay, so workers across the industry must fight to rebuild solidarity and put an end to fear-based repression.

The first place this rebuilding must occur is within the UAW itself. The tiered wage structure, in combination with expanding numbers of temporary workers, has greatly undermined solidarity within the union. Rank and filers in the UAW recognize this fact and have taken the lead in rebuilding solidarity since the crisis. At an Indianapolis stamping plant last year, GM workers, despite heavy pressure from GM and the UAW International, voted overwhelmingly against reopening their contract to allow buy-downs and tiering. And in a historic turnaround, in the fall of 2009 Ford workers voted against a national contract demanding additional concessions. After GM and Chrysler emerged from bankruptcy in 2009 with more concessions than Ford, the company argued that its workers should agree to further concessions to even the score and make Ford more competitive. In particular it demanded limits on the right to strike, a wage freeze, and the removal of restrictions on entry-level hires. But Ford workers had had enough. When Bob King gathered workers together on the shop floor of Dearborn Truck to convince them to vote in favor of the concessions, he didn't get past his first sentence. According to UAW activists, when King asked members if they could hear him, a worker shouted "No!" sparking a chorus of noes, foot stomping, and clapping. King left without another word. The contract was rejected by over 70 percent of membership in production and 75 percent in skilled trades, with some locals rejecting it by 90 percent.[52]

The recent crisis demonstrates that the UAW's strategy to battle neoliberalism and globalization through concessions is untenable. Concessions have been unable to preserve jobs, wages, or benefits, and in the long run have ultimately threatened the very survival of the unionized auto sector. As Marx and Schumpeter emphasized long ago, capital continually reinvents itself. Auto manufacturing in the US will evolve and continue to experience cycles of decline and growth, but it is here to stay. If auto unions are to recover from the crisis they must also reinvent themselves and fight back against fear-based repression. Rank-and-file workers are taking the lead in this process, even as they face opposition from the UAW leadership. To succeed workers must rebuild solidarity within the union by reversing the tiered wage system and demanding equal pay for equal work. And rather than looking for "big" victories like unionizing the foreign assemblers, workers should start organizing drives at the hundreds of nonunion suppliers in the US where workers are desperate for a union. At the same time, workers and the union must also look to the future of the industry and become advocates of more sustainable transportation, placing themselves in the vanguard of green technology development. Doing so will restore the power of autoworkers and in the process help to revitalize the US labor movement.

CRISIS AS CAPITALIST OPPORTUNITY: THE NEW ACCUMULATION THROUGH PUBLIC SERVICE COMMODIFICATION

Ursula Huws

I.

This essay argues that 2008 marked a turning point for international capital, with the financial crisis providing an unprecedented opportunity to embark on a new phase of accumulation, based not on what might be called "primary primitive accumulation" (the generation of new commodities from natural resources or activities carried out outside the money economy) but on the commodification of public services.* In this commodification process, which might be regarded as a kind of "secondary primitive accumulation," activities already carried out in the paid economy for their use value (such as education, or healthcare) are standardized in such a way that they can be traded for profit and appropriated by capital: use value is thereby transformed into exchange value.[1] This secondary form of accumulation is based on the expropriation, not just of nature or unalienated aspects of life, nor of unpaid domestic labor, but of the results of past struggles by workers for the redistribution of surplus value in the form of universal public services. It thus constitutes a *re*appropriation and, as such, its impacts on working-class life are multiple and pernicious.

For the workers actually delivering public services, new forms of alienation are introduced and there is generally a deterioration in working conditions. However, there are also larger implications for workers

---

*   This essay was first published in *Socialist Register 2012* (London: Merlin Press, 2012).

in other sectors, because public sector workers are, in most developed economies, the last remaining bastion of trade union strength and decent working conditions, setting the standards for other workers to aspire to. This means that the erosion of the bargaining position of public sector workers also represents a defeat for all workers in their capacities *as* workers. At an even more general level, past gains are snatched from the working class as a whole (including children, the elderly, the sick, and the unemployed). This last effect cannot, of course, remain invisible and understandably becomes a focus of opposition. However, a political strategy based only on "fighting the cuts" risks giving the impression that it is simply the scale of state expenditure that is in contest, rendering invisible the underlying logic of commodification and the new reality that public services themselves have become a site of accumulation that is crucial for the continuing expansion of international capital. The new reality is one in which large sections of capital actually have a vested interest in an *enlarged* public service sector, but one in which services are standardized and capable of being delivered by a compliant and interchangeable workforce, embedded in a global division of labor and subjected to the discipline of that global labor market. This raises new contradictions for the relationship between the state and capital.

It is increasingly difficult, if not impossible, to separate "finance capital" from "productive capital" either analytically or empirically.[2] I will not attempt here to disentangle the complex interactions between the lead-up to the financial crisis and the restructuring of transnational organizations, or the ways in which the holding companies that own supposedly nonfinancial organizations are increasingly behaving like financial ones. Nevertheless, in order to understand this phenomenon, it is necessary to outline some of the background conditions that have led to the emergence of the new breed of multinational corporations currently waxing fat on the commodification of public services.

II.

The 2008 financial crisis coincided with a crisis of profitability for international capital, which was already undergoing massive restructuring. One aspect of this restructuring was a huge growth in the concentration of capital. The year 2007 represented a peak in global investment flows, with global foreign direct investment (FDI) flows reaching their highest level ever ($1.8 trillion), surpassing the 2000 peak.[3] There was also a record level of cross-border mergers and acquisitions, with the number rising by 12 percent and the value (some $1.6 trillion) up 21 percent on the previous year.[4] The UN Conference on Trade and Development (UNCTAD) estimated that the total sales of 79,000 transnational corporations and their 790,000 foreign affiliates amounted in that year to $31 trillion—a 21 percent increase over 2006—while the total number of their employees rose to some eighty-two million. The 100 largest TNCs, in particular, strengthened their global grip, with combined foreign assets estimated at $570 billion.[5] However, despite this huge growth, the number of greenfield FDI projects actually *decreased*—from 12,441 in 2006 to 11,703 in 2007.[6] This indicates that while the process of concentration was accelerating, there was actually a slowdown in the generation of new production. In other words, the largest TNCs were sustaining their profits not so much as a result of new production but through the cannibalization of preexisting production capacity. Without some new source of commodities from which to generate surplus value, the preconditions were in place for a decline in profitability. When few parts of the world were left outside the scope of global capitalism, where might these new commodities be found?

Associated with this trend was a major reorganization of value chains. Facilitated by a combination of neoliberal trade policies and the widespread introduction of the information and communications technologies that make it easy to relocate economic activities and manage them remotely, the previous decade had seen an acceleration of the trend to modularize business processes in such a way that they could be reconfigured in a variety of different contractual and spatial permutations and combinations. In the late 1990s, "offshore outsourcing" still seemed something of a risky experiment.[7] A decade later it had come to seem such a normal part of business as usual that US and European managers were expected to justify why they had *not* opened call centers in India, shared service centers in Russia, or design studios in Vietnam, alongside their production facilities in China. Most large corporations had systematically anatomized their business processes, broken them down into standardized units and, unit by unit, decided whether to concentrate them on a single site or distribute them around the world, whether to keep them in-house or outsource them, and whether to search for the lowest price or the highest quality or some complex combination of these things. In aggregate, these decisions had brought about major upheavals. By 2008 a new global division of labor had emerged,[8] with new patterns of regional specialization and new corporate and sectoral configurations. As more and more economic activities became tradable, large companies embarked upon a dual process of disaggregation and aggregation, shuffling and reshuffling these activities into new combinations.[9] While some companies continued to focus on their traditional strengths in manufacturing or the extraction of natural resources, others consolidated their positions as suppliers of services. By 2006, one in five (20 percent) of the one hundred largest nonfinancial TNCs listed by UNCTAD was a company providing services, compared with only 7 percent in 1997.

As these huge service companies expanded their markets, the services they supplied became more generic, increasingly developing the character of standard commodities—so standardized that, in many cases, it was possible to supply essentially the same services (for instance IT services, payroll administration, or customer services) to client companies regardless of which economic sector they were in: manufacturing, retail, utilities, or other sectors. Most of their customer companies were no longer, as they might have been in the past, operating in a buyer's market, acquiring bespoke services tailored to their individual needs; rather, they were becoming like shoppers in a chain store, selecting from among a range of standard models offered by the seller. Once such a supply reaches critical mass, a harsh economic logic sets in: the larger the market for these services is, and the more that standardization can be achieved, then the lower the price will become. Soon, even customers whose preference might be to continue to produce these services for themselves in-house, or to buy them tailor-made from a small local supplier, are driven by the relentless logic of the market (in which the relative cost of customization has become exorbitantly expensive compared with the purchase of standard products) to realize that such personalization is a luxury, and to follow the crowd to the cheapest supplier. In IT-based business services, in particular, this logic has been given an extra push through the dominance of standard software packages (such as those supplied by Microsoft) or platforms (such as those supplied by SAP Business Management Systems) and the ways that these may be bundled in with the services supplied by global suppliers of telecommunications, energy, or other infrastructure services. However, IT-enabled industries are by no means the only examples of sellers' markets in the supply of services; large multinational corporations are also increasingly involved in supplying manual labor, either through labor-only subcontracting by temporary employment agencies or through the outsourced provision of, for instance, security, care, or cleaning services. Increasingly prominent among the customers of these service companies, over the past decade, have been public sector organizations.

In the early years of the twenty-first century, these trends reinforced each other, producing a situation whereby large service supply companies (with their own internal global divisions of labor) were desperate to expand. With limited opportunities to grow through acquisition and merger, and markets in many other sectors nearing saturation, the public sector offered a tempting new field for expansion. By 2008, according to a report published by the UK government, outsourced public services accounted for nearly 6 percent of GDP in the UK, directly employing over 1.2 million people, with a turnover of £79 billion in 2007–2008—an increase of 126 percent over the estimated £31 billion in 1995–96. The report dubbed this rapidly expanding sector "the public services industry" (PSI) and noted that, in terms of value added, it "is significantly larger than 'food, beverages and tobacco' (£23bn in 2006), 'communications' (£28bn), 'electricity, gas and water supply' (£32bn) and 'hotels and catering' (£36bn)." This phenomenon is not peculiar to Britain. As a share of GDP, the PSI sector was estimated in that year to be even higher in Sweden and Australia. In absolute terms, the UK PSI market, at £79.4 billion, was second only to that of the United States (at £393 billion), but the sector was nevertheless significant in scale elsewhere, with an estimated value, for instance, of £44.8 billion in France, £32.2 billion in Australia, and £24.7 billion in Spain. If a somewhat-broader definition were to be applied, encompassing former public utilities like post, telecommunications, water, and energy, these figures would be considerably larger.[10]

Large though these sums are, they represent only a fraction of the total value of public services. Despite the neoliberal anti–"big government" rhetoric of the last quarter century, despite the very real cutbacks in services that have been experienced by working people as a withdrawal of state support, and despite the sale of public assets,[11] government spending has risen inexorably in all OECD countries, both in absolute terms and as a percentage of GDP. Whereas in 1960 government spending was on average 28.4 percent of GDP across the OECD, by 1980 this had risen to 43.8 percent, since when it has continued to creep up to reach 47.7 percent in 2009. This varies somewhat by country, with Japan at 39.7 percent, the United States at 42.2 percent, and Canada at 43.8 percent relatively near the bottom of the range, and the Netherlands, Sweden, France, Austria, Belgium, and Italy near the top, each with government spending between 50 percent and 54 percent of GDP. The UK and Germany are close to the average, at 47.2 percent and 47.6 percent respectively.[12] An analysis based on government spending per person produces a different ranking, with the United States (where total government spending is estimated at nearly six trillion dollars) above Italy, Canada, Britain, and Japan, partly because of its much-higher military spending.[13] However the figures are broken down, this represents a potential field for expansion which is staggering in its scale, a market which, ironically enough, with the notable exception of the militarized United States, is proportionally largest in precisely those countries that, as a result of democratic pressure from below, have built the most comprehensive welfare states. This is how social democratic Sweden, regarded by Esping-Andersen[14] and others as having achieved the highest degree of decommodification of any developed capitalist economy, contrived to top the list of countries with the largest share of outsourced government services in 2008: the more decommodification, the more scope for recommodification.

III.

How has this market been levered open? Procurement of services from external providers is not new, of course. For centuries governments have commissioned buildings, roads, bridges, and other "public works," and purchased goods, ranging from paper clips to fire engines, from private suppliers. And for just as long there have been scandals relating to the greasing of public servants' palms by suppliers to acquire these lucrative contracts. However, it is probably most useful to date the origins of the current wave of outsourcing to the early 1980s. In the UK, the Conservative government pioneered two distinctively different forms of privatization. One of these was the direct sale of public assets, originally promoted as sales to individual citizens rather than to companies. The most high-profile of these were the sales of council houses to their tenants and, starting in 1984, of public utilities—telecommunications, gas, and electricity—via widely publicized share issues, which the general public were invited to buy. Associated with the latter, though less well-publicized, was the opening up of telecommunications and energy markets to competition from private companies. The other form of privatization (not involving a total change of ownership) was the government-enforced introduction of "compulsory competitive tendering," first into local government and then into the National Health Service (NHS). While this did not necessarily mean that the services in question *had* to be carried out by external contractors, in-house departments, employing public servants, were now obliged to compete with private companies in order to be able to continue providing the service in question. This brought downward pressure on wages and conditions and introduced a new precariousness: jobs were no longer necessarily "for life" but only guaranteed for the duration of the contract.

This first swathe of competitive tendering involved mainly manual tasks such as construction work, waste disposal, and cleaning, perhaps not coincidentally also the areas where public sector unions were strong, and had demonstrated this strength in the widespread strikes of the "winter of discontent" of 1978–79 that directly preceded Thatcher's election victory. Much of the rhetoric surrounding this enforced outsourcing centered not just on the supposed efficiencies that would be gained through the delivery of services by private companies, unconstrained by the "restrictive practices" of public sector manual unions, but also on a discourse of "enterprise": the external provision of these services, it was claimed, would create openings for new small firms. In reality, the majority of the contracts went to large, often multinational, companies. In 1984–85, for instance, while public attention was focused on the national strike by coal miners—the other group of organized workers directly targeted by Thatcher's Tories—another long-running strike was taking place at Barking Hospital in East London. The striking cleaners at this hospital were employed by a subsidiary of the Pritchards Services Group, a transnational corporation with fifty-eight subsidiaries in fifteen countries, employing seventeen thousand people in 430 hospitals worldwide, including Saudi Arabia, South Africa, New Zealand, France, Germany, and the United

202 SOCIALIST REGISTER READER

States.[15] Interestingly enough, from 1983 to 1994, Thatcher's husband, Denis, was vice-chairman of Attwoods PLC, a large international waste-management company which stood to gain from precisely this form of privatization. A detailed study of the impact of compulsory competitive tendering in local government in the UK carried out in 1993–94 concluded that women were much more adversely affected than men, with female employment in local government declining by 22 percent compared with 12 percent for male employment, as well as a much-steeper decline in earnings for women than for men. There was also a substantial fall in trade union membership. However, the cost implications for the state were actually *negative*. While neoliberal proponents of the policy (in the World Bank, IMF, and OECD, as well as the UK government) were claiming that the policy would bring savings of 20 to 25 percent; in reality the savings averaged only 6.5 percent. In the thirty-nine case study authorities studied, this amounted to an estimated £16 million. However, the estimated total public costs (taking into account lost national insurance contributions and the cost of related unemployment benefit) were estimated at £41 million (of which £32 million was accounted for by women's employment). Extrapolated to a national level, this was estimated at savings of £124 million and losses of £250 million, leading to a net national loss of £126 million.[16]

Each of these forms of privatization had parallels elsewhere. In Europe, Britain played an important role in pushing through a liberalization agenda which led to the compulsory selling off first of national telecommunications providers, then of publicly owned energy companies, and the opening up of postal services to the market. There had been EU regulation of public procurement since 1966 (in Directive 66/683, which prohibited rules favoring national suppliers over foreign ones within the single European market). The turn to neoliberalism brought much-broader deregulation in the mid-1980s. The Single European Act of 1986 introduced a new regime in which open tendering procedures were established as the norm for all public supplies in the EU and negotiated procedures were allowed only in exceptional circumstances. The first Utilities Directive (90/351) removed market access barriers to energy, telecommunications, transport, and water, and in 1992 the Services Directive (92/50) extended the principles that had governed the procurement of goods, works, and public utilities to public services more generally.[17]

. Meanwhile, the Uruguay round of the General Agreement on Tariffs and Trade, which commenced in 1986 and culminated in GATT 1994, brought services (along with capital and intellectual property) within the scope of global trade agreements. The year 1992, in which the International Telecommunications Union was established, initiated an era of global telecommunications deregulation which in turn opened up the enabling infrastructure for cheap global transfer of digitized information. This was also the year in which India was able to start exporting its software services freely, through the removal of export barriers that had originally been designed to protect an indigenous industry as part of an import substitution strategy. In the early 1990s, the stage was therefore set for global companies to provide a range of services across national borders, bulldozing their way through any restrictions that might have been set up to protect national companies or local workforces.[18]

These developments coincided historically with the formal ending of the Cold War after 1989. Not only did this open up the countries of the former Soviet bloc as new markets for Western capital; it also removed any remaining reasons for employers, in collaboration with national governments, to strike the sort of special deals with labor that characterized the third quarter of the twentieth century (variously described as "Fordism," the "golden age," the "postwar Keynesian national welfare state," et cetera).[19]

IV.

The erosion of these special deals forms part of the context of the development of the new global division of labor practiced by the new business services multinationals. Whether these companies achieve their economies of scale by sending jobs to the places where the skills are abundant and cheap ("offshoring") or by bringing cheap labor to the sites where the work is carried out, for instance through the use of migrant workers, they are adopting what is in effect the same strategy: drawing on a global reserve army of labor. Their choices are not, of course, entirely unconstrained. They have to operate within limits set by, for instance, the supply of suitable skills and qualifications; national regulations which restrict the movements of labor, set minimum wages, or impose particular quality standards; and the extent to which the existing labor force is able to put up a fight. Nevertheless, to the extent that employers can draw on alternative sources of labor, this poses a threat to the wages and conditions of existing workforces and acts as a disciplinary force on them.

The existence of this new global reserve army seems directly associated with the long, slow unraveling of labor standards in capitalism's privileged core workforce, with its expectations of job security, promotion, employer-provided pension schemes, paid holidays, sickness compensation, maternity rights, and the other benefits won by workers in the third quarter of the twentieth century. This development cannot, of course, be attributed entirely to the globalization of labor; the direct attacks on organized labor under Thatcher and Reagan, for instance, also clearly played a major role. However the existence of a global reserve army of labor is certainly a major factor in explaining the failure of workers, even workers who have historically been highly skilled and well organized, to resist the deterioration in their working conditions and wages of the last two decades, a deterioration that is clearly measurable in terms of longer hours, worsening physical and mental health, lower purchasing power of wages, loss of pension coverage, and contractual impermanency. It is hard to escape the conclusion that workers' bargaining position with their employers has been severely undermined by the knowledge that there are other workers out there quite capable of doing their jobs.

It should be noted that, in most developed countries, up to 2008 the major exception to this trend of erosion was among public sector workers. In many countries, during the last two decades public sector workers became not just the most strongly unionized part of the workforce,[20] but also nearly the only remaining carriers of a set of models of what decent work might look like. Public sector workers have taken the lead in, for instance, negotiating equal opportunities agreements, trade-offs between time and money that promote a better work–life balance and the reinforcement of standards that place the quality of service to clients higher than financial considerations.

This is not the place to argue whether a single "Fordist model" of postwar industrial relations can be said to have existed. Whatever particular compromises had been struck between capital and labor in differing national contexts, and whatever the extent to which neoliberal policies had already begun to dismantle them during the 1980s, it can be safely asserted that 1989 marked a moment when the pressures to move toward a convergent global employment model began, almost universally, to exert greater force than any countervailing pressures from labor to protect or extend previous gains.

This process has not been entirely negative for all workers, of course. Because of huge disparities between countries and the strongly segmented nature of labor markets, as well as the very different degrees with which labor has been able to resist, these leveling processes have represented a relative improvement for some, even while they have been experienced as a deterioration in wages and working conditions by others. In particular, women and people from Black and ethnic minorities, part-time and temporary workers, and workers in countries with a history of very poor employment protection benefited, for instance, from various International Labour Organization or European directives against discrimination during the 1990s. Nevertheless, an important part of the context of the opening up of public services to the market has been the simultaneous erosion of employment protection and easing of access to a global pool of labor: a reserve army not just of manual workers but also of "information workers" who, thanks to the standardization of white-collar work through the introduction of information and communications technologies, are increasingly able to carry out the tasks that had previously formed part of the job descriptions of civil servants or other public sector bureaucrats. Standardization of tasks and the increasingly generic nature of white-collar labor processes (combined with the ease with which digitized information can be transmitted across distance) have rendered office workers newly substitutable for each other, undermining their bargaining power with employers, whether public or private.

V.

Far from modifying the more pernicious effects on labor of the marketization of public services of the 1980s and early 1990s, the New Labour government elected to power in the UK in 1997 aggressively pursued further privatization. In local government, for instance, it replaced what the Conservatives had called "compulsory competitive tendering" with its own "Best Value" initiative, which placed a legal duty on local councils to secure the most economic, efficient, and effective services and demonstrate that they had compared all their services with those of other private and public providers. It also introduced a regime of continuous audit and control, reducing the scope for the exercise of individual professionalism and workers' ability to respond directly to the needs of clients. While there was less apparent and immediate legal requirement to outsource, the general legal obligations were broader (and some of the penalties for failing to demonstrate "Best Value," just as punitive, if not more so). Perhaps more importantly, the introduction of this policy involved a change of mindset, with local authorities, of whatever political persuasion, being forced into a process of internalizing the values imposed by the system. Even if services were not outsourced, they had to be managed as if they were, with public servants increasingly placed under the discipline of the market. A precondition for making the required comparisons was that services were defined in standardized ways. "Best Value" can thus be seen as one of the drivers of a process of routinization and standardization of tasks, accompanied by the introduction of performance indicators and protocols, enabling them to be monitored statistically and providing the basis for quality standards to be inscribed in the contracts or "service-level agreements" that define the terms on which private companies provide these formerly public services.

Since standardization is a prerequisite for commodification, such New Labour policies thus played a crucial role in the commodification of public services that underpins their transformation into units of exchange in a global market.[21] Local government was not the only target: New Labour also introduced major reforms that developed a market for private companies in the National Health Service,[22] education, prisons, and legal services.[23] In each case, the process of transforming part of a public service into a tradable commodity passes through the same stages: standardization, the creation of demand, persuading the workforce to accept the changes and the transfer of risk.[24] These developments were not, of course, unique to New Labour, or to the UK. However, their enthusiastic endorsement by social democrats in Britain, as in Scandinavia and elsewhere, played an important role in creating a new common sense, whereby it is seen as both natural and inevitable that norms are set by the market.

In the case of complex personal services (such as teaching, nursing, or social work) involving a large body of contextual and tacit

knowledge, communication skill and "emotional work,"[25] the standardization processes that underpin commodification are by no means
easy to achieve, involving many steps during the course of which: tacit
knowledge is progressively codified; tasks are standardized; output
measures are agreed; management processes are reorganized; organizations are broken down into their constituent parts; these constituent
parts are formalized, sometimes as separate legal entities; and mar-
ket-like relationships are introduced between them. All this may well
be preparatory to a change of ownership or an opening up for external
tender. Only when the activity has been actually or potentially transformed into something that can be made or sold by a profit-making
enterprise is the ground prepared for further restructuring in ways that
form part of the normal practices of multinational companies: mergers,
acquisitions, reconfiguration of parts in new combinations, and the
introduction of a global division of labor.[26]

The decade from 1997 to 2007 saw these standardization and internationalization processes proceeding apace. By 2000, an enormous
new array of global protocols and quality standards had been put into
place. These include the ISO quality standards.[27] Here, quality management systems requirements grew from 46,571 in 1993 to 1,064,785
in 2009—a staggering nearly twenty-three-fold increase over a six-
teen-year period.[28] The global growth in environmental standards was
equally dramatic—from 13,994 in 1999 to 223,149 a decade later, a
sixteen-fold increase in just ten years. In the meanwhile, millions of
workers around the world gained certificates accredited by Sun, Ora-
cle, Cisco, Microsoft, or other IT companies, enabling them to enter
a transparent global job market in such a way that their skills were
interchangeable with those of others and clearly understood by employers. It is possible for a newly qualified holder of a Cisco certificate, for instance, to go to a website and discover that it will earn its
holder an average annual salary of US$69,401 in the UK or an aver-
age of US$14,518 in India. Those who cannot sell their skills to large
multinational corporations can auction them to the highest bidder on
websites like oDesk.[29] To give an indication of the scale of the global
reserve army created in this way, it can be noted that just one Microsoft
certificate, the Microsoft Certified Professional was held at the time of
writing by 2,296,561 workers. For an occupation that, as recently as

the 1980s, was the preserve of an elite few with considerable bargaining power,[30] this number is staggering.

VI.

Many of the companies for whose employ these white-collar workers are competing have grown exponentially over the last quarter century, sometimes with origins in the service divisions of manufacturing companies but sometimes with roots in financial or business-services companies. They include Siemens Business Services, Accenture, Capgemini, and Capita, with a historical base in Europe or North America. But they also include Infosys, Wipro, and Tata Software Consultancy, companies that originated in India, at first providing relatively low-level IT services but soon able to move rapidly up the value chain to become global leaders in the supply of offshore business process outsourcing. There are also companies that focus more on the supply of manual workers, such as Manpower and Group 4 Securicor [now G4S], and companies that specialize in certain sectors or types of service (such as Vertex, which supplies outsourced call center services), as well as others that span many types of activity, such as Serco and ISS.

These companies are not passive players in the global economy. They actively market their services to governments and lobby vigorously for an expansion of outsourcing, either individually or through business associations such as, in the UK, the Business Services Association and National Outsourcing Association. Many have consultancy divisions that advise government bodies on how to "modernize" their services, recommending with one hand the sorts of outsourcing strategies from which they, and other companies, benefit with the other. These consultants are particularly active in emerging markets, such as Vietnam,[31] where the large scale of state services offers rich pickings. Serco has even set up a "Serco Institute," which describes itself as "a UK think tank offering research and thought-leadership on the use of competition and contracting in public service reform and the development of sustainable public service markets."[32] Leys and Player have anatomized the extraordinarily aggressive lobbying of the New Labour and coalition governments in the UK that shaped the 2011 proposals for NHS reform.[33]

Increasingly, their market relationship with the governments that are their customers is changing from one where the buyers wield the power to a sellers' market. One of the factors bringing about this shift of power is the changing nature, and ownership, of the skills and knowledge of the workforce. Traditionally, many public service workers (including teachers, social workers, and health workers) have brought a complex array of skills to their work and have been able to exercise a degree of autonomy in responding individually to their clients. Even in highly bureaucratized, rule-driven environments, such as tax offices,[34] many public workers have possessed a considerable amount of specialist knowledge derived from their experience, much of it not written down. The quality of services has therefore depended crucially on the existence of a stable, committed workforce, often with strongly enforced professional and ethical standards developed within communities of practice with a degree of self-regulation.

The processes that form part of the preconditions for commodification involve an analysis of these skills and the tasks associated with exercising them, breaking them down into their component parts, setting explicit standards for their performance, and, often, introducing an elaborated division of labor whereby the more routine tasks are transferred to less skilled workers. Internalized forms of control exercised by workers themselves and monitored either by their own motivation or through feedback from colleagues or line managers are thus replaced by externally dictated ones. This process takes time, often requiring the gradual handover of work to a new, and differently trained, cohort of workers.

It is not only the workforce that has to be retrained, either: service users also have to become accustomed to being treated as consumers in a mass market rather than individual clients. In the early stages of outsourcing, this process is by no means complete. Considerations both of political expediency and of efficiency demand a smooth and seamless transfer, which is experienced by service users as representing in its early stages no deterioration and, if possible, in some respects an improvement, compared with its "wasteful" and "bureaucratic" predecessor. The easiest way to bring about such a transition is to use the same staff to deliver the same service. Thus a typical first outsourcing of any given service (much like a typical corporate takeover) involves not mass redundancies but rather a transfer of personnel from one employer to another. In Europe, this is eased by TUPE, the EU's Transfer of Undertakings (Protection of Employment) Directive (EC Directive

2001/23). This provides legal protection for transferred employees with
respect to their working conditions, including pension entitlements.
TUPE's existence has led to a situation where the trade union reaction
to outsourcing is often not to resist it outright but to focus on ensuring
that transferred employees are fully covered by the TUPE regulations.
Industrial action in public sector outsourcing situations is comparatively rare, though by no means nonexistent.[35] As a result of successive
transfers, in the locations where outsourcing has first taken place, such
as the UK, the skilled workforce of the outsourcing multinationals has
expanded not so much through new recruitment in the labor market
as through transfers. In a department providing IT services, for instance, or a large outsourced call center, sitting alongside each other,
and with very different terms and conditions of employment inherited
from their previous employers, may be found workers whose previous
employment might have been in a variety of different central or local
government departments or in banks, manufacturing companies, or
service companies. Once employed by the outsourcer, they may find
that their work undergoes a further series of changes, with some tasks
moved to other branches of the company in other regions or countries
and, for those remaining, new performance indicators or targets to be
met, and new requirements to be available at what were formerly regarded as unsocial hours for working. Since outsourcing contracts are
generally of quite a short duration, each contract renewal will involve
further restructuring.

In one case study in the UK, a local government IT department was
first outsourced to a large European-based global IT firm (Company
A). Some employees took redundancy, while others transferred their
employment to this company. After a few years, the contract came up
for renewal and was won by a smaller UK-based company (Company
B). Some of the originally transferred employees remained in Company A, reabsorbed into different roles; some took redundancy; and
some were employed by Company B. Company B was then bought
up by a US-based multinational with a strongly anti-union tradition
(Company C). The remaining workforce (still providing the same IT
service to the same local authority) had thus been employed by four
different employers in less than a decade. Although there did not appear to have been any formal breach of TUPE regulations, there had
been a steady decline in the quality of working life and in working

conditions over this period. One worker, whose child was dying of cancer, asked permission of the new management at Company C to work from home a couple of days a week (something that would have been normal under the old local authority collective agreement) and was refused permission by a manager who told him that, "If the work can be done from home, it can be done from India."

Even more invidious for many public sector workers is the shift in values from a public service ethos, where work is felt to have some intrinsic meaning, to a commercial environment where the work leads only to "filling the pockets of the shareholders," in the words of one IT technician. Many have consciously made a choice to work in the public sector, sacrificing promotion possibilities for what is seen as a secure and rewarding job that makes a contribution to the community.[36] They may make disgruntled employees, refusing to acquire the "lean and mean" attitudes that command respect in the multinational companies for which they now work, but to the company, this does not much matter. Once their expertise has been acquired by the company, they can be replaced by a younger, more malleable workforce, grateful for whatever security it can get. In the UK, the Labour government did provide some protection for second-generation employees in out-sourced public services, with a "two-tier" code on terms and conditions in outsourced services that ensured that new employees working alongside former public sector workers received the same pay and pensions. However, this code was withdrawn in December 2010 by the incoming coalition government.[37] A comparison of working conditions in the same occupations in the public, private, and voluntary sectors in the UK, using data from the Labour Force Survey, found that in each case conditions were worse in the private sector. For instance, only 3 percent of prison officers in the public sector have job tenure of less than a year, compared with 11 percent of those in the private sector and 10 percent of full-time healthcare and personal service workers in the private sector work more than forty-eight hours per week, compared with only 2 percent in the public sector.[38]

Once the knowledge of former public sector workers has been stripped and coded and placed in standard databases it can not only be transferred to cheaper employees, it can also be used as an asset by the new employer. For instance, a company that has already gained the experience of running a local government helpline, managing the HR system of a university, supplying the IT to run a tax system, or providing the laundry service for a hospital is then able to market this service aggressively to other potential public customers, in other regions or countries. Commodified workers' knowledge thus provides the raw material for expansion.

VII.

There is now a sufficient accumulation of such knowledge to propel a huge extension in the scope and scale of outsourcing. In the targets of the PSI companies are a wide range of services with education and health seen as offering the greatest scope for growth.[39] A particularly tempting prize is the British NHS, the third-largest employer in the world (after the Chinese Red Army and the Indian State Railways).[40] The aftermath of the 2008 financial crisis has provided exactly the right conditions for such explosive growth. The need to reduce the state deficits (the debts run up by bailing out the banks) legitimates cost cutting and the search for "efficiencies" and economies of scale. This is bolstered by a rhetoric of shrinking the state. A new model is being promoted in which the function of government is no long to deliver services but to procure them. This model has already been enthusiastically taken up by some. For instance, in October 2010, Suffolk County Council in the UK announced plans to become a "virtual council" and outsource all its services, including administrative functions, moving from a directly employed workforce of twenty-seven thousand to around three hundred employees.[41] Barnet Council is already well advanced on this path, with its "Future Shape" policy, announced in 2008, which has been shown to have made few real savings, partly because of the high cost of consultancy, while leading to a drastic drop in the quality of services, as well as job losses.[42] (An even more dramatic, though smaller-scale, example is the tiny city of Maywood in Los Angeles County, which, since July 1, 2010, has had no employees whatsoever, with all its services provided by independent contractors or staff on loan from the neighboring city of Bell).[43]

In the UK, 2010 Tory-Liberal coalition government provided an extreme example of this new thinking. The rhetoric surrounding these developments has been confused, on the left, by a focus on "cuts" that suggests the issue is simply one of the size of the budget devoted to public services, and, on the right, by rhetoric about the "Big Society."

This rhetoric does not speak of handing public assets over directly to multinational corporations to manage (though this option is not excluded) but suggests that they will be taken over by volunteers. The *Modernising Commissioning* Green Paper published by the UK government in 2010 quotes the *Liberal Democrat Manifesto*'s commitment to "support the creation and expansion of mutuals, co-operatives, charities and social enterprises, and enable these groups to have a much greater involvement in the running of public services." It goes on to say that "these reforms are fundamental to achieving the *Power Shift* to which this government is committed, transferring power away from central government to local communities."[44]

To what extent this is a simple smoke screen and to what extent a new role may be opening up for nongovernmental organizations in the provision of services is a moot point. Globally, the role of NGOs has changed considerably in recent years. Not only are many in partnership with multinational corporations in varying degrees of closeness (for instance, the Aga Khan Foundation providing nursing training in Tanzania funded by Johnson & Johnson),[45] many NGOs are entirely funded by multinationals. For example the *New Citizen Life Center*, which provides health services and help with finding employment to destitute migrant workers in the Guijing migrant village in Pudong, on the outskirts of Shanghai in China, is entirely funded by GlaxoSmithKline, where it serves to help promote the company's products as well as to project a positive image of the company in particular, and of capitalism in general.[46] It seems likely that a similar blurring of roles will increasingly take place elsewhere. Even if services are run by NGOs, it is unclear to whom they will be accountable, and how. In the short term, the involvement of voluntary organizations may soften and humanize the impact of the changes; in the longer term, it seems likely that multinational companies will end up taking over the running of any operations likely to be profitable, simply by exploiting the economies of scale they can achieve. There is little question that the main impact of the new approach will be a massive transfer of public assets to corporations that can use them to generate profit. In the process, the public sector workforce will be subsumed into a larger mass of interchangeable labor: dispensable, precarious and—since workers will increasingly be employed by bodies with intermediate positions in shifting global value chains—without a stable framework for collective representation and negotiation.

This situation is not without its contradictions, however. For the state, there are tensions between its role in attracting and controlling capital on its territory on the one hand and, on the other, its role in opening up a new field of expansion for capital. Within national ruling elites, there are tensions between those who want a smaller role for governments, tout court, and those (representing the companies that profit from supplying public services) who would like to see an enlarged public sphere, albeit one that is opened up for profit. There are also contradictions between the national interest in preventing unemployment from reaching unmanageable levels and the interest of global companies in searching out the cheapest workforce, wherever it may be based. What is clear, however, is that if workers are to claw back any returns for the working class from the next wave of accumulation (based as it is on the expropriation of their own past collective efforts at redistribution), new forms of organization will be required: forms of organization that recognize the common interests of a global proletariat, with globally organized employers.

THE WALMART WORKING CLASS

Arun Gupta

In April 2012 my partner, Michelle Fawcett, and I were preparing to embark on a road trip around the United States.* We were planning to visit Occupy Wall Street camps as a follow-up to our journey in late 2011 that took us to occupations in twenty-seven different cities. Wanting to avoid eating overpriced, greasy restaurant food, we decided to purchase a cooler, plates, glasses, cutlery, and cleaning supplies to prepare meals out of a car. As many retailers now carry these items, we popped into a CVS in a strip mall outside San Diego. I was struck by how expensive all the items were, which would strain our budget earned from freelance journalism. We decided to try our luck elsewhere, and upon exiting we noticed a Walmart in the distance. "No," I said. "I've never been in a Walmart, and I'm not about to start now." We found a Walgreens and futilely repeated the exercise. "Okay," I muttered as we exited and the Walmart loomed closer. "Let's just check it out." Inside it was a consumer wonderland as everything was half or even a third the price at the other retailers. Soon we were piling our cart with goods. Michelle remarked, as we grabbed twenty-five-cent forks and spoons, "It's so cheap it might as well be free." The whole process was efficient, and we spent fifty dollars for dozens of items, less than a cooler would have cost at the other chain stores.

This was confirmed by my visits to five other Walmart stores since then. Intellectually, I knew Walmart ruthlessly rationalized global

---

*   This essay was first published in *Socialist Register 2014* (London: Merlin Press, 2014).

supply chains, pushed the flight of US manufacturing, and normalized precarious low-wage jobs. But as a consumer I discovered that Walmart is unmatched for the low cost and ease of social reproduction. Or as one worker put it, "Walmart is cheap as shit and it's convenient."

Walmart accounts for about 13 percent of the $2.53 trillion US retail market, and 140 million Americans shop at Walmart weekly, more people than voted for Barack Obama and Mitt Romney combined in 2012. It employs almost 1 percent of the US workforce, with 1.3 million workers, and claims another 3 million US jobs are dependent on it. At 3 percent of US GDP ($466 billion in fiscal year 2013), its net sales were on par with GM's postwar peak. Almost 80 percent of its $27.8 billion in operating profits came from domestic sales ($274.5 billion, plus $56.4 billion for over six hundred Sam's Club outlets). In 2007 the Walmart family wealth was greater than the combined wealth of the bottom 30 percent of American families, and by 2010 it had grown to more than 41.5 percent of all families, making Walmart an unambiguous measure of class polarization in US society.[1]

Walmart aims to offer the lowest-priced goods, relying on high volume to compensate for razor-thin margins, so from the start its model has been to maximize labor productivity by minimizing pay, benefits, and workplace rights. This process has intensified during the economic downturn that began in 2007 as Walmart has cut an average of fifty-seven employees per US outlet.[2] Even as same-store sales have stagnated since 2008, it is increasing profits by cutting staff and benefits, forcing the remaining workers to speed up their work pace through strict time-management software. Internal Walmart memos reveal poorly stocked stores and for six years it has been "placed last among department and discount stores in the American Customer Satisfaction Index."[3] Indeed, Walmart may no longer be able to maintain a significant price advantage over other grocery stores and discount retailers, and is being pressured by Amazon in e-commerce. Walmart is a victim of its own success as it has eliminated "a raft of salesmen, jobbers and other supply-chain middlemen, squeezed the manufacturers by shifting every imaginable cost, risk, and penalty onto their books, and taught the entire retail world how the bar code and data warehouse could finally put real money on the bottom line."[4] To add just twenty-four full-time employees per US store would cost it $2.1 billion, or 10 percent of its domestic profits.

This is the context in which a new struggle by Walmart workers—the national campaign led by Organization United for Respect (OUR Walmart) and the Chicago-based Warehouse Workers for Justice (WWJ) and its organizing arm, the Warehouse Workers Organizing Committee (WWOC)—has emerged since 2009. It was very much on the minds of the eleven Walmart retail and warehouse workers with whom I conducted in-depth interviews in May and June 2013. While the only workers I found willing to talk were disgruntled—using terms like "prison," "serfs," and "company town"—and expressed contempt for Walmart as an employer and shopping destination, evidence indicates discontent is widespread. As if confirming what interviewees told me about being "overworked," and "pulled in too many directions," one former Walmart store manager explained to the *Huffington Post*: "People don't line up for those jobs. You can make the same thing at a 7-Eleven or flipping burgers but you don't have to work nearly as hard."[5] A 2011 survey of 501 "associates" (as Walmart calls its workers) found "84 percent say they would take a better job if they could find one."[6]

Despite having been told or believing that any attempt to unionize or even discuss unions at work would result in being fired, all eleven workers are pro-union. One is organizing his workplace as part of OUR Walmart, and all four warehouse workers participated in a semi-successful 2012 strike against Walmart and its subcontractors in massive distribution facilities outside of Chicago. OUR Walmart and WWOC coincide with organizing efforts in Walmart warehouses in New Jersey and California, the Walmart supply chain along the Gulf Coast, and the national "Fight for $15" campaign—an unabashed drive by the Service Employees International Union (SEIU) to unionize low-wage workers with the slogan "$15 and a union." One burning question before the left today is whether these campaigns in the low-wage sectors can revitalize the American labor movement, especially after the Occupy Wall Street movement injected class politics back into popular discourse with talk of the 99 percent and the 1 percent.

THE WALMART EFFECT

Walmart's uniqueness as a general discount merchandizer by the beginning of the twenty-first century could be measured by its annual revenue—more than the next-four-largest global retailers combined.[7] Founded as a discount retailer in 1962—the same year as more than twenty other retail chains began discount operations, including Kmart and Target—it soon compelled "many competitors and suppliers . . . to adjust their business models to conform to Walmart."[8] It "forced its suppliers to cut costs, made it more difficult for companies to compete on any terms other than price, and made it close to impossible for manufacturers and service providers to pass on the cost of improvements in products and services to consumers in the form of price increases."[9]

Taking advantage of new technology, as well as "concentration in the retail sector and the rise in global competition in suppliers" industries," Walmart pioneered the late-twentieth-century merchant-led "drive to rationalize market institutions."[10] This logistics revolution induced a shift from a "push" system "dominated by large consumer-goods manufacturers [with] long production runs in order to gain efficiencies of scale and minimize unit costs" to a "pull" system in which retailers used bar codes, scanners, and computers to scrutinize point-of-sale consumer behavior and share that information with vendors to "coordinate production with actual sales, minimizing inventory buildup anywhere in the chain . . . which cuts costs for both manufacturers and retailers." By acting as a monopsony, which can set prices for vendors, and by becoming an operations specialist with "core competencies" in "purchasing, warehousing, distribution, [and] trucking," Walmart devised an answer (along the lines of Japan's just-in-time production system) to capitalism's chronic "disjuncture between production and distribution, or supply and demand." It has "organised and rationalized global supply chains; established trade standards and logistics solutions, and even ventured into product development."[11]

Given Walmart's role as a motor force in "American-led globalization" and as the largest private sector employer of African Americans, with two hundred fifty-five thousand associates in 2013, the origins of its proletariat and ideology are steeped in irony. Walmart was founded in the Ozarks, the populist "heartland of anti-monopolism" and movement against chain stores. Sam Walton tapped into populist discontent by promising to keep "Ozarks dollars in the Ozarks," and later positioning Walmart as "a populist multinational." While the nineteenth-century Populist movement was anti-corporate to the bone, it supported government largesse to promote economic activity, "so long as it acted on behalf of the mythic original citizen, the yeoman." Walmart benefited from this history, as well as the New Deal, which served as a welfare state for whites by excluding "African Americans from the new federal bounty [like] Social Security, minimum wages, healthcare, [and] education." New Deal credit programs "subsidized free enterprise" in the underdeveloped South, a process that spread during the Cold War as federal money flowed to employers that were allowed to deny social claims. And the Labor Management Relations Act of 1947, known as Taft-Hartley, encouraged Sun Belt states to pass anti-union "right-to-work" legislation, with Arkansas becoming one of the first to pass such a law.[12]

Along with these elements, Walmart benefited from a racially homogenous Ozarks that witnessed anti-Black pogroms around the turn of the twentieth century. Walmart was founded in the early sixties in Benton County, Arkansas, "which had but 23 blacks, most elderly servants." This helped it dodge civil rights protests targeting anti-integration businesses. Almost all of its first hundred stores were in this "homogenous homeland" that "precisely coincided with the territory that had generated so many sundown towns" starting in the 1890s. Walmart was an economic and cultural lifeline for "farm wives and daughters displaced by the agricultural revolution," not unlike the "Lowell Mill girls of the early nineteenth century." Combined with the dominant Christian and patriarchal culture, Walmart enclosed "a rural Protestant family ideology and a female work culture based on 'people skills.'" It replaced the male-dominated industrial economy with a "patriarchal organization of work" that extended from the store floor to apparel sweatshops. "The industrial economy's scorn for women's work skills meant they could be had for a bargain price." By offering social value to rural women entering the workforce, while emphasizing "Every Day Low Prices" for the same women looking to economize in service to their family, Walmart generated unusual loyalty while exploiting underpaid female workers. From the start Walton squeezed labor costs by creating shell companies to evade minimum-wage laws in the 1960s.[13]

During its explosive growth in the 1970s and '80s, Walmart took advantage of inflation spikes to attract newly price-conscious consumers, as well as global trends toward waning union strength and labor process restructuring, including the "deskilling" and "reskilling" of jobs.[14] Walmart is also a virtuoso in manipulating regulation. It benefited from the 1970s property tax revolt as local governments turned to siting big-box retailers to increase tax revenue, and it aggressively sought development subsidies, with one study uncovering more than one billion dollars in public largesse by 2004, while systematically challenging property tax assessments to reduce payments to local governments.[15] At the heart of Walmart's model are distribution centers (serving up to 150 retail stores to keep "commodities in motion" as quickly as possible from manufacturer to stores), which are "built deep in the countryside where wages are low and workers largely anti-union"; and it supplemented this with a profit-sharing system (eliminated in 2011) as a means of not only "linking the employees to the fate of the company, but also justifying the self-exploitation that was integral to the Walmart culture."[16] Its "well-organized anti-unionization policy [which] set the standard for other retailers and industrialists" involves taking such union avoidance so seriously that it "maintains a staff of 200 in its labor relations department, many available to fly to any store" whenever the "Union Probability Index" (keyed to "factors measuring morale, complaints, turnovers and other problems") hits a prescribed level.[17] The success of this was such that an independent Walmart effect on the economy—and the working class—could be discerned, "where the jobs are traps: low wages, miserly benefits, stultifying work, no respect, no future."[18]

THE WALMART PROLETARIAT

Some economists contend the Walmart effect is positive because benefits accrue to all of society, particularly to low-income households that can save up to 25 percent on food costs from lower prices offered by supercenters and increased competition with other supermarkets.[19] It was also claimed that Walmart was single-handedly responsible for much of the late-1990s surge in US productivity because its "success forced competitors to improve their operations."[20]

Whatever the accuracy of such claims, they sidestep the role Walmart has played in shifting working-class employment from stable medium-wage jobs to a precarious low-wage service sector. Walmart's assertion that it "create[s] quality jobs," or any jobs for that matter, does not hold up to scrutiny.[21] The most detailed study of Walmart's effects on local labor markets found that each Walmart job cost 1.4 retail-sector jobs, or nearly 150 jobs on average in affected counties. There was "a 2.7 percent reduction in retail employment attributable to a Walmart store opening," as well as "declines in county-level retail earnings of about $1.4 million, or 1.5 percent."[22] The Walmart effect is especially pronounced among supermarkets whose unionization rates were traditionally much higher than general merchandizers like Walmart. In 1988 Walmart opened its first grocery store and discount supercenter to capture more revenue as consumers "shop for food on average about 2.5 times a week" compared to once a month at a drugstore or retailer. By 2012 groceries accounted for 55 percent of Walmart's US sales, and by one estimate it has acquired a breathtaking 33 percent market share. One Walmart study revealed that it paid supercenter workers up to $3.50 an hour less than unionized supermarket workers.[23] Thus if Walmart has reduced consumer good prices for the entire US economy, it has also reduced wages and benefits for entire sectors. If a state had fifty Walmarts, which was the average in 2000, wages dropped 10 percent and health insurance coverage shrank 5 percent among all retail workers in that state.[24]

Even if an average family buys all its food, clothing, electronics, and furnishings from Walmart, they will still spend twice as much on healthcare, education, transportation, and housing.[25] Plus, consumers are not purely rational agents who will buy the same amount of goods if they switch to Walmart and pocket the savings. Some vendors discovered their sales increased dramatically after becoming Walmart suppliers with no other explanation than consumers were buying more products, replacing them more often, and consumption was being "driven strictly by price and impulse."[26] By one estimate Walmart has directly pushed twenty thousand families into poverty nationwide.[27] At the same time, and by no means unrelated, Walmart has been fingered as responsible for 10.5 percent of the rise in obesity from 13 percent to 34 percent among Americans from 1960 to 2006 due to innovations "in *distribution* technology that lower the prices of food and other consumer goods."[28]

With its anti-union, low-wage strategy, Walmart exploited neoliberal "attacks on the welfare state, deregulation, and increased international free trade that began in the 1970s."[29] Just like nineteenth-century industrialists who pitched free trade as a boon for workers,[30] Walmart fiercely pushed the North American Free Trade Agreement (NAFTA) and subsequent free trade agreements, claiming this would lower prices and create jobs. Instead it accelerated the loss of US manufacturing and middle-income jobs.[31] The relation between lower-cost goods and lower wages is symptomatic of an era that's "a golden age" for corporate profits. During the third quarter of 2012, corporate profits' share of national income reached 14.2 percent, "the largest share at any time since 1950, while the portion of income that went to employees was 61.7 percent, near its lowest point since 1966."[32]

No less than 26 percent of US private sector jobs, held by 29.1 million workers, pay less than ten dollars an hour, and most of these jobs are precarious.[33] The low-wage workforce includes both the poor and "near poor"—those who earn up to 200 percent of the poverty threshold—which together number 106 million Americans, or 34 percent of the US population. Of 10.2 million families (47.5 million people) classified as working poor, an estimated 61 percent "had a high housing cost burden," meaning they spent more than 33 percent of their income on housing, while low-income families spent 8.6 percent of their income on gasoline as opposed to 2.1 percent for higher-income families. As of 2011, 48.6 million Americans lacked health insurance, including 28 million workers.[34]

Walmart associates average $8.81 an hour, more than cashiers average at Target and Kmart, $7.96 and $7.59 respectively.[35] An internal wage guide dated February 2012 "details a rigid pay structure for hourly employees that makes it difficult for most to rise much beyond poverty-level wages."[36] The wage guide was developed to cut costs and provide objective measures for pay "as a response to a landmark class action lawsuit, *Dukes v. Walmart Stores Inc.*, which accused the company of discriminating against women in pay and promotion."[37] (That suit was dismissed by the US Supreme Court in 2011.) The guidelines create an incentive to push out higher-waged workers. Walmart acknowledged this in a 2006 internal memo: "[T]he cost of an Associate with 7 years of tenure is almost 55 percent more than the cost of an Associate with 1 year of tenure, yet there is no difference in his or her productivity."[38]

In 2013 Walmart admitted "disproportionately" hiring part-time workers without fixed hours, possibly to circumvent the Affordable Care Act that would, starting in 2015, require businesses with more than fifty workers to offer health insurance to employees who work at least thirty hours a week.[39] In fact, a Walmart memo from 2005 explicitly laid out a strategy for slicing healthcare costs by "hiring more part-time workers and discouraging unhealthy people from working

at Walmart."[40] This memo exposed the fact that in 2004 the number of Walmart associates and their children on Medicaid was about
25 percent higher than the national average. They spent 8 percent of
their income on healthcare, "nearly twice the national average," and
38 percent of enrolled employees spent more than one-sixth of their
income on healthcare. It noted Walmart "workers are getting sicker
than the national population, particularly with obesity-related dis-
eases" like diabetes and heart disease.[41] Ironically, the Supplemental
Nutrition Assistance Program benefits (food stamps)—which one in
seven Americans receive and amounted to $74.6 billion in 2012—is a
vital source of revenue for Walmart, which admits that a "significant
percentage of all SNAP dollars are spent in our stores"; nine of its
supercenters in Massachusetts received $33 million in SNAP in one
year; and in Oklahoma it raked in 42 percent of all SNAP monies
($506 million) over one twenty-one-month period.[42] In Wisconsin, it
has been estimated that a worker in a three-hundred-employee Walmart supercenter requires at least $3,015 and up to $5,815 in public
aid once subsidized school meals, childcare, housing, energy assistance,
food stamps, healthcare, and tax credits are taken into account.[43] The
shreds of social welfare that backstop millions of service sector workers
thus also subsidize Walmart as well as other big global corporations like
McDonalds, Wendy's, and Burger King. "Walmart transfers income
from the working poor and from taxpayers through welfare programs
directed at the poor to stockholders and the heirs of the Walmart fortune, as well as to consumers."[44]

Ultimately, "Walmart management may well have more power than
any other entity to 'legislate' key components of American social and
industrial policy."[45] And this includes shaping a workforce that serves
its interests—one that is precarious, on the cusp of poverty, lacks any
semblance of workplace rights and minimal social solidarity, and above
all, lives in fear.

WALMART WORKERS SPEAK

Interviews with seven current and former Walmart retail workers
and four warehouse workers (six of whom are twenty-six years old or
younger) flesh out what life is like for this segment of the proletariat.[46]
Everyone said a Walmart store or warehouse is the one place nearly anyone can get work, and often it's a job of last resort. The retail workers

earned between $7.85 and $9.50 an hour, apart from one with eleven years' experience who makes $12 an hour. The warehouse workers made $9 to $11.50 an hour. Their time in the labor force ranges from four to thirty-six years. Each of the retail workers has had at least five jobs, mainly in fast food, retailing, bookstores, supermarkets, convenience stores, telemarketing, and drugstores, while the warehouse workers lean toward physical labor, equipment operators, or trades, though one is currently working in fast food. One former retail worker now earns $35 an hour as a part-time unionized stagehand, and one warehouse worker once made $17.50 an hour as an apprentice electrician, but none of the others ever made over $15 hourly. Most earned under fifteen thousand dollars annually and only one makes above twenty thousand. All describe "anxiety about financial issues." When asked how much they think they should be paid, the range was one to four dollars an hour extra.

One former retail worker and all four warehouse workers lack healthcare; the rest have it through family, spouses, or the government, and one through Walmart. Five retail workers live in multigenerational households of adults, indicative of the 22.3 million shared households, an increase of 13 percent since 2007.[47] Among workers with more than one year tenure, only one receives any paid vacation; two say they are working injured because of the inability to take time off; and three report attempts at wage theft involving managers demanding cashiers stay later to check out customers because of chronic understaffing, and then at the end of the pay period managers pressure workers to delete the overtime and work off the clock. Others say managers would tell them to go home early or take longer lunches to eliminate overtime. One said managers told him to follow the example of other workers who "skip breaks to get their products in the shelves." Five say they were "coached" repeatedly, or written up. Nearly all say they're overworked as a result of understaffing, and that managers can be verbally abusive or condescending, especially in the warehouses. Other than the bakery worker, retail workers know their schedules only two weeks in advance and shifts are unpredictable, which affects their ability to plan their lives. If they take unpaid leave for even a day their hours may be cut. In essence Walmart treats labor as another just-in-time commodity.[48] Steve, forty-four, successfully managed to get his job back after being fired by appealing to higher levels of management on the basis of

Walmart's vaunted "open-door" policy of listening to employee complaints; but he says he had never been fired in more than twenty-five years of working prior to that, and there was a "constant threat of losing your job. They tolerate bad behavior so they can fire them when they don't need them anymore. The whole purpose is not to have to pay unemployment."

Aaron, who lives in St. Petersburg, Florida, says human resources staff at his former Walmart store "made sure to tell everyone if you needed help with housing assistance or food stamps they would help you get that stuff." He echoes other workers when he says employees and customers are captive of Walmart: "It's like the old company town. The minute workers get their paycheck, they spend their money right there." Many are frustrated at being perceived as "stupid" or "dumb" for working at Walmart. "Low wages don't mean low intelligence," says one. Tim Adams, a "Marxist and pro-union" cashier and college student in Columbus, Ohio, says about his coworkers, "there's not much energy, or excitement, or happiness. . . . It does seem like a lot of workers are depressed about their conditions."

Perhaps because they are hidden from public view, the warehouse workers, known as "lumpers," live and toil in particularly onerous conditions. The four I interviewed were all temps, classified as "material movers," and none had paid time off, healthcare, or other benefits. This is the norm in the Chicago area, according to the Warehouse Workers for Justice study "Bad Jobs in Goods Movement": 63 percent of warehouse workers are temps; 78 percent are male; the average wage is $9 an hour, $3.48 an hour less than those who work directly for Schneider Logistics, Walmart's warehouse management firm; and "only 5 percent of temps had sick days and 4 percent health insurance." The four men I talked with are all single and rent houses with other single men or live in a Catholic Worker house, which has aided the organizing effort. Phillip, thirty-eight, said some workers squat in abandoned homes and one lived in a tent in the woods for a few weeks.[49] All four earned under twenty thousand dollars in 2012, and say on workdays lumpers survive on fast food because "you can eat for $5 or $6 a day." One said, "You see a lot of people in the break rooms not eating, and that's the saddest thing you could ever see." Mike, thirty-five, says managers would eliminate breaks "if they said our cartons per hour were too low. I've never seen the quota so vigorously enforced as in Walmart.

You'd be working a fourteen-hour day and they would come by your trailer and say, 'You're eight minutes off pace.'" At age thirty-eight, Phillip has left the industry because "the pace was pretty fast and brutal. It's back-breaking. During the summer it's 120 or 130 degrees in the back of the truck trailer. People routinely fall out in the summer from dehydration or exhaustion. They would pass out, they would have heat strokes. . . . I'm too old. You're in serious pain every day you do that." Joseph, twenty-five, says minor injuries happen every day: "Your shin gets cut, jam fingers, sprain something, neck pulls, back pulls." Nor was management sympathetic, according to James, twenty-six: "The supervisors would basically say, 'You need a job, here's how many boxes you have to throw an hour. You can't do it, we'll find somebody else.'" WWJ's study found one-third of workers were fired or disciplined for reporting injuries.

In any case, few report the injuries, says James, because "they immediately take you for a drug test, and if you fail it you're fired and they don't pay your medical bills." Indeed, James and others say drug use is pervasive. "At least 80 percent do drugs. Most people smoke weed, a lot of people take prescription painkillers on the docks, some people do coke. Adderall was really common. It would focus you and keep you awake." Because of high unemployment and high turnover, warehouse jobs attract everyone from parolees, former union plumbers, carpenters, and machinists to university graduates. Mike, who's worked in warehousing since 1996, says employers "feed off people who are on their last legs, who are struggling. These jobs are easy to get if you have a criminal background. I'd say close to 50 percent of temps have a criminal record. One temp agency specialized in parolees; they bused all of them in. There's guys who've worked there five years and are temps, they're perma-temps. There's no such thing as a raise, no such thing as vacation, no such thing as benefits." All claim wage theft is systematic. Mike says, "Every pay period people would complain about being shorted hours. Sometimes people were missing a whole day on their check. One guy was missing a whole weekend." One of the chief complaints was irregular hours. James says, "You would come in at 6 a.m. and sometimes you'd be sent home in a couple of hours or sometimes you'd be there for fourteen hours." Some temp agencies use a morning "shape up" and regularly send home workers "who drove there from wherever with no pay," which is illegal. He says, "These management tactics are letting you know that you don't have any rights."

This especially applies to women who work in the warehouses, who are not only often paid less but also subject to sexual harassment, assault, and battery by coworkers and supervisors. WWJ spokesperson Leah Fried says, "We surveyed fifty-three women and found about 50 percent reported sexual harassment, and 82 percent reported gender discrimination." When women would report the incidents to management, responses allegedly ranged from, "I didn't see that," to assigning them the most difficult jobs, to supervisors asking the worker "out on a date," to one company allegedly retaliating by accusing a 19-year-old woman of criminal acts with the result she was imprisoned for sixteen days.[50]

Retail workers face their own set of difficulties. Ally is a married 26-year-old female who has worked at a Kentucky Walmart for more than two years. She began working at age sixteen, and makes $8 an hour for thirty-four hours a week, while her husband works in a factory at $17.50 an hour. She's worked in supermarkets and pharmacies, and the most she ever earned was $12.75 an hour. They pay $600 for housing and her husband pays another $600 a month in student loans. "My husband and I argue a lot because we don't have enough money for the bills to go around. We've had to go to McDonald's and take napkins to use as toilet paper for the last week. My shoes fell apart and I had to rubber-band the soles back on. For the two of us we spend fifty dollars a week on groceries, sometimes twenty-five. For lunch I'll bring a Michelina frozen dinner—it costs 98 cents. I would like to eat healthier, but we can't afford to eat healthier. Almost everything we eat is a frozen TV dinner or canned food. Every work shirt has holes in them."

Ally has considerable credit card debt and says ten creditors are demanding one thousand a month in payments total, but she can't afford to hire a lawyer to discharge the debt. "The stress in my life is ridiculous. [The job] is making me mentally exhausted, emotionally exhausted. It sucks you into such a deep rut you can't look for another job." In terms of the workplace, "Walmart is the first place I've worked where no one ever tries to stab you in the back because Walmart does it enough for you. It feels like a prison movie. It feels like the Walking Dead. . . . Every day when I go in, I dread going into work because I have to deal with crap. I don't hate the customers. I hate Walmart because they're an evil corporation. I work my butt off every single day, and they tell you, 'If you work hard, we'll promote you,' and that's not true."

As for workplace issues, Ally has an irregular schedule, often works weekends and holidays, and has not accrued vacation time in two years. She can take unpaid days, but says, "[When] I requested one day off, they scheduled me only for two days the next week." She pulled a muscle in her arm at work and has been working injured for two months because her schedule conflicts with doctor's appointments. She complains about understaffing, poorly stocked shelves, and broken equipment around the store. The work is monotonous: "All you do is stand in one spot; you don't do anything." But at the beginning of the month, "you're lucky to get your break. We live in a poor part of town, a lot of people on welfare, WIC, food stamps. There's a big rush when they get their aid. When I ring up other employees almost everyone uses food stamps."

Ally says, "A lot of customers complain" about Walmart's dependence on goods from China, while coworkers complain about schedules, low pay, working on holidays, and the cost of healthcare. Once or twice a month Ally is forced to work through a paid fifteen-minute break. Management has "told us if any employees are heard talking about a union they will be fired." She describes management as abusive: "I've never been at a job where a manager can call you stupid, calls you retarded, screams at people."

Ally previously worked in a unionized supermarket and didn't like paying dues. "I don't think I would get better benefits with a union, because I made minimum wage there." But, she adds, "I'd rather pay union dues and be treated like a human, rather than being treated like an insect. I support OUR Walmart whether they help or not. I'd like knowing someone is standing up to Walmart. We can't just be treated like crap forever." As for the possibility of organizing, coworkers are "afraid of losing their job. Walmart would need to come to some kind of standstill. I don't see it happening, because they know they are too big to do that."

Janet, a fifty-something mother, has worked for Walmart in Missouri for eleven years, currently as a baker earning twelve dollars per hour. She applied to more than one hundred businesses but says no one else would hire her because of her age. Her husband Brad's three-thousand-dollar monthly pension is their main source of income. But he is in failing health and says, "If I can last until Janet's sixty-five, then she will get my pension." Janet earns about two thousand dollars a month. After out-of-pocket medical expenses, deductions for healthcare, and taxes, her take-home pay is about $900 a month. The couple, who live with an adult child who works sporadically, paid off their mortgage and "wiped the slate clean" after Brad's father, a unionized auto worker, left them an inheritance when he died in the early 2000s. Janet's been working with an injured leg for more than a month and is afraid to take sick days to recover, after a coworker with twenty years on the job was replaced because she missed her scheduled return date after surgery.

"The work is horrible, and the pay's no good. You have to push hard to get everything done. It makes me feel stressed. There's a lot of pressure put on the people that can be tracked by the computers. Anything that can be monitored, they monitor. The fact that it's not paying that much makes you feel worthless. Walmart is like a company town. We're entering a new stage of feudalism. It's the corporation that's the baron and the workers are the serf. To be honest I can't afford the meat anymore. We have a garden; that helps. Our idea of meat anymore is bacon, hotdogs, canned meat." The store is "understaffed continually" and workers are "pretty dissatisfied with what's going on. We don't get the equipment we need. We're trying to do too much. Everyone feels overworked." She says people work there mainly for the healthcare and the paycheck, and want to be paid more.

"My coworkers don't have any hope in government, not anymore. They're pretty sure government is in the pocket of corporations. I brought up the factory collapse in Bangladesh, and no one heard about it. They said, 'You've got it be kidding. I'll believe it if it's Walmart.' They are so fixated on their survival. They talk about how Walmart is essentially a sweatshop operation. 'They should bring it back and be made in America.' A lot of my coworkers shop at Walmart. They don't have a choice about it. A lot of younger woman with small children talk about money problems. None of them have any hope of getting into a house unless their husbands have a really good job. Most are on food stamps, and get childcare from the state. They get a lot of state-based assistance. Everything is a strain for them. They have to wait weeks to get their cars fixed. They get together and if one of them gets into a jam they loan them money, and they pass it around."

Janet is adamantly pro-union. "When I was growing up, my dad belonged to the union. It was called 'the union,' and it did good things for workers. The union gave my dad a well-paying job that took care of five kids and my mom. We had good medical because of them." Her coworkers' opinions vary. "A lot of my coworkers are very conservative. They don't want to give their money to a union, taking money out of their mouths to give it to a union to influence political rallies." She says that in terms of participating in OUR Walmart strike actions, "many workers wished they could just go ahead and walk out. They thought it would serve Walmart right, but they're terrified of losing their jobs. We're talking about people who literally live from paycheck to paycheck. These discussions would take place very quietly at the cash register. To try to organize a union they would have to be assured they had a job if Walmart fired them. It's economic fear above all else. I don't think there's anti-union sentiment nearly as badly as anyone thinks among Walmart employees."

For her part, Janet dismisses Walmart's famous "open-door" policy, which allegedly allows any worker to "take their complaint straight to a top executive in Bentonville."[51] "[It's] bullshit. If you use the open-door policy they will tell you why it's done the way it's done and then they close the door in your face." She's still angry about an incident in which a male coworker revealed Walmart "paid him $1.50 more an hour because he had a family to support. That really pissed me off. I was taking care of my brother's four children, my children and a husband." And she claims the only way she gets a raise is through class-action suits. "I got forty cents per hour from one lawsuit." But she also sees Walmart as part of any solution: "Walmart could do so much good if they tried. I think it's just about profits. It's all about greed right now. Look at all the influence they got. They could green the world. If they gave everybody a raise, the economy would boom. A lot of customers say unions have outlived their usefulness." Though they ask, "'Why can't they buy stuff made in America, why can't they support American jobs?' But a lot of times customers are in the same boat as us and they have no choice. When you're poor you go to the lowest price place, period."

Gabriel is a 31-year-old resident of Apple Valley, Minnesota, working on a BS in math communications, and in addition to working at Walmart he's a DJ. He's worked there since August 2011, is an electronics associate earning $9.00 an hour, and is involuntarily part-time at twenty to twenty-five hours per week. He's worked since he was fourteen; previous employers include Kmart, Best Buy, and a bank; and the most he's ever earned is $11.75 an hour as a manager of GameCrazy. Gabriel lives with his two parents, who are homeowners with a remaining mortgage of approximately fifty thousand dollars. He receives low-income healthcare and food stamps, and has twenty thousand dollars in student loans in deferral.

Gabriel sought employment at Walmart because "it was a hard time, I needed the money, and I was having trouble finding work." His weeklong orientation included a "full day of discussion and video about how unions take your money and do nothing for you. Managers used scare tactics: 'You could lose health benefits. Unions cause business to go down, so we will have to cut back on hours.'" The orientation included "role-playing and skits, where someone would play an organizer and the employees were taught how to respond. It was a lot of words and training in our heads." Gabriel says at first he didn't care about the anti-union ideology. "I was raised Republican, not to be fond of unions."

He says: "I don't have money to buy clothes, and I'm ashamed. I have a '92 Dodge Caravan I call Big Bertha, and if she breaks down we have to see if we can do without things to pay for repairs." In terms of benefits, "I don't get any paid vacation from Walmart. If I take vacation, I take unpaid leave. I don't get any sick days. That's how Walmart saves money, by keeping us part-time."

Gabriel's decision to join OUR Walmart began after he was on the job three months and was having difficulty learning the stocking system. "A manager started yelling at me in front of the customers because I was working slower. First I took it, and was very upset. That night I looked for chat boards or groups to see if there were other associates being treated this way. And I happened upon OUR Walmart. I started reading the testimonials. I clicked the link to be contacted, and I left my number but a fake name. They called back after a few days. At first I was very scared and worried. We had it drilled into our heads you don't go outside to organize. We have the 'open door.'"

Then in December 2011 while at work he started urinating blood and nearly collapsed because of "major kidney stones." As a coworker helped him, a manager said, "'You can leave whenever you want, but we can't okay the absence.' I was very surprised." These incidents and discussions with an organizer convinced him to join OUR Walmart. He's taken part in two walkouts in 2012, and two worker-led protests in Bentonville. He says in October 2012, when he went on strike to travel to Bentonville to protest an investors' meeting, "I saw a bunch of passionate people who were trying to make things better for our fellow coworkers, so they don't have to rely on food stamps and housing assistance. When I went on strike, everybody thought I was going to get fired. When I came back I thought people would be upset, angry. They gave me handshakes and said, 'This is a long time coming, thank you for standing up for us.' I had one manager pull me aside, who said: 'I totally believe in what you're doing, keep it up, Gabe. A couple of other managers believe the same thing." Everybody at Walmart knows how bad it is."

During breaks and after-hours, he talks extensively with other workers: "We talk about wages, being underpaid, understaffed; how do you pay the bills and mortgage, or do you buy food. We talk about people who feel like they're being retaliated against or mistreated. Given too much work knowing it's not going to get done, so a write-up ensues, on the floor being micro-managed and critiqued." Gabriel says some workers told him after he went on strike, "You leave more work for the rest of us," and that instead he "should talk to management and use the open door." He responded, "If Walmart staffed the way it should, we wouldn't have this problem, but it wants to use the least workers possible." He also told them: "The open door can't get more pay for us. The open door can't make staffing better and get us more hours. The open door can't get better healthcare for us. We need a stronger fix."

He claims, "Everyone that's joined has come to me. They say, 'We saw how you went on strike, and you weren't fired.' I was the only worker that went on strike. The way people are joining I can guarantee next time it will be ten to fifteen workers on strike." But he also acknowledges, "Until we educate the public they're not going to care, and Walmart's going to keep pushing." Perhaps one of the most important effects of the organizing campaign is the sense of meaning and self-worth workers derive from their involvement. Gabriel says the "strategy is to have associates stand up and live better," a play on Walmart's slogan, "Save money, live better." "You can go talk to your boss without fear of retaliation. You can have better pay, better health benefits, better schedules so you can attend your son's baseball games."

And he adds: "God sent me down for a reason. He's got a path laid out for us. I'm very proud to be part of this movement. I now have people looking up to me. When my kids read in the history books about this, I'll be able to tell them I was there, and that makes me feel good. I want to be able to go into work with my head held high, do my job, and provide for my family. That's all any of us wants to do."

OUR WALMART

The United Food and Commercial Workers launched Organization United for Respect at Walmart in 2011 through social media and personal outreach by about one hundred staff and union members. It builds on an attempt launched in 2005 to build a workers' association in Florida by UFCW, SEIU, and the now-defunct ACORN association of community groups. The campaign hindered Walmart's expansion in the state, and the national attention, including from the Federal Reserve, it drew to its demands for better hours and pay for its workers apparently motivated Walmart to raise wages in more than five hundred stores in 2006. Yet the same year the workers' association collapsed, in part due to union infighting.[52]

OUR Walmart began with a flurry of optimism, with organizers saying they had "more than fifty members at some stores," and they hoped to "soon have tens of thousands of members." Its first action was one-day strikes at stores in October 2012, involving eighty-eight workers across twenty-eight stores. The impetus was to protest Walmart firing and punishing OUR Walmart members, and it came on the heels of strikes in September at Walmart warehouses in Mira Loma, California, and in Elwood, Illinois, as well as a strike by eight "guest workers" at a Walmart supplier, CJ's Seafood in Louisiana, in June 2012.[53] In November OUR Walmart organized community-based protests in one hundred cities in forty-six states on Black Friday, the annual shopping frenzy at US retail stores, that drew thousands of demonstrators, including five hundred striking workers. It also organized three protests in Bentonville, Arkansas, during Walmart shareholder and investor meetings in 2012 and 2013.[54] Smaller actions took place, and in April 2013 a meeting was held in Los Angeles bringing together Walmart supply chain workers from Chicago warehouses, the Gulf seafood industry, and Bangladeshi garment factories.[55] By the summer of 2013 at least a thousand workers (including some former workers) were dues-paying members (at five dollars or more a month), while perhaps five times that many were active in OUR Walmart. Yet, the effort was slow going. As one union staffer put it: "It's extremely difficult to organize low-wage workers period, much less low-wage workers who are working among an extremely hostile company with a sophisticated union-avoidance strategy."

This difficulty is also a product of the weakness of US labor law. A survey of 1,004 National Labor Relations Board (NLRB) elections from 1999 to 2004 found "employers threatened to close the plant in 57 percent of elections, discharged workers in 34 percent, and threatened to cut wages and benefits in 47 percent of elections."[56] A 2007 Human Rights Watch report explained US laws allowed for "a wide range of employer tactics that interfere with worker organizing," while imposing only "weak" penalties to "deter employers from breaking the laws," allowing them to "violate their employees' basic rights with virtual impunity." Walmart, the report stated, "takes full advantage" of that process.[57] This highlighted how far "the welter of laws, board decisions, judicial decisions, and contractual obligations . . . ensnared the modern labor organization" since the passage of Taft-Hartley. That act banned secondary strikes, excluded foremen and supervisors from labor law, legalized "employer free speech" and right-to-work laws, and stoked internal warfare against the labor left by requiring union officers to file "non-Communist affidavits."[58]

Once Taft-Hartley had reversed successful organizing among Black workers in the South, most unions proved ill-equipped to embrace African American workers seeking an equal footing in core industries. While public sector unionism grew dramatically starting in the sixties, unions largely ignored the growing private service sector that relied on part-time female workers. Slow to embrace rank-and-file democratic movements, or to respond effectively to the neoliberal counterattack, yet desperate to stay relevant, organized labor has banished most talk of the working class in favor of the poll-tested middle class. Its call for "good jobs," "fair wages," and "a level playing field" romanticize a corporatist past where national capital can be cajoled to bring good-paying jobs back home.

Walmart's anti-union strategies smashed earlier attempts at unionization. In 1978 the International Brotherhood of Teamsters found a receptive audience of workers fed up with low pay, a high rate of injury, and unresponsive management at a Walmart distribution center in Searcy, Arkansas. Nearly half of the 415 employees at Searcy signed union cards. On the eve of the vote, after delaying it for years, Sam Walton and his brother Bud parachuted into Searcy and threatened to fire workers, eliminate profit sharing, and close the facility (all in violation of labor law). The Teamsters lost the vote by a more than three-to-one margin, and pro-union employees were fired.[59] But having been spooked, Walmart elevated its drivers "to something resembling a labor aristocracy" by paying them union-scale wages, giving them high-quality equipment, and no longer requiring them to load and unload their trailers. As a result, annual turnover among Walmart truckers declined to single digits and it achieved an "astounding" on-time store delivery rate of 99.8 percent.[60]

In 2000, when UFCW organized nine butchers in a Texas Walmart into a bargaining unit, the company eliminated all meat cutters at several hundred US supercenters, which was "almost certainly a form of illegal retaliation." The same year when UFCW filed a petition to prepare an NLRB election for eighteen tire-and-lube workers in a Kingman, Arizona, store, Walmart dispatched a labor team within twenty-four hours, eventually flooding the store with more than twenty outside managers. Regular staff "watched anti-union videos and attended near-daily captive meetings," a new set of cameras were trained on the tire-and-lube shop, and hourly managers were told they were part of management and required to report any union activity despite repeated NLRB rulings against this tactic. After the "UFCW organizing drive collapsed in inglorious defeat . . . the labor board eventually ruled, at Kingman and elsewhere, that Walmart had systematically harassed and spied upon numerous workers, that it had threatened employees with a loss of benefits and raises if they supported the union, and that the company had fired key labor partisans outright."[61] In 2005 another UFCW organizing drive in a Colorado store wilted after Walmart "employed its sophisticated array of anti-union tactics that go to the very brink of what weak U.S. labor law allows."[62]

The Walmart effect on unionized workers was clearly seen after it announced in 2002 it would build forty supercenters in California. Since Walmart has "a decisive competitive advantage" over supermarkets when it comes to labor costs, wages, and benefits, Safeway and Kroger used the mere announcement as an excuse "to chop wages, and reduce retirement and healthcare benefits." In October 2003 more than fifty-nine thousand workers with the UFCW went on strike or were locked out for 145 days. The strike leaders "made a hash of the epic confrontation," which ended "in a decisive defeat" after the union accepted a two-tier wage structure, smaller pensions, and higher healthcare premiums and expenses. The lesson for the entire labor movement was ominous: "union organizing and collective bargaining . . . were ineffective, if not obsolete, in that huge sector of the economy where Walmart cast such a large shadow."[63]

OUR Walmart is thus the third phase of UFCW attempts to organize Walmart workers, incorporating lessons from past union drives and recent corporate campaigns. One source explained why the union has scrapped traditional organizing: "We would lose, and even if we won, Walmart would close the store, fire the workers, and thumb its nose at the rulings." OUR Walmart avoids the trap of a traditional NLRB election by striking over "unfair labor practices," the same innovative tactics used by the United Electrical, Radio, and Machine Workers of America (UE) involvement in the Warehouse Workers Organizing Committee to unionize Walmart warehouses west of Chicago, and by SEIU's "Fight for $15" campaign to organize low-wage workers in cities nationwide. Labor law allows companies to "permanently replace" workers who strike over economic issues or for union recognition, but not those who picket over unfair labor practices. Although all three campaigns admit companies have fired pro-labor workers, particularly after the walkouts, this tactic has nevertheless enabled workers to conduct strikes in which they returned to their jobs, establishing credibility among coworkers that collective on-the-job action is possible without immediate retaliation, thereby increasing the possibility of larger actions in the future. Notably, all three campaigns were influenced by community-level workers centers and Occupy Wall Street.[64]

The UFCW along with SEIU broke from the AFL-CIO to form the Change to Win labor federation in 2005, and OUR Walmart includes former SEIU organizers who were hired because of their experience with corporate campaigns, which is "a multidimensional campaign that attacks an adversary from every conceivable angle, creating relentless pressure on multiple individual and institutional targets."[65] One union staffer says that when the UFCW and SEIU organized corporate campaigns in the mid-2000s like Walmart Watch and Wake Up Walmart, this was designed to force the company to "agree to some form of organizing conduct, or at least tarnish their brand and make it harder for them to expand into other markets. Those campaigns were geared toward public relations strategies, anti-trust work, targeting the company's vulnerabilities in relation to the gender discrimination lawsuit. Unfortunately there was not enough of a worker base." By contrast, OUR Walmart is a nontraditional model using traditional union tactics with lots of union resources, but it's not creating a dynamic where the company can call for an election and then crush the organizing attempt in that store. There are corporate campaign elements targeting the company's expansion into urban markets and its attempts to rebrand itself as green and socially responsible through counter-marketing tactics that benefit significantly from workers who can challenge that image. Workers are organizing but they're not seeking to gain majority recognition status in any worksite. They're calling on the company to hear the concerns that they're raising, but they have to be very careful about not making union demands around economics. The strikes over the last year are unfair labor practice strikes based on retaliation against workers who are exercising their rights to speak out about those issues.

Spread across hundreds of stores, OUR Walmart is a classic example of "minority unionism," in which a core of passionate, militant workers can exert pressure across the whole company, win demands, and attract more workers to their movement, slowly building their ranks until they can win an election. To this point, it's been more effective than previous unionization drives. One union staffer says: "It's succeeded in placing Walmart at the center of the debate about the low-income economy, worker rights, fairness and equity in the workplace, and just what it's like trying to be a low-income worker in today's economy." The strikes are historic as there's "never been a group of workers at Walmart that have engaged in this type of action. It has been very important in capturing the imagination of the Walmart workforce and the public," and it appears to have had an impact, along with the Bangladesh factory collapse and fires, in Walmart's declining reputation among consumers. Despite lacking "anywhere the numbers to affect retail operations," this union staffer says that OUR Walmart "continues to be a thriving organization that can engage with company officials in a public way and raise issues that resonate with a significant part of the workforce."

OUR Walmart faces an uphill climb, however. Walmart treated the first strike cautiously in October 2012, circulating a memo that told salaried managers strikes were generally "protected concerted activity," and not to discipline associates for walking off the job or discussing work stoppages on break time.[66] In advance of Black Friday, Walmart filed charges with the NLRB to stop OUR Walmart picketing, claiming the UFCW was engaged in illegal representational actions. In January 2013, in order "to avert likely charges from regulators that it engaged in weeks of illegal picketing at Walmart stores," the UFCW announced it was not trying to unionize Walmart.[67] Since then all its communications have included a disclaimer like: "UFCW and OUR Walmart have no intent to have Walmart recognize or bargain with UFCW or OUR Walmart as the representative of Walmart employees."[68] Because labor law "requires the NLRB to prioritize employers' allegations of illegal picketing over other charges," injunctions against picketing are usually issued within days while workers who are fired for union activity usually languish months without remedy.[69]

Around the time of the June 2013 shareholder meeting, Walmart started firing and disciplining OUR Walmart members, and by late June the worker organization claimed the company had retaliated against thirty-six members, including eleven who were fired.[70] As a UFCW source put it: "We're now going to have a new test of the NLRB to see if they respond in a timely fashion and reinstate workers who appear to have been illegally fired, and if they don't then this more adaptive tactic of striking over ULP [unfair labor practices] and US labor law may prove ineffective in the face of Walmart's aggression. . . . We've yet to see the board do anything substantive to protect Walmart workers." There's also the issue of top-down organizing strategy. While OUR Walmart foot soldiers like Gabriel are on the front lines recruiting and organizing other workers, it's doubtful they have input in a strategy determined by lawyers, pollsters, senior union officials, and outside consultants like ASGK Public Strategies, "the media and branding firm started by David Axelrod, a senior political adviser to President Obama." According to *Bloomberg Businessweek*, ASGK conducted "opinion research about how to effectively reach Walmart employees," decided to use social media, "helped name the movement and craft" the logo, and determined that the campaign should recruit "dedicated employees" whose chief complaints included a lack of respect from managers and low wages.[71]

ORGANIZING THE WAREHOUSE

Like OUR Walmart, the Chicago-area Warehouse Workers for Justice was set up by a union, in this case UE. Unlike OUR Walmart, WWJ is explicitly a workers center that aims to educate workers about "workplace rights, unite warehouse workers to defend their rights on the job, build community support for the struggles of warehouse workers and fight for policy changes to improve the lives of warehouse workers and members of our communities."[72] The union established WWJ after UE Local 1110 successfully occupied a window factory in 2008, winning back pay owed to more than two hundred workers. The Warehouse Workers Organizing Committee, with about three hundred active members, is also backed by UE and since 2009 has served as the labor-organizing arm to WWJ's community activism. Leah Fried, spokesperson for WWJ, explains that UE (for whom she is a staffer) is taking a long-haul approach in working with the WWOC. The UE-led campaign is also noteworthy for its commitment to developing rank-and-file organization, leadership, and democracy, with workers deciding the tactics and broader strategy. The UE's decision to create a strike fund for nonunionized workers is a very rare and especially important step in the North American labor movement.

WWOC focuses on organizing in the warehouses located in Will County, Illinois, where some thirty thousand clerks, truck drivers, material movers, and package handlers work. The Chicago-Naperville-Joliet metropolitan area is the only place in North America where six class 1 railroads converge along with four interstate highways. Walmart relies on two intermodal facilities with 3.4 million square feet of space to process a phenomenal 70 percent of its imported goods sold in the United States.[73] The four warehouse workers I interviewed all temped in a Walmart warehouse in Will County, Illinois. James, who helped organize workers there, says Walmart uses subcontractors to shield it from liability: "Walmart owns the warehouse, Schneider Logistics runs it, subcontracts for labor to Roadlink Workforce Solutions, and Roadlink will then subcontract some workers to other temp agencies." He says, "The strategy is to build a militant minority union, and over many years to build density because of the high turnover."

Joseph says they want to eliminate the temp agencies and get directly hired by Schneider because "it's much more vulnerable to a union drive. It's much more difficult for Walmart to cut their ties with them." Workers say after UE first started organizing "Schneider raised wages and improved benefits."

Matters came to head in 2012 with a 21-day strike by thirty-eight workers, about 10 percent of the workforce there. James says it began "in mid-September when about forty to fifty workers from two docks were delivering a petition to Roadlink. A supervisor charged with a forklift, cut off half the group, and threatened to fire the rest if they kept going. The petition had basic things like living wage, safety, face masks and shin guards, set hours per day." After a confrontation with management, the workers went out on strike, which was unplanned but eventually drew substantial support, including a march of six hundred people followed by civil disobedience in early October. The combination of bad publicity for Walmart, as well as claims that eight million dollars was lost as a result of management's decision to close the warehouse, led Roadlink to agree to let the workers return.[74]

Prior to this, rank-and-file organizers built a core group with tactics like handing out "know your rights" flyers, which Mike says helped people get over the fear of being fired. Joseph, who was active in Occupy Wall Street, took a position in the warehouse specifically for the purpose of organizing. He says "Pointing to space heaters that cost sixty-five dollars each, talking about how many there are, how much Walmart makes, is a really effective way to explain you're being stolen from. 'So in five minutes we've unloaded enough for a day's pay.'" Organizing softball games provided an opportune place to bend coworkers' ears outside the workplace. Once the strike occurred, UE, in a highly unorthodox gesture, gave "picket pay" of two hundred dollars a week to workers not even in the union. Bailey says, "We considered ourselves union, but were not part of a recognized union. None of it would have been possible without WWJ being there."

James says while few workers were "actively anti-union," the company used plants and spies to sow fear and disrupt organizing. Mike says rank-and-file organizers would "share notes on people we thought were spies. We really watched what we said around them." James says "the real problem is most people have so much shit on their plate they don't have time to organize. They're dealing with children, taking care of parents, paying off a mortgage, the car just broke down. They're homeless, recovering from an addiction." Another issue, says Mike, is that "more than anti-union, there's a lot of ignorance and misinformation about unions."

Joseph says the strike "was a huge bonding experience; there was a lot of pride. We had consolidated and done something, the bosses were afraid of us." After they returned to work, they were put on the same dock. As the workforce is over 80 percent Black and Latino, and strikers were mostly white, managers tried to divide workers along racial lines. Mike says, "We're already divided, so there was definitely a sense from Black workers that it's those crazy white kids on strike." Joseph adds, "Schneider keeps the line divided. They don't like the temps talking to the direct hires." But returning gave the strikers credibility. Joseph says, "We went in with another petition and it went faster. People were much more aware of their rights and were not afraid to sign their names like the first time. We should have taken our time when we went back in to develop the conversations, but we were also under pressure. For those not striking, there was lots of confusion, questions, misunderstandings, fear."

Ultimately, says Joseph, the warehouse is "still the same shop floor. You're in physical confrontation with your bosses. There's someone breathing down your neck telling you to work faster all the time. You're all mad together. It could lead to the kind of militancy that you don't get in other sectors." But he argues workers internalize precarity: "The job creates a feeling of insecurity, dispensability. You have to accept that 'I work here in this warehouse, and I'm going to make this job better no matter how long it takes.' The general attitude among workers is that the job is temporary.'

James notes, "There is rudimentary class consciousness. The workers are aware of their own conditions, and how economic forces affect them. But expanding it to how this affects all the working class, and I should unite with them—not even close." Mike adds, "A majority of the workers see management as the enemy. I was surprised by how many people would say, 'Fuck the Waltons.' But they . . . don't realize what could be accomplished with collective bargaining. They feel powerless in their own country, what can they do across the ocean?" In his view militant solidarity gives labor its power. "You can't wait on the NLRB to reinstate your jobs. You have to organize the shop floor so if anyone gets fired or threatened for organizing, everyone should walk off the job. That's the way it's always been done. It's a cat-and-mouse game." After returning to work the four were among nine workers illegally fired for union activity by Roadlink. The NLRB ruled in their favor, but Roadlink had not settled the case as of July 2013. As Roadlink's contract with Schneider ended April 30, Bailey points out it has to compensate workers only for back pay up to April 30, and if anyone found a job in the meantime that's when the back pay ends. "Labor law is extremely weak. It's a completely rigged system in the favor of the employer," he laments. Most are also part of a separate class-action suit charging wage theft.[75] Mike says, "For now it appears the company won. They got the organizers out of the warehouse. Even if we win and get our back pay and jobs reinstated, they put an end to the organizing for a while." Joseph is more optimistic: "I don't feel defeated. In the warehouse it's like organizing sand. We learned a lot from the first attempt. You have to build relationships and trust" before you build class solidarity. Indeed, Joseph is essentially reviving an old form of labor organizing known as "colonizing" or "salting," in which militant pro-labor activists take jobs "organizing the unorganized" from the inside. This strategy was used effectively in the thirties and to a lesser degree in the seventies in heavy industry. As Steve Early notes in his book *Save Our Unions*, nothing can replace salting "in teaching young organizers, largely from a non-working-class background, what the working class is about and how to talk and especially listen to workers. Salting needs to become fashionable again for young people politically committed to reinvigorating the labor movement."[76]

FIGHT FOR $15

The SEIU's "Fight for $15" campaign kicked off in November 2012 when about two hundred workers joined "a day of walkouts and rallies at dozens of Burger King, Taco Bell, Wendy's, McDonald's and other fast-food restaurants" in New York City, and by the summer of 2013 similar walkouts had spread to ten cities total, with a coordinated national strike planned for July 2013.[77] According to *Labor Notes*, the campaign is "part of a coordinated effort by SEIU, which has been providing funds as part of its two-year-old project 'Fight for a Fair Economy.'" The Fight for $15 campaign mobilizes community groups, clergy, politicians, and unions in the same manner as corporate campaigns and worker centers. Most target cities have a "Workers Organizing Committee" that brings the workers together, but SEIU provides strategic direction and funding, and hires the paid organizers, eight to twelve per city, except in New York, which has forty organizers devoted to the effort. Reports claim New York Communities for Change (a successor to the ACORN community group in that city) is organizing workers. But SEIU is behind this, with NYCC, and funds the organizers. In fact, one labor organizer in New York confided that the organizers themselves were discussing forming their own union because of low wages and sixty-hour work weeks.[78]

SEIU organizers say after finding "large majorities" in favor of unionization in New York and Chicago, the first two cities targeted, the project was expanded and similar one-day walkouts have occurred in Detroit, St. Louis, Milwaukee, Washington, DC, and Seattle, while similar campaigns were being nurtured in Arizona, Colorado, and South Carolina. In addition to agitating for $15 an hour, more than double the federal minimum wage of $7.25 in 2013, the campaign wants to ensure workers can organize without fear of retaliation and to stop the employer practice of shorting workers hours or overtime pay, common forms of "wage theft." A report by the SEIU-funded Fast Food Forward found 84 percent of five hundred workers surveyed in New York City were victims of wage theft.[79] SEIU is using an industrial union approach that welcomes any low-wage workers who work for chains in apparel, retail, drug stores, convenience stores, discounters, or similar enterprises.

Fight for $15 draws on a December 2009 SEIU proposal, "A Plan for Organizing Post-Labor Law Reform."[80] After spending $450 million during the 2008 election cycle, unions were banking on Obama to secure passage of the Employee Free Choice Act, which would have legalized card-check unionization, imposed binding mediation if contract talks stalemated, and enhanced penalties against employers who illegally retaliated against workers.[81] Eyeing forty million low-wage workers, SEIU saw EFCA as "the best opportunity the union has had in decades to once and for all turn the tide in favor of America's workers," but the act died in the Senate in 2010 after being sidelined by Obama.[82] Nonetheless, the 2009 plan appears to guide current strategy. It proposed concentrating on one or two geographic areas before

expanding. Cities were chosen for "favorable local political environment and workforce composition," and targets limited to seven to ten
of the largest chains. The campaign aimed to build support for workers
via extensive community outreach and work "with prominent local
elected officials, deploying the call for 'a living wage' as a vehicle to
build momentum, including by building worker lists and identifying
potential leaders who would potentially support collective bargaining.

One SEIU organizer outlines the thinking behind the drive: "The
labor movement is dying. The only way to turn it around is by organizing the low-wage sector. How do we organize outside the traditional
NLRB model? How do we build minority unions to fight? Rather
than sitting back and waiting for the government to say you're a union,
we say we're a union. Labor is often afraid of using the strike; we're
using the strike to try to win. Can we create a crisis? Let's set the
bar high: fifteen dollars an hour and the right to form a union without retaliation. Post-Occupy, how do we start something in cities like
New York, Seattle, Chicago, Detroit? Can we inspire other cities as
well? Can we build a toolkit for a small town in Kansas to do a strike
themselves?"

SEIU has apparently devoted the equivalent of one to two hundred
full-time staff to the project, which is in line with the 2009 proposal.
There's an attempt to try to create an Occupy-like uprising, which is
one reason why SEIU is not taking center stage. Given the ambitious
scope of the campaign and SEIU's top-down organizing style, where
strategy is kept under wraps, there is considerable speculation as to
the real goals. No one believes wages will suddenly leap to fifteen
dollars an hour. One organizer says workers know this. "They want
to make fifteen an hour, but they realize that's not going to happen
overnight. It doesn't hurt that President Obama has talked about raising the minimum wage, but not a single worker thinks nine dollars
is nearly enough." Some organizers think "SEIU will strike a deal
like in the healthcare industry, where they agree to organize one city,
but nowhere else." But another organizer responds, "That would be a
high-quality problem. We're not even close to that." Steve Early, the
author of *The Civil Wars in US Labor*, points out that it was the SEIU
model to unionize nursing homes, but only because it could convince
employers: "We can add value, we're going to be a corporate partner
by lobbying for more money in the state legislature."[83]

Bill Fletcher Jr., who at the time headed the National Retail Justice Alliance, a UFCW-backed think tank and advocacy group, suggested the fifteen-an-hour slogan was misleading: "If the objective is really to raise the minimum wage, it's important that workers know that that's what they're fighting for."[84] Indeed, Fight for $15 revived criticisms of SEIU, such as its disdain for internal democracy.

One organizer describes the cross currents: "A lot of these folks are pissed off and have been struggling for all of their lives, for some it's a generational thing. This campaign is giving them a spark of hope for a better life in America. We've had over a hundred workers in the room. Enthusiasm is high, but everyone's on edge. The workers have day-to-day issues, family stuff, paying rent. They're all scared if they lose their bread and butter they'll be out on the street in two weeks. The agenda is pretty top-down, such as strike dates. The organizers say, 'All the other cities have decided to go on strike on this date, do you want to join them?' And the workers are like, 'Yeah!' Do I think it's ideal? No. But do I have any better ideas? No, and that's the problem."

Speaking of protests at fast-food shareholder meetings, the same organizer says, "They shuffle the workers in, shuffle them out, tell them what to say, what makes the best story for the media, not necessarily what the truth is." SEIU organizers say the union campaign "is looking at models of minority unionism and worker centers with the workers driving the fight." But even more than UFCW, SEIU treats minority unionism as a tactic, rather than a strategy, taking a bureaucratic, even corporate approach. Workers centers and a few unions send "salts" into workplaces to build rank-and-file democracy, worker consciousness and organic leaders. This contrasts with SEIU, which is "very quick to hire organizers and turn them into full-time doorknockers."[85] This creates a disconnect as organizers are often unaware of day-to-day issues facing workers or downplay them in favor of strategy determined by a remote leadership. The fact that organizers were guessing as to the strategy shows how removed they are from the decision making, and workers even more so.

There is obvious overlap between the Fight for $15 campaign and SEIU's earlier Fight for a Fair Economy initiative in 2011 to mobilize "mostly low-wage minority workers in 10 to 15 cities" with high numbers of SEIU members and threatened by cuts to the public sector. Steve Early explained that Fight for a Fair Economy never achieved much visibility: "The campaign looked good on paper, but was top-down, staff-driven and [had] a consultant-shaped message that was boilerplate union rhetoric."[86] Early also criticized SEIU's tendency to jump from one campaign to the next, while one former SEIU organizer who praised the low-wage worker campaign nevertheless fretted that the union was "fickle," and "subject to entering and leaving a project at whim, given its panic and lack of anything like consistent social vision, its internecine fights exemplary of paranoia, its fear of its own membership and failed track record of cultivating member consciousness." One organizer is worried the union will call off the campaign if it isn't working, leaving the workers in the lurch, and another organizer indicates SEIU may pull the plug within two years if it's not meeting expectations: "The money going into this is a gamble. These workers aren't paying dues; they're not financing this right now."[87] At the same time, workers have notched victories in cities like Chicago, where workers report pay increase of ten cents to two dollars an hour, more regular scheduling, increased hours, improved break rooms, and better treatment from managers.[88]

A LABOR RENAISSANCE? BEYOND WORKERS CENTERS AND OCCUPY

It is notable that in all three campaigns discussed above, the unions place themselves in the background, downplaying their involvement. While unions have a 51 percent favorability rating in polls, only 20 percent of the public expresses confidence in them, slightly behind banks, televised news, and big business. At the same time, Blacks and Hispanics combined are twice as favorable toward unions as unfavorable, and women nearly 50 percent more favorable, while men and whites are almost exactly evenly split.[89] In this light it's logical to organize sectors that are disproportionately female and people of color.[90] There is no doubt, in this respect, that the new union campaigns reflect the influence of workers centers. These are new types of community-based, rather than workplace-based, organizations that support low-wage workers by raising wages, improving working conditions, advocating for immigration reform, and addressing issues like housing, education, and healthcare for immigrant communities, which can be considered a revival of social unionism.[91] They've grown from 5 nationwide in 1992 to 139 by 2005, 88 percent of which work "specifically with immigrants," and emphasize "leadership development and democratic decision-making."[92] Workers centers also organize across borders, often through the supply chain of a corporation, and ally with religious, governmental, community, and labor organizations. Seeing the growth and opportunity afforded by workers centers, "the AFL-CIO has formal partnerships with the National Day Worker Organizing Network, Interfaith Worker Justice, the Domestic Workers Alliance and the National Guestworkers Alliance."[93]

But workers centers are a far cry from the type of labor organization that can unionize millions of workers, as the Congress of Industrial Organizations (CIO) did in the 1930s. At a time when their proportion of the workforce has fallen to under 12 percent, the lowest in almost a century, Early says if the 14.3 million US workers in unions had "a movement worth its salt [there wouldn't] be any need for foundation-funded worker centers."[94] He sees an inherent problem with them: "They have very high turnover. People pay dues, get active for a while, but then they get another job. If people aren't paying dues to a workers center, how is it their organization? The organizations workers do pay dues to are hard enough to control." However, Early also notes that one advantage of workers centers is that they "organize without regard to employer, industry wide." Insofar as big initiatives like Fight for $15 are "following the worker center model," Early says, "unions are finally taking a creative approach . . . but it's also a recognition that traditional labor organizing is all but dead." Unions have an advantage in being able to marshal money, organizers, and public support to allow for these strike waves. "It allows workers to walk out for a day and there's enough community pressure so that the workers keep their jobs."

One of the most significant influences on new labor organizing was Occupy Wall Street as it opened space for militancy and creative actions. When activists occupied Zuccotti Park, near Wall Street, on September 17, 2011, organized labor was absent, but unions quickly climbed aboard as Occupy spread like wildfire. Unions provided Occupy camps around the country with camping supplies, office space, and even a small park for the Charleston, West Virginia, group. Jackie DiSalvo, a New York labor activist and retired professor, said labor gave "Occupy a broader constituency than the young people sleeping in Zuccotti who were precarious workers, unemployed, or students."

When New York Mayor Michael Bloomberg attempted to shut down the camp in October 2011, hundreds of union members joined the thousands who showed up to successfully defend the park. In numerous cities organizers said Occupy influenced labor talks, such as in Philadelphia, where one thousand staff at a major arts center and twenty-five hundred office cleaners in a hundred corporate high-rises won better-than-expected contracts. In New York City, Occupy activists joined with Teamsters to thwart union busting by the Sotheby's auction house and participated in the Laundry Workers Center campaign that helped twenty-three mostly undocumented workers at the Hot and Crusty bakery chain win union recognition after they briefly occupied their workplace and the sidewalk in front of a Manhattan outlet. Most dramatically, Occupy Oakland in twelve days went from its first public action to drawing tens of thousands of people into the streets for a general strike endorsed by local unions.[95]

Labor groups and workers also adopted the tactic of occupying public space in continuous protest. In Freeport, Illinois, Sensata Technologies workers, aided by SEIU organizers, erected an Occupy-style camp outside their factory during the 2012 election campaign. Protesting the transfer of 170 jobs and the physical factory to China by the private equity firm Bain Capital, which Mitt Romney cofounded, the workers drew national support and backing from dozens of unions and Occupy movements. In West Virginia, retirees with an average age of seventy have set up an "Occupy Century Aluminum" outpost in two consecutive years, first for seventy-five days in the winter of 2012, to protest the company's cancellation of their health benefits. A more radical approach has been taken by the SEIU-backed "We Are Oregon" community organization, which supported homeowners in foreclosure who stay in their homes, and has even helped families reoccupy homes after being evicted. In fact, it was a labor struggle that presaged the Occupy movement. In 2008 workers with UE Local 1110 in Chicago illegally occupied their window-making factory after being laid off without proper notice, and again in 2012, eventually forming the worker-owned New Era Windows Cooperative. After their 2008 occupation became a national sensation, a group of workers embarked on a national tour to spark more militant labor action, but as local 1110 president Armando Robles admits, they found that other workers were reluctant to engage in any actions that might be illegal.[96]

A few high-profile incidents soured many Occupiers on working with labor. In West Coast cities, attempts by Occupiers to stage actions at ports led to conflicts with West Coast longshore workers. In Los Angeles many Occupiers claimed labor organizers tried to hijack the movement by setting up an alternative occupation. And in New York City on November 17, 2011, days after police evicted the Occupation, unions led a march of thirty thousand protesters into Brooklyn while Occupiers wanted to use the numbers to march on Wall Street and potentially retake the park. But Occupy also failed to create an organizational infrastructure that could mobilize a mass constituency around inequality or labor issues.

If organized labor is to have a renaissance, it has to go far beyond selectively picking from a buffet of activist tactics. It needs to revive tactics like sit-down strikes that enabled a new labor formation such as the CIO to exploit the organizing possibilities of the thirties and forties, whereas the conservative American Federation of Labor (AFL) fumbled numerous opportunities. Of course, it was spurred by pressures from below reflecting greater rank-and-file democracy, and further aided by broad public support, sympathetic politicians and media, and new labor laws like the National Labor Relations Act. There is all too little like this visible as yet. This is not to say organized labor is doomed, but its resurrection is unlikely to come from unions that have presided over more than half a century of decline. It will depend on the rebirth of a strong left in large enough numbers, with a vision that points the way beyond wages and consumption to economic democracy, to spur militant class consciousness and create the social space for it to spread.

RECONSIDERATIONS OF CLASS:
PRECARIOUSNESS AS PROLETARIANIZATION

Bryan D. Palmer

The positing of the individual as a worker, in this nakedness, is itself a product of history.

Karl Marx[1]

The experience of class conflict, proletarian mobilization, and class consciousness—so clearly visible in 1917–21, 1934–37, and 1946–48—was very much on the twentieth century's calendar again in the mid-1960s, when the *Socialist Register* was founded.[*] Shop stewards' movements and discussions of workers' control animated much of the left in the United Kingdom. With the Labour Party in power, there was spirited debate aimed at developing a program for socialist advance, as opposed to the reformist inclination of collapsing strategic sensibility into the cul-de-sac of an incomes policy.[2] In the United States and Canada, rising discontent in labor circles took many forms. A mid-1960s wildcat wave was eventually tamed,[3] but was soon followed, into the early 1970s, by much talk of "blue-collar blues" at General Motors plants like the sprawling assembly-line complex in Lordstown, Ohio.[4] Detroit gave birth to the League of Revolutionary Black Workers.[5] The Ben Hamper–designated "Rivethead" phenomenon of counter-planning on the shop floor was governed less in this period by an individualist credo of escape from work than it was by an edgy class antagonism.[6]

---

[*]   This essay was first published in *Socialist Register 2014* (London: Merlin Press, 2014).

May 1968 had witnessed the coming together of workers and students in massive protests in France,[7] while Edward Heath's governing Tories across the channel were toppled in 1974. An upsurge of class conflict in the first four years of the decade beat back anti-union legislation, broke a wage freeze, and unleashed militant factory occupations in opposition to plant closures. Two miners' strikes—one in 1972, another in 1974—finally sealed the fate of the Conservatives. They helped bring the Labour Party back into government, with the militant rhetoric of a "fundamental shift in class power" advanced by those in its ranks a source of visible discomfort to its tepid leadership.[8] This "moment" of class struggle, reaching from 1965–74 was, arguably, labor's last stand in the faltering economic climate of the post–World War II "long boom" that was obviously winding down. For by the mid-1970s, the terms of trade in the class war had shifted. Working-class victories—registering in militant extra-parliamentary mobilizations of class struggle as well as the incremental creep of union densities that saw, over time, the percentage of the nonagricultural workforce associated with labor organizations climb to 35 percent even in that bastion of ostensible "exceptionalism," the United States—slowed, stalled, and sputtered. Oppositional political formations—Militant Tendencies, anarchist collectives, and aspiring vanguards of "new communists"—came into being, made their voices heard, and then, all too often, disintegrated. The routine tempo of class conflict downshifted into a climacteric that would, over decades, see union densities plummet to one-third the percentage of earlier, better, times. Working-class combatants almost everywhere had the lifeblood of militancy sucked out of them, and confidence in labor circles waned as the advantage was seized by class adversaries. From 1975 to the present, capital has rewritten the script of class relations in the developed capitalist economies of the West, using to good effect a series of deepening and ongoing crises to discipline not only labor, but all dissident forces, drawing on the myriad powers of the state and unleashing material and ideological assaults of unprecedented vigor.

The result: declining material standards of the working class as a whole; the domestication of a once-combative trade unionism to a machinery of concession bargaining; a generation of young workers robbed of a sense of class place, its future marked by insecurity, with employment prospects understood to be precarious. Working-class defeats have, after decades of retrenchment, taken on a cumulative character, and the result is a class too often stripped of its seeming capacity to fight, its leadership increasingly characterized by caution and the sensibilities of an ossified officialdom. To be sure, there are, on a global scale, indications of class mobilizations that threaten to break out of these doldrums. Mike Davis writes, for instance, that "two hundred million Chinese factory workers, miners and construction laborers are the most dangerous class on the planet. (Just ask the State Council in Beijing.) Their full awakening from the bubble may yet determine whether or not a socialist Earth is possible."[9] Davis's optimism is refreshing, but a certain pessimism may well also be in order. The class consciousness and appetite for militancy within the Chinese proletariat is subject to a number of constraints, including limitations on working-class agency characteristic of class relations forged in the cauldron of a Stalinist-Maoist state moving away from its planned economy roots toward integration into a global capitalist order with which it has yet to fully align.

In any case, the developing world and the nature of its class formations certainly reinforces the contemporary significance of proletarian precariousness. The International Labor Organization has recently estimated that what might be called the global reserve army of labor is now larger than the approximately 1.4 billion workers who are totally dependent on wage labor for subsistence. This reserve now extends well beyond the roughly 218 million unemployed, an astronomical 1.7 billion workers being designated "the vulnerably employed." A significant portion of this reserve is undoubtedly wageless, composed of members of marginal domestic economies who eke out material being through unpaid labors, scavenging, and other illicit endeavors of the kind associated with life in the favelas, barrios, and shantytowns of Latin America, Asia, and Africa. Often this segment of the dispossessed scratches its day-to-day remunerations out of an *informal* economy where the struggle for subsistence relies as much on the trappings of petty, self-exploiting entrepreneurialism as on anything approximating waged labor.[10] Precariousness is axiomatic. What Davis calls the "global informal working class"—a socioeconomic stratum that he sees "overlapping with but non-identical to the slum population"— now surpasses one billion in number, "making it the fasting growing, and most unprecedented, social class on earth."[11]

But does precariousness, per se, constitute a *separate and distinct class formation*? If it does, then precarious employments, across a spectrum of almost infinite possibilities, are, in their fragmentations, constitutive of specific and particular classes, which then necessarily occupy different class places, with counterposed class interests, from those in other employment sectors. It is the purpose of this essay to suggest that this kind of thinking, which has of late gathered momentum, is antagonistic to foundational Marxist understandings and will, inevitably, have consequences in terms of struggle and practice that are divisive and counterproductive.[12]

PRECARIOUSNESS AS SOCIAL CLASS

Leading the analytic charge to declare precarious workers a *new class force*, one that must be reckoned with in the social struggles of our times, is Guy Standing. Standing, for instance, insists that in our current reconfigurations of work and everyday life, "the precariat is in the front ranks, but it has yet to find the voice to bring its agenda to the fore. It is not the 'squeezed middle' or an 'underclass' or 'the lower working class.' It has a distinctive bundle of insecurities and will have an equally distinctive set of demands."[13] Such claims rest on understandings of a *hierarchy of differentiated class formation* in which a new neoliberal global economy has forever gutted both the old, drab, Fordist regime of factory-driven accumulation and the routine conception of employment as a nine-to-five undertaking, defined by continuous work relations that were ordered, in part, by union protections. Stable working-class identities have been swept aside; a sense of proletarian power as a transformative agent of social relations of exploitation and oppression is now ended.

This new installment to what is by now over a three-decades-old "retreat from class"[14] is ironically centered on insisting that old class structures and agencies have been replaced by new ones, albeit class formations that are defined by their distance from structures of class place and the many destabilizations that separate this new precarious class from all previous touchstones of working-class identity. Standing posits the existence of a ladder of stratification that orders the lower classes of contemporary society into distinct components: the manual working class; the army of the unemployed; the social misfits living a thoroughly marginalized existence; and the youth-dominated precariat.

Beyond the intellectual grid of Standing's Weberian / Lloyd Warne-rian classifications lie a graveyard of political implications, in which are buried the possibilities of a past written off as finis. A sclerotic laborist politic, according to Standing, is simply antiquated in modern times, a residue of a tired social democracy, its affiliation with a dying labor movement little more than a hangover of a previous era. As a separate youth-led precariat emerges as a distinct class force, according to Standing, it will scale the heights of new mobilizations, creating struggles and corresponding slogans that leave older injunctions, such as "Workers of the world, unite!," discarded as useless impediments. The precariat is now the truly dangerous class, threatening disorder, a body of nomads coalescing under the banner, "Denizens, unite!" In-sisting that with the dismantling of the public sector, the rising signif-icance of black markets, and generational tensions associated with the young resenting their elders living off of state subsidies, such as lavish pensions, the precariat is a unique and distinct class entity, Standing urges this powerful force to make the turn to utopianism, calling on all right-thinking advocates of multiculturalism to rally to its standard as a matter, almost, of natural selection. "The precariat is not victim, villain, or hero," he writes, "it is just a lot of us.'

Standing's response to capitalist crisis, the intensification of expro-priation, the dismantling of working-class entitlements, and the assault on the material well-being of the working class that manifests itself in a growing insecurity of waged employment—all of which, and more, constitute a revived class war from above—is nothing less than an *ide-ology*. It is, to be sure, appealing in its simplified identification of the young, the restless, and the insecure as the foundation of a new move-ment of resistance. Nonetheless, for all of its attractiveness to an increas-ingly volatile global sector of the working class, the end result of being drawn into this ideology will be to fragment the potential power of an amalgamation of the dispossessed by hiving off a sector of this class from all other components with whom this contingent might ally, thereby weakening the forces of anti-capitalism. The suggestion that class, its composition and its strategic importance, has somehow changed in the recent past, because work is no longer secure, represents a retreat into fragmentation, rather than a creative response to it. It is also a funda-mentally ahistorical argument, for work has never been anything but a precarious foundation of life lived on the razor's edge of dispossession.

Claims of a new precariat class grow logically out of the "post-Marxist postmodernism" that has, since the 1980s, reveled in study of marginality, repudiating the "totalizing" master narratives of class and class struggle that animate the desire not only to interpret the world, but to change it. The tragedy is that this ideological posture is likely to gain traction precisely because the established trade union leaderships have ossified to the point that they cannot reclaim the sensibility that prodded the labor movement into being, the understanding that "An injury to one is an injury to all." With the revolutionary left largely moribund, moreover, there are precious few forums in which class mobilizations are hailed as stepping stones in the creation of new organizations, parties, and structures of opposition that can truly become "tribunes of the people," expressions of the need to resist capitalist encroachments in the name of a wide-ranging socialist agenda. Instead, there are European examples, like Portugal and Spain, where the marginally, casually, and insecurely employed are an expanding and increasingly significant percentage of the working class (upward of 40 percent), exhibiting organizational initiatives (such as the formation of the Precári@s Inflexiveis movement) that reflect this reality.[15]

For Marxists, the existence of such organization of the precariously employed is heartening. Yet this is no substitute for a powerful coming together of *all* components of the working class, which must be united in their struggles against capitalism and staunch in their refusals of division, driven by capitalism's conveniences rather than the needs of socialized humanity. In this sense, resisting the ideology of *precariousness as class formation* is a theoretical point of departure. Doing this necessitates going back to the original theoretical foundations of historical materialism, and addressing the extent to which dispossession (from which flows all manner of insecurities and all manner of precariousness in the wage relation) has always been *the fundamental feature of class formation* rather than the material basis of a new, contemporary class, with an agenda silent on the necessity of socialism.

DISPOSSESSION AS SOCIAL CLASS: THE ORIGINS OF HISTORICAL MATERIALISM

In the 1873 afterword to the second German edition of *Capital*, Marx declared that

the contradictions inherent in the movement of capitalist society im-
press themselves upon the practical bourgeois most strikingly in the
changes of the periodic cycle, through which modern industry runs,
and whose crowning point is the universal crisis. That crisis is once
again approaching, although as yet but in its preliminary stage; and
by the universality of its theatre and the intensity of its action it will
drum dialectics even into the heads of mushroom upstarts.[16]

Capitalist progress was thus premised on capitalist destruction. "The
growing incompatibility between the productive development of society and its hitherto existing relations of production expresses itself
in bitter contradictions, crises, spasms," Marx wrote in the *Grundrisse*,
concluding that, "the violent destruction of capital not by relations external to it, but rather as a condition of its self-preservation, is the most
striking form in which advice is given it to be gone and give room to a
higher state of social production."[17]

Socialism, Marx and Engels reasoned, was necessary if humankind
was ever to transcend the destructive logic of the profit system, which
was "too narrow to comprise the wealth" that it created: "And how
does the bourgeoisie get over these crises? On the one hand, by enforced destruction of a mass of productive forces; on the other, by the
conquest of new markets, and by the more thorough exploitation of
the old ones. That is to say, by paving the way for more extensive and
more destructive crises, and by diminishing the means whereby crises
are prevented."[18] Class formation, about which Marx wrote relatively
little, was never separable from this understanding of *capitalism as crisis*. Earlier epochs had seen society fragmented into "various orders, a
manifold gradation of social rank [composed of] . . . patricians, knights,
plebeians, slaves . . . feudal lords, vassals, guild-masters, journeymen,
apprentices, serfs." Capitalism, in contrast, "simplified the class antagonisms." Under the revolutionizing drive of the bourgeoisie, civil society was split into "two great hostile camps, into two great classes
directly facing each other: Bourgeoisie and Proletariat." This was, for
Marx and Engels, the fundamental sociopolitical fact of the human relations of capitalism. As much as the working classes, pluralized in the
mainstream language of the epoch, were fragmented by identities of
nationality, religion, morality, and status, Marx and Engels insisted that
the proletarians, recruited from all previous classes of the population,
were finally brought together in inevitable association because of what

they lacked: property. An original expropriation, generalized (some-times over generations) to dispossession, defined the mass of humanity as inherently opposed to the propertied and powerful minority, and the isolations of laboring life would eventually give way "to revolution-ary combination." Capitalism and the bourgeoisie had produced their "own gravediggers." This was fundamental to what Marx and Engels insisted was a process, spawned in all that was once solid melting into air, of men and women at last being "compelled to face with sober senses" their "real conditions of life."[19]

In hindsight, and with a historical appreciation of the longue durée of class formation, it is clear that Marx and Engels wrote at a specific juncture, preceded by the dissolution of feudal relations and followed by the consolidation of increasingly structured capitalist social rela-tions, of which differentiated labor markets were an integral part. To be sure, Marxist analysis of class relations necessarily addresses value, extraction of surplus, and regimes of accumulation, but the prior (and always historically ongoing)[20] process, on which all of this is premised, is necessarily expropriation and, in the long term, the continuity of dispossession. Thus, in Chapter 23 of *Capital*, Marx declares, in his discussion of simple reproduction and the relations of seigneurs and serfs, "[I]f one fine morning the lord appropriates to himself the land, the cattle, the seed, in a word, the means of production of this peasant, the latter will thenceforth be obliged to sell his labour power," while in Chapter 25, on "the general law of capitalist accumulation," Marx crit-icized (but drew upon) Sir Fredrick Morton Eden's book, *The State of the Poor; Or, an History of the Labouring Classes of England* (1797). Against Eden's view that those emerging capitalists who commanded the pro-duce of industry owed their exemption from labor "to civilization and order," Marx argued that

> the reproduction of a mass of labour-power, which must incessantly re-incorporate itself with capital for that capital's self-expansion; which cannot get free from capital, and whose enslavement to capi-tal is only concealed by the variety of individual capitalists to whom it sells itself, this reproduction of labour-power forms, in fact, an essential of the reproduction of capital itself. Accumulation of capital is, therefore, increase of the proletariat.

Marx quoted the eighteenth-century satirist, philosopher, and political economist Bernard de Mandeville, who noted, "[I]t would be easier, where property is well secured, to live without money than without the poor; for who would do the work?" Dispossession, then, is the basis of all proletarianization, which orders accumulation. Only socialism can end this cycle of dispossession/accumulation/crisis/disorder, the partial and temporary resolution of which, under capitalism, can only be achieved by the bloodletting of another round of violent dispossession.[21]

DISPOSSESSION AS SOCIAL CLASS: WHAT'S PAST IS PRECARIOUSNESS

From the vantage point of Marx, schooled by Eden's marshaling of evidence and other sources, proletarianization flowed historically, a trickle that commenced in antiquity and had grown to a stream by the seventeenth century. Christopher Hill describes the masterless masses who provided the shock troops of Digger and Leveller contingents in the 1640s, the "surplus" population that created the surplus out of which the capitalist class would coalesce. He refers to a "seething mobility of forest squatters, itinerant craftsmen and building labourers, unemployed men and women seeking work, strolling players and jugglers, pedlars and quack doctors, vagabonds, tramps: congregated especially in the big cities, but also with footholds wherever newly-squatted areas escaped from the machinery of the parish or in old-squatted areas where labour was in demand." It was from this "underworld" that ships' crews and armies were recruited, and out of which the migratory settlement that peopled the New World was fashioned.[22]

By the mid-nineteenth century this stream of dispossession had become a torrential river of class formation, fed by underground currents of enclosures, wars, technological displacements of handicraft labors, and other forces of expropriation and displacement. Marx and Engels can perhaps be excused for seeing proletarianization at this time as a maturing process, rather than one that was, in fact, only coming into its adolescence. In the decades that would follow, class formation would consolidate, indeed harden. Yet this would be an extremely uneven project, and never one in which anything approximating "stabilization" occurred. Dispossession was always disorderly: the old jostled with the new, layers of labor were structured into seemingly contradictory locales, with their designations running from the aristocratic (the black-coated worker) to the derogatory (the dangerous classes, the residuum).[23] And complicating this chaotic making and remaking of class experience was the potent disruption of capitalism's persistent underside: crisis.

A working class conceived as forged out of the process of dispossession is thus central, not only to the thought of Marx and Engels, but to the monumental achievement of E. P. Thompson's *The Making of the English Working Class*, which in 2013 celebrated a fiftieth anniversary of its original date of publication. Indeed, Thompson explored the crucible of class formation in England in the years 1790–1830 by accenting how a mass of previously differentiated *employments*, in which variegated occupational labors evolved, had come, through struggle and crisis, to be *a working class*. He drew on Henry Mayhew, whose writings on London labor and the poor emerged at roughly the same time as the commentaries of Marx and Engels. Mayhew had suggested the extent to which the capitalist employment marketplace was structured in a series of arbitrary ways. It was dependent on work that could only be conducted seasonally, reliant on fashion and accident, ordered by overwork and scamp work in the cheap trades, constantly reconfigured by the dilution of skills that saw women and children introduced into specific handicrafts in order to depress wages and restructured by machinery and managerial innovations. Recruited to the metropolis by the dissolution of landed relations and the destruction of village handicrafts, waged workers struggled, through time, with impersonal disciplines of a labor market always cramped by acute limitations. Mayhew concluded that regular employment was available to roughly 1.5 million laborers, while half-time work might accrue to a further 1.5 million, with 1.5 million more either wholly unemployed or working occasionally only by displacing those who considered specific jobs to be their terrain.

This might seem to be anything but a coherent grouping, the "working classes" that it designated a "bundle of discrete phenomena." Thompson nevertheless argued that it was *a working class* that was indeed made in the cauldron of the Industrial Revolution and the counter-revolution of property, both historical processes either ridden forcefully or instigated by the bourgeoisie, and both either dependent upon or directed against those who were, increasingly, dispossessed of property and power over their lives. Class constituted an "identity of interests . . . of the most diverse occupations and levels of attainment," and it was forged in antagonism to the attempts to make of all of these components "a sort of machine." If class was composed of various parts, drawn from a plethora of experiences of dispossession, both Marx and Engels's and Thompson's understandings converged: all of these layers of class formation were drawn together, not so much because they had come from or were embedded in absolute sameness, but because their life courses were being determined by ultimately similar processes and outcomes.[24]

The point, as a rich historiography reveals, and as is evident in Thompson's *Making*, with its accounts of proto-industrialization and outworkers, field laborers, declining crafts, "church and king mobs," opaque societies of machine breakers, the denizens of "Satan's strongholds," and metropolitan artisans, is that there is nothing new about fragmentations of class experience. Class has always embodied differentiation, insecurity, and precariousness. Just as precariousness is historically inseparable from class formation, there are invariably differentiations that seemingly separate out those with access to steady employments and secure payments from those who must scramble for work and access to the wage. Expropriation, then, is a highly heterogeneous experience, since no individual can be dispossessed in precisely the same way as another, or live that process of material alienation exactly as another would. Yet dispossession, *in general*, nonetheless *defines proletarianization*. It is the metaphorical mark of Cain stamped on all workers, regardless of their level of employment, rate of pay, status, waged placement, or degree of wagelessness.[25]

This has been a premise of much Marxist analysis, evident, for instance, in the (admittedly gendered) title of Martin Glaberman's essay on the American working class in the 1960s, "Be His Payment High or Low." Glaberman noted, decades ago, that "what is involved in industry after industry is not simply the replacing of men by automated machines but the discarding of men, the moving of others and the bringing of still others into the industrial working class and the reorganisation of the work process."[26] This kind of constant restructuring is precisely what animated Harry Braverman's concern with the degradation of work in the twentieth century.[27] Although, as Braverman argued, the process of change in the relations of production intensified in the twentieth-century age of monopoly, it had been around for decades. It astounded even early capitalists, who could not quite fathom the "moral economy" of Adam Smith. "It is vain to read his book to find a remedy for a complaint which he could not conceive existed, vis. 100,000 weavers doing the work of 150,000," wrote one humane English employer early in the nineteenth century. This man's inability to understand "that the profits of a Manufacture should be what one Master could wring from the hard earnings of the poor, more than another" led to his ruin.[28]

It is in this context that capitalist crisis has become something of a fountainhead from which spring all manner of theoretical musings on new class formations. Capitalist crisis, for instance, ushered into being new class struggle initiatives on the part of the bourgeoisie. It has often called forth new tactics and strategic reassessments on the part of the working class. The *ahistorical* claim that the precariousness of modern labor is something dramatically new, necessitating a revision of all that has been solid in the Marxist approach to class, however, must be refused. Acknowledging the extent of precariousness in the contemporary trends of global class formation does *not* necessitate a conceptual and political rupture with understandings of the possibilities of a unity of the dispossessed, which remains the only hope for a socialist humanity.

PROLETARIAN SURPLUS, PRECARIOUSNESS, AND PAUPERIZATION

A stable working class identity or, dichotomously, a precarious one—these are not the defining features of class difference, one designated *proletarian*, the other defined as *precariat*. Rather, as a deep structure of being, dispossession itself is fundamental and throughout history has been a continuous thread that ties together exploitation *and* oppression. Marx noted this in *Capital*, writing that capitalist enrichment was premised on "the condemnation of one part of the working class to enforced idleness by the over-work of the other part," accelerating "the production of the reserve army on a scale corresponding with the advance of social accumulation." Every proletarian can thus be categorized, not so much according to their waged work, but to the possible forms of surplus population, which Marx labeled "the floating, the latent, and the stagnant." This is why the accumulation of capital is also the accumulation of labor, but the Malthusian multiplication of the proletariat does not necessarily mean the working class will, in its entirety, be waged. As Marx wrote:

The lowest sediment of the relative surplus-population finally dwells in the sphere of pauperism . . . the quantity of paupers increases with every crisis. . . . Pauperism is the hospital of the active labour-army and the dead weight of the industrial reserve army. Its production is included in that of the relative surplus population, its necessity in theirs; along with the surplus population, pauperism forms a condition of capitalist production, and of the capitalist development of wealth. It enters into the *faux frais* of capitalist production.[29]

As John Bellamy Foster, Robert W. McChesney, and R. Jamil Jonna note in the November 2011 issue of *Monthly Review*, Marx's way of seeing class formation was much ahead of his time, anticipating how modern imperialism and the relentless march of capital accumulation on a world scale would result in the quantitative expansion and qualitative transformation of the global reserve army of labor.[30] This massive reserve, from which capital draws such sustenance for its accumulative appetite, now numbers in the billions, and as it has grown so too have the dimensions of misery of the dispossessed expanded, as Marx predicted.[31] Jan Breman, writing of exploitation, expropriation, and exclusion in India, declares, "[A] point of no return is reached when a reserve army waiting to be incorporated into the labor process becomes stigmatized as a permanently redundant mass, an excessive burden that cannot be included now or in the future, in economy and society. This metamorphosis is, in my opinion at least, the real crisis of world capitalism."[32] What this suggests is that in any analytic grappling with the historical record of class formation, it is mandatory to see proletarianization whole. Historians are beginning to appreciate, as indicated by the interpretive excursions of Michael Denning into wagelessness and Mike Davis into slummification, that it is imperative not to center our studies of labor in the logic of capital's validations. The working class does not only achieve visibility and become invested with political relevance to the extent that it is *waged*. Expropriation is being, and even in the throes of dispossession, work is necessary for the vast majority of humanity, regardless of whether or how it is remunerated. Indeed, as feminists have long insisted in their accounts of unpaid reproductive labor, a perspective on class formation bounded only by the wage will inevitably be blinkered in all kinds of ways.[33]

PRECARIOUSNESS AND THE LUMPENPROLETARIAT:
THE POLITICS OF CLASS AFFILIATION

In circles uninfluenced by Standing's approach to the precariat as a
separate social class there is nonetheless a congruent, if seemingly unrelated, interest in Marx's ostensible dismissiveness of precariousness,
especially as it manifested itself in jaundiced comments on the lumpenproletariat. There is no doubt that, writing as a Victorian, Marx often
lapsed into moralistic judgement with respect to the most marginalized, often criminalized, subcultures of the dispossessed. The further
one gets from the core capitalist economies of the advanced capitalist
Western nations, the more apparent it is that class formation is often
structured around wagelessness and subcultures of the marginally employed: transitions in and out of penny capitalism, criminality, and
hybrid existences in which peasant subsistence and temporary proletarianization congeal are almost routine.

Historians interested in class formation on a world scale, and especially the importance of wagelessness in the developing world, have
necessarily confronted the prejudice in selective comments by Marx
on a class stratum he was prone to denigrate as the lumpenproletariat.[34]
Nonetheless, for all that Marx (and Engels) can be castigated for the
"political incorrectness" of their comments on the lumpenproletariat, it
is crucial to recognize that this loose term of abuse was situated within
a particular context and was not necessarily a way of separating out
one portion of the dispossessed from others in class terms. Given that
Marx's coining of the term lumpenproletariat was as much metaphorical trope as it was a rigorously developed analytic category, claims that
Marx erred in writing out of the proletariat the criminalized and destitute who were divorced from the productive relations of developing
capitalism may well be overstated. Indeed, a close reading of the entire
oeuvre of Marx and Engels suggests four things.[35]

First, even within the political writings of the 1840s, where there
is no doubt that the term "lumpenproletariat" is used to designate de-
rogatorily sectors of the dispossessed that cast their political lot with
the project of reaction and restoration of class privilege, it is obviously
the case that use of the prefix "lumpen" is meant to convey debasement rather than a hardened class place. This is evident in how Marx
affixes the lumpenproletarian adjective to Bonaparte himself, who is
the principal object of Marx's revulsion in "The Eighteenth Brumaire

of Louis Bonaparte" and *Class Struggles in France*. Bonaparte was met-
aphorically castigated as the princely *"chief of the lumpenproletariat,"* a
scoundrel who recognized in the "scum, offal, refuse of all classes the
only class upon which he [could] base himself unconditionally."[36] One
literary theorist has commented that "Marx must have lived the history
of France from 1848 to 1852 – the revolution careening backwards – as
resembling nothing so much as a latrine backing up."[37] Understanding
this, it would seem, might temper the ways in which contemporary
scholarship evaluates the birth of a term such as "lumpenproletariat,"
which truly did enter the world amid the death agonies of revolutionary
possibility. As Hal Draper has suggested, Marx's utilization of the prefix
"lumpen" was a way of labeling an individual or a social grouping as
knave-like or odious,[38] and this means, I would suggest, that the term
is far less a rigorous classification of analytic substance than it is an adjective of vitriol. This surfaces in Marx's pillorying of a particular kind
of mid-nineteenth-century French financial aristocracy, a rakish layer
of bourgeois society that is presented as having risen to commanding,
parasitic heights, gorging itself on wealth produced by others, exhibiting an "unbridled display of unhealthy and dissolute appetites." Such an
aristocratic layer, characterized by pleasure becoming *"crapuleux,* where
gold, dirt, and blood flow together," was, in Marx's view, "nothing
but the resurrection of the lumpen proletariat at the top of bourgeois
society."[39] Second, inasmuch as this debasement is, in the passions of
an 1848–51 defeat of working-class revolution, Marx's way of locating
how sectors of the dispossessed opted to struggle in ways that secured
the privileges of power and money rather than challenging them, the
central issue in approaching the lumpenproletariat must be a consideration of how the lowest of the low act in moments of class struggle.
Even Fanon—whose validation of the "pimps, the hooligans, the unemployed, and the petty criminals" as a revolutionary contingent seems
at odds with Marx's less salubrious approach to people identified in
this way—understood that colonial authority might well be "extremely
skilful in using [the] ignorance and incomprehension of the *lumpenproletariat."* Unless organized by revolutionary activists, Fanon feared that
the lumpenproletariat would "find itself fighting as hired soldiers side-
by-side" with the troops of reaction, and he cited instances in Angola
and the Congo where precisely this had indeed happened.[40]

Third, even when he is, as in the writings relating to France between 1848–51, disparaging the lumpenproletariat as a force of reaction, Marx hints at the extent to which the sectors of the dispossessed
were not so much acting as a distinct class apart from the proletariat,
but were, rather, individuals *directed* in this way by bourgeois forces.
When Marx writes in *The Class Struggles in France* that the twenty-four
battalions of the Mobile Guards were set up by the Provisional Government, and that they were (rightly or wrongly) composed of young
men from fifteen to twenty years of age who "belonged for the most
part to the *lumpenproletariat*," he prefaces this reading of historical development with the statement that it came about because of bourgeois
need.[41] With the bourgeoisie no "match for the proletariat" in 1848,
it embarked on establishing "a hundred different obstacles" to curb
working-class power. When these efforts failed "there consequently
remained but one way out: to set one part of the proletariat against
the other," a conclusion that can certainly be interpreted as acknowl-
edgment that Marx did not consider the lumpenproletariat and the
proletariat as irreconcilably divided, but part of a continuum of the
same dispossessed class. But consciousness of class place/interests is
never simply a fait accompli. Because this must be built, and is part of
the project of making socialism by making socialists, it is possible, in
periods of intense struggle to see individuals cross class lines and act
in ways that pit them against members of their class. The language of
antagonism is then often quite harsh, as the designation "scab" reveals.

Fourth, inasmuch as Marx never wrote the decisive volume on labor
that might well have at least addressed, if not clarified, the meaning
of lumpenproletarianization, it is surely critical to acknowledge that
Marx's perspective shifted gears through and over time. His assessment
of the lumpenproletariat reached, to be sure, something of a nadir with
Bonaparte's coup d'état, orchestrated by the so-called Society of December 10, composed, in Marx's words, of

> ruined and adventurous offshoots of the bourgeoisie . . . vagabonds,
> discharged soldiers, discharged jailbirds, escaped galley slaves,
> swindlers, mountebanks, *lazzaroni*, pickpockets, tricksters, gam-
> blers, *maquereaus*, brothel-keepers, porters, *literati*, organ-grinders,
> rag-pickers, knife grinders, tinkers, beggars – in short, the whole
> indefinite, disintegrated mass, thrown hither and thither, which the
> French term *la bohème*.[42]

This rhetoric of revulsion notwithstanding, there are passages in both earlier and later writings, distanced from the immediacy of Marx's 1848–51 political disappointment, that exhibit a more analytic understanding. As Peter Haynes suggests, Marx recognized well the ways in which the dispossessed were victimized by capitalism's capacity to criminalize and punish the poor. In later writings, Marx drew explicitly on Thomas More, for instance, whose *Utopia* was a source utilized in the writing of *Capital*, and who had represented the dispossessed as "dryven to this extreme necessitie, firste to steale, then to dye."[43]

For all that Marx and Engels could write in the pejorative language of their times about what would later be called "the underclass,"[44] they were also not unaware of how the "residuum" was reciprocally related to the stalwart proletarians on whom they based their hope for socialism. Engels's *The Condition of the Working-Class in England in 1844* had much of moralistic condemnation in it, especially with respect to immigrant Irish labor, but this did not mean that he saw the most downtrodden sectors of the proletariat as irredeemably separated out from the working class. Indeed, in an 1892 preface to his Manchester study, Engels recorded with considerable optimism the extent to which socialism's advance in England had registered even in a former bastion of lumpenproletarianization, London's East End. "That immense haunt of misery is no longer the stagnant pool that it was six years ago," Engels wrote. "It has shaken off its torpid despair, has returned to life, and has become the home of what is called the 'New Unionism,'" he continued, adding, "that is to say the organisation of the great mass of 'unskilled' workers."[45]

Marx understood well, as Michael Denning has recently noted, that

> political economy . . . does not recognize the unemployed worker, the workingman, insofar as he happens to be outside this labour relationship. The rascal, swindler, beggar, the unemployed, the starving, wretched and criminal workingman – these are *figures* who do not exist *for political economy* but only for other eyes, those of the doctor, the judge, the grave-digger, and bum-bailiff, etc.; such figures are spectres outside its domain.[46]

Marx, of course, also had considerable empathy for what was *done to* the dispossessed, as is more than evident in his condemnation of the "barbarity in the treatment of the paupers" and his recognition of the "growing horror in which the working people hold the slavery of the workhouse," which he dubbed a "place of punishment for misery."[47] In his 1842–43 *Rheinische Zeitung* articles on the debates in Germany over the law on the theft of wood, moreover, there is ample suggestion that Marx appreciated the ways in which capitalism's socioeconomic trajectory tended in the direction of wider criminalization of behaviors of the poor that were themselves critical to the survival of the dispossessed. Separated first from nature, the dispossessed then found themselves expropriated from the institutionalized protections of civil society.

State formation, in Marx's view, proceeded on this basis: ruling-class power and institutions subservient to such authority's ends made the law into a vehicle driving forward the expanding nature of dispossession, turning the apparatus of governance into a mailed fist of privileged interests. As Peter Linebaugh pointed out in the mid-1970s, Marx's writings on the thefts of wood provide a jumping-off point for a discussion of class formation that necessitates analysis of the meaning of Marxist understandings of the lumpenproletariat, a term that can only be interrogated when "the principle of historical specification" and "the concept of class struggle" are central to analysis.[48] In discussing the issue of access to the fallen wood of the forest, Marx contended that "just as it is not fitting for the rich to lay claim to alms distributed in the street, so also in regard to these *alms of nature*," and he insisted on the need for a universal set of "customary rights of the poor."[49] Needless to say, nothing of the sort materialized in the cauldron of capitalist class formation, and Marx concluded that the state had been turned into a servant of property.

Marx thus addressed proletarianization as a dual process, the creation of labor as both "free" *and* outlawed.[50] But if there is honor among *some* thieves, not all who have been placed beyond the boundary of respectability exhibit admirable traits.[51] Marx appreciated, in a way that many contemporary scholars who romanticize segments of society driven to

> incorrigibility fail to discern, that extreme and long-term dispossession could well deform a section of the proletariat politically, reducing it to an adjunct of reaction. This matter was still being posed in the 1930s, with activists and Left Book Club authors such as Wal Hannington, a founding member of the Communist Party of Great Britain and organizer of the National Unemployed Workers' Movement, asking worriedly, "Is there a Fascist danger amongst the Unemployed?"[52]

Debates over lumpenproletarianization, like discussions of precariousness, highlight the reality of status differentiation within the dispossessed, illuminating the importance of conscious identifications on the plane of class-struggle politics among sectors of the working class. As difficult as is the project of uniting the expropriated, many of whom can be incorporated into the hegemonic and ideological edifice of acquisitive individualism, this can never be the foundation of a materialist separation of layers of the dispossessed into distinct classes.

CLASS POLITICS AND PRECARIOUSNESS

Expropriation is not in and of itself a guarantee of behaviors that will advance humanity. It is in uniting the dispossessed in struggles that can realize a new social order, one premised not on expropriation, exploitation, and oppression, but on collective productions for the use and benefit of all, that constitutes the only possibility for meaningful progress.

On a global scale, dispossession is accelerating. A crisis-ridden capitalism necessarily intensifies expropriation and expands the boundaries of immiseration. The necessity of orchestrating a collective response to this quickening pace of material alienation is most urgent, yet analytic thought in our times trends in the direction of accenting the fragmentations and divisions that incapacitate the working class, in all its gradations, rather than forging it into a fighting tribune for all of the world's exploited and oppressed. At its most populist, such thought, articulated most clearly by Guy Standing, stresses the unique constellation of a new class force, the *precariat*. Radical revisionists, animated by the need to address class formation on a global scale and cognizant of the importance of marginalization in the making of the world's proletariat, have turned away from some of Marx's insights, fracturing the experience of the waged and the wageless, questioning Marx's failure to create a sense of class premised on inclusivity.

These developments, largely confined at this point to theoretical discussions and academic treatises, are nevertheless paralleled in the actual world of class politics and praxis by a deepening structural and institutional separation of the fragments of the working class. Trade unions atrophy, both in terms of their capacity to organize labor, and with respect to their willingness to put forward a politics of class that extends past the constrictions of business unionism, which focuses narrowly on specific occupational jurisdictions of waged employments.

The revolutionary left, never weaker over the course of the last century than it is now, is a tragically understated presence in contemporary class relations, and has been usurped, as a critical political voice, by identity-driven social movements that reproduce the fragmentations inherent in capitalism's tendency to divide the better to conquer. And the working class appears as more and more fractured, divided against itself, and less and less able to utilize the precarious conditions of its material life to sustain structures of resistance.

Understanding this tragic set of parallel trajectories, it is imperative that those on the socialist left—as well as those working in unions, social movements, and all manner of campaigns that see themselves challenging capital and the state in the interests of the dispossessed—reassert what is most solid in the Marxist tradition. What is more than ever needed is a politics of class that speaks directly to the betterment of humanity through insistence that the expropriated are as one in their ultimate needs. The reciprocal powers (however subjectively and seemingly different) of the waged and the wageless must be organized and utilized to speak to the debilitating consequences of precariousness as well as the exploitative nature of all productions, payments, and pro-hibitions. Transcending an imposed and ultimately artificial difference is central to breaking the chains that keep workers separated from their collectivity, and bind them to the isolations that seal their subordina-tion. In the recent words of the East European dissident, G. M. Tamás, "Vive la difference? No. Vive la Commune!"[53]

Once it is grasped that all proletarians suffer precariousness, and all of those constrained by precariousness in their working lives are indeed proletarians or have interests that coincide directly with this class of the dispossessed, it is clear that there are expanding possibilities for more effective politics based on class struggles in our times. And it is indeed class struggle—rooted in expropriation and forged in the increasingly agitated crises of capitalism—that remains the ultimate basis for chang-ing the world through a transformative politics.

CLASS THEORY AND CLASS POLITICS TODAY

Hugo Radice

In the spring of 2013, the BBC unveiled a major survey of the class structure of modern Britain, prepared by a team of sociologists led by Professor Mike Savage of the London School of Economics.* The survey sought to broaden the traditional occupational analysis of class by more fully taking into account "the role of cultural and social processes in generating class divisions," and the authors argued that "this new seven class model recognises both social polarisation in British society and class fragmentation in its middle layers."[1]

These two observations—of polarization and fragmentation—will certainly strike a chord with any casual observer of social change. In recent years, in many countries around the world, inequality of income, wealth, and power has undoubtedly been increasing; for example in Britain, where the rise of inequality has been widely studied, often connecting inequalities of income and wealth to those in health, housing, education, and other quality of life issues.[2] At the same time, the increasingly complex configurations of class, as understood in the LSE survey, have also been evident. What has traditionally been understood as the working class has been seen by many as fragmenting

* This essay, first published in *Socialist Register 2015* (London: Merlin Press, 2015), is part of a larger project on the critique of political economy and the prospects for socialism (see the citations in notes 7, 17 and 37). For advice and encouragement I am grateful to Logie Barrow, Anthony Barzey, Paul Blackledge, Dave Byrne, David Camfield, Daniele Tepe-Belfraege, Alfredo Saad-Filho, the editors of the *Socialist Register* and members of the CSE Transpennine Working Group.

into layers defined as much by social standing, spending patterns, and welfare dependency as by the more traditional attributes of occupation and income.[3] Meanwhile, the middle class has remained, as it has always been, hard to define with any clarity: it includes small business owners, professionals, managers, and higher-skilled or supervisory workers across all sectors of the economy, public and private.

The authors of the LSE survey identify their classes in terms of people's experiences, attitudes, and lifestyles, and relate these to underlying economic and social trends. Such an approach is attractive because it roots class identity in something common to all of us, namely a life path that can be mapped out and analyzed, and because the data generated in such a survey can then be subjected to sophisticated statistical analysis. The elements selected for recording are underpinned by a particular conceptual framework, developed some thirty years ago by Pierre Bourdieu.[4] In this approach, individuals are differentiated by their possession of economic, cultural, and social capital in different quantities and proportions—the three forms of capital being in principle independent of each other. The data are then analyzed in order to identify clusters of individuals—eventually, in this case, seven in number—who broadly share the same economic, social, and cultural characteristics.

While such a survey provides an informative snapshot of these clusters, it leaves open the question of what social processes are shaping how we cluster in this way, and how these classes-as-clusters interact with each other.[5] Some of the forces shaping the clusters are treated as distinct, if interacting, and in the final analysis attributable to factors such as technology or resource constraints that are seen as external. However, the survey is in essence a heuristic exercise rather than one of testing distinct hypotheses about social change, and the main outcome is a mapping of how the various observable changes are compatible with each other; it remains very hard to ask really important questions about society as a whole, and how social differentiation changes through time.

But the current renewed preoccupation with class also raises important questions about whether and how we can challenge the present social order. If society is really as fragmented as it immediately appears, what chance can we ever have of once again promoting the progressive ideals of democracy, equality, and solidarity pursued by socialists—in the broadest sense—for the last two hundred years? The wider political environment is hardly helpful, given ever-deepening global integration that seems to undermine any sense of local or national political agency; the pervasive fracturing of most if not all societies along lines of gender, race, sexuality, and religion; and the looming problem of climate change that threatens the entire relation of humanity with nature. After decades of retreat in the face of such obstacles, the unfolding of the great financial crisis after 2007 led to many disparate initiatives across the world, but not as yet to any significant renewal of the left, or at least one sufficiently unified, sustained, and widespread to provide cause for real optimism.

On the contrary, whether in the supposedly more advanced rich countries or elsewhere, neither social democracy nor state socialism have been able to withstand the political consequences of the new circumstances, and we have hardly begun to respond creatively. We still too readily turn to the old playbooks, clinging to the belief that the problem does not lie in how we as socialists have translated our political ideals into an effective left politics, but rather in failures of leadership, or deficiencies in our unresponsive fellow citizens. It is indeed hard, these days, to talk about socialism as any kind of real alternative, let alone to map out a politics that can build prefigurative institutions and practices that will in turn persuade others, in meaningful numbers, of the possibility of a better world.

So where do we begin? Surely, we have to campaign on many fronts. The renewed interest in inequality (such as Piketty's *Capital*)[6] is having an impact on public debate in many parts of the world. Sadly, this is not because of a real sea change in opinion—let alone political action— among the public at large, for they display that mix of aspiration and resentment usually attributed to them by the commentariat. Rather, it is largely because to the political elites, whether liberal, social democratic, or authoritarian, the gap between rich and poor has grown so wide that they fear aspiration faltering and resentment deepening into disenchantment and revolt—as much from the "new middle classes" as from the poor and excluded.

The starting point of this essay is the proposition that the question of class is central, as argued in the preface to last year's *Socialist Register*.[7] This is not because I want in any way to suggest that it must take precedence over other issues; on the contrary, it seems obvious that the counterposing of "class politics" against "social movements" has been one of the main obstacles to left renewal now for forty years or more.[8] Instead, in what follows I want to argue that the painful experiences of this whole period can only be resolved through a thorough critique of the ways class has been understood.

In order to do this, I propose first to revisit Marx's original relational understanding of class, and how that understanding was taken up by later generations in the Marxist tradition, especially in the revival of debate about class from the 1960s to the 1980s. In the following sections, I look first at the analyses of the middle classes in relation to Marx's two-class model, in which the New Left sought to respond to claims that their growth had confounded Marx's expectations of social polarization. I then examine the related question of whether in any case the working class was (or still is) a revolutionary subject capable of overthrowing the capitalist order. This, then, sets up the problem of how far class relations can really be understood in relation to labor within capitalist production alone, rather than embracing also labor and other activities taking place elsewhere in society, or what has come to be called the sphere of social reproduction. Here I suggest an alternative understanding of production and labor that can effectively integrate the sphere of reproduction, and provide a better way of deploying class as a critical concept. This approach is then applied in the last section to political practice in the contemporary world, the aim being to shed light on the changes that have taken place in the neoliberal era and the political consequences that now confront us.

Finally, this essay is deliberately open and exploratory in nature. It is futile to imagine that locked within the past contributions of scholars or activists is a key that can unlock a better future. Equally futile is the time-honored method of argument-by-quotation, with the implicit assumption that every proposition must be justified by appeals to authority, related to the study of time-honored questions, and deploying approved terminology. That method may safeguard a tradition, but at the cost of reducing still further its appeal to a society that has plainly rejected the failed socialisms of the past.

CLASS ANALYSIS IN THE MARXIST TRADITION

For Marx there were two great classes in capitalist societies, the capitalist class (or bourgeoisie) and the working class (or proletariat), bound together in the social relation of capital. In this view, capitalists own the means of production, and purchase labor power from workers with the purpose of increasing their wealth by extracting surplus value and accumulating it as capital; workers have been dispossessed of direct access to the means of subsistence through self-activity, and therefore must sell their labor power in order to subsist. The two classes in relation to each other constitute the relations of production in capitalism, which is a historically distinct mode of production that emerges from a preexisting feudal order undermined by economic, social, and technological change. Its own development, in turn, entails a growing economic polarization between the two great classes; this generates a political consciousness uniting the working class in collective action to overturn the capitalist order and usher in a classless society.

This core "Marxist theory of class" has been challenged and qualified on a great variety of grounds, precisely because it stands at the heart of the political theory and practice of his followers. Theoretically, the two classes and the relationship between them are co-constituted with the concepts of mode of production, relations of production, value, capital, surplus value, labor process, accumulation—and necessarily also the forms of law and state that ensure the political rule of the capitalist class. Practically, socialism as a political movement rests on the belief that there exists a common interest across the working class, on which a unity of action can be built, first for resistance and then for revolution; this directs attention to the empirical configurations of class, the determinants of belief and behavior, and the strategies and tactics of political mobilization.

Before turning to the main critical challenges to the two-class model, it is worth setting out the positive case for it, and especially for the idea of the working class as agent of social change. There is no question that Marx and his successors argued repeatedly that the dynamics of capital accumulation would tend to generate increasing social polarization between capitalists and workers. Even in the first volume of *Capital*, these tendencies find empirical specification in the account of how, after its initial phase of "primitive accumulation," in which the means of production are appropriated by the rising capitalist class, both the production of commodities and their circulation are transformed by the drive to accumulate. In production, the key argument is that the "formal" subsumption of labor to capital, in which capitalists assume control of

substantively unchanged material production processes based on handicraft methods, tends to be transformed toward a "real" subsumption
of labor, entailing the development of first a detailed division of labor
in factory production, and then the application of science and technology to the development of machine-based production. As Braverman,
Gorz, and others reminded us in the 1970s, this transformation of the
capitalist labor process tends to reduce an increasing proportion of the
direct labor force within the capitalist workplace to an undifferentiated
mass of unskilled (or, more euphemistically, "semiskilled") workers,
subjected to the relentless discipline of mechanical or chemical processes designed and policed by capitalist managers.

At the same time, competition in the marketplace reinforces this
process. In the labor market, technological change in production, ap-
pearing for capital in the form of increased labor productivity, continually leads to reductions in the demand for labor, and thereby a reserve
army of labor that depresses wages and undermines attempts to organize opposition on the shop floor. In product markets, competition leads
inevitably to the concentration and centralization of capital: the scale of
production tends to grow faster than sales, leading to concentration in
ever-larger units, while the development of credit and financial markets encourages the centralization of capital through the creation and
merger of joint-stock companies.

But do these developments lay the foundations for the self-organization and growth of the working class as a collective actor? The conventional understanding within Marxism has always been that the
collective experience of class struggle brings home to workers their
shared class interest, encouraging self-organization and political contestation. Marx and Engels themselves left no systematic account of
how this might transpire, but their writings abound in concrete analyses of the political activities of the working class, analyses that necessarily can only be undertaken by successive generations in response to the
contingencies of time and place. Such contingencies evidently include
a vast array of natural, social, and cultural factors that stand alongside
the reproduction and accumulation of capital, shaping the thinking
and the actions of different groups within the working class. It is this
unavoidable gap between abstract theory and concrete self-activity that
later Marxists summed up in the formula that the "class in itself" had
to become a "class for itself" equipped with a collective understanding

of their circumstances.[9] This gap can only be navigated by developing and contesting political strategies for overthrowing capitalist rule and ushering in a classless society. It is in this context that the validity of the two-class model has been questioned.

THE MIDDLE CLASSES

A first important challenge to the two-class model has been the existence of social groups that appear to stand between capital and labor. The empirical existence of "middle classes" was clear to Marx and Engels themselves, and has been the subject of periodic debates ever since.[10]

Capitalism had emerged over a long historical period from societies of a very different kind, building upon components in a social division of labor that was dominated politically by a land-owning ruling class and characterized by its own distinctive relations of production. The transition to capitalism entails the continuing coexistence of earlier institutions, cultures, and practices with the emerging capitalist order, and this hybridity is remarkably persistent; but in addition, the spread of capitalism generates rapid economic growth, new patterns of international trade, and continuous technological change. These transform the division of labor both in society at large and within workplaces: new occupations arise and old occupations are brought within the scope of capitalist production, not only affecting the makeup of the two new great classes, but also continually generating an ill-defined border zone between them. Furthermore, these complexities are never observable in isolation from the processes of social contestation that accompany the development of capitalism.

Thus in the late nineteenth century, socialists recognized the political importance of both a "labor aristocracy" and a "petty bourgeoisie." The former was made up of workers organized both to defend the skill-based material privileges that they retained from their artisanal origins, and to establish shop floor control within the new industries of the Second Industrial Revolution. Their generally higher levels of education and income ensured that they played a disproportionate role in the development of trade unions and social democratic parties, but it was open to such workers to pursue their own interests at the expense of the working class as a whole. This could be achieved both individually through promotion within the workplace,[11] and collectively through maintaining separate "craft" unions and pursuing demarcation disputes against management attempts to deskill their work.

As a result, they could be drawn into political alliances with liberal reform. The petty bourgeoisie, the small proprietors in industry and commerce, were capitalists by definition, but in the face of market competition and the development of large-scale industry and finance in this period, their position became increasingly precarious, especially at times of economic crisis. They therefore gravitated politically toward populist alliances with the working class, but on the other hand, political ideologies of nationalism, racism, or imperialism could suffice to keep them loyal to the haute bourgeoisie and the capitalist state.

Of greater interest in more recent debates have been other intermediate groups, such as managers and technical specialists in capitalist production; independent professionals such as lawyers, accountants, doctors, artists, journalists, clergy, et cetera; and managers within the public sector and the state apparatus. There is no question that the occupational groups in question expanded greatly in the twentieth century in the advanced capitalist countries, and indeed in the Soviet bloc and other state-socialist countries also. At the turn of the century, Thorstein Veblen had already identified the potential antagonism between businessmen and engineers in large-scale industry, and the work of Berle and Means and James Burnham in the 1930s launched the idea of the "managerial revolution."[12] By the 1960s, even mainstream economists and sociologists were heralding a "postcapitalist" order based on technical rationality and economic efficiency, and it is hard to find much difference in this respect between the "new industrial state" of J. K. Galbraith and the ostensibly Marxist analysis of "monopoly capital" in the work of Baran and Sweezy.[13]

In relation to these middle-class elements, Marxists have followed two main analytical strategies. One strategy is to attribute to these groups, or even by extension the middle classes as a whole, a set of activities and beliefs that seem to define a distinct location within the class structure of capitalism, which then becomes a three-class model. The second is to argue that the various components of the middle classes have no distinct function or purpose, but instead occupy a collectively ambiguous position; rather like the traditional labor aristocracy and petty bourgeoisie, they align with either the capitalist class or the working class, most visibly in periods of crisis. Both strategies were extensively deployed in European and North American debates in the 1960s and '70s.

A well-known example of the first strategy was the thesis of the professional-managerial class, or PMC, posited in 1977 by Barbara and John Ehrenreich.[14] They distinguished the PMC from the traditional petty bourgeoisie of small proprietors, and included in it a wide range of salaried white-collar workers, including scientists, engineers, managers, public officials, teachers, journalists, accountants, lawyers, and the medical professions. Citing E. P. Thompson's view that class could only be understood as a historical relationship, they argued that the specific class role of the PMC was primarily one of reproducing capitalist social relations. The occupational, educational, social, and economic diversity of the PMC was no obstacle to its identification, and in any case no greater than the diversity of the capitalist class or the working class. Its rapid expansion during the post-1945 boom years was closely linked to the consolidation of monopoly capitalism and the expansion of the state, but also to the renewal of middle-class radicalism in the form of the New Left. This allowed the possibility of the PMC becoming a "class for itself," developing a distinct political voice and purpose, and even potentially taking over the role of revolutionary agency traditionally attributed to the working class. In all respects, this placed the putative PMC of the 1970s firmly in the American progressive tradition. It also stood alongside a growing literature in mainstream US sociology that advanced "new class" theses,[15] as well as echoing parallel thinking among dissident Marxists in Eastern Europe on the role of the intelligentsia.[16]

In contrast to the depiction of the PMC as a distinct if related class, other writers used various arguments to claim either that the occupational groups contained within it were liable to absorption into either the capitalist or the working class, or that they remained unable to cohere into a class-for-itself and were therefore irrelevant to the prospects for revolutionary change.[17] Braverman's deskilling thesis, though much misrepresented, provided ammunition to the prediction that intermediate groups were liable to undergo the same process of polarization that the original two-class model entailed. After all, the principles that Marx applied to the appropriation of workers' skills in the development of the capitalist labor process could be applied just as well to mental as to manual workers, and therefore to the various occupations included in the

PMC. Since the 1970s, many low- and mid-level technical, professional, and managerial occupations have indeed become more routinized, and their workers subjected to the steady erosion of the advantages that they once enjoyed in the labor market. Elements of the process of deskilling long identified in blue-collar work now apply not only to low-level clerical or retail jobs, but also to supposedly higher-level jobs. The close monitoring of work processes in graduate professions such as university teaching undermines the traditional ideology of professionalism, creates antagonism between staff and senior management, and encourages traditional responses such as trade union activism.

At the same time, in the higher reaches of the PMC, the once-feted managerial revolution has very largely been reversed. In the private sector, the revival of shareholder power, the use of stock options, and widespread privatization of state enterprises have drawn the highest levels of management firmly into the capitalist class. In the public sector also, the wholesale adoption of management techniques from the private sector has steadily undermined the traditional ideology of public service, installing instead apparatuses of strategic management based on top-down executive hierarchies and financial incentives. This has been accompanied by the outsourcing of everything from policy design through to routine service provision, overseen by growing two-way managerial traffic between the public sector and its private contractors. Today, it would be hard to argue that there exists a class, in the Marxist relational sense, that is distinct from the working class and the capitalist class. The trends that have brought about the demise of the PMC are part of the wider turn to neoliberalism in recent decades, although it could still be argued that there *really was* a nascent PMC in the period from the 1920s to the 1970s.[18]

THE FRAGMENTATION OF THE WORKING
CLASS AND THE PROBLEM OF AGENCY

If the working class in Marx's sense can now be understood once more to be overwhelmingly predominant in terms of numbers, it remains the case that the concept of the middle classes is very widely accepted in public debate; and the course of the global crisis since 2008 shows all too clearly how far we are from an effective class-based socialist politics. This brings us to the second critical issue for Marxist class theory, namely the question of agency: can either side of the two-class model really be seen as a historical subject? As far as the capitalist class is concerned, this centers on the historical development of capitalism, and the economic and political processes by which the capitalist class becomes hegemonic in relation to landed interests as well as subordinate classes. There is a long tradition of debate on divisions within the capitalist class, most notably between industry and finance, as well as on the institutions and practices through which individual capitals or "fractions" of capital overcome the antagonisms generated by their competitive struggles and arrive at some form of hegemonic strategy to sustain their class rule. Any historical inquiry into these issues unavoidably has to take fully into account the development of the capitalist state, which like class was vigorously debated in the 1970s and '80s, but more recently has been relatively neglected; the main exception being the focus on the states system in arguments over globalization.[19]

Problematic though the relation between capital and the state remains, however, the question of working-class agency is far more challenging. As noted earlier, the standard formula for this has traditionally been to distinguish between the "class in itself" and the "class for itself": while accumulation expanded the ranks of the working class as a structural category and concentrated them in ever-larger production sites, it would then take the active organization of workers to transform them from victims of exploitation into agents of social transformation. This analytical distinction played a crucial part in shaping socialist politics, especially in ensuring the ascendancy of political parties, whether ostensibly reformist or revolutionary, over alternative working-class agencies such as trade unions that focused either on labor market conditions or on workplace struggles. Most damaging to the grassroots political engagement of workers at large was the concept of "false consciousness," used to justify the elimination of rank-and-file democracy in workers' organizations of all kinds.[20] But although the in-itself/for-itself distinction appears to have been largely rhetorical, it does direct us to the fragmentation of the working class across society at large, as well as the advances that have historically been achieved through party politics.

That the proletariat is differentiated in a great variety of ways is indeed clear, not least in the empirical evidence on which Marx himself drew in analyzing capitalist production in *Capital*. The social division of labor between branches of production, coupled with the technical division of labor within the workplace, means that wage laborers are highly differentiated by location, income, skill, and authority, in complex combination with dimensions of difference such as gender, ethnicity, and religion whose origins appear to lie outside the capitalist production process as such. In his analysis of the evolution of capitalist production from simple cooperation to manufacture to modern industry, Marx places considerable emphasis on how in the latter two stages the drive to extract relative surplus value entails the transfer of immediate control over production from workers to capital and its agents.[21] This leads not to the reduction of all to interchangeable general laborers, but to the decomposition of earlier forms of hierarchy and division of tasks and their recomposition as elements, no less hierarchical and diverse, within the collective laborer of developed capitalist production. At the same time, he sees the shedding of employment by large-scale modern industry as providing the basis for a continuous renewal of small-scale and less technically advanced fields of production; for example, the widespread existence of adjunct production formally outside the factory, such as homework in the textiles industry, allows factory owners to transfer to petty producers the financial consequences of periodic crises. Labor shedding constantly feeds into the broader reserve army of the unemployed, but they too are differentiated into what Marx dubs the floating, the latent and the stagnant.

Despite this obvious diversity within the mid-nineteenth-century workforce, there is little doubt that traditionally the primary reference point for assessing the unity and cohesion of the working class was the large factory. In his general discussion of the development of machinery in *Capital*, Marx argues that once machine-based production takes hold of an industry, the relation between the workers and their instruments of labor becomes inverted: the worker becomes the adjunct of the machine.[22] With further evolution toward a unified machinery system, workers are bound together by its preordained rhythm: the collective character of labor confronts the workers as a technical necessity. This vision of increasingly automated flow production reflects the early development of assembly-line technology, which reaches its apotheosis in the early twentieth century in Ford's Highland Park plant and in continuous-flow production in the chemical and related industries; it becomes a primary subject for the analysis of modern capitalist production, whether from cheerleaders or critics, as well as a cultural reference point when contrasted with the supposed idyll of artisanal production, as in Fritz Lang's *Metropolis* or Chaplin's *Modern Times*. In Marxist scholarship, this model of mass production is seen as dramatically accentuating the contradictions of capitalism. The need to valorize vast amounts of fixed capital accelerates the trend toward monopoly, the rise of trusts and cartels aimed at controlling markets; and at the same time, flow production systems make the collective nature of exploitation immediately apparent to the workers involved, encouraging thereby collective resistance on the shop floor and the rise of shop stewards and other forms of bottom–up self-organization. For example, Alfred Sohn-Rethel argued that the contradiction between the normal ebb and flow of price-competitive markets and the require-ment of continuity of flow production amount to a "dual economics of transition," which he identified historically in the support given by German heavy industry to the forms of state coordination and sector planning adopted by the Nazis.[23]

However, as is readily apparent to anyone examining more broadly the nature of capitalist labor processes, very few wage laborers in cap-italism actually find themselves subordinated to a machine-based col-lective process in this way. Even within the engineering industries, heartland of the machine-paced assembly line, at the peak of manu-facturing employment in the UK it was estimated that such systems covered only 30 percent of workers.[24] The reality is that the disposition of labor in the modern workplace is for the most part not shaped by technology into an inflexible form that contradicts the fluidity that money capital seeks. As the pioneers of labor process studies showed in the 1970s, it is shaped by the choices of capitalist management and the resistance, whether individual or collective, of workers.[25] As we have seen only too clearly in recent decades, even the most apparently stable oligopolies, whether in manufacturing or services, are open to fundamental disruption through not only technological change, but also organizational innovations such as the relocation or outsourcing of production; the use of complex incentive schemes; the ever-closer monitoring of production activity through information systems; and above all, the constant and recently all too successful efforts of employ-ers to remove hard-won legal rights from trade unions.

Already in 1986, Peter Meiksins suggested that the debates on class, and specifically the relation between the "polar" model and the evident vertical and horizontal fracturing of the workforce in capitalism, required that "the relationship between production relations and specific, historical patterns of class conflict needs to be reconsidered."[26] Yet with the general decline in interest in class, these adjustments have not taken place, or at least not with the positive outcome that Meiksins hoped for. Indeed, the lack of progress is reflected in the similar call made nearly twenty years later by David Camfield, who draws attention not only to the continuing need to situate classes historically, but also to "consciously incorporate social relations other than class, such as gender and race."[27] In the remaining sections I will try to explain this and to suggest ways to begin to effect such changes in theory and in practice, and particularly to overcome the divisions that currently beset us in challenging the present social order.

CAPITALIST PRODUCTION AND SOCIAL REPRODUCTION

While the 1970s debates on the capitalist labor process certainly included consideration of this fragmentation of the working class, the turn to analyzing production and work also coincided with the rise of Marxist and feminist (including explicitly Marxist-feminist) work on the political economy of gender, where an important topic was the role of unwaged household work in capitalism, and more generally the reproduction of labor power outside the direct production and sale of commodities.[28] One way of looking at reproduction was in terms of the vexed question of productive and unproductive labor, but looking back it is clear that the valiant attempts to sort this out by close study of Marxist texts never got very far. The role of nonwage labor in reproducing capitalism could not be denied, but as with work on the labor process, its critical analysis did not fundamentally transform Marxist theory and analysis as might have been expected.

In a 2014 essay, Nancy Fraser seeks to explore the reasons why "we are living through a capitalist crisis of great severity without a critical theory that could adequately clarify it . . . we lack conceptions of capitalism and capitalist crisis that are adequate to our time."[29] She sees Marx's analysis as attributing four key features to capitalism: in order of precedence, they are private property, which presupposes the standard two-class division; the free labor market, through which noncapitalists must secure their subsistence and reproduction; the capitalists' compulsive pursuit of the accumulation of self-expanding value; and the distinctive role of markets, which allocate inputs to commodity production and determine how society's surplus is invested. This last element, she argues, should not be understood as an "ever-increasing commodification of life as such," because the overall reproduction of capitalist society actually depends on a wide range of activities that do not take place within the production and exchange of commodities.[30] While Marx goes behind the appearance of capitalist markets as equal exchange by finding the secret of exploitation in the hidden abode of production, Fraser identifies social reproduction in abodes that are in turn hidden behind production. She argues that Marx only broaches such issues in his historical introduction to the rise of capitalism in Part 8 of *Capital*, Volume 1 and we now need to explore these yet-more-hidden abodes. Social reproduction, she argues, is an "indispensable background condition for the possibility of capitalist production . . . moreover, the division between social reproduction and commodity production is central to capitalism – indeed, is an artefact of it."[31] The remainder of her essay then explores these doubly hidden abodes, setting out a range of propositions on their relation to capitalist production and their role in capitalist crisis.

While I sympathize with Fraser's rejection of the "dystopian fantasy" of ever-increasing commodification, her analysis of Marx ignores some very important elements in his critique of political economy—elements that, if restored to consideration, do much to soften the impact of her arguments, and point to a different way of placing social reproduction firmly at the heart of the analysis of class and of crisis. Fundamentally, this concerns Fraser's characterization of Marx's critique of capitalist production as "economic" in content, and implicitly structural-functionalist rather than historical in method. The four features that she ascribes to Marx are set out in the opening two parts of *Capital*, which are highly abstract in content. However, if we read on into the later parts, we find not only the famous hidden abode of production, but also precisely Fraser's doubly hidden abodes of social reproduction. There we can find ample evidence that Marx's critique incorporated concretely not only aspects of the social order that would be understood, in the fragmented obscurity of bourgeois thought, as social, political, cultural, or technological, but also the relation of humanity to nature. This is certainly not "economics" as mainstream social science would define it; on the contrary, in discussing issues like the length of the working day, the forms that wages take in capitalist employment, or the effects of machinery on workplace relations, Marx draws extensively on the concrete experiences of workers, and on the social conditions that they endure at home, in their communities and in their relations with the state.

None of this is to claim that reading *Capital* is all we need to do, that somehow from Marx's brow there sprang forth a complete workshop manual for revolutionaries that would forever suffice us; or indeed that the task he bequeathed to us was simply to write the remaining books that he indicated (in a few casual passages that he himself never revised for publication) would round out the analysis. It is obvious, given the history of the twentieth century, not only that it is impossible to derive a completion from the fetishistic search for truth in Marx's own writings, but also that whole swathes of historical change have occurred that were not visible in Marx's lifetime—not least, the progress that has been made in addressing sources of oppression that lie outside capitalism as such. But that is precisely why the main benefits to be derived from studying Marx lie in his *method* of inquiry, which is developed in the opening chapters of *Capital* and exemplified not only in the historical account of the closing chapters, but also the chapters of concrete analysis of his own time that lie between.

So how does Marx go about his critique? There is a vast literature on Marx's method available for those who wish to mull over the many ways of answering this question, but I think it really boils down to a few basic principles. First, historical materialism entails locating social inquiry in historical context, using the principle of identifying those institutions, ideas, and practices that together constitute distinct ways in which humanity structures its relationship to nature, that is, social reproduction. Social reproduction is indeed the primary purpose of social inquiry, and Fraser is right to privilege it over production insofar as she sees production as a narrowly economic process. Second, the historical thread running through Marx's analysis of the capitalist mode of production is not to be identified with specific visible features of capitalism (as in Fraser's list of property, free labor, accumulation, and markets). Rather, it consists in the possibility of historical transcendence, of humanity developing a conscious and collective self-control, which Marx traces from its most abstract representation in the form of the commodity through to its most concrete historical manifestations in struggles over the organization of social reproduction.

Marx's *Capital* is not built around a historical account of capitalism, but around a critique of political economy, that is, the core ideology of the ascendant capitalist class. At the heart of this ideology, he reasons, lies the concept of the self-regulating market, freed from bondage to sovereign or state, and therefore his analysis begins with the commodity as the object of market exchange. He uncovers first the dual nature of commodities as useful objects (use value) and as the carriers of exchange value. He suggests that the exchange of two distinct use values in definite quantities indicates that they have something in common, namely that they are products of labor. The value of a commodity is the amount of socially necessary labor embodied in it, abstracting from the specific or concrete labor that makes the product useful in meeting social needs. The labor undertaken by a worker in producing a commodity likewise has a dual character, as concrete useful labor, and as abstract value-producing labor, a distinction that is specifically absent in the apologetics of bourgeois political economy. The significance of this is brought out in the section on the fetishism of commodities, where he makes repeated presentations of the point from different perspectives.

This dual character of labor provides the starting point from which Marx elaborates his critique.[32] The elaboration follows a very specific sequence of concepts, first in the sphere of circulation, from the commodity to labor to money to capital to surplus value and exploitation. Then he goes into the sphere of production, where the labor process reproduces not only the commodities that go into it, but also capitalists, the workers, and the social relations between them, through the extraction of surplus value and the subsumption of labor to capital. Finally, he returns in Part 5 to circulation, where that surplus value is realized, distributed, and accumulated as capital. The way the analysis unfolds mirrors deliberately the circuit of capitalist production, because that is the reality that lies behind the veil of commodity fetishism, the "magic of the market." Along the way there emerges not only the capitalist, but also the worker; not only individuals pursuing their personal self-interest through free exchange, but capital and labor as social categories and as classes; not only the freedom of the market, but the coercion of the state; not only the apparent and commonsense logic of capital accumulation as organizing the production and sale of useful commodities, but the division of society into exploiters and exploited, the ravaging of communities and of nature, and all the hidden injuries of class.

However, there also appears at every stage of the argument the possibility of a different social order that humanity could establish, not on ideals plucked from the air, but on the basis of negating capitalist commodity production.[33] As a historical mode of production, capitalism contains within it not only the realm of value, the relentless logic that bourgeois political economy represents and tries to naturalize, but also the realm of use value. In every facet of social production and reproduction, these two realms coexist: the one driven by the imperative of capital accumulation, and the other by the application of labor time to nature to meet humanity's transhistorical need for subsistence.

Where does class, in the sense of the two-class model, fit into this? Surely it is part of the realm of value; and just as surely, the potential for its negation—a classless society—lies in the realm of use value, where concrete useful labor is expended to meet social needs. When Marx's two-class model is situated within the duality revealed by his critique of bourgeois thought, the historical character of its imposition upon society is revealed, and the possibility of its supersession also. Precisely because the capitalist form of class rule is co-constituted with the realm of value and capital, the starting point for its supersession must lie outside it, in aspects of society that must continue beyond capitalism, albeit in a different form. To envision socialism as a realm of freedom, and develop social practices that can begin to realize it, we have to start from use values, concrete labor, and social needs. This is what the critics of class politics have been arguing for; but it does not require the ditching of Marx's analysis of capital and class, only its reinterpretation as a critique of political economy rather than as Marxist economics.

FINDING BRIDGES TO SOCIALISM IN CAPITALISM TODAY

If the investigation of method in the previous section allows us to integrate the politics of production and of reproduction, then equally it can be argued that Marx's relational model of class, which is historically specific to capitalism, is generally compatible with sociological delineations of classes based, like that of Savage and his collaborators, upon the identification of clusters of economic, social, and cultural characteristics within society. More than that, the integration of the two approaches to class into a single ontological and epistemological framework allows the weaknesses of each to be addressed. On the one hand, the real fragmentation of the "relational" working class clearly bedevils attempts to develop an emancipatory politics of sufficiently wide appeal to mount a serious challenge to capitalism as it actually exists and as it is perceived. On the other hand, as noted at the outset, starting from the subjective attitudes and social practices of different segments of society makes it hard to see the wood for the trees—to grasp the commonalities that are concealed by a hegemonic common sense centered on individual aspirations in relation to property and consumption.

Nowhere has this been more visible recently than in the frustrating inability of "the 99 percent" identified by the Occupy movement to develop from a visceral hostility to the remaining 1 percent into a serious political challenge to neoliberalism. The newer slogans of the social movements seem to have little more purchase than the older ones of the traditional labor movement, even when the two are able to coalesce at least in identifying the object of their wrath, as they did for a few years following the Battle of Seattle in 1999. What is more, as the current crisis has gone on, the common experience of shock and dislocation following the financial crash has been replaced by marked differences in how the resolution of the crisis affects different groups: not only between employed and unemployed, or skilled and unskilled, but between different countries and regions. In pre-Brexit Britain, the government and most of the media have scapegoated welfare recipients (whether unemployed, or receiving incomes so low that they must be topped up with state benefits) and above all immigrants, in a deliberate divide-and-rule strategy. Meanwhile, German workers protected from austerity policies have shown little or no solidarity either with their less protected fellow Germans, or with workers in the Eurozone "periphery" whose governments have been blamed for the crisis and forced to impose unprecedented cuts in living standards and state provision alike. The differential economic impact of crisis policies on women has also been widely noted.[34] Across the globe, employers and governments alike beat the drum of "international competitiveness": work harder and longer, do as you're told, invest in skills (at your own expense), and then, just maybe, you can avoid losing your job to those industrious Chinese (Mexicans, Turks, et cetera). Further, a crucial feature of capitalism in its modern neoliberal form is that the individualistic logic of competition is imposed far beyond the realm of capitalist production alone: such as within the higher education sector that employs many of you reading this, and even, it now seems, in the "production" of protest.[35]

But this is the ideology of capital, the world seen from the standpoint of the law of value and the compulsion of profit. Meanwhile, within not only capitalist production, but also within the spheres of reproduction that lie outside the factory or office—those that Fraser identifies as doubly hidden—other forces are at work in contradiction to that ideology. In capitalist production, the relentless drive to deskill and control workers runs up, with equal necessity, against the capitalist's unavoidable dependence upon human beings. In his critique of the Ehrenreichs' thesis that the work of engineers essentially reproduces the pursuit of profit and thus the rule of capital, David Noble insisted on the continuing ideology of professionalism that remains rooted in the exercise of scientific and practical knowledge, and the nonpecuniary satisfactions obtained from such work.[36] Much further down the workplace status hierarchy, Paul Durrenberger and Dimitra Doukas have argued that a "gospel of work" continues to act as a counterweight to the "gospel of wealth" among the US working class.[37]

More generally, the apparently abstract concept of the "collective laborer" developed by Marx in his analysis of machinery and modern industry does not simply represent, as many people claim, the strategy of "capital in command"; it also contains within it the necessity for elements of that collective laborer—in other words, individual workers—to combine their concrete activities creatively. Outside of the much-mythologized but rarely achieved "fully automated" production process, most of us have to exercise our imagination and combine our talents with those of others in tasks from the most mundane to the most esoteric. If socialism is the "free association of producers," then the capitalist workplace willy-nilly provides a foretaste of it. Nearly fifty years ago, in a relatively short chapter near the end of his study of Marx's *Capital*, Roman Rosdolsky examined what he called "the historical limits of the law of value."[38] He argued that contrary to the usual assertion that Marx was unwilling to make any predictions about a future socialist society, we "constantly encounter discussions and remarks in *Capital*, and the works preparatory to it, which are concerned with the problems of a socialist society." His suggestion that Marx's method both directs our attention to the historical past and posits the "historic presuppositions for a new state of society" supports the idea that bridges can indeed be found toward socialism within everyday capitalist production.

What about the work of social reproduction that takes place in households, in recuperative leisure activities, or in voluntary associations of all kinds that supplement or even replace the state-funded provision of goods or services? Surely it demonstrates also the unavoidable dependence of tasks, however mandated and whomever by, upon concrete labor that entails forethought, initiative, and creativity by individuals, typically exercised in cooperation with others. Insofar as such forms of labor shift to and fro across the boundary between capitalist and noncapitalist production, there is little change in the concrete labor performed; what changes is whether it generates pecuniary reward, and how far that reward is diminished by the interposing of private capital in the production process.

We should therefore look upon the world of work—by which I mean *all* kinds of work, not just that which takes place in the framework of capitalist wage labor—not only as an external and alienating form of subordination to the other. It is equally, as Marx put it, "the everlasting Nature-imposed condition of human existence, and therefore is independent of every social phase of that existence, or rather, is common to every such phase."[39] But this very universality needs to be recognized, and to be seen as fundamental to the construction of a movement whose class purpose is, quite simply, the abolition of class society.

At this point we have to return to the vexed question of politics—no longer a politics "of" class or a "working-class politics," but a politics *against* class. This requires, in the first place, that we stop being coy about our eventual purpose, and start to spell out what exactly we envisage as the constitutive features of a postcapitalist society. By breaking this down into a picture of social needs and creative activities under socialism that people can compare directly with their day-to-day experiences under capitalism, we can challenge the relentless drumbeat of "there is no alternative." Capitalism is not a natural order, it is a social order; constructed by people in interaction with each other, it can equally be demolished and replaced. This is nothing more nor less than the original purpose of the Social Forum movement, to all appearances sidelined by the crisis of 2007–2008 and its aftermath, but even at its most vigorous, bedeviled by the remnants of the failed party politics of the last century.

This leads to a second requirement: that we face up to the painful lessons of those failures. How can the grotesque inequalities of wealth and power in capitalism be challenged politically, if not by a robust insistence on the equal participation of all in any meaningful movement for change? This has to be rooted in the principles of citizenship and democracy that drove the pursuit of social justice in centuries past: there must be no more easy dismissal of "bourgeois democracy," or insistence that enlightenment can only be brought to "the masses" by a party elite. How many more attempts will be made to establish parties on the left in pursuit of the holy grail of a revolutionary politics that will brook no compromise with bourgeois politics? If we accept that bridges exist in day-to-day life that can help us to develop a popular and powerful movement for socialism, then there is nothing to be lost by working within existing organizations, whether parties, unions, or social movements of all kinds. Given the compromises that we are forced to make every day of our lives, surely we can live with compromises in our political work; in many countries we have opportunities to do this in social democratic or green parties in which we will find people who share some vision of a better world. Above all, no amount of work to develop a more enlightening analysis of present-day capitalism is going to deliver a political awakening without a great deal of hard graft in the real world of compromised lives and confused aspirations. Perhaps it is time to read and write less, and instead plunge into that world.

NOTES

The Economics of Neo-Capitalism

1   Fully developed in "Die langen Wellen der Konjunktur," *Archiv für Sozialwissenschaft und Sozialpolitik (Tübingen)* 56:3 (December 1926), pp. 573–609.

2   Leon Trotsky, *The First Five Years of the Communist International*, Vol. 1 (New York: Pioneer Publishers, 1956), pp. 201, 205–6.

3   The "boom" of the civilian electronics industry has been mainly sustained by military orders, e.g., in the United States.

4   "Statistiques Industrielles," *OSCE* 3–4 (1963).

5   One should add that the change in the structure of popular demand, with the proportion of the family budget devoted to buying food declining rapidly, is an additional explanation of some aspects of the boom (for instance, the greatly increased demand for durable consumer goods). Of course, this has been compensated by a permanent crisis in agriculture.

6   Some striking examples of wrong forecasts: the Belgian ministry of Economic Affairs, under the influence of the Suez crisis, thought that coal output would have to be increased from 30 to 40 million tons; it was, in fact, reduced from 30 to 21 million tons within a few years' time. The fourth French "plan" foresaw a big increase in refrigerator output, and it discounted foreign competition; in fact, Italian imports have cut French output by nearly 25 percent.

7   Other examples from Western Germany: the precision industry just kept its output from 1961 to 1962; but employment fell by 2.3 percent. The iron and steel industry increased its output by 7.9 percent between 1960 and 1962 but reduced total employment by 2.8 percent; the musical instruments and sports equipment industry increased its output by 22.7 percent between 1956 and 1962, but employment fell by 6.3 percent. All these employment figures are global, i.e., they apply to the sum total of manual workers, white-collar workers, and technicians. The fall in production workers' employment is of course much greater.

8   *US News and World Report*, May 25, 1956, and March 11, 1955.

9   Günter Friedrichs, *Automation und technischer Fortschritt in Deutschland und den USA* (Frankfurt: Europäische Verlagsanstalt, 1963), p. 127.

10   *11e rapport general sur l'activite de la Communaute (ler fevrier 1962 – 31 janvier 1963)*, EU Commission working document (Luxembourg: May 1963), available at aei.pitt.edu/40270/.

11   Agence Europe, "Les problèmes de l'industrie automobile européene en 1963," *Documents* 179, January 4, 1963.

12   Thomas Balogh, *Planning for Progress, Fabian Tract 346* (London: Fabian Society, 1963), pp. 46–47.

Professor Galbraith and American Capitalism

1   John Kenneth Galbraith, *The New Industrial State* (London: Hamish Hamilton, 1967), p. 427.

2   Galbraith, *The New Industrial State*, pp. 74–75.

3   Galbraith, *The New Industrial State,* pp. 71 and 69.

4   The fact that power is "obscured" (if it is a fact) would not, one would have thought, mean that it does not exist, but simply that it is more difficult to perceive, which is something very different.

5   Galbraith, *The New Industrial State*, p. 268.

6   Robert Sheehan, "Proprietors in the World of Big Business," *Fortune*, June 15, 1967, p. 178.

7   Sheehan, "Proprietors," pp. 179, 180, 182.

8   Gabriel Kolko, *Wealth and Power in America* (New York: Praeger, 1962), p. 13. See also C. Wright Mills, *The Power Elite* (New York: Oxford, 1956) and Don Villarejo, "Stock Ownership and the Control of Corporations," *New University Thought* 2 (Autumn 1961 – Winter 1962). For Britain, a survey of share owning, published in 1955, showed that directors of companies held shares to an average value of twenty-eight thousand pounds, and that this was the largest average holding of all the groups about which information was available (Bulletin of the Oxford Institute of Statistics, November 1965, cited in Perry Anderson and Robin Blackburn, eds., *Towards Socialism* [Ithaca: Cornell University Press, 1965], pp. 116–17).

9   Robert L. Heilbroner, "The View from the Top: Reflections on a Changing Business Ideology," in Earl F. Cheit, ed., *The Business Establishment* (New York: John Wiley & Sons, 1960), p. 25.

10   Earl F. Cheit, "The New Place of Business: Why Managers Cultivate Social Responsibilities," in Cheit, *The Business Establishment*, p. 178.

NOTES 295

11 Adolf A. Berle and Gardiner C. Means, *The Modern Corporation and Private Property* (New York: Macmillan, 1932), p. 84.

12 Clive S. Beed, "The Separation of Ownership from Control," *Journal of Economic Studies* (University of Aberdeen) 1:2 (1966), p. 31, original emphasis.

13 Villarejo, "Stock Ownership," p. 52.

14 Beed, "Separation of Ownership," note 22.

15 Beed, "Separation of Ownership," p. 32, original emphasis.

16 Galbraith, *New Industrial State*, p. 93.

17 The argument that there is no display of greed and graspingness would seem a poor basis for the claim that it does not exist. It could, after all, be that "greed and graspingness" are now simply less ostentatious, better concealed, not least by a vast public relations industry of which many academic economists appear to be honorary members.

18 Carl Kaysen, "The Social Significance of the Modern Corporation," *American Economic Review* 47:2 (May 1957), pp. 313–14.

19 C. A. R. Crosland, *The Conservative Enemy: A Programme of Radical Reform for the 1960s* (Anne Arbor: University of Michigan Press, 1962), pp. 88–89.

20 *Industry and Society: Labour's Policy on Future Public Ownership* (London: Labour Party, 1957), p. 48.

21 Sheehan, "Proprietors," p. 242. See also my earlier references to gains through stock options and Villarejo, "Stock Ownership," Part 3.

22 Kolko, *Wealth and Power*, p. 65.

23 Paul A. Baran and Paul M. Sweezy, *Monopoly Capital* (New York: Monthly Review, 1966), pp. 39–40.

24 Kaysen, "Modern Corporation," pp. 313, 315.

25 Sheehan, "Proprietors," pp. 183, 242.

26 James S. Earley, "Contribution to the Discussion on the Impact of Some New Developments in Economic Theory: Exposition and Evaluation," *American Economic Review* 47:2 (May 1957), pp. 333–34.

27 Galbraith, *New Industrial State*, pp. 162, 163, my emphasis.

28 Galbraith, *New Industrial State*, p. 163.

29 Galbraith, *New Industrial State*, pp. 138, 141, 161.

30 Galbraith, *New Industrial State*, pp. 356, 105.

31 Galbraith, *New Industrial State*, pp. 229, 341, my emphasis.

32 Galbraith, *New Industrial State*, p. 345.

33 John Kenneth Galbraith, *The Affluent Society* (New York: Houghton Mifflin Harcourt, 1958), p. 254, my emphasis.

34 Galbraith, *Affluent Society*, p. 254.

35 Harry Magdoff, "Problems of United States Capitalism," *Socialist Register 1965* (London: Merlin Press, 1965), p. 73. "Deprivation" was held by the conference to include people living above the stark poverty level but below what a Labour Department investigation found to be a "modest but adequate" worker's family budget. See also, e.g., Baran and Sweezy, *Monopoly Capital*, Chapter 10, and Michael Harrington, *The Other America* (New York: Macmillan, 1962).

36 Galbraith, *New Industrial State*, p. 356.

37 Galbraith, *New Industrial State*, pp. 137, 263, 294.

André Gorz and His Disappearing Proletariat

1 André Gorz, *Farewell to the Working Class: An Essay on Post-Industrial Socialism* (London: Pluto Press, 1982).

2 For example, Mark Abrams and Richard Rose, *Must Labour Lose?* (New York: Penguin, 1960). The notion that "affluence" and "embourgeoisement" had destroyed workers' readiness to support Labour was confronted in a massive research study, the results of which appeared only after Wilson's two election victories had already given a practical refutation; see John H. Goldthorpe et al., *The Affluent Worker: Political Attitudes and Behaviour* (Cambridge, UK: Cambridge University Press, 1968).

3 Such revisionism (in some respects the linear antecedent of the SDP breakaway from Labour) was most elegantly proposed in the writings of C. A. R. Crosland; in particular *The Future of Socialism and The Conservative Enemy* (London: Cape, 1956 and 1962).

4 For instance Eric J. Hobsbawm's 1978 lecture and the subsequent debate, published in *The Forward March of Labour Halted?* (London: Verso, 1981); and Tony Lane, "The Unions: Caught on the Ebb Tide," *Marxism Today*, September 1982 (and the ensuing controversy).

5 For the first fifteen years of *Les Temps Modernes*, Sartre had been sole editor.

6 Examples are *Strategy for Labor: A Radical Proposal* (Boston: Beacon, 1964); *Socialism and Revolution* (Norwell, MA: Anchor, 1973); *The Division of Labour: The Labour Process and Class Struggle in Modern Capitalism* (Sussex: Harvester Press, 1978); and *Ecology as Politics* (Boston: South End Press, 1980).

7 Gorz, *Farewell*, p. 4.

8   Ivan Illich, *Tools for Conviviality* (London: Calder & Boyars, 1973).

9   Gorz, *Farewell*, pp. 7, 8, 9, 11–12.

10   Gorz, *Farewell*, pp. 14–15.

11   Karl Marx and Friedrich Engels, *Collected Works*, Vol. 4 (London: Lawrence & Wishart, 1975), p. 37.

12   Gorz, *Farewell*, pp. 27–8.

13   Gorz, *Farewell*, pp. 32–3.

14   Gorz, *Farewell*, p. 35.

15   Gorz, *Farewell*, pp. 48, 52.

16   Gorz, *Farewell*, pp. 64, 65.

17   Gorz, *Farewell*, pp. 67–68.

18   Gorz, *Farewell*, pp. 70, 71.

19   Gorz, *Farewell*, pp. 73, 74.

20   Gorz, *Farewell*, pp. 73, 74.

21   Gorz, *Farewell*, pp. 78, 79–80.

22   Gorz, *Farewell*, p. 82. Gorz makes no explicit reference here to the more bucolic utopian vision outlined in *The German Ideology*, but it surely lies behind this passage.

23   Gorz, *Farewell*, pp. 87, 90.

24   *Capital*, Vol. 3 (London: Lawrence & Wishart, 1959), p. 820.

25   The parallel with Durkheim's discussion of "mechanical solidarity" is presumably not accidental.

26   Gorz, *Farewell*, pp. 115, 116.

27   Gorz, *Farewell*, p. 134.

28   Presumably this is a deliberate allusion to *The German Ideology*, in which Marx and Engels refer to "Saint Max" Stirner.

29   One of the first popular assertions of this theme was in Robert C. Tucker, *Philosophy and Myth in Karl Marx* (Cambridge, UK: Cambridge University Press, 1961).

30   Rudolf Bahro, *The Alternative in Eastern Europe* (London: New Left Books, 1978), p. 195.

31   Gorz, *Farewell*, p. 16.

32   Hal Draper, *Karl Marx's Theory of Revolution*, Vol. 1 (New York: Monthly Review, 1977), pp. 136–37.

33   Notably in Marx's peroration to the penultimate chapter of Volume 1 of
     Capital, reproducing two decades later the revolutionary scenario of the
     Communist Manifesto.

34   Shlomo Avineri, *The Social and Political Thought of Karl Marx* (Cambridge,
     UK: Cambridge University Press, 1968), p. 144.

35   Georg Lukács, *History and Class Consciousness* (London: Merlin Press, 1971),
     p. 79.

36   Gorz gives several references to the *Grundrisse*; the only other text
     specifically mentioned is the *Critique of the Gotha Program*. In neither
     work, as far as I can see, does Marx posit the emergence of a polytechnic
     worker within capitalism. What he does argue in the *Grundrisse* (New York:
     Penguin, 1973) is that the productivity resulting from advanced technology
     "will redound to the benefit of emancipated labour, and is the condition of
     its emancipation" (p. 701); that is, after the abolition of capitalist production
     relations. For a similar argument see *Capital*, Vol. 1 (New York: Penguin,
     1976), p. 618.

37   *Capital*, Vol. 1, pp. 548–49. For additional examples of the same argument,
     see *Grundrisse*, pp. 692–94, 700–9; *Capital*, Vol. 1, pp. 483, 526–27, 544–45,
     559, 619, 667; *Inaugural Address* and *Critique of the Gotha Program in The First
     International and After* (New York: Penguin, 1974), pp. 77–78, 352.

38   Notably Serge Mallet, with his notion of the "new working class" of
     technically qualified workers. For critical discussions of this approach, see
     Michael Mann, *Consciousness and Action among the Western Working Class*
     (New York: Macmillan, 1973); Michael Rose, *Servants of Post-Industrial
     Power?* (New York: Macmillan, 1979); Richard Hyman and Robert Price,
     The New Working Class? (New York: Macmillan, 1983).

39   See for example his essay "Technology, Technicians, and Class Struggle" in
     The Division of Labour

40   Harry Braverman, *Labor and Monopoly Capital: The Degradation of Work in the
     Twentieth Century* (New York: Monthly Review, 1974).

41   Gorz, *Farewell*, pp. 39–40.

42   London Edinburgh Weekend Return Group, *In and Against the State*
     (London: Pluto Press, 1980), p. 130.

43   London Edinburgh Weekend Return Group, *In and Against*, pp. 76–77.

44   Bahro, *The Alternative*, p. 253

45   Bahro, *The Alternative*, pp. 405–7.

46   Gorz, *Ecology as Politics*, p. 3.

47   Gorz, *Farewell*, p. 63. "Capital is, therefore, not a personal, it is a social
     power" (Karl Marx and Friedrich Engels, *Manifesto of the Communist Party*,

in *Collected Works,* Vol. 6 [London: Lawrence & Wishart, 1976], p. 499). "[C]ompetition subordinates every individual capitalist to the immanent laws of capitalist production, as external and coercive laws" (*Capital,*Vol. 1, p. 739).

48   See, for example, Göran Therborn's discussion "Finding the Ruling Class," in *What Does the Ruling Class Do When It Rules?* (London: New Left Books, 1978).

49   Gorz, *Farewell,* p. 74.

50   *Farewell,* pp. 11, 116.

51   I do not mean to overlook the involvement of many union activists in both the practical and the theoretical aspects of "workers' alternative plans" or the initiatives of some left-wing Labour councils; here, one suspects, is a source of some of the cadres of the "movement" to which Gorz refers. At the same time, it is necessary to recognize the extent to which such activities are patronized, ignored, or opposed by the official union hierarchies.

52   Ivor Clemitson and George Rodgers, *A Life to Live: Beyond Full Employment* (Toronto: Junction Books, 1981). The book carries a foreword by Neil Kinnock; it will be interesting to see what becomes of his endorsement of a "life ethic" rather than a work ethic.

53   Hilary Wainwright, cited in Hobsbawm, *The Forward March of Labour Halted?,* p. 132.

Marx, the Present Crisis, and the Future of Labor

1   See, among others: André Gorz, *Adieux au prolétariat* (Paris: Éditions Galilée, 1979); Daniel Bell, *The Post-Industrial Society: The Evolution of an Idea* (London: Ilford House, 1971); Ralf Dahrendorf, in *Geht uns die Arbeit aus?* (Bonn: Verlag Bonn Aktuell, 1983); Eric Hobsbawm, "The Forward March of Labour Halted?," *Marxism Today,* September 1978.

2   Joseph Huber, *Die verlorene Unschuld der Oekologie* (Frankfurt: Fischer, 1982); Ivan Illich, *Le travail fantôme* (Paris: Seuil, 1981); Club of Rome, *The Limits to Growth: A Report for the Club of Rome's Project on the Predicament of Manking,* (London: Earth Island, 1972); Rudolph Bahro, *From Red to Green: Interviews with New Left Review* (London: New Left Review, 1981); Gorz, *Adieux au prolétariat.*

3   OECD, *Robots industriels,* (Paris: OECD, 1983).

4   Obviously, this does not imply that in given branches of industry (e.g., coal mining) there is no absolute decline in world employment, or in others (like textiles, shoe industry, shipbuilding, steel) a decline in employment in certain regions (US, Western Europe) and a rise in others (Asia).

5   See the excellent study by Winfried Wolf, "Volkswagen's Robots," *Was Tun?*, December 1983.

6   This phenomenon expresses itself among other things in the rise of drug addiction in the United States, hooliganism in Britain, et cetera.

7   Saga Ichiro, "The Development of New Technology in Japan," *Bulletin of the Socialist Research Centre*, Hosei University, Tokyo, November 1983.

8   *Japan Economic Journal*, February 21, 1984.

9   Karl Marx and Friedrich Engels, *Marx-Engels-Werke*, Volume 16 (Berlin: Dietz-Verlag, 1962), pp. 12–13, 322, 192, my translations. In his pamphlet *Value, Price, and Profit [Lohn, Preis und Profit]*, Marx stated equally: "In their attempts at reducing the working day to its former rational dimensions, or, where they cannot enforce a legal fixation of a normal working day, at checking overwork by a rise of wages, a rise not only in proportion to the surplus time exacted, but in a greater proportion, workingmen fulfil only a duty to themselves and their race. They only set limits to the tyrannical usurpations of capital. Time is the room of human development. A man who has no free time to dispose of, whose whole lifetime, apart from the mere physical interruptions by sleep, meals, and so forth, is absorbed by his labour for the capitalist, is less than a beast of burden. He is a mere machine for producing foreign wealth, broken in body and brutalised in mind." *Selected Works* (Moscow: Foreign Languages Publishing House, 1968), p. 329.

10 It is especially developed in Karl Marx, *Zur Kritik der Politischen Oekonomie [A Contribution to the Critique of Political Economy]* (1861–1863), in *Karl Marx-Friedrich Engels Gesamtausgabe (MEGA)*, Vols. 1–6, Part 2.3 (Berlin: Dietz-Verlag, 1976–1982). First comments on this hitherto-unknown manuscript of Marx can be found in *Der Zweite Entwurf des "Kapitals"* (Berlin: Dietz-Verlag, 1983).

11 Karl Marx, *Grundrisse* (London: Pelican Marx Library, 1973), pp. 704–5.

12 Marx, *Grundrisse,* p. 705.

13 Ernest Mandel, *Late Capitalism* (London: New Left Books, 1975), p. 207.

14 A workers and trade-unionist group in France, writing under the pseudonym of Adret, published a book in 1977 under the title *Travailler deux heures par jour* (Paris: Seuil), which has had too little echo. It showed the material possibility of a radical reduction of the workday, even before the appearance of robotization.

15 See in that respect the very subdued conclusion of a recent conference on robotics: Patrick H. Winston and Karen Prendergast, eds., *The AI Business: The Commercial Use of Artificial Intelligence* (London and Cambridge, MA: MIT Press, 1984).

16   What most advocates of the capacity of capitalism to "regulate" its present crisis forget is the fact that *every* step forward in mechanization, and certainly of automation, is accompanied by a *huge increase in the mass of goods produced* (see Marx, *Grundrisse,* p. 325 and *MEGA,* II, 3.6, p. 2164), *which have to be sold* before capital can realize and appropriate produced surplus value.

17   Aristotle drew attention to the fact that those who deal with politics and science (i.e., those who "administer," "accumulate" in the Marxist sense of the word) can only do so because *others* produce for them their livelihood.

18   Marx, *Grundrisse,* p. 708.

19   *MEGA,* II, 3.6, p. 2164.

20   In his *Nicomachean Ethics,* Aristotle had already developed a view of the relationship between labor and leisure that comes near to that of Marx's *Grundrisse* and *Capital.* One should remember the etymology of "leisure": the latin word licere, i.e., to be free to act as one likes.

21   See on this subject Danièle Linhart, "Crise et Travail," *Temps Modernes* 450, (January 1984).

22   Barry Commoner, *The Closing Circle* (London: Jonathan Cape, 1972).

23   Karl Marx, *Capital,* Vol. 1, Pelican Library ed. (London and New York: Penguin, 1976), p. 638.

24   Marx, *Capital,* Vol. 1, pp. 562–63.

25   See David F. Noble, *Forces of Production* (New York: Knopf, 1984).

26   "World Markets Forecast," *Electronics Week,* January 1, 1985.

27   See on this subject Reinhard Breuer, *Die Pfeile der Zeit* (Munich: Meyster Verlag, 1984).

28   A. J. Ayer has dealt with the same question in a review of J. David Bolter's book *Turing's Man: Western Culture in the Computer Age* (Chapel Hill: University of North Carolina Press, 1983), which appeared in the *New York Review of Books,* March 1, 1984.

29   "*Denning Mobile Robotics* Inc., Woburn, Mass., said it had signed an agreement to provide Southern Steel Corp. with up to 680 robots for prison guard duty over the next three years. It said the contract was worth between $23 million and 30 million" (*New York Times,* January 9, 1985).

"Competitive Austerity" and the Impasse of Capitalist Employment Policy

1   John Maynard Keynes, *The General Theory of Employment, Interest, and Money* (London: Macmillan, 1936), p. 381.

2   See Bob Rowthorn and Andrew Glyn, "The Diversity of Unemployment Experience since 1973," in Stephen Marglin and Juliet Schor, eds., *The Golden Age of Capitalism* (Oxford: Clarendon, 1990).

3   See Fritz Burchardt et al., *The Economics of Full Employment* (Oxford: Basil Blackwell, 1944); David Worswick, "Jobs for All?" *Economic Journal* 95 (March 1985); and Robert Solow, "Unemployment: Getting the Questions Right," *Economica* 53 (1986), supplement.

4   Keynes, *General Theory,* pp. 33–34.

5   See: Milton Friedman, "The Role of Monetary Policy," *American Economic Review* 58 (March 1968); and Michael Bruno and Jeffrey D. Sachs, *The Economics of Worldwide Stagnation* (Oxford: Oxford University Press, 1985).

6   Joseph Schumpeter, *Business Cycles, Vol. 2* (New York: McGraw-Hill, 1939), p. 515. See also OECD, *Employment Growth and Structural Change* (Paris: OECD, 1985).

7   Harry Braverman, *Labor and Monopoly Capital* (New York: Monthly Review Press, 1974).

8   Michael Piore and Charles Sabel, *The Second Industrial Divide* (New York: Basic Books, 1984).

9   On the different factors shaping the skilling process, see Stephen Wood, ed., *The Degradation of Work* (London: Hutchinson, 1982); Eric Batstone et al., *New Technology and the Process of Labour Regulation* (Oxford: Clarendon, 1987), Ch. 1; and Robert Allen, "The Impact of Technical Change on Employment, Wages and the Distribution of Skills: A Historical Perspective," in W. Craig Riddell, ed., *Adjusting to Change: Labour Market Adjustment in Canada* (Toronto: University of Toronto Press, 1986). Especially fascinating on this issue, in relation to economic performance, is Theo Nichols, *The British Worker Question* (London: Routledge, 1986).

10 Richard Hyman and Wolfgang Streeck, eds., *New Technology and Industrial Relations* (Oxford: Basil Blackwell, 1988); Arndt Sorge and Malcolm Warner, *Comparative Factory Organization* (London: Gower, 1986); and Marc Maurice, François Sellier, and Jean-Jacques Silvestre, *The Social Foundations of Industrial Power* (Cambridge, MA: MIT Press, 1986).

11 Michael Storper, "The Transition to Flexible Specialization in the US Film Industry," *Cambridge Journal of Economics* 13:2 (1989), p. 197.

12 For surveys see Adrian Ziderman, *Manpower Training: Theory and Policy* (London: Macmillan, 1978); Mark Blaug, "The Empirical Status of Human Capital Theory: A Slightly Jaundiced Survey," *Journal of Economic Literatur,* 14 (1976); and David Gordon, *Theories of Poverty and Underemployment* (Lexington: D. C. Heath, 1972). It should be noted that human capital theory, in its early or more recent variations, is more concerned with market-based

financing of training than with the dynamic relationship between skills and production. Entrepreneurs are responsible for innovations. But new developments in neoclassical economics are beginning to raise some similar concerns. See: Francis Green, "Neoclassical and Marxian Conceptions of Production," *Cambridge Journal of Economics* 12:3 (1988).

13   "Investment in Human Capital," *American Economic Review* 51 (1961), p. 3.

14   See Assar Lindbeck and Dennis J. Snower, *The Insider-Outsider Theory of Employment and Unemployment* (Cambridge, MA: MIT Press, 1988).

15   See Gordon, *Theories of Poverty*, pp. 92–94 and 122–24; and Glen G. Cain, "The Challenge of Dual and Radical Labour Market Theories to Orthodox Theory," *Journal of Economic Literature* 14 (1976).

16   Ziderman, *Manpower Training*, 34–39; and James Davies, "Training and Skill Development," in W. Craig Riddell, ed., *Adapting to Change: Labour Market Adjustment in Canada (Toronto, University of Toronto Press, 1986)*. The problem may also be stated as follows: the contradiction between the generality of a particular skill in terms of its training content (potential transferability) and the generality of the investment (potential mobility of the trainee).

17   Gary Becker, *Human Capital* (New York: National Bureau of Economic Research, 1964).

18   The theoretical points in contention can be seen in Ziderman, *Manpower Training*, pp. 48–54; Davies, "Training," pp. 182–84; and Wolfgang Streeck, "Skills and the Limits of Neo-Liberalism: The Enterprise of the Future as a Place of Learning," *Work, Employment, and Society* 3:1 (1989), pp. 92–97.

19   Streeck, "Skills and the Limits of Neo-Liberalism," p. 94.

20   Streeck's case is most directly presented in his "Skills and the Limits of Neo-Liberalism." See also Peter Senker, "Technical Change, Work Organization, and Training," *New Technology, Work, and Employment* 4:1 (1989).

21   Streeck, "Skills and the Limits of Neo-Liberalism," pp. 96–99.

22   Although differing in their assessment of flexible automation, several authors note the new skills profiles: Raphael Kaplinsky, "Industrial Restructuring: Some Questions for Education and Training," *IDS Bulletin*, 20:1 (1989); A. J. Phillimore, "Flexible Specialisation, Work Organization and Skills," *New Technology, Work, and Employment* 4:2 (1989); and Philippe Méhaut, "New Firms' Training Policies and Changes in the Wage-Earning Relationship," *Labour and Society* 13:4 (1988).

23   Sorge and Warner, *Comparative Factory*, pp. 173–80; and Christel Lane, "Industrial Change in Europe: The Pursuit of Flexible Specialization in Britain and West Germany," *Employment, Work, and Society* 2:2 (1988).

24   *Empowering Workers in the Global Economy: A Labour Agenda for the 1990s* (Toronto: United Steelworkers of America, 1991), pp. 16–17, 26.

25 Robert Boyer, ed., *The Search for Labour Market Flexibility* (Oxford: Clarendon Press, 1988), p. 260. This choice has been discussed with respect to Canadian trade unions in: Gregory Albo, "The 'New Realism' and Canadian Workers," in Alain G. Gagnon and James Bickerton, eds., *Canadian Politics* (Peterborough: Broadview Press, 1990).

26 See especially Manfred G. Schmidt, "The Politics of Unemployment," *West European Politics* 7:3 (1984); Göran Therborn, *Why Some Peoples Are More Unemployed Than Others* (London: Verso, 1986); and Fritz W. Scharpf, *Crisis and Choice in European Social Democracy* (Ithaca: Cornell University Press, 1991).

27 See Leo Panitch, *Working Class Politics in Crisis* (London: Verso, 1986).

28 This view has been developed in: Manfred Bienefeld, "The International Context for National Development Strategies: Constraints and Opportunities in a Changing World Economy," in Manfred Bienefeld and Martin Godfrey, eds., *The Struggle for Development: National Strategies in an International Context* (London: John Wiley & Sons, 1982); and Alain Lipietz, *Towards a New Economic Order* (New York: Oxford University Press, 1992).

29 The problem of planning employment is linked to the reformation of the left's position on state administration. For a recent effort to do so see: Gregory Albo, David Langille, and Leo Panitch, eds., *A Different Kind of State? Popular Power and Democratic Administration* (Toronto: Oxford University Press, 1993).

30 The diversity of employment experiences through the 1980s has also amply illustrated that the labor supply must be considered as at least a medium-term policy target. That is, countries have handled quite differently the size and composition of the labor supply in terms of access to paid, full-time work. As we confront the crisis of work, this needs to be brought more clearly into democratic deliberation, in terms of paid work as a right of citizenship for all ages, and the extent to which the national market should be open to labor flows, before the worst aspects of sexism, ageism, and xenophobia develop.

31 See: Ken Coates and Michael Barratt-Brown, eds., *A European Recovery Programme* (Nottingham: Spokesman, 1993); Michael C. Webb, "International Economic Structures, Government Interests, and International Coordination of Macroeconomic Adjustment Policies," *International Organization* 45 (1991); Stuart Holland, *Out of Crisis: A Project for European Recovery* (London: Spokesman, 1983); John Williamson, "Global Macroeconomic Strategy," in Institute for International Economics, *Promoting World Recovery* (Washington: Institute for International Economics, 1982); and Fritz W. Scharpf, *Crisis and Choice in European Social Democracy* (Ithaca: Cornell University Press, 1991), pp. 259–69.

32   Joan Robinson, *What Are the Questions? And Other Essays* (Armonk: M.E. Sharpe 1980), p. 30.

33   Keynes, *General Theory*, pp. 382–83.

The Making of a Cybertariat? Virtual Work in a Real World

1   *Analytica*, e-mail newsletter, March 2000.

2   E-mail from Alice de Wolff, April 2000.

3   Rosemary Crompton and Gareth Stedman Jones, *White-Collar Proletariat: Deskilling and Gender in Clerical Work* (London and Basingstoke: Macmillan, 1984).

4   Duncan Gallie, *In Search of the New Working Class: Automation and Social Integration within the Capitalist Enterprise* (Cambridge, UK: Cambridge University Press, 1978).

5   Nicos Poulantzas, *Classes in Contemporary Capitalism* (London: New Left Books, 1975).

6   Erik Olin Wright, "The Class Structure of Advanced Capitalist Societies," in *Class, Crisis, and the State* (London: Verso, 1979).

7   Karl Marx, *Capital*, Vol. 3 (London: Lawrence & Wishart, 1974), pp. 299–300, quoted in Crompton and Jones, *White-Collar Proletariat*, p. 8.

8   Gordon Marshall, Howard Newby, David Rose et al., *Social Class in Modern Britain* (London: Hutchinson, 1988), p. 23.

9   C. Wright Mills, *White Collar: The American Middle Classes* (New York: Oxford University Press, 1951).

10   David Lockwood, *The Black-Coated Worker* (London: George Allen & Unwin, 1958).

11   Quoted in Harry Braverman, *Labor and Monopoly Capital: The Degradation of Work in the Twentieth Century* (New York: Monthly Review Press, 1974), p. 296.

12   Wright Mills, *White Collar*, pp. 352–53.

13   Marshall et al., *Social Class*, p. 68.

14   Richard Sennett and Jonathan Cobb, *The Hidden Injuries of Class* (New York: W.W. Norton & Co., 1972).

15   Braverman, *Labor and Monopoly Capital*.

16   John H. Goldthorpe, *Social Mobility and Class Structure in Modern Britain* (Oxford: Clarendon Press, 1980); and "On the Service Class: Its Formation and Future," in Giddens and Mackenzie, eds., *Social Class and the Division of Labour* (Cambridge, UK: Cambridge University Press, 1982).

17   I have discussed some of these ideas at greater length in Ursula Huws, "Reflections on Twenty Years Research on Women and Technology," in Swasti Mitter and Sheila Rowbotham, eds., *Women Encounter Technology* (Maastricht: UN University Institute of Technology, 1995; and London: Routledge, 1995).

18   Jean Tepperman, *Not Servants, Not Machines: Office Workers Speak Out* (Boston: Beacon Press, 1976); Judith Gregory, *Race against Time* (Cleveland: 9 to 5, 1981); Marianne Craig, *The Office Worker's Survival Handbook* (London: BSSRS, 1981); Rosemary Crompton and Gareth Jones, *White-Collar Proletariat: Deskilling and Gender in Clerical Work* (London and Basingstoke: Macmillan, 1984); Ann Game and Rosemary Pringle, *Gender at Work* (London: Pluto Press, 1984); Louise Kapp Howe, *Pink Collar: Inside the World of Women's Work* (New York: Avon, 1977); Robert Howard, *Brave New Workplace* (New York: Viking, 1985); Lenny Siegel and John Markoff, *The High Cost of High Tech* (New York: Harper & Row, 1985); Heather Menzies, *Women and the Chip: Case studies of the Effects of Informatics on Employment in Canada* (Quebec: Institute for Research on Public Policy, 1982).

19   These are discussed in Ursula Huws, Nick Jagger, and Siobhan O'Regan, *Teleworking and Globalization* (Brighton: Institute for Employment Studies, 1999), and include Annie Posthuma, *The Internationalization of Clerical Work: A Study of Offshore Office Services in the Caribbean*, SPRU Occasional Paper 24 (Brighton: University of Sussex, 1987); Antonio Soares, "The Hard Life of the Unskilled Workers in New Technologies: Data Entry Clerks in Brazil" in H. J. Bullinger, ed., *Human Aspects in Computing* (Amsterdam: Elsevier Science Publishers, 1991) and "Telework and Communication in Data Processing Centres in Brazil" in Urs E. Gattiker, ed., *Technology-Mediated Communication* (Berlin and New York: Walter de Gruyter, 1992); Dennis Pantin, *Export-Based Information Processing in the Caribbean, with Particular Respect to Offshore Data Processing* (Geneva: FIET, 1995); Ruth Pearson, "Gender and New Technology in the Caribbean: New Work for Women?," in Janet Momsen, ed., *Gender Analysis in Development*, UEA Discussion Paper 5 (Norwich: University of East Anglia, 1991); and Ruth Pearson and Swasti Mitter, "Employment and Working Conditions of Low-Skilled Information Processing Workers in Less Developed Countries," *International Labour Review* 132:1 (April, 1993).

20   Exceptions to this are Christopher May's analysis in *The Rise of Web-Back Labour: Global Information Society and the International Division of Labour* (University of Plymouth: Plymouth International Studies Centre, 1999) and the pioneering field studies of Jan Sinclair Jones, in various unpublished papers and in "First You See It, Now You Don't: Home-Based Telework in the Global Context," working paper presented to the Australian Sociology

Association Conference, Monash University, Melbourne, December 5–7, 1999.

21 Braverman, *Labor and Monopoly Capital*, p. 303.

22 Marx, *Capital*, Vol. 3, pp. 299–300, quoted in Crompton and Jones, *White-Collar Proletariat*, p. 9.

23 See my "Material World: The Myth of the Weightless Economy," *Socialist Register 1999* (London: Merlin Press, 1999).

24 I have written about this process at greater length elsewhere. See, for instance, my "Challenging Commoditization: Producing Usefulness outside the Factory," in Collective Design, eds., *Very Nice Work if You Can Get It: The Socially Useful Production Debate* (Nottingham: Spokesman Books, 1985), pp. 149–67.

25 Strategic alliances are discussed, inter alia, by John H. Dunning in *The Globalization of Business* (London: Routledge, 1993).

26 Frank Parkin, *Marxism and Class Theory* (London: Tavistock, 1979).

27 Edward Wolff and William Baumol, in Lars Osberg et al., eds., *The Information Economy: The Implications of Unbalanced Growth* (Montreal: Institute for Research on Public Policy, 1989).

28 Marie Lavoie and Pierre Therrien, *Employment Effects of Computerization* (Ottawa: Human Resources Development Canada Applied Research Branch, 1999).

29 European Labour Force Survey data, Eurostat.

30 M. Campbell and M. Daly, "Self-Employment: Into the 1990s," *Employment Gazette*, June 1992.

31 Nigel Meager and Janet Moralee, "Self-Employment and the Distribution of Income," in John Hill, ed., *New Inequalities* (Cambridge, UK: Cambridge University Press, 1996).

32 Meager and Moralee, "Self-Employment."

33 Amin Rajan and P. van Eupen, *Tomorrow's People* (Kent: CREATE, 1998).

34 I have explored this idea in greater depth in my "Terminal Isolation: The Atomization of Work and Leisure in the Wired Society," in Radical Science Collective, eds., *Making Waves: The Politics of Communications* (London: Free Association Books, 1985), pp. 9–25.

35 UK Labour Force Survey 2000, Office of National Statistics, UK; analysis by Ursula Huws and Peter Bates, Institute for Employment Studies, July 2000.

36 Quoted in Barbara Ehrenreich and Deirdre English, *For Her Own Good* (London: Pluto Press, 1979).

37 E-mail from Gerard Greenfield, *Globalization Monitor*, Hong Kong, June 2000.

38 Quoted in Theo Nichols, "Social Class: Official, Sociological, and Marxist" in John Irvine, Ian Miles, and Jeff Evans, eds., *Demystifying Social Statistics* (London: Pluto Press, 1979), p. 159.

39 Crompton and Jones, *White-Collar Proletariat*, p. 27.

40 Eurostat data, 1999.

41 UNCTAD and PIKOM data, quoted in Swasti Mitter and Umit Efendioglu, "Relocation of Information Processing Work: Implications for Trade between Asia and the European Union," unpublished paper (Maastricht: UN University Institute of Technology, 1997).

42 Sunil Khilnani, *The Idea of India* (Delhi: Penguin, 1998), p. 148.

43 E-mail from Sujata Gothoskhar, June 2000.

44 Jones, "Home-Based Telework."

45 This point is made by Peter Lloyd in *A Third-World Proletariat* (London: George Allen & Unwin, 1982).

46 Pearson, "Gender and New Technology."

47 Soares, "Data Entry Clerks in Brazil."

48 Jones, "Home-Based Telework."

No-Collar Labor in America's "New Economy"

1 Lawrence Mishel, Jared Bernstein, and John Schmitt, *The State of Working America* (Armonk, NY: M.E. Sharpe, 1997), pp. 258–73.

2 AnnaLee Saxenian, *Regional Advantage: Culture and Competition in Silicon Valley and Route 128* (Cambridge, MA: Harvard University Press, 1994).

3 This notorious estimate is the work of Daniel Pink, operator of FreeAgentNation.com, and chief promoter of the concept in the dizzy pages of the industry rag *Fast Company*. Nina Munk, "The Price of Freedom," *New York Times Magazine*, March 5, 2000, p. 52.

4 Bureau of Labor Statistics, *Contingent and Alternative Employment Arrangements*, December 1999.

5 Michael Lewis, "The Artist in the Gray Flannel Pyjamas," *New York Times Magazine*, March 5, 2000, p. 46.

6 Munk, "The Price of Freedom," p. 54.

7 For a fuller analysis of this point and others in this essay, see Andrew Ross, "The Mental Labor Problem," *Social Text* 63 (Summer 2000), pp. 1–31.

8   See NEA Research Division, "Artist Employment in America," 1997, available at www.arts.endow.gov.pub.

9   NEA Research Division Note 73, April 1999, available at www.arts.endow. gov.pub.

10 Randy Martin, "Beyond Privatization: The Art and Society of Labor, Citizenship, and Consumerism," *Social Text* 59 (Spring 1999), pp. 38–39.

11 Lois Gary and Ronald Seeber, *Under the Stars: Essays on Labor Relations in Arts and Entertainment*, (Ithaca: Cornell University Press, 1996), p. 6.

12 David Bacon, "Silicon Valley Sweatshops: High-Tech's Dirty Little Secret," *Nation*, April 19, 1993, p. 517.

13 Andrew Ross, "Jobs in Cyberspace," in *Real Love: In Pursuit of Cultural Justice* (New York: NYU Press, 1998), pp. 7–34; and "Sweated Labor in Cyberspace," *New Labor Forum* 4, (Spring 1999), pp. 47–56.

14 Estimates based on annual reports on new media employment, Coopers and Lybrand/PriceWaterhouseCooper. New York New Media Industry Survey: *Opportunities and Challenges of New York's Emerging Cyber-Industry*, New York New Media Association, 1996, 1997, and 1999. There is no data on comparative compensation levels in the 1999 report, but PriceWaterhouse confirmed to me that, without accounting for stock equity, the ratios for 1998 full-time employees are about the same as for previous years: $40,000 for new media; $83,500 for advertising; $84,000 for TV.

15 Bill Lessard and Steve Baldwin, *NetSlaves: True Tales of Working on the Web* (New York: McGraw-Hill, 2000), p. 246. For an active website, see "NetSlaves: Horror Stories of Working on the Web" at www.disobey.com/ netslaves.

16 Data are from the 1987 and 1997 National Survey of Postsecondary Faculty (NSOPF), conducted by the National Center for Education Statistics of the Department of Education.

17 "AUP, Annual Report on the Economic Status of the Profession 1999–2000," *Academe* 86:2 (March–April 2000).

A Tale of Two Crises: Labor, Capital, and Restructuring in the US Auto Industry

1   In this essay, use of the term "foreign" generally refers to firms not of US origin that operate or invest in the United States.

2   United States Government Accountability Office, *Summary of Government Efforts and Automakers' Restructuring to Date*, report to Congressional committees, GA-09–553, 2009.

3   USGAO, *Summary of Government Efforts.*

4   USGAO, *Summary of Government Efforts.*

5   In June 2011 Fiat bought the US government's share of Chrysler and began negotiations to buy out both the Canadian government's and the UAW VEBA's share.

6   Ford sold Aston Martin in 2007.

7   James M. Rubenstein, *A Changing US Auto Industry: A Geographical Analysis* (New York: Routledge, 1992).

8   Carl H. A. Dassbach, *Global Enterprises and the World Economy: Ford, General Motors, and IBM; The Emergence of the Transnational Enterprise* (New York: Garland Publishing, 1989).

9   Stan Luger, *Corporate Power, American Democracy, and the Automobile Industry* (Cambridge, UK: Cambridge University Press, 2000); Alex Taylor, "The Death of the Sport-Utility Vehicle Foretold," *Fortune,* July 8, 1996, p. 22.

10   The data tracks all openings, expansions, closings and downsizings reported in every issue of the weekly trade journal *Automotive News* from 1988 to 2006. The AIP database is intended to illustrate *trends* in investment over time and space rather than a census of all events. Nicole M. Aschoff, *Globalization and Capital Mobility in the Automobile Industry,* PhD thesis, Johns Hopkins University, Baltimore, 2010. Refer to Chapter 2 and Appendix 1 for a detailed discussion of the AIP database.

11   Aschoff, *Globalization and Capital Mobility;* Thomas Klier and James Rubenstein, *Who Really Made Your Car: Restructuring and Geographic Change in the Auto Industry* (Kalamazoo: W. E. Upjohn Institute for Employment Research, 2008).

12   Julie Froud, Sukhdev Johal, Adam Leaver et al., *Financialization and Strategy: Narrative and Numbers* (New York: Routledge, 2006).

13   Restructuring in the auto industry rarely follows a coherent long-term plan, because competition and the cyclicality of the industry force assemblers to please the markets through frequent, high-visibility restructuring programs. As Froud et al. argue: "[T]he stock market can often change its shallow, collective mind much more rapidly than giant firms can change their strategies. Thus, in a first period, the market may encourage or even demand supposedly value-creating moves by individual firms which may then in a second period provide the basis for general condemnation of the industry and a call for strategy reversal." Froud et al., *Financialization and Strategy,* p. 44.

14   "De-verticalization" refers to the process by which vertically integrated firms such as GM and Ford outsourced in-house production to independent suppliers.

15 The automotive industry is commonly divided into the categories of original equipment manufacturers (OEMs) who manufacture cars and their original equipment suppliers. Parts that are installed on cars outside the factory, after the sale, are considered part of the aftermarket (AM) production network. Original equipment suppliers fall into three tiers. Tier 3 suppliers are generally the smallest and produce individual parts such as hoses, gaskets, et cetera. Tier 2 suppliers are larger and produce a range of products that include more complicated components and sometimes modules. Tier 1 suppliers are the largest suppliers and produce a wide range of parts, components, and modules. Tier 1 suppliers are now often delegated responsibility for organizing tier 2 and 3 suppliers by assemblers, and sometimes produce entire systems for cars.

16 Timothy Sturgeon and Richard Florida, *Globalization and Jobs in the Automotive Industry*, study by Carnegie Mellon University and the Massachusetts Institute of Technology, final report to the Alfred P. Sloan Foundation, March 2000.

17 Froud et al., *Financialization and Strategy*.

18 Richard J. Anderson, Cristina Muise, and David Gancarz, "Partial Divestitures as an M&A Alternative: The Case of GMAC," *Journal of Corporate Accounting* 21:2 (January–February 2010).

19 Anderson et al., "Partial Divestitures."

20 Greta Krippner, *Capitalizing on Crisis: The Political Origins of the Rise of Finance* (Cambridge, MA: Harvard University Press, 2009), p. 224.

21 Gerald F. Davis, *Managed by the Markets: How Finance Reshaped America* (Oxford: Oxford University Press, 2009).

22 Anderson et al., "Partial Divestitures."

23 Anderson et al., "Partial Divestitures."

24 As US assemblers adjust their plants and products in line with their decreasing market share, investment seems to be shifting away from Canada and back toward the United States, reversing investment trends of the 1980s, when Canada was a favored destination of new investment.

25 David Welch and Dakin Campbell, "Why Ally Financial and GM, Once Family, Are Now Rivals," *Markets and Finance* 24 (February 2011).

26 James Sherk, "Auto Bailout Ignores Excessive Labor Costs," Heritage Foundation, November 19, 2008, available at www.heritagefoundation.org; Sven Gustavson, "Auto Bailout Shifts to Political Assault on UAW," 2009, available at www.mlive.com.

27 The far-reaching concessions agreed to by the UAW put a great deal of pressure on Canadian autoworkers to agree to similar give-backs. In March

2009 the CAW agreed to a wage freeze and other concessions but has thus far resisted a tiered wage structure such as the one adopted by the UAW.

28 In March 1996 Delphi workers went on strike in Dayton, Ohio, at two GM brake plants, shutting down sixty-one Delphi plants within a week. Two years earlier, the union had agreed to reorganize production, implementing work teams and flexible "production cells" in exchange for a promise of substantial investment in the plant by GM. GM failed to keep its part of the agreement, outsourcing new brake contracts for the 1998 Chevrolet Camaro and Pontiac Firebird to Robert Bosch instead.

29 Office of Aerospace and Automotive Industries, *US Automotive Industry Employment Trends*, US Department of Commerce, March 30, 2006.

30 See Aschoff, *Globalization and Capital Mobility*, for a detailed case study of Delphi.

31 Delphi cut five thousand jobs shortly after it was spun off from GM in 1999.

32 This illustrates the short-term thinking of the union. The company decided to close these plants anyway (just two years later), but achieved the historic feat of the tiered wage system.

33 Form 8-K Current Report, Securities and Exchange Commission, March 1, 2005; Form 8-K Current Report, Securities and Exchange Commission, June 8, 2005.

34 Joseph B. White, "Delphi Negotiates with GM, UAW about Big Revamp," *Wall Street Journal*, August 5, 2005.

35 Jeffrey McCracken and Lee Hawkins Jr., "Delphi Asks Union for Deep Cuts as Chapter 11 Deadline Nears," *Wall Street Journal*, October 7, 2005.

36 Jeffrey McCracken, "Delphi Seeks Further Concessions: In Addition to Wage Cuts, Greater Leeway is Requested to Hire Non-union Workers," *Wall Street Journal*, October 28, 2005.

37 Edward Lapham, "Delphi's Wage War Will Reshape US Labour Market," *Automotive News*, November 14, 2005.

38 The only challenge from labor the company faced was from a group of dissident workers inside the UAW called the Soldiers of Solidarity, whose efforts achieved the few benefits Delphi workers received during the bankruptcy proceedings.

39 Jeffrey McCracken, "In Shift, Auto Workers Flee to Health-Care Jobs," *Wall Street Journal*, September 11, 2007.

40 The VEBA was a boon for Detroit automakers. In 2007 the UAW agreed to take on the cost (and risk) of healthcare for workers and retirees in exchange for a lump sum and company stock. The nature of the transfer,

especially the agreement to receive payment in the form of stocks, made UAW members extremely vulnerable to the ups and downs of share prices in a notoriously cyclical industry. During the 2009 bankruptcy restructuring, GM and Chrysler were able to decrease their financial obligations to the VEBA in exchange for an increase in preferred stock, decreasing the likelihood that theVEBA will be able to cover the healthcare costs of UAW members and retirees in the years to come.

41   Sherk, "Auto Bailout Ignores"; Steve Finlay, "Kiss Babies, Bash Auto Industry," *Ward's Auto World,* June 1, 2008; Clive Crook, "Does Obama Still Want Stronger Unions?," *National Journal,* November 22, 2008.

42   USGAO, *Summary of Government Efforts,* p. 26.

43   USGAO, *Summary of Government Efforts,* p. 27.

44   The concessions were negotiated first àt Ford and then expanded at GM and Chrysler prior to bankruptcy. The Jobs Bank was also eliminated in late 2008.

45   Jane Slaughter, "UAW Members Protest 50% Wage Cut at GM Plant, Demand a Vote," *Labor Notes,* October 21, 2010.

46   David Barkholz, "Detroit 3 are Expected to Add 36,000 Tier 2 Jobs by 2015," *Automotive News,* April 12, 2011.

47   Detroit has been slowly increasing the number of temporary workers it employs, especially since 2007. See Jane Slaughter, "Auto Workers Stuck in Two-Tier System," *Automotive News,* May 2011, p. 8.

48   While GM and Toyota have historically paid comparable wages in the US, GM's total compensation costs have been much higher than Toyota because of its large number of retirees. This cost disparity worsened as GM's active working population decreased over the past three decades due to productivity gains and decreased market share, while its retiree pool increased. However, recent concessions in combination with the VEBA have largely eliminated this cost differential.

49   Louis Uchitelle, "Unions Yield on Wage Scales to Preserve Jobs," *New York Times,* November 19, 2010.

50   Dee-Ann Durbin, "GM, Chrysler Investing in New Small Cars," *Associated Press,* October 31, 2010.

51   Jane Slaughter, "UAW Says It Will Go 'All In' to Organize Foreign-Owned Auto Plants," *Labor Notes,* January 24, 2011.

52   Brent Snavely, "UAW Members Defeat Proposed Changes to Ford Contract," *Detroit Free Press,* November 2, 2009; Brett Hoven, "Ford Workers Reject New Concessions—Build a Movement to Change the UAW," November 5, 2009, available at www.socialistalternative.org.

Crisis as Capitalist Opportunity: The New Accumulation through Public Service Commodification

1   Or, perhaps more precisely, it could be said that uncommodified use values are being transformed into commodified use values, giving them exchange value in the market.

2   See Claude Serfati, "Transnational Organisations as Financial Groups," *Work Organisation, Labour, and Globalisation* 5:1 (2011), for an interesting discussion of the convergence between nonfinancial and financial TNCs.

3   UNCTAD, *World Investment Report* (Geneva: UNCTAD, 2008), p. 3.

4   UNCTAD, *World Investment Report*, p. 4.

5   UNCTAD, *World Investment Report*, pp. xv–xvi.

6   UNCTAD, *World Investment Report*, p. 4.

7   For instance, when it was introduced during the late 1990s, in the IT industry for labor-intensive programming tasks such as converting European company accounting systems to cope with the introduction of the euro, or averting the catastrophes it was predicted would be caused by the "millennium bug."

8   I have written extensively elsewhere about the long development of this new global division of labor from the 1970s on in, for instance, *The Making of a Cybertariat* (New York: Monthly Review Press, 2003); "Fixed, Footloose, or Fractured: Work, Identity, and the Spatial Division of Labour," *Monthly Review* 57:10, 2006; Ursula Huws and Jörg Flecker, eds., *Asian Emergence: The World's Back Office?*, IES Report 419 (Brighton: Institute for Employment Studies, 2005).

9   This process is described in more detail in my "The Restructuring of Global Value Chains and the Creation of a Cybertariat," in Christopher May, ed., *Global Corporate Power: (Re)integrating Companies into International Political Economy* (Boulder: Lynne Rienner Publishers, 2006), pp. 65–84.

10   DeAnne Julius, *Public Services Industry Review* (London: Department for Business Enterprise and Regulatory Reform, 2008).

11   Including post and telecommunications, energy and water networks, formerly publicly owned airlines, state-owned banks, and public housing stock.

12   OECD data, quoted in "A Special Report on the Future of the State," *Economist*, March 19, 2011, p. 4.

13   IMF data, quoted in "A Special Report," p. 5

14   Gøsta Esping-Andersen, *The Three Worlds of Welfare Capitalism* (Princeton: Princeton University Press, 1990).

15   Ursula Huws, "Move Over Brother," *New Socialist*, January 1985.

16 Equal Opportunities Commission, *The Gender Impact of CCT in Local Government* (Manchester: Equal Opportunities Commission, 1995).

17 Subsequently, this process culminated in the 2006 Services Directive (2006/123), which came into force on December 28, 2009, effectively removing any national barriers within the EU to companies wishing to tender for public services.

18 Again, this set the scene for further liberalization of international trade in services under the GATS. In the words of the WTO: "The Uruguay Round was only the beginning. GATS requires more negotiations which began in early 2000 and are now part of the Doha Development Agenda. The goal is to take the liberalization process further by increasing the level of commitments in schedules." "Understanding the WTO: The Agreements," WTO, available at www.wto.org.

19 Bob Jessop, *The Future of the Capitalist State* (Oxford: Polity Press, 2002).

20 Union density is significantly higher among public sector workers than their private sector counterparts in every European country other than Belgium. See V. Glassner, *The Public Sector in the Crisis*, Working Paper 2010.07 (Brussels: European Trade Union Institute, 2010), p. 15.

21 I have written at greater length about this process in, for instance, *The Making of a Cybertariat*; and "The New Gold Rush," *Work Organisation, Labour, and Globalisation* 2:2 (2008).

22 For a detailed anatomization, see Stewart Player and Colin Leys, *Confuse and Conceal: The NHS and Independent Sector Treatment Centres* (London: Merlin Press, 2008).

23 See Dexter Whitfield, "Marketisation of Legal Services," *Legal Action*, March 2007.

24 Colin Leys, *Market-Driven Politics* (London: Verso, 2003).

25 Arlie Russell Hochschild, *The Managed Heart: The Commercialization of Human Feeling* (Berkeley: University of California Press, 1983).

26 The question is sometimes raised whether there is any improvement in the quality of services that have been standardized, commodified, and outsourced. The implication is that, if this is the case, then the benefits to service users may outweigh any disadvantages to workers. In fact it is extremely difficult to make such comparisons for a number of reasons. First, restructuring is often introduced in situations where services are already deteriorating because of spending cuts. Second, the change processes associated with commodification make it difficult to compare like with like. Third, the obsessive focus on quantitative indicators that is an essential underpinning of commodification renders invisible many of the qualitative changes that may be experienced negatively by service users.

Nevertheless, there is a considerable body of research that suggests there
is a deterioration (see for example Colin Leys and Allyson Pollock, *NHS
Plc: The Privatisation of Our Health Care* (London: Verso, 2004); Player and
Leys, *Confuse and Conceal*; Dexter Whitfield, *Global Auction of Public Assets*
(London: Spokesman, 2009). It is perhaps no accident that John Hutton,
secretary of state for business enterprise and regulatory reform in the New
Labour government in 2008, stopped even arguing that the main advantage
of outsourcing was to bring efficiency savings. The public services industry,
he said, should be encouraged because "[t]here is significant export
potential in this growth industry. Encouraging and assisting UK firms to
make the most of these opportunities will generate substantial benefits not
only for UK firms but also for the UK economy. The Review concludes
that the best way that government can support the PSI abroad is through
maintaining a competitive framework for public services which fosters a
dynamic and thriving PSI in the UK." See the executive summary in the
introduction to Julius, *Public Services Industry Review*, p. v.

27   The International Organization for Standardization, which has
     2,700 technical committees, subcommittees and working groups, sets
     international technical standards for a large range of different industrial
     processes. The existence of these standards means that it is possible to
     trade with, or outsource to, an ISO-certified company in the confidence
     that the outputs will be predictable and standardized, removing the need
     for detailed supervision, in just the same way that, for instance, electrical
     standards make it possible to plug an appliance into a standard socket in the
     confidence that it will function correctly.

28   ISO survey, 2009, available at www.iso.org.

29   Brett Caraway, "Online Labour Markets: An Enquiry into oDesk Providers,"
     Work Organisation, Labour, and Globalisation 4:2 (2010), pp. 111–25.

30   I have written in greater depth about the changing occupational identities
     of IT workers in the context of globalization in "New Forms of Work:
     New Occupational Identities," in Norene Pupo and Mark Thomas, eds.,
     Interrogating the "New Economy": Restructuring Work in the 21st Century
     (Peterborough, Ontario: Broadview Press, 2010).

31   See Chris Dixon, "The Reformatting of State Control in Vietnam," *Work
     Organisation, Labour, and Globalisation* 2:2 (2008), pp. 101–18.

32   Available at www.serco.com.

33   Colin Leys and Stewart Player, *The Plot Against the NHS* (London: Merlin
     Press, 2011).

34   For a detailed description of the impact on workers' skills on the "call-
     centerization" of the Danish tax system, see Pia Bramming, Ole Sørensen,
     and Peter Hasle, "In Spite of Everything: Professionalism as Mass-

Customised Bureaucratic Production in a Danish Government Call Centre," *Work Organisation, Labour, and Globalisation* 3:1 (2009), pp. 114–30.

35   See Pamela Meil, Per Tengblad, and Peter Docherty, *Value Chain Restructuring and Industrial Relations: The Role of Workplace Representation in Changing Conditions of Employment and Work*, WORKS Project, Higher Institute of Labour Studies (Leuven: HIVA, 2009).

36   This case study is described in greater detail in Simone Dahlmann, "The End of the Road: No More Walking in Dead Men's Shoes: IT Professionals' Experience of Being Outsourced to the Private Sector," *Work Organisation, Labour, and Globalisation* 2:2 (2008), pp. 148–61.

37   Howard Reed, *The Shrinking State: Why the Rush to Outsource Threatens our Public Services*, report for Unite (London: Landman Economics, 2011), p. 13.

38   Reed, *The Shrinking State*, p. 18.

39   Julius, *Public Services Industry Review*.

40   Sam Lister, "NHS Is World's Biggest Employer after Indian Rail and Chinese Army," *Times Online*, March 20, 2004.

41   Anna Bawden, "Suffolk Council Plans to Outsource Virtually All Services," *Guardian*, September 22, 2010, *guardian.co.uk*.

42   Dexter Whitfield, *Analysis of Development and Regulatory Services Business Case* (London: European Services Strategy Unit, 2011).

43   "There Goes Everybody," *Economist*, July 8, 2010.

44   Cabinet Office, *Modernising Commissioning: Increasing the Role of Charities, Social Enterprises, Mutuals, and Co-operatives in Public Service Delivery*, Cabinet Office Green Paper, London, 2010, p. 5, original emphasis.

45   Aga Khan Development Network, "Upgrading Nursing Studies: Strengthening the Health-Care System in Tanzania," October 2007, available at www.akdn.org.

46   Brett Neilson, "Guijing Migrant Village," *Transit Labour* 2 (December 2010), pp. 33–35.

The Walmart Working Class

1   The data in this paragraph were gleaned from *Walmart 2013 Annual Report*, pp. 17–20 ("Walmart US Stores"), available at corporate.walmart. com; "Supply Chain Graphic of the Week: A Detailed Look at Walmart Statistics in Chart Form," *Supply Chain Digest*, August 1, 2012, available at www.scdigest.com; Linton Weeks, "Is Walmart a Magnet for American Mayhem?," *National Public Radio*, September 14, 2011, available at www. npr.org; "NRF Forecasts Retail Industry Sales Growth of 3.4 Percent in

2012," National Retail Federation, January 16, 2012, available at www.nrf. com; Elizabeth Flock, "Walmart Heirs Net Worth Equals Total of Bottom 30 Percent of Americans," *Washington Post*, December 9, 2011; Charles Fishman, *The Walmart Effect: How the World's Most Powerful Company Really Works—and How It's Transforming the American Economy* (New York: Penguin, 2011), p. 7; Josh Bivens, "Inequality Exhibit A: Walmart and the Wealth of American families," Economic Policy Institute, July 17, 2012, available at www.epi.org.

2   Stephanie Clifford, "Walmart Strains to Keep Aisles Fresh Stocked," *New York Times*, April 3, 2013.

3   Renee Dudley, "Walmart Faces the Cost of Cost-Cutting: Empty Shelves," *Bloomberg Businessweek*, March 28, 2013. The *New York Times* reported that other confidential memos indicated similar problems such as poor stocking, poor quality, and low consumer confidence. See Clifford, "Walmart Strains."

4   Nelson Lichtenstein, *The Retail Revolution: How Walmart Created a Brave New World of Business* (New York: Metropolitan, 2009), p. 35. See also "Comparable Store Sales," Walmart, June 2013, available at stock.walmart. com.

5   Alice Hines and Christina Wilkie, "Walmart's Internal Compensation Documents Reveal Systematic Limit on Advancement," *Huffington Post*, November 16, 2012, available at www.huffingtonpost.com.

6   John Marshall, "The High Price of Low Cost: The View from the Other Side of Walmart's 'Productivity Loop,'" *Making Change at Walmart*, 2011, p. 10, available at makingchangeatwalmart.org.

7   Misha Petrovic and Gary G. Hamilton, "Making Global Markets: Walmart and Its Suppliers," in Nelson Lichtenstein, ed., *Walmart: The Face of Twenty-First Century Capitalism* (New York: The New Press, 2006), pp. 110–15.

8   Anita Chan, ed., *Walmart in China* (Ithaca: Cornell University Press), 2011, p. 2. See also Anthony Bianco, *Walmart: The Bully of Bentonville* (New York: Currency, 2006), p. 13.

9   Edna Bonacich and Jake B. Wilson, *Getting the Goods: Ports, Labor, and the Logistics Revolution* (Ithaca: Cornell University Press, 2008), p. 7.

10   Petrovic and Hamilton, "Making Global Markets, p. 110.

11   See Nelson Lichtenstein, "Walmart's Long March to China," in Chan, *Walmart in China*, pp. 21–22; Bonacich, *Getting the Goods*, pp. 4–5; Petrovic and Hamilton, "Making Global Markets," p. 111; Fishman, *The Walmart Effect*, p. 83.

12   Bethany Moreton, *To Serve God and Wal-Mart: The Making of Christian Free Enterprise* (Cambridge, MA: Harvard University Press, 2009), pp. 24–40; Lichtenstein, *The Retail Revolution*, pp. 53–84.

13   For Blacks, a "sundown town" was literally a town where they may have
      been in physical danger if still there after sundown. Many towns literally
      had signs posted at their limits reading, "Nigger, don't let the sun go down
      on you in . . . ." Lichtenstein, *The Retail Revolution*, pp. 39, 62–64, 89–90.
      See also James W. Loewen, *Sundown Towns: A Hidden Dimension of American
      Racism* (New York: The New Press, 2005); and Moreton, *To Serve God and
      Walmart*, pp. 49–65, 84. Walmart also claims to employ more than 169,000
      "Hispanic associates." See "Our People," Walmart, available at corporate.
      walmart.com.

14   Arindrajit Dube, Barry Eidlin, and Bill Lester, "Impact of Walmart Growth
      on Earnings throughout the Retail Sector in Urban and Rural Counties,"
      Institute of Industrial Relations Working Paper Series, University of
      California at Berkeley, 2005, p. 3, available at economics.ucr.edu.

15   Clarence Y. H. Lo, *Small Property versus Big Government: Social Origins of the
      Property Tax Revolt* (Berkeley: University of California Press, 1990); Barnaby
      J. Feder, "Walmart's Expansion Aided by Many Taxpayer Subsidies," *New
      York Times*, May 24, 2004; David Cay Johnston, "Study Says Walmart Often
      Fights Local Taxes," *New York Times*, October 10, 2007.

16   See Lichtenstein, *The Retail Revolution*, pp. 36–39; 125–26, 141; Matthew
      Boyle and Duane D. Stanford, "Walmart to End Employee Profit-Sharing
      in February," *Bloomberg Businessweek*, October 9, 2010.

17   Wade Rathke, "A Walmart Workers Association? An Organizing Plan," in
      Lichtenstein, *Walmart*, pp. 268–70.

18   Fishman, *The Walmart Effect*, pp. 3–9.

19   Jerry Hausman and Ephraim Leibtag, "Consumer Benefits from Increased
      Competition in Shopping Outlets: Measuring the Effect of Walmart,"
      National Bureau of Economic Research Working Paper 11809, December
      2005, available at www.nber.org. Hausman and Leibtag also claim a
      bias against using Walmart in inflation data causes the US government
      to overstate increases in the consumer price index by 15 percent. Jerry
      Hausman and Ephraim Leibtag, "CPI Bias from Supercenters: Does the
      BLS Know that Walmart Exists?," National Bureau of Economic Research,
      August 2004, p. 29. Another analysis concludes prices decline 1.5 to 3
      percent in the short run and 7 to 13 percent in the longer run: Emek
      Basker, "Selling a Cheaper Mousetrap: Walmart's Effect on Retail Prices,"
      Journal of Urban Economics 58:2 (September 2005).

20   Michael Schrage, "Walmart Trumps Moore's Law," *MIT Technology Review*,
      March 1, 2002, available at www.technologyreview.com.

21   "Walmart US to Create more than 22,000 Jobs in 2009," Walmart, June 4,
      2009, available at news.walmart.com.

22   David Neumark, Junfu Zhang, and Stephen Ciccarella, "The Effects of Walmart on Local Labor Markets," *Journal of Urban Economics* 63 (2008), available at socsci.uci.edu. See also Dube et al., "Impact of Walmart Growth," esp. pp. 1, 28–30.

23   Tim Sullivan, "In Bitter Strike, Grocery Workers Lost Ground," *High Country News*, June 7, 2004, available at www.hcn.org; Stephanie Clifford, "Big Retailers Fill More Aisles with Groceries," *New York Times*, January 16, 2011.

24   Arindrajit Dube, T. William Lester, and Barry Eidlin, "A Downward Push: The Impact of Wal-Mart Stores on Retail Wages and Benefits," UC Berkeley Center for Labor Education and Research, December 2007, pp. 6–7, available at laborcenter.berkeley.edu.

25   Jared Bernstein, L. Josh Bivens, and Arindrajit Dube, "Wrestling with Walmart: Trade-offs between Profits, Prices, and Wages," Economic Policy Institute, June 15, 2006, pp. 4–5. For example, median gross rents rose 45 percent from 1970 to 2000 in inflation-adjusted dollars. "Historical Census of Housing Tables: Gross Rents," US Census Bureau, available at www.census.gov.

26   Fishman, *The Walmart Effect*, pp. 69–70.

27   Fishman, *The Walmart Effect*, pp. 163–66.

28   Charles Courtemanche and Art Carden, "Supersizing Supercenters? The Impact of Walmart Supercenters on Body Mass Index and Obesity," September 10, 2010, p. 29, available at papers.ssrn.com, original emphasis.

29   Bonacich, *Getting the Goods*, p. 5.

30   Friedrich Engels, "History of the English Corn Laws," *Telegraph für Deutschland*, December 1845, available at www.marxists.org.

31   Moreton, *To Serve God and Walmart*, pp. 248–63.

32   Nelson D. Schwartz, "Recovery in US Is Lifting Profits, but Not Adding Jobs," *New York Times*, March 3, 2013.

33   "Big Business, Corporate Profits, and the Minimum Wage: Executive Summary," National Employment Law Project, July 2012, available at nelp.org. It's unclear if NELP includes farmworkers, and seasonal migrants in the United States, who are an integral part of the Walmart supply chain. One estimate puts their numbers at more than three million, with one of the highest poverty rates of any sector at 23 percent. "Table B-1. Employees on Nonfarm Payrolls by Industry Sector and Selected Industry Detail," Bureau of Labor Statistics, June 2013, available at www.bls.gov. "Farmworker Health Factsheet," National Center for Farmworker Health, Inc., August 2012.

34 The most precise data are in Carmen DeNavas-Walt, Bernadette D. Proctor, and Jessica C. Smith, "Income, Poverty, and Health Insurance Coverage in the United States: 2011," US Census Bureau, September 2012, pp. 17–24, available at www.census.gov. See also Sabrina Tavernise and Robert Gebeloff, "New Way to Tally Poor Recasts View of Poverty," *New York Times*, November 8, 2011; Jason DeParle, Robert Gebeloff, and Sabrina Tavernise, "Older, Suburban, and Struggling, 'Near Poor' Startle the Census," *New York Times*, November 18, 2011; "Low-Income Working Families: The Growing Economic Gap," The Working Poor Families Project, Winter 2012–13, p. 3, available at www.workingpoorfamilies.org.

35 Courtney Gross, "Is Walmart Worse?," *Gotham Gazette*, February 14, 2011, available at old.gothamgazette.com.

36 See Hines and Wilkie, "Internal Compensation Documents"; "Field Non-exempt Associate Pay Plan FY 2013," Sam's Club, published by the *Huffington Post*, February 11, 2012.

37 Hines and Wilkie, "Internal Compensation Documents."

38 Susan Chambers, "Reviewing and Revising Walmart's Benefits Strategy: Memorandum to the Board of Directors," Walmart Stores, Inc., 2006.

39 Dhanya Skariachan and Jessica Wohl, "Walmart Only Hiring Temporary Workers in Many US Stores," *Reuters*, June 13, 2013.

40 Steven Greenhouse and Michael Barbaro, "Walmart Memo Suggests Ways to Cut Employees Benefit Costs," *New York Times*, October 26, 2005.

41 Chambers, "Walmart's Benefits Strategy."

42 Michele Simon, "Food Stamps: Follow the Money. Are Corporations Profiting from Hungry Americans?," *Eat, Drink, Politics*, June 2012, pp. 15–17, available at www.eatdrinkpolitics.com. See also Leslie Dach, "Partnership for a Healthier America Remarks," Walmart, November 29, 2011, available at www.news.walmart.com.

43 Democratic Staff of the US House Committee on Education and the Workforce, "The Low-Wage Drag on Our Economy: Walmart's Low Wages and Their Effect on Taxpayers and Economic Growth," May 2013, available at democrats.edworkforce.house.gov.

44 Stephan J. Goetz and Hema Swaminathan, "Walmart and County-Wide Poverty," Department of Agricultural Economics and Rural Sociology, Pennsylvania State University, October 18, 2004, p. 12. This study was later published in *Social Science Quarterly* 87:2 (2006).

45 Lichtenstein, *The Retail Revolution*, p. 8.

46 The interviews were conducted over the phone, with the exception of two in person. Most workers asked for anonymity due to fear of losing their job or being blacklisted; as such, identifying information has been changed.

Some of the quotes are edited and condensed from the transcript. Nearly two dozen other Walmart workers were contacted, including many who said "I'm interested in telling my story," but who did not make or keep appointments for interviews. From discussions with interviewees and some who backed out, it is clear that many workers fear retaliation by Walmart or other employers, even though they were promised full anonymity.

47   DeNavas-Walt et al., "Income, Poverty and Health Insurance," pp. 18–19.

48   Jenny Brown, "In Walmart and Fast Food, Unions Scaling Up a Strike-First Strategy," *Labor Notes*, January 23, 2013, available at www.labornotes.org.

49   Paul Harris, "Walmart Supply Chain: Warehouse Staff Agencies Accused of Theft," *Guardian*, October 18, 2012. Bailey told me the same anecdotes when I interviewed him by phone.

50   "Women at Work, Women at Risk: Sexual Harassment and Assault in Will County Warehouses," Warehouse Workers for Justice, March 8, 2012, available at www.warehouseworkersunited.org.

51   Lichtenstein, *The Retail Revolution*, p. 66.

52   Brown, "In Walmart and Fast Food"; Steven Greenhouse, "Walmart Workers Are Finding a Voice without a Union," *New York Times*, September 3, 2005; Liza Featherstone, "Walmart Workers Walk Out," *Nation*, October 17, 2012, see also "Meeting of the Federal Open Market Committee," May 10, 2006, available at www.federalreserve.gov. The entire board of governors, including Chair Ben Bernanke and Vice Chair and Treasury Secretary Timothy Geithner, were present during the discussion where it was revealed Walmart was raising wages "because of all the controversy about Walmart."

53   Steven Greenhouse and Stephanie Clifford, "Protests Backed by Union Gets Walmart's Attention," *New York Times*, November 18, 2012; Josh Eidelson, "Walmart Strikes Spread to More States," *Salon*, October 9, 2012; and his "Walmart Punishes Its Workers," *Salon*, July 26, 2012, available at www.salon.com. See also Featherstone, "Walmart Workers Walk Out"; and Gabriel Thompson, "The Big, Bad Business of Fighting Guest Workers Rights," *Nation*, July 3, 2012.

54   Alice Hines and Kathleen Miles, "Walmart Strike Hits 100 Cities, But Fails to Distract Black Friday Shoppers," *Huffington Post*, November 23, 2012; Greenhouse and Clifford, "Protests Backed by Union"; Susan Berfield, "Walmart vs. Union-Backed OUR Walmart," *Bloomberg Businessweek*, December 13, 2012.

55   "Global Supply Chain Workers Pressure Walmart to Get Serious about Labor Conditions," Warehouse Workers United, April 9, 2013, available at www.warehouseworkersunited.org.

56 Kate Bronfenbrenner, "No Holds Barred: The Intensification of Employer Opposition to Organizing," Cornell School of Industrial and Labor Relations, May 20, 2009.

57 Carol Pier, "Discounting Rights: Walmart's Violations of US Workers' Right to Freedom of Association," Human Rights Watch, May 2007, p. 3, available at www.hrw.org.

58 A good summary of how the Taft-Hartley Act reshaped organized labor is Rich Yeselson, "Fortress Unionism," *Democracy*, Summer 2013, available at www.democracyjournal.org.

59 Bianco, *Walmart*, pp. 111–12.

60 Lichtenstein, *The Retail Revolution*, pp. 128–31.

61 The preceding quotes in this paragraph are from Lichtenstein, *The Retail Revolution*, pp. 137, 143–47.

62 Pier, "Discounting Rights," pp. 100–11.

63 Lichtenstein, *The Retail Revolution*, pp. 135, 230–31. Sullivan, "Bitter Strike."

64 This was confirmed by a dozen union staffers (including ones from all three unions in question) and close observers of the US unions (including Steve Early, Jenny Brown, and Ari Paul) that I interviewed.

65 "What We Do," Corporate Campaign, Inc., www.corporatecampaign.org.

66 Walmart, "Response to Walkout/Work Stoppage—Salaried Management Talking Points," published by the *Huffington Post*, October 8, 2012.

67 Josh Eidelson, "Walmart Asks a Judge to Block Historic Strikes," *Nation*, November 19, 2013; Steven Greenhouse, "Labor Union to Ease Walmart Picketing," *New York Times*, January 31, 2013.

68 Organization United for Respect at Walmart, www.forrespect.org.

69 Eidelson, "Walmart Asks a Judge to Block Historic Strikes."

70 Josh Eidelson, "Walmart Fires Eleven Strikers in Alleged Retaliation," *Nation*, June 22, 2013; Ned Resnikoff, "Walmart Workers' Campaign Targets Yahoo's Marissa Mayer," June 27, 2013, MSNBC, available at tv.msnbc.com.

71 Berfield, "Walmart vs. Union-Backed OUR Walmart."

72 Warehouse Workers for Justice, available at www.warehouseworker.org.

73 "NAI Hiffman/NAI Global Logistics assists Wal-Mart with a 3.4 Million Square Foot MEGA Distribution Center," NAI Hiffman, available at www.hiffman.com.

74 Micah Uetricht, "Strike Supporters Shut Down Illinois Walmart Warehouse," *Labor Notes*, October 2, 2012.

75 Josh Eidelson, "Labor Board Alleges Repeated Retaliation at Walmart's Top US Warehouse," *Nation*, March 20, 2013; Alexandra Bradbury, "Walmart Warehouse Strikers Return to Work with Full Back Pay," *Labor Notes*, October 9, 2012. Information on the NLRB case and class-action suit is from a follow-up phone interview with Phillip Bailey, July 5, 2013.

76 Excerpt from *Save Our Unions: Dispatches from a Movement in Distress* (New York: Monthly Review Press, 2014).

77 Steven Greenhouse, "With Day of Protests, Fast-Food Workers Seek More Pay, *New York Times*, November 29, 2013.

78 Jenny Brown, "Fast Food Strikes: What's Cooking?," *Labor Notes*, June 24, 2013; Josh Eidelson, "In Rare Strike, NYC Fast-Food Workers Walk Out," *Salon*, November 29, 2012; "Strike Wave by Fast Food and Retail Workers Spreads to Chicago," Workers Organizing Committee of Chicago, April 24, 2013, available at www.commondreams.org. An SEIU organizer provided information on the planned national strike. The labor organizer who claims NYCC organizers want to unionize is involved in a different fast-food worker campaign in New York. The Association of Community Organizations for Reform Now was born during the sixties welfare reform movement and grew into a national organization known for direct-action style campaigns around housing, living wage, and social welfare issues, as well as voter registration drives. ACORN founder Wade Rathke drafted the initial plan for a Walmart Workers Association. ACORN collapsed in 2010 after a right-wing media sting operation presented flimsy video evidence that low-level employees were advising clients on how to hide criminal financial activity, but this came right after news that ACORN had hushed up nearly one million dollars in embezzlement by Rathke's brother Dale in 1999 and 2000. Rathke, "A Walmart Workers Association?"; Stephanie Strom, "Funds Misappropriated at 2 Nonprofit Groups," *New York Times*, July 9, 2008.

79 Josh Eidelson, "Fast Food Walkout Planned in Chicago," *Salon*, April 23, 2013; Fast Food Forward, "Wage Theft and NYC's Fast Food Workers: New York's Hidden Crime Wave," 2013; Saki Knafo, "Seattle's Fast-Food Workers Strike as National Movement Begins to Claim Small Victories," *Huffington Post*, May 30, 2013.

80 "Recommendation to the Property Services Division Leadership Board: A Plan for Organizing Post-Labor Law Reform," SEIU, December 2009.

81 Steven Greenhouse, "After Push for Obama, Unions Seek New Rules," *New York Times*, November 8, 2008.

82 Adam Turl, "Who Killed EFCA?," *Socialist Worker*, July 23, 2009.

83 Interview with Steve Early, May 29, 2013.

84 Brown, "Fast Food Strikes."

85   Interview with Steve Early, May 29, 2013.

86   Interview with Steve Early, January 27, 2012.

87   Kris Maher, "Big Union to Step Up Recruiting," *Wall Street Journal*,
      February 11, 2011; Arun Gupta, "What Occupy Taught the Unions," *Salon*,
      February 2, 2012. The email note from the former SEIU organizer was
      sent to a listerv and the author was forwarded a copy.

88   Ellyn Fortino, "Chicago Fast Food and Retail Workers Win Victories
      after April Strike," Progress Illinois, July 10, 2013, available at www.
      progressillinois. com.

89   "Favorable Views of Labor, Business Rebound," Pew Research Center for
      the People and the Press, June 27, 2013, available at www.people-press.
      org; Elizabeth Mendes and Joy Wilke, "Americans' Confidence in Congress
      Falls to Lowest on Record," *Gallup Politics*, June 13, 2013, www.gallup.com.

90   SEIU organizers note that in many cities the percentage of the workforce
      and strikers who are African American is as high as 90 percent, and women
      make up two-thirds of the fast-food workforce. As for Walmart, data
      turned over in the gender discrimination class-action suit on 3.9 million
      personnel employed from 1996 to 2002 found that by the end of 2001,
      64 percent of active retail positions were filled by women. See Richard
      Drogin, "Statistical Analysis of Gender Patterns in Wal-Mart Workforce,"
      Drogin, Kakigi & Associates, February 2003.

91   Charles Post, "Social Unionism without the Workplace?," *New Politics*,
      Winter 2013, available at www.newpol.org.

92   Janice Fine, "Workers Centers: Organizing Communities at the Edge of
      the Dream," Economic Policy Institute, December 13, 2005, pp. 2–5.

93   Steve Early, "Can Workers Centers Fill the Union Void?," *New Labor Forum*,
      Summer 2006, www.newlaborforum.cuny.edu; John Garvey, "The New
      Worker Organizing," *Insurgent Notes*, March 11, 2013, insurgentnotes.com.

94   Interview with Steve Early. See also Steven Greenhouse, "Share of the
      Work Force in a Union Falls to a 97-Year Low, 11.3 percent," *New York
      Times*, January 23, 2013.

95   Gupta, "What Occupy Taught the Unions"; Steven Greenhouse,
      "Occupy Movement Inspires Unions to Embrace Bold Tactics," *New York
      Times*, November 8, 2011; Gabriel Thompson, "Occupy Oakland Calls
      for a November 2 General Strike," *Nation*, November 1, 2011; Gayge
      Operaista, "The Oakland General Strike: The Days Before, the Days After,"
      Autonomous Struggle of the Glittertariat, November 6, 2011, available at
      glittertariat.blogspot.com; Nick Pinto, "Hot and Crusty Bakery Employees
      Go from Lockout to Victory in One Week," *Village Voice*, September 10,
      2012, available at blogs.villagevoice.com.

96   Arun Gupta, "What Happened to the Green New Deal?," *Truthout*, November 16, 2012, www.truth-out.org; Zach Roberts, "Corporate Giant vs. Retirees in West Virginia," *Mudflats*, May 1, 2013, www.themudflats.net; Arun Gupta, "Freeport Is Not a Democrat vs. Republican Issue," *Progressive*, November 2, 2012.

Reconsiderations of Class: Precariousness as Proletarianization

1   Karl Marx, *Grundrisse: Foundations of the Critique of Political Economy* (Harmondsworth: Penguin, 1973, p. 472.

2   See, for instance, the discussions of "Incomes Policy" by A. J. Topham, "Background to the Argument"; Ken Coates, "A Strategy for the Unions"; and Ralph Miliband, "What Does the Left Want"; in *Socialist Register 1965* (London: Merlin Press, 1965), pp. 163–94; as well as Richard Hyman, "Workers' Control and Revolutionary Theory," *Socialist Register 1974* (London: Merlin Press, 1974), pp. 241–78.

3   Bryan D. Palmer, "Wildcat Workers: The Unruly Face of Class Struggle," *Canada's 1960s: The Ironies of Identity in a Rebellious Era* (Toronto: University of Toronto Press, 2009), pp. 211–41.

4   Barbara Garson, "Luddites in Lordstown," *Harper's Magazine*, June 1972, pp. 68–73; Judson Gooding, "Blue-Collar Blues on the Assembly Line," *Fortune*, July 1970, pp. 112–13; Jefferson Cowie, *Stayin' Alive: The 1970s and the Last Days of the Working Class* (New York and London: New Press, 2010).

5   James A. Geschwender, *Class, Race, and Worker Insurgency: The League of Revolutionary Black Workers* (Cambridge, UK: Cambridge University Press), 1977.

6   Bill Watson, "Counter-planning on the Shop Floor," *Radical America*, May–June 1971; and Ben Hamper, *Rivethead: Tales from the Assembly Line* (Boston: Warner, 1991).

7   Daniel Singer, *Prelude to Revolution: France in May 1968* (Boston: South End Press, 2002); Kristin Ross, *May '68 and Its Afterlives* (Chicago: University of Chicago Press, 2002).

8   On class conflict see Richard Hyman, "Industrial Conflict and the Political Economy," *Socialist Register 1973* (London: Merlin Press, 1973), pp. 101–54, which surveys the 1960s and early 1970s. Note, on the 1972 miners' strike, E. P. Thompson, "A Special Case," in *Writing by Candlelight* (London: Merlin Press, 1980), pp. 65–76. See also, Leo Panitch, *Social Democracy and Industrial Militancy* (Cambridge, UK: Cambridge University Press, 1976), 204–34.

9   Mike Davis, "Spring Confronts Winter," *New Left Review* 72 (November–
      December 2011), p. 15. See also Kwan Lee, *Against the Law: Labour Protests
      in China's Rustbelt and Sunbelt* (Los Angeles: University of California Press,
      2007).

10   Early comment on the growing significance of the informal economy
      appeared in Manfred Bienefeld, "The Informal Sector and Peripheral
      Capitalism," *Bulletin of the Institute of Development Studies* 4 (1975), pp. 53–
      73; and the importance of this informal sector in terms of African class
      formation is much discussed in Bill Freund, *The African Worker* (Cambridge,
      UK: Cambridge University Press, 1988).

11   Mike Davis, *Planet of Slums* (London and New York: Verso, 2006), p. 178.

12   Not all recent writing on precariousness is wrongheaded. Although
      approaching the issue from an entirely different vantage point than the
      current essay, addressing precarity from a cultural studies perspective
      and placing far more emphasis on "the knowledge economy," "creative
      industries," and "cultural revolutions," Andrew Ross refuses both the
      suggestion that a precariat is necessarily a cross-class formation and
      that there is nothing to unite those in work sectors associated with the
      traditional, unionized proletariat and those who find themselves in more
      precarious employments. See his *Nice Work If You Can Get It: Life and Labor
      in Precarious Times* (New York and London: New York University Press,
      2009).

13   Guy Standing, *The Precariat: The New Dangerous Class* (London and New
      York: Bloomsbury Academic, 2011). For the quotations in this and the
      following paragraphs, see esp. pp. vii, 8–9, 154, 159, 183.

14   Note, for instance, Ellen Meiksins Wood, *The Retreat from Class: A New
      "True" Socialism* (London: Verso, 1986); and Leo Panitch, "The Impasse of
      Working Class Politics," *Socialist Register 1985/6* (London: Merlin Press,
      1986); as well as the subsequent essays on "The Retreat of the Intellectuals,"
      Socialist Register 1990 (London: Merlin Press, 1990).

15   See Ricardo Antunes, "The Working Class Today: The New Form of Being
      of the Class Who Lives from its Labour," *Workers of the World: International
      Journal on Strikes and Social Conflict*, 1:2 (January 2012).

16   Karl Marx, *Capital: A Critical Analysis of Capitalist Production*, Vol. 1 (Moscow:
      Foreign Languages Publishing House, n.d.), p. 20.

17   Marx, *Grundrisse*, pp. 749–50.

18   Karl Marx and Frederick Engels, *Manifesto of the Communist Party*, in *Selected
      Works* (Moscow: Progress Publishers, 1968), pp. 36–46.

19   Marx and Engels, *Manifesto*.

20 See Bryan D. Palmer, "Social Formation and Class Formation in Nineteenth-Century North America," in David Levine, ed., *Proletarianization and Family History* (New York: Academic Press, 1984), pp. 229–308.

21 Marx, *Capital*, pp. 568, 612–16. See also, Marx, *Grundrisse*, esp. pp. 483–509.

22 Christopher Hill, *The World Turned Upside Down: Radical Ideas during the English Revolution* (New York: Viking, 1972), p. 39.

23 The literature that could be cited is immense, and for London alone is benchmarked between 1850 and 1890 by the pioneering sociological inquiries of Henry Mayhew and Charles Booth. See, for other useful commentary, Raphael Samuel, "Workshop of the World: Steam Power and Hand Technology in Mid-Victorian Britain," *History Workshop Journal* 3 (1977), pp. 6–72; Gareth Stedman Jones, *Outcast London: A Study in the Relationship between Classes in Victorian Society* (Oxford: Oxford University Press, 1971); and for France, Louis Chevalier, *Laboring Classes and Dangerous Classes in Paris during the First Half of the Nineteenth Century* (New York: Howard Fertig, 1973); Robert Stuart, *Marxism at Work: Ideology, Class and French Socialism during the Third Republic* (Cambridge, UK: Cambridge University Press, 1992), pp. 127–79.

24 E. P. Thompson, *The Making of the English Working Class* (Harmondsworth: Penguin, 1968), esp. pp. 9–11, 276–77, 887–88. This is not to deny what Thompson would later stress, and that is congruent with subsequent writings of Michael Lebowitz and David Harvey, that Marx, in his fixation on creating an *anti-structure* counterposed to the structure of conventional political economy, failed to adequately theorize class formation as something other than the object of capital's accumulative appropriation of surplus. See E. P. Thompson, *The Poverty of Theory and Other Essays* (London: Merlin Press, 1981), pp. 60–65; Michael Lebowitz, *Beyond "Capital": Marx's Political Economy of the Working Class* (Basingstoke: Palgrave Macmillan, 2003); Lebowitz, *Following Marx: Method, Critique, and Crisis* (Leiden and Boston: Brill, 2009), pp. 308–11; David Harvey, *The Limits to Capital* (Chicago: University of Chicago Press, 1982), p. 163.

25 For a useful attempt to wrestle with the ever-present tension between "universalist" and "exceptionalist" understandings of labor, see Dipesh Chakrabarty, *Rethinking Working-Class History: Bengal, 1890–1940* (Princeton: Princeton University Press, 1989), esp. pp. 219–30.

26 Martin Glaberman, "Be His Payment High or Low: The American Working Class in the Sixties," *International Socialism* 21 (Summer 1965), pp. 18–23. Glaberman, of course, drew directly on Marx: "It follows, therefore, that in proportion as capital accumulates, the lot of the laborer, be his payment high or low, must grow worse" (Marx, *Capital*, p. 645).

27 Harry Braverman, *Labor and Monopoly Capital: The Degradation of Work in the Twentieth Century* (New York and London: Monthly Review Press, 1974).

28   Quoted in Thompson, *Making*, p. 309.

29   Marx, *Capital*, pp. 641, 643–44.

30   John Bellamy Foster, Robert W. McChesney, and R. Jamil Jonna, "The Global Reserve Army of Labor and the New Imperialism," *Monthly Review* 63 (November 2011), available at monthlyreview.org.

31   Marx, *Capital*, p. 644–45.

32   Jan Breman, *The Labouring Poor in India: Patterns of Exploitation, Subordination, and Exclusion* (New York: Oxford University Press, 2003), p. 13.

33   Particular contributions to this literature were made by Canadian feminists. See Meg Luxton, *More Than a Labour of Love: Three Generations of Women's Work in the Home* (Toronto: Women's Press, 1980); Bonnie Fox, *Hidden in the Household: Women's Domestic Labour Under Capitalism* (Toronto: Women's Press, 1980); Michèle Barrett and Roberta Hamilton, eds., *The Politics of Diversity: Feminism, Marxism, and Nationalism* (London and New York: Verso, 1986).

34   See, for instance, Michael Denning, "Wageless Life," *New Left Review* 66 (November–December 2010), pp. 79–87; Marcel van der Linden, *Workers of the World: Essays toward a Global Labor History* (Leiden and Boston: Brill, 2008), pp. 10, 22–27, 267, 298; van der Linden, "Who Are the Workers of the World? Marx and Beyond," *Workers of the World: International Journal on Strikes and Social Conflicts* 1 (January 2013), pp. 55–76. Unease with Marx's seeming dismissiveness of the so-called lumpenproletariat has long been evident among Africanists, and was posed forcefully in Peter Worsley, "Frantz Fanon and the 'Lumpenproletariat,'" *Socialist Register 1972* (London: Merlin Press, 1972), pp. 193–229.

35   See especially Hal Draper, "The Lumpen-Class versus the Proletariat," *Karl Marx's Theory of Revolution: The Politics of Social Classes*, Vol. 2 (New York: Monthly Review Press, 1978), pp. 453–80. Draper's discussion is informed and invaluable, and contains many important insights and analytic nuances. Nonetheless, while I draw on this account I also depart from some of its claims.

36   Karl Marx, "The Eighteenth Brumaire of Louis Bonaparte," in Marx and Engels, *Selected Works*, p. 44.

37   Jeffrey Mehlman, *Revolution and Repetition: Marx/Hugo/Balzac* (Berkeley and London: University of California Press, 1977), pp. 24–25.

38   Draper, *Marx's Theory of Revolution*, esp. pp. 628–34.

39   Karl Marx, *The Class Struggles in France (1848–1850)* (New York: International Publishers, n.d.), p. 36.

40   Quoted in Stuart Hall et al., *Policing the Crisis: Mugging, the State, and Law and Order* (London: Macmillan, 1978), p. 385, which has a useful discussion

of *The Wretched of the Earth*, pp. 381–89. See Frantz Fanon, *The Wretched of the Earth* (New York: Grove, 1966), pp. 103–9.

41   Marx, *Class Struggles in France*, p. 50.

42   Marx, "Eighteenth Brumaire," p. 138. On Marx, the lumpenproletariat, and the economic analysis of *Capital*, see Draper, *Marx's Theory of Revolution*, pp. 469–71.

43   Peter Hayes, "Utopia and the Lumpenproletariat: Marx's Reasoning in 'The Eighteenth Brumaire of Louis Bonaparte,'" *Review of Politics* 50 (Summer 1988), esp. p. 458.

44   The "underclass," an early twentieth-century sociological designation that would be excavated in Robert Roberts's *The Classic Slum: Salford Life in the First Quarter of the Century* (Manchester: Manchester University Press, 1971), is not unrelated to the continuity of precariousness in proletarian life.

45   Frederick Engels, *The Condition of the Working-Class in England in 1844* (London: Swam Sonnenschein, 1892). Six years earlier Engels had written in correspondence to Laura Lafargue and August Bebel in ways that suggested a problem in seeing "barrow boys, idlers, police spies, and rogues" as sources of support for socialism. He referred to "numbers of poor devils of the East End who vegetate in the borderland between working class and lumpen proletariat." Engels to Laura Lafargue, February 9, 1886; Engels to August Bebel, February 15, 1886, in Karl Marx and Frederick Engels, *Collected Works*, Vol. 47, *1883–1886* (New York: International Publishers, 1995), pp. 403–10. See also Stedman Jones, *Outcast London*; and Arthur Morrison, *A Child of the Jago* (London: Methuen, 1896).

46   Karl Marx, "Economic and Philosophic Manuscripts of 1844," in Marx and Engels, *Collected Works*, Vol. 3, *1843–1844* (New York: Lawrence & Wishart, 1975), p. 284.

47   Among many passages that might be cited, see Marx, *Capital*, pp. 653–54; as well as the following discussions of "The Badly Paid Strata of the British Industrial Working Class" (pp. 654–63), "The Nomad Population" (pp. 663–7), and "The British Agricultural Proletariat" (pp. 673–712).

48   See Karl Marx, "Proceedings of the Sixth Rhine Province Assembly. Third Article Debates on the Law on Thefts of Wood," in Marx and Engels, *Collected Works*, Vol. 1, *1835–1843* (Moscow: Progress Publishers, 1975), pp. 224–63; Teo Ballvé, "Marx: Law on Thefts of Wood," July 12, 2011, available at territorialmasquerades.net; Peter Linebaugh, "Karl Marx, the Theft of Wood, and Working Class Composition: A Contribution to the Current Debate," *Crime and Social Justice* 6 (Fall–Winter 1976), pp. 5–16; Erica Sherover-Marcuse, *Emancipation and Consciousness: Dogmatic and Dialectical Perspectives in the Early Marx* (New York: Blackwell, 1986).